Continued on next page

THE BEACON
HANDBOOK

THE **BEACON HANDBOOK**

THIRD EDITION

ROBERT PERRIN

Indiana State University

Chapter 32 by Chris Hall of Wright State University

Houghton Mifflin Company   Boston   Toronto
Geneva, Illinois   Palo Alto   Princeton, New Jersey

Contents

The Composing Process   2

Contents

Contents

Contents

Contents

Contents

Contents

Preface

The primary goal of *The Beacon Handbook* is to offer students clear, succinct, accessible explanations of the basic issues of grammar, usage, punctuation, and mechanics within the larger context of writing to communicate meaning.

Recognizing that although a handbook must be complete and accurate to be useful, it must be accessible to be used, *The Beacon Handbook* includes several features designed to enhance both content and accessibility.

Accessibility

"Quick Reference." A "Quick Reference," placed near the beginning of each chapter, abstracts and presents succinctly the most important information in that chapter. "Quick References" can be used to preview or review chapters as well as drawn on for quick answers to students' pressing questions.

Clear Explanations. Students are introduced to grammatical terms and principles through definitions and explanations couched in everyday language. Sample sentences, many accompanied by specific parenthetical explanations, illustrate discussions.

Tables and Other Graphic Displays. Numerous tables, charts, lists, and checklists, present information clearly and concisely. Checklists are especially useful for students working independently.

Thematic Exercises. Each exercise, whether in sentence or paragraph format, treats a single topic, allowing students to apply newly learned information and skills within a realistic, coherent context of written expression.

Word Processing. Because of their versatility and ease of use as a tool for learning and writing, computers have introduced new possibilities for exploration and control of writing by writers at every level of experience. *The Beacon Handbook* offers specific, practical information and advice for using a word processor to make writing easier. Word-processing advice, clearly marked with the symbol ▓ , is incorporated into the text where it is most directly helpful, either within text discussions or in separate sections. Some advice, particular to a specific problem, will benefit only a few students; other advice will be of use to all students with access to a word processor; but even students without word processors may find it useful to adapt to paper some of the techniques described for the screen. Exercises marked with the computer symbol are available in ASCII files.

Content

The Writing Process. *The Beacon Handbook* emphasizes the writing process — the discovery of meaning, expression, and form through planning, drafting, and revising — providing thorough grounding in writing the essay and the research paper, two formats typical in college writing.

Critical Thinking and Writing. Chapter 5, "Critical Thinking and Writing," leads students through some of the basic concepts underlying critical thinking and writing skills, emphasizing the importance to communication, whether spoken, read, or written, of logical sequences of ideas, clearly and correctly articulated assertions, and apt and adequate supporting evidence.

Professional Samples. Paragraph-length samples from respected writers such as Henry Thoreau, E. B. White, Martin Luther King, Jr., and Joan Didion provide students with interesting reading as well as effective, varied models.

Samples of Full-length Papers. *The Beacon Handbook* includes a full-length model of each of the three types of paper discussed in detail: the essay, the argument, and the research paper. "The Composing Process" follows Jacob, a student writing on film adaptations of novels, through his planning, drafting, and revising to his final paper. "Critical Thinking and Writing" contains Norman Ornstein's essay "You Get What You Pay For,"[1] annotated to show use of logical strategies. The research process and final paper of Michele, a student writer, illustrate "Research"; the paper, on intelligence testing, is annotated to show Michele's rhetorical, stylistic, and technical choices.

The Research Paper. *The Beacon Handbook* describes and illustrates the entire research process, beginning with the selection and evaluation of potential topics and sources and ending with

1. Norman Ornstein, "You Get What You Pay For," *Newsweek* 16 Jan. 1989: 10.

preparation of the final copy. Through the model of one student's research and paper, students see the relation among all stages and the bearing of each on the final paper. Coverage of proper documentation forms includes both the Modern Language Association of America[2] style and, in an appendix, American Psychological Association[3] style.

Writing About Literature. New to this edition is a brief guide to writing about literature (Appendix E). Written by Deborah Barberousse, it offers practical advice in writing papers of explication, analysis, and comparison and includes sample papers.

Instructional Supplements

The Beacon Workbook, by Cynthia Lynch Frazer, Old Dominion University. A collection of 180 supplemental exercises accompanied by an instructor's manual with answers to all exercises.

Beacon Exercises and Review. A grammar and review program of nearly three hundred exercises available in computerized form for IBM[®] and Macintosh[®] computers.

Beacon Editing Exercises. Sixty-five thematic exercises available in computerized form as ASCII files.

Also of interest to those using computers is *Fine Lines* by William H. Koon and Peter L. Royston, a writing-process software program available for IBM[®] computers.

2. Joseph Gibaldi and Walter S. Achtert, *MLA Handbook for Writers of Research Papers,* 3rd ed. (New York: MLA, 1988).
3. *Publication Manual of the American Psychological Association,* 3rd ed. (Washington: APA, 1983).

ACKNOWLEDGMENTS

I am indebted to the following teachers for their advice in planning this and previous editions:

Kit Adkins, Piedmont Technical College, SC
Brenda Ameter, Indiana State University
Ted Atkinson, Edinboro University of Pennsylvania
Linda Bannister, Loyola Marymount University, CA
Larry Beason, Eastern Washington University
Alexander Belroy, Cerritos College, CA
Josephine Bloomfield, University of California, Davis
Judith L. Burken, Kellogg Community College, MI
Joan Bush, The University of Michigan-Dearborn
Patsy Callahgan, Central Washington University
Janet Carr, Northeastern University, MA
Janice U. Clayton, San Antonio College, TX
Susanna Clemans, Cerritos College, CA
Catherine Cox, University of Florida
Margaret DeHart, Trinity Valley Community College, TX
Bob Freud, Bergen Community College, NJ
Ray Frisch, Brainerd Community College, MN
Tahita Fulkerson, Tarrant County Junior College, TX
Douglas R. Garrison, College of the Desert, CA
Clark Germann, Front Range Community College, CO
Peter Gingiss, University of Houston, TX
César A. González-T, San Diego Mesa College, CA
Norma Cruz-Gonzales, San Antonio College, TX
Patricia H. Graves, Georgia State University
William H. Green, Chattahoochee Valley State College, AL
Huey S. Guagliardo, Louisiana State University
Judith Halden-Sullivan, CUNY/LaGuardia, NY
Gary M. Heba, Purdue University, IN
Peggy Jolly, University of Alabama
Howard Jones, Allan Hancock College, CA
Linda Julian, Furman University, SC

Frederica Kaven, Ithaca College, NY
Elizabeth Keating, San Diego City College, CA
Edward Klonoski, University of Hartford, CT
Betty Koch, York Technical College, SC
Anne Legge, Lord Fairfax Community College, VA
Leonard Lizak, California University of Pennsylvania, CA
Helen Lojek, Boise State University, ID
Irma Luna, San Antonio College, TX
John Markley, San Diego City College, CA
Joanne H. McCarthy, Tacoma Community College, WA
Douglas J. McMillan, East Carolina University, NC
Alice C. McWaters, Rose State College, OK
Gary Myers, Mercyhurst College, PA
Gwen Neary, Santa Rosa Junior College, CA
Gretchen Niva, Western Kentucky University
Kim H. Noling, Hartwick College, NY
Katherine Parrish, Southeast Missouri State University
William Peirce, Prince George's Community College
Karen Propp, University of Lowell, MA
Marie Saunders, Central State University, Edmond,OK
Jes Simmons, University of Findlay, OH
Joel Super, University of Illinois at Urbana-Champaign
John W. Taylor, South Dakota State University
Sally Taylor, Brigham Young University
Susanna Tracy, Cerritos College, CA
Robert S. Utterback, Owens Technical College, OH
Stephan L. Waterworth, El Camino College, CA
Thomas A. Westerfield, University of Northern Iowa
John O. White, California State University, Fullerton
Xiao-Ming Yang, Ocean County College, NJ
Jane Yarbrough, University of Wisconsin Center-Marinette
James Zoller, Houghton College, NY

In addition I would like to acknowledge several people who offered help with specific sections of the book. Raymond Dolle, Indiana State University, provided useful suggestions for improving Appendix D, Business Writing. My students have also offered useful comments on the effectiveness of explanations and exercises. In particular, I would like to thank Michele Newton for allowing me to use her preliminary research work and her research paper as the basis for much of the discussion in the research unit.

As always, I wish to thank Judy, Chris, and Jenny for their patience, encouragement, and support.

R.P.

To the Student

The Beacon Handbook combines a brief introduction to writing with a complete yet compact reference to the conventions of standard English, the expected means for communication in college and the work place. Parts 1 and 7 cover the process of writing essays and research papers, respectively; parts 2, 3, 4, 5, and 6 describe and illustrate the conventions of English grammar, usage, punctuation, and mechanics.

Designed to be used efficiently, *The Beacon Handbook* organizes information in a consistent format. After reviewing *The Beacon Handbook's* organization and learning to use its features, you will see that you can easily find the information you need, even when you are not sure what information you are looking for. And after you have found what you are looking for, *The Beacon Handbook's* features also help you to understand clearly and apply effectively the principles of good writing.

Finding Information

Organization. The seven parts of *The Beacon Handbook* are divided into thirty-five chapters, each treating a specific aspect of composition or English grammar and usage. Each chapter is divided into precepts (rules to guide your work), coded with the chapter number and a letter of the alphabet; up to three levels of headings may subdivide precept sections. Look, for example, at Chapter 15, "Fragments": the first precept, coded 15a, reads "Revise fragments that are phrases.' Two headings at the same level, "Fragments Lacking Subjects" and "Fragments Lacking Verbs," subdivide the discussion. For an example of subdivisions at more than one level, see precept 22d.

Note that precept numbers appear in the top outside corner of each page. These work like the guide words at the tops of dictionary pages; the precept number at the top of the left page indicates the first precept on that page, and the precept number at the top of the right page indicates the last precept on that page.

Guides to the Organization. The inside covers contain a brief outline of the book and a list of correction symbols similar to those your instructor will use to comment on your papers, with cross references to relevant text sections.

The table of contents provides a complete outline of the text. See pages v–xv.

Two indexes, one to word-processing information (see pages 655–57) and a general index (see pages 658–90), provide detailed, alphabetical listings of the text's contents.

"Quick References." "Quick References," located near the beginning of each chapter list in a clear, brief, accessible format the most crucial information in the chapter. See pages 75 and 324.

Appendixes and Glossaries. The appendixes and glossaries provide useful information in accessible locations and formats. Four appendixes are included: Appendix A, on preparing typed and handwritten manuscripts (see pages 577–81); Appendix B, on the basic features of the American Psychological Association documentary style (see pages 582–99); Appendix C, on writing essay examinations (see pages 600–605); and Appendix D, on the basic forms of business letters and resumes (see pages 606–16).

Two glossaries are included: the Glossary of Usage explains troublesome or often-confused words and provides examples of correct usage (see pages 617–34); and the Glossary of Grammatical Terms defines grammatical terms used in the book and provides an example of each (see pages 635–54).

Using Information

Examples, Tables, and Special Notes. Throughout the text, examples, tables, and special notes augment definitions and explanations. Use them to assure your understanding of and as convenient references to chapter concepts and information.

Examples, set off with extra space and distinguished by typeface and labels, illustrate the principle under discussion. Explanation of examples may follow in parentheses, when needed, to point out the pros and cons of specific choices. See page 211 for sample.

Tables, charts, and lists present crucial information succinctly in an easily located, readable format. See pages 139, 245, and 415–23.

Special notes, marked with the symbol **》》》** **《《《**, describe exceptions to rules or offer hints for applying specific principles in your writing. See pages 282 and 331.

Computer Notes, Boxes, and Exercises. Advice for using a word processor to improve your writing appears in computer notes within discussions (see page 10) or separate computer boxes (see pages 40–42); both are marked with the symbol ▪. Choose among the strategies suggested according to your needs as a writer or the nature of a particular project. Try all of the strategies; by playing with the computer you will find your own best strategies and style of working.

You will notice that some of the exercises in *The Beacon Handbook* are marked with the disk symbol. This means that those exercises may be available on disk from your instructor or in your writing lab. If so, you can complete the exercises using your word-processing program, which will enable you to correct, revise, and rewrite freely, without retyping. If the disk version is not available or you do not have access to a word processor, you can, of course, still complete the computer exercises as you would any of the others, by recopying them.

Whether you are using *The Beacon Handbook* as a text, with chapters assigned by your instructor, or as a reference, using it as necessary when you are writing for any of your courses or for your own reasons, a preliminary review of its features and information will give you increasing control of your writing.

R.P.

THE BEACON HANDBOOK

THE
COMPOSING
PROCESS

1 Planning

Before sitting down at a desk or computer to write, most writers make plans. Whether those plans are formulated in the mind or on paper, writers begin to focus on particular subjects and make choices about ways of exploring them. Writers typically vary their planning strategies with each project as they respond to its individual requirements and challenges. This chapter explores some common and consistently helpful planning strategies.

Quick Reference

Planning strategies encourage exploration and discovery. Use the following approaches to think about your subject:

> *Be open-minded about potential subjects.*

> *Do not select a specific topic until you have explored the general subject from a variety of perspectives.*

> *Develop topics that interest you. Your enthusiasm will come through in your writing and will engage your readers.*

> *After determining your topic, clearly state the main idea in a working thesis statement that expresses the appropriate tone and any necessary qualifications.*

1a ⟩ To begin, select a general subject.

Because the most effective writing develops from a writer's inter-

Note: The exercises in Chapters 1, 2, and 3 will take you from idea to final paper. Keep the work from each exercise to use in later exercises.

est in or commitment to a subject, select a general subject that appeals to you as you begin to plan your paper. **》》》** *Often in academic and professional writing, circumstances or other people will determine your subject. In these cases, start with the strategies described in section 1b.* **《《《**

When beginning to select a subject, do not limit your thinking. Instead, keep an open mind and consider various general subjects, such as the following, before selecting one.

Regular activities. Think of your routine activities: working, studying, listening to music, shopping, watching television, eating, exercising, reading. Any of these routines can yield interesting topics if thoughtfully explored.

General reading. Thoughts about, associations with, and responses to your general (non-course-related) reading in books, magazines, and newspapers can lead to interesting subjects.

Special interests. Do you see every foreign film that comes to local theaters or every television documentary on ecology? Can you write computer programs to track baseball statistics or compile a club newsletter? Such special interests make good subjects because the more you know about a subject, the more you will have to write about it.

People you know. The appearance, personality, behavior, and beliefs of the people you know can provide interesting subjects. Consider anyone you know — a newspaper vendor, your landlord, a professor — not just close friends and family.

Places you have visited. Have you been to Spain, Montreal, or the Grand Canyon? What about a relative's farm or business, your city's police station, or the weight room at the local gym? Both familiar and unfamiliar places, explored in detail and without preconceptions, make interesting subjects.

Unusual experiences. If you have had experiences that most others have not had, you have the beginning of a good subject. Exploring these experiences on paper may lead you to insights both you and others will appreciate.

Problems people face. Personal, social, economic, and political problems demand attention. Serious problems to which you have given or would like to give serious thought can be provocative subjects.

Changes in your life. Think about significant changes in your life: going to college, getting a job, adjusting to the aging or death of a parent. Exploring the feelings and thoughts you had during and after these changes may provide a rewarding subject.

Likes and dislikes. Consider things you find appealing or unappealing: the network news, mystery novels, reunions, jazz. Consider especially the underlying attitudes and values that your preferences reveal, and be willing to discuss them openly.

Strong opinions. What strong opinions do you hold on important matters like censorship, U.S. immigration policy, or nuclear disarmament? Consider writing about the opinion that usually starts the liveliest discussions with relatives or friends.

Social, political, and cultural events. Local, national, and international issues and events can be fascinating to write about, whether the topic is the politics of the Olympics, the collapse of a local bridge, or the latest Broadway musical hit. Consider especially events that you have followed closely.

Academic courses. The information, insights, and associations that you have absorbed in academic courses make productive subjects to explore in writing. Remember that not everyone learns the same things, even in the same courses.

EXERCISE 1.1 ❯ *General subjects*

> *For each of the twelve general subjects presented above, list at least two potential subjects for a paper, a total of twenty-four.*

| 1b | ❯ | **Develop ideas through planning.** |

Most writers do not move directly from selecting a general subject to writing a paper or an article. Rather, they take time to explore a general subject, to select and develop a manageably narrow topic by focusing on one aspect of the subject, to consider their knowledge of and opinion about the topic, and to explore alternative ways to develop ideas related to the topic. This multifaceted approach to planning leads to better writing by encouraging writers to think, make choices, reconsider emphases, and arrange ideas.

Planning strategies provide opportunities to think about a subject and explore ideas. When you have the freedom to select first your own subject and then your narrowed topic, these strategies will help you to decide what to write about. When you work from an assigned general subject or narrow topic, these strategies will help you to discover ways to clarify and develop your ideas about it. Sometimes completing one activity will be enough; sometimes you will need to try several.

Planning Strategies

Freewriting	Looping
Journal writing	Clustering
Journalists' questions	Brainstorming

Freewriting

Freewriting means writing spontaneously for brief, sustained periods of ten or fifteen minutes. Freewriting can be *unfocused* if

▎! *Basics for composing on the word processor*

Writers experienced in using word processors follow the steps below to avoid losing or misplacing their work.

Save your work frequently. Every fifteen to twenty minutes and whenever you leave your computer, however briefly, use the "save" command to ensure that your work will be stored in the computer's memory.

At the end of every writing session, print a paper copy, known as a *hard copy,* of your work. If the electronic version is lost, you will still have your work, and a hard copy will be useful when your reread and revise.

At the end of every writing session, make a backup disk copy of your work. Store your disks carefully to avoid damage from liquids, dust, heat, magnetism, and so on.

Provide distinctive, easily recognizable names for each file, clearly indicating the project and its stage of development. When you revise, copy and rename the file before working on it.

Arrange the stages of your projects into logical directories and subdirectories that can be easily located. Regularly print hard copies of your directories so that you can locate material at a glance even when you are not at your computer.

Identify your work by placing its directory and file name at the bottom of the last page. You will then easily be able to locate the electronic file corresponding to any hard copy.

Date drafts of your projects so that you can determine the most recent version.

you are searching for a subject, or it can be *focused* if you know the subject but are deciding how to approach it. Freewriting generally uses full, linked sentences, but because it does not require any other formal constraints, it gives you an opportunity to relax and write down ideas that might not otherwise occur to you.

To begin, think briefly about your subject and then start writing about it. (If you do not have a subject, simply begin writing down whatever comes to mind.) Write quickly. Do not worry about grammar or mechanics, neatness or form. Avoid any urge to revise your sentences or to worry about logical connections among ideas. Write down all your thoughts; write until you can think of nothing else to say.

Consider this freewriting sample, which helped Jacob, a student writer, to identify a general subject for a paper assigned in his English class:

Yesterday Todd and I went to The Video Station to get a tape. We headed straight to the "action/adventure" section and picked out something that would be fun to see — relaxing, not demanding. As we walked back to the counter to pay for the tape, I got sidetracked in the "classics" section. I looked at the display boxes: Great Expectations, The Grapes of Wrath, To Kill a Mockingbird, Romeo and Juliet, and lots of others. Todd came to get me. "Gimme a break, Jay," he said. "We don't want any of those." I agreed at the time, but that action/adventure film turned out to be a bust — repetitive, chaotic, unbelievable, boring — and I got to thinking about those classics — good films that have been around awhile. Lots were based on novels and plays that I'd read — some in lit. class, some on my own — and I'd seen quite a few of the films. Sometimes the book was best, but sometimes the film was. I mentioned to Todd that the next time we got a tape I wanted to get one of those. "Ah, Jay," he moaned, "that'd be like being in class on the weekend." I thought to myself that it might be, but that wasn't so bad. I want real entertainment when I punch the "play" button on the VCR — and maybe something more.

Notice that Jacob's word choices are sometimes colloquial and vague, his sentences sometimes informal, and his ideas only loosely linked. But his ideas are flowing, and he is getting them down on paper.

> **!** To avoid mulling over the right word or revising a sentence until it is perfect — tendencies that interfere with the quickness and spontaneity that freewriting requires — turn off your computer screen or dim it so that words cannot be read. Then simply type, free from the urge to pause or tinker. You will be surprised by how much writing you will do, and you can revise or correct the text later if you wish.

Journal Writing

Keeping a journal means recording your thoughts and observations regularly, for your own use, usually in a notebook kept for the purpose. Like freewriting, journal writing gives writers a chance to record ideas for later evaluation; journal writing, however, more often focuses on and systematically develops a specific topic or event. Reflective by definition, journal writing offers you the chance to explore privately and in detail thoughts and feelings about people, actions, events, ideas — in short, anyone or anything of interest or concern. Writers who regularly keep a journal find that it leads to ideas, insights, and further observations that they would not otherwise have had.

To make the best use of this strategy, try to write in your journal every day. You might try carrying your notebook with you, writing briefly or at length whenever a thought occurs to you or an event or comment interests you. Or you might try writing in your journal by appointment, choosing a convenient time such as first thing in the morning or just before dinner. Whenever and wherever you write in your journal, give it a long trial, perhaps a month, of making regular entries. Journal writing may seem awkward at first, but it is likely to become easy and pleasurable as you find your own best method of working.

Jacob wrote systematically in his journal about one aspect of his freewriting:

> *Reading a novel or play and seeing a film adaptation do not produce similar responses in me — and they should not because the forms are different. Yet each experience can be rewarding. I can remember times when I was thrilled with a book and unimpressed by the film and vice versa. But why? I find some novels — especially long, compli-cated ones like* Great Expectations *— more enjoyable to read be-cause I can move slowly through the story, reread sections to pick out details I might have missed, and concentrate on the details that place the story in its context. A film adaptation, even a very long one, must move quickly to include even the most basic elements of the plot, and except on video, viewers cannot go back to "spot check" a missed de-tail. Yet I must admit that films can do some things that novels can't. For example, I can't imagine (as Dickens' first readers could) what London streets looked like in Pip's day, but the film can show me. The challenge of adapting a novel for film must be enormous, and for the viewer, understanding and appreciating both forms is a big challenge as well.*

Jacob's journal entry, though not fully focused or developed, draws connections more clearly than did his freewriting as he ex-plores the facets of film adaptation that interest him most.

Journalists' Questions

For decades, journalists have used a reliable set of questions — *who, what, when, where, how,* and *why* — to explore their subjects and to uncover the specific, detailed information that their readers want to know. By using these questions as prompts and refining them to suit your needs, you can pinpoint various aspects of your subject, finding pertinent and interesting connections and information that you didn't know you knew.

Jacob specifically modified the journalists' questions to extend his exploration of his subject, producing these notes:

Literary Works and Film Adaptations

Who sees films and reads novels? Lots of people: students, certainly, but others, too; Todd; my parents; people who read the book first and see the film second; people who see the film and then read the book.

What kinds of works are effectively adapted? Both classic and popular works: novels and plays; Romeo and Juliet, To Kill a Mockingbird, Sophie's Choice, A Streetcar Named Desire, Amadeus.

When do people become aware of adaptations? People see films of famous works during school; later in life, too, when they go out to a theater or watch TV.

Where do people see film adaptations? At school, at movie theaters, and at home on the TV, especially on cable channels, and on VCRs.

How are books modified? Plots are shortened, simplified; characterization is altered; themes are modified; visual images are emphasized; settings are changed.

Why are the changes necessary? Production costs; need for clear narrative pattern; time restrictions; mass distribution; visual nature of film; producer or director's interpretation.

Some of Jacob's questions yield more ideas than others. *What, how,* and *why* provided particularly specific and useful responses. The questions most useful for a given subject will vary, though any might provide useful details or lead to an interesting, focused topic.

Looping

Looping helps you to move from a general subject to a narrow topic through a series of progressively more specific freewritings.

To loop, begin with a general subject and freewrite for five to ten minutes. Then circle one element or detail and freewrite again, focusing on it. Repeat the process as often as necessary until you decide on a specific, restricted topic within your original, general subject.

Jacob's looping produced this series of brief paragraphs:

Freewriting

The nature of a literary work often changes in a film adaptation. Sometimes plots get simplified or secondary plots get dropped altogether. Sometimes directors alter characterizations to produce roles to suit specific actors or to make the characters more acceptable to a general audience. Sometimes even the locale or time period is changed, creating a different context.

Loop 1

Characterizations often change in film adaptations. Directors and actors may "soften" a pivotal negative character to make him or her more appealing to a mass audience. Sometimes a character that was well rounded (having both positive and negative qualities) in a novel or play becomes wholly positive. Sometimes secondary characters may disappear completely.

Loop 2

In film adaptations done in the 1940s and 1950s, negative characters tended to be "cleaned up." For instance, in the film version of the play A Streetcar Named Desire*, Stanley is loud and verbally abusive but not as physically violent as he is in the original version. His behavior is so repugnant in the play that Stella leaves at the end; in the film version produced for American distribution, he is not so despicable, and Stella stays.*

Notice the pattern in Jacob's looping: he writes first on a general subject, then on a specific topic, and finally on a specific example. Looping frequently, though not always, follows this sequence, allowing a writer to explore a subject and perhaps to select a topic and method of development.

> The dimmed-screen approach described on page 9 works well with looping. Complete the first freewriting with the screen dimmed. Then turn the brightness up, read what you've typed, and select an aspect for further exploration. Turn the brightness down again and freewrite on your new topic. Repeat the process as often as is useful.

Clustering

Clustering, because it combines verbal with visual prompts, can lead to more flexible, nonlinear planning that emphasizes associations among rather than hierarchies of ideas. This free-form approach encourages some writers to pursue looser, more creative exploration of their subjects.

Begin a cluster with a circled key word or phrase in the center of a sheet of paper. Associating ideas freely, add lines radiating from the central idea leading to circled words or phrases that describe, define, or explain it. These ideas in turn will prompt further associations that branch from them. Continue adding ideas and connections as they occur to you. Evaluate your finished cluster. Use another color ink or pencil to trace the most interesting development and to cross out ones that did not work. Look for self-contained satellite clusters that move beyond the original idea. Consider whether portions of your cluster correspond to portions of the paper you are planning, thus indicating an organization. Finally, consider clustering around a new idea suggested by your first cluster.

Jacob, for example, began his clustering with the word *classics,* which he had used repeatedly in his other planning, and produced the cluster shown on page 14.

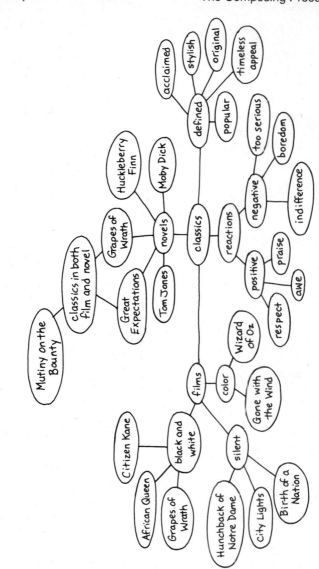

Analyzing his cluster, Jacob concluded that the branches "novels" and "films," by producing more specific and varied examples, illuminated *classics* and each other intriguingly.

Clustering may not always produce ideas that you will be able to use in a paper, but because of its flexible, nonlinear form, it can lead you to surprising discoveries and provocative associations.

Brainstorming

Use **brainstorming** to produce a list of everything you can think of that is related to your subject. A brainstorming list generally comprises freely associated ideas expressed in words and phrases. It may be developed by an individual writer or by a group working together on one project.

Begin a brainstorming list by thinking briefly about your subject. Then write without pausing, using single words or short phrases, until you run out of ideas. Brainstorming should be done rapidly and spontaneously, so do not pause to evaluate, analyze, or arrange your ideas.

Although lists are the most commonly used format for brainstorming, some writers prefer other, more graphic formats. They may organize their ideas into trees, showing ideas branching out of one another, or into clusters, in which ideas radiate from and circle around the main idea. Use any format that is comfortable for you and that encourages the lively generation of ideas.

Jacob's brainstorming produced this list:

Film Adaptations of Literature

classic and popular works

directors change plot

actors change characterization

larger audience

from mental to visual form

Romeo and Juliet

The Wizard of Oz

Frankenstein

Moby Dick

To Kill a Mockingbird

Sophie's Choice

viewers' reactions

subplots eliminated

settings changed

Todd

personal interpretation

public version

good film / weak book

good book / weak film

Jacob's long and varied list shows that he looked at his subject from many angles. The list reveals some connections among ideas but shows no formal arrangement.

To use a brainstorming list, arrange items in groups unified by a common idea or theme. Do not let your original list limit your thinking while grouping ideas. Drop items that do not fit your groups, repeat items in several groups if appropriate, and add new items whenever you think of them.

Grouping Ideas

Classify by topics.

Identify examples.

Arrange chronologically.

Compare or contrast.

Classify by Topics

Items from your list will generally suggest logical classes or categories into which to subdivide your subject. Group items from your list into the appropriate categories. Sometimes an item from your list will be a comprehensive category that in turn suggests additional items. At this point in planning, categories need not be logically related.

Items from Jacob's list suggested many categories, two of which are shown here.

Specific works

Romeo and Juliet

The Wizard of Oz

Frankenstein

To Kill a Mockingbird

Sophie's Choice

Kinds of changes

directors change plot

actors change characterization

mental to visual form

subplots eliminated

setting changed

Identify Examples

Specific examples make writing livelier than do abstract discussions. Use examples drawn from your brainstorming list to focus your topic, adding details as you think of them.

Jacob mentions several films in his brainstorming list. Discussing them could unify his ideas or stimulate new ones. Here is a sample:

Frankenstein

a classic work

directors changed plot

actors changed characterization

themes eliminated

seldom-read novel — quite good

often-seen film — entertaining but not good

Arrange Chronologically

Many subjects suggest a chronological, historical, or narrative pattern in which a series of events or the stages in a single event are recounted in sequence.

Jacob's subject, for example, could be developed chronologically:

1920s and 1930s

early reliance of filmmakers on literary sources and models

some successful adaptations of traditional narratives

emphasis on epic events

All Quiet on the Western Front

Gone with the Wind

1940s and 1950s

refinements in filmmaking led to more subtle adaptations

successful adaptations of psychological novels

emphasis on character, personal narratives

<u>*All the King's Men*</u>

<u>*Hamlet*</u>

<u>*On the Waterfront*</u>

1960s and 1970s

new techniques split traditional from innovative films

continued attempts

adaptations often remakes of classic films

themes, issues of central importance

<u>*Elmer Gantry*</u>

<u>*To Kill a Mockingbird*</u>

<u>*Dr. Zhivago*</u>

Compare or Contrast

Often, similarities or differences among items on your brainstorming list will suggest logical groupings. Comparing similar items or contrasting dissimilar ones may lead to an interesting perspective on, or to new items relevant to, your subject. Parallel lists, as in the following example, may be used to explore these relations. Revise your original entries, as necessary, to emphasize the points of comparison or contrast.

Books	**Adaptations**
complicated plots	*simplified plots*
many characters	*reduced number of characters*
unique themes	*mainstream themes*

mental images	visual images
(vary with reader)	(specified by director)
extended experience	restricted experience
(time)	(time)
reader's interpretation	director's or producer's interpretation

EXERCISE 1.2 ❯ *Planning strategies*

Using several of the general subjects you listed in Exercise 1.1, try each of the planning strategies: freewriting, journal writing, journalists' questions, looping, clustering, and brainstorming-grouping.

| 1c | ❯ | **Select a specific topic for your paper.** |

Having explored your general subject and discovered the aspects of it that interest you most, you should now work toward identifying a specific, narrowed topic.

To begin, review your planning materials. Then use these questions to decide on an effective topic:

Which topic seems most original? Look for interesting ideas, unusual connections, or unique observations.

Which topic interests you most? Notice recurrent ideas, repeated phrases, or often-used examples.

About which topic are you most informed? Notice your use of examples, specific details, facts, and names.

Which topic is the most useful? Look for problems to solve or contradictions to explore.

Which topic can you cover best in the space allowed for your paper? Consider a simple issue for a short paper but a complex issue for a long paper.

Finally, state your chosen topic in a sentence.

Reviewing his planning using the questions listed above, Jacob discovered several distinct patterns. Specific examples, appearing in different planning contexts, suggested that Jacob had extensive knowledge of and a keen interest in novels and their film adaptations. Jacob also saw that he had many ideas and opinions about the pros and cons of adaptation. On the basis of these discoveries, Jacob chose to contrast novels and their film adaptations, omitting references to plays. He would thus be able to use his experience, knowledge, and ideas to write a focused paper

EXERCISE 1.3   ❯   *A specific topic*

Review your planning materials and select a specific topic. Then write a brief paragraph describing how you arrived at your selection. Describe your review of your planning materials; comment on how you selected ideas and rejected others; and end the paragraph by stating your topic in a sentence.

1d	Identify your role, your readers, and your purpose.

As you narrow your topic and develop and arrange the ideas of the paper, consider in detail the context for your writing — your role, your readers, and your purpose.

Your Role as a Writer

Consider your perspective on your topic. If you are writing about horse racing, are you writing from your experience as a spectator or as a jockey? Do you own a racehorse or oppose horse racing? What knowledge of and attitude toward the sport does each of these positions involve? Defining your individual perspective on your topic — whether you are writing as an authority, an unbiased observer, or a probing nonspecialist — will help you to make choices of content and presentation.

Jacob enjoys both original literary works and their film versions and can write without bias on their relative merits. His familiarity with a number of novels and their screen adaptations allows him to choose appropriate examples and discuss them in detail. He can write open-mindedly and with a broad perspective.

Your Readers

Consider carefully the expectations, concerns, and knowledge of your audience. To do this, first identify your readers by answering these questions:

What are the probable age, educational level, and experience of your audience?

What information, concerns, and interests do your readers probably share?

What choices of tone and language will best communicate with your audience?

For example, twenty-year-olds and forty-year-olds have different experiences and concerns, so they are likely to know and be interested in different examples. Jacob might discuss Greta Garbo in *Anna Karenina* for an older audience and Meryl Streep in *Out of Africa* for a younger one. Similarly, appropriate tone and language can vary with audience; one audience might understand and enjoy reading current slang, while another might be confused by it. Differences in education and information require differences in the amount of detail offered in explanations. An informed audience may realize at once that *The Wizard of Oz* was a popular children's book by L. Frank Baum long before it was a movie starring Judy Garland; an uninformed audience might not.

> **!** Dim the screen on your computer and freewrite for five minutes about your audience. Using specific details, describe your audience as completely as possible — age, education, opinions, activities, favorite television shows — as if you were writing quickly to a friend. When you have finished, turn the brightness up, read what you have written, and introduce italic or boldface codes to highlight the most revealing details about your readers.

Jacob decided that the audience for his paper — his teacher and college classmates — ranged in age from seventeen to forty-five, though most fell between seventeen and twenty-two. Seeing films based on books was a common experience for this group, but to avoid lengthy descriptions, he decided to concentrate on well-known films. Jacob thought the novels would be less familiar, however, and would require fairly detailed descriptions. Finally, concluding that he had a serious point to make on an academic topic, he decided that his readers would expect a serious tone and somewhat formal language.

Your Purpose

Your purpose for writing is never simply to fulfill a course requirement. Any time you write with careful attention to your thoughts, information, and audience, an organizing purpose will emerge.

Most writing has one of four general purposes: expressive, referential, persuasive, or argumentative. Writing for college courses may serve any of these purposes. In **expressive writing,** writers express their individuality by sharing experiences, opinions, perceptions, and feelings. Expressive papers explore the writer's perspective. **Literary writing,** not covered in this book, is a form of expressive writing in which writers share perceptions and insights using artistic forms such as the short story, poem, novel, or play. In **referential writing,** writers share information and ideas, often gathered through systematic research. A writer's focus in a referential paper is on the topic and often on specialists' views, which must be carefully documented. (For a discussion of documentation, see section 32g.) In **persuasive writing,** writers present information and opinions intended to alter readers' views or perceptions. A persuasive paper relies on evidence to convince readers to rethink the topic; some research (properly documented) may be required. Finally, in **argumentative writing,** writers present their opinions on arguable topics, topics on which there are many possible viewpoints, supporting their positions using ideas, information, experience, and insights. A writer's focus in an argumentative paper is on the issues.

Begin thinking about your specific purpose by deciding which general purposes suit your needs. In most writing, the general purposes overlap. Most persuasive writing is also expressive, and referential writing is often persuasive. As you develop a paper and make choices about structure, content, and style, you will discover how purposes blend naturally.

Jacob, for example, decided that his paper would be primarily referential because it would be based on a nonjudgmental assessment of the nature of film adaptations of novels and on facts such as copyright and film release dates. The paper would have an expressive element as well, for it would reveal his taste and perspective. Jacob was unsure whether he would develop a persuasive element in his paper.

EXERCISE 1.4 ❯ *Role, readers, and purpose*

Make a list that characterizes your role, readers, and purpose for the paper you have been planning. Consider how the results of this analysis will influence further planning and drafting.

Example

    Role: a lover of both books and film adaptations; someone familiar with many pairs of works.

    Readers: teacher and classmates; ages 17–45; most have seen film adaptations; some have read the corresponding original works; many may be unaware of what occurs in adaptation.

    Purpose: to write a referential paper but express my views.

1e ⟩ Write a working thesis statement.

After narrowing your topic and characterizing your role, readers, and purpose, you should be able to formulate a **working thesis statement** — a brief statement of your topic and your opinion on it — to guide your draft. Later in the writing process you will want to refine your working thesis into a **final thesis** — generally a single sentence near the end of the introductory paragraph — that will guide readers in reading your paper

    In finished paragraphs and even in papers, writers sometimes omit their thesis statements. The writer builds meaning implicitly through examples, details, or description, leaving it to the reader to formulate the meaning explicitly. Such works are said to have an **implied thesis.** This method generally works best for very personal descriptive or narrative papers. For most writing, a thesis statement helps both the writer and the reader understand the organization and follow the development of ideas. And even writers who, in their finished papers, rely on an implied thesis may have used a working thesis statement to help focus their thinking during planning, drafting, and revising. (See page 79 for an example of a paragraph that has no thesis statement.)

    After a thoughtful review of your planning materials, moving from your topic to a working thesis statement should be a simple step. A review of your planning materials, concentrating on recurrent or especially fully developed ideas, may help you to pinpoint your opinion about your topic. From your analysis of your role, your readers, and your purpose, you know the general approach you want to take. Now consider how best to achieve that approach. Ask yourself what you want your readers to know or think about your topic and try to express the answer in a single sentence.

An effective thesis statement has three essential characteristics and may have three optional characteristics:

Essential

Identify a specific, narrow topic.

Present a clear opinion on, not merely facts about, the topic.

Establish a tone appropriate to the topic, purpose, and audience.

Optional

Qualify the topic as necessary, pointing out significant opposing opinions.

Clarify important points, indicating the organizational pattern.

Take account of readers' probable knowledge of the topic.

Carefully planned and written working thesis statements help writers to control their material by suggesting a focus for their thinking and a structure for their writing. In the final paper, a good thesis statement will prevent confusion by clarifying for readers the paper's central idea. Ineffective thesis statements like these do not help the writer or readers:

Attics are places to store belongings.   (This topic lacks an opinion; it merely states a fact.)

Cats make weird pets.   (This narrowed topic contains an opinion, but it is imprecise, is stated too informally, and fails to qualify its criticism for readers who like cats.)

Liquor advertisements glamorize the drinking that leads to thousands of highway deaths each year.   (The topic and opinion are clear, but this thesis statement ignores the variables in a controversial issue.)

First drafts of thesis statements are often as vague and incomplete as these. Careful writers, however, revise weak thesis statements by using the guidelines listed on page 26 and, often, by doing some additional planning. The weak thesis statements shown above were rewritten to produce these improved versions:

Attics are great places to store useless belongings.   (The inclusion of *great* and *useless* defines the writer's opinion and establishes a humorous tone.)

Cats make unusually independent pets.   (*Independent* is more precise and therefore clearer than *weird*. The change in wording creates the formal tone appropriate to a college paper.)

Although some advertisements now include warnings not to drink and drive, most continue to glamorize the drinking that leads to thousands of highway deaths each year.   (This thesis statement still expresses a strongly held opinion, but the introductory qualification and the inclusion of *most* help make it more judicious than the original version.)

Here are Jacob's attempts to write an effective thesis statement:

First attempt
Film adaptations vary considerably from the original novels they are based on.

(The topic is vague, and the sentence presents a fact, not an opinion.)

Second attempt
Film adaptations distort the original novels they are based on but create workable equivalents to the originals.

(The topic is clearer and an opinion is stated, but the thesis statement is still imprecise and ineffectively worded.)

Third attempt

Although film adaptations of novels may seem to distort original works, the adaptations often create worthy counterparts to the originals.

(The topic is more explicit, and placing the qualification first creates emphasis at the end.)

> **!** When writing working thesis statements, use to your advantage the computer's capability to copy easily. Type a first attempt at a thesis statement. Then copy it several spaces below (use the "block" and "copy" commands). Leaving the original version in place, analyze and revise the copy. Copy the second version and revise it to produce the third, and so on. Keeping all versions will allow you to reexamine your choices of wording and tone without substantial retyping or a clutter of markings. You may want to return to earlier versions to reclaim discarded phrases or words.

EXERCISE 1.5 ❯ *Thesis statements*

Briefly evaluate each of the following thesis statements. Note the strengths and weaknesses of each. Revise any ineffective thesis statements by narrowing and focusing the topic, changing the tone, or adding an opinion or any necessary qualifications.

1. Some critics maintain that the *Iliad* and the *Odyssey* are the foundation works on which all subsequent literature in the Western tradition are based.

2. The 1988 Winter Olympics were held in Calgary.

3. Contrary to commonly held opinion, anti-Communist hysteria in the United States predated the rabid speeches and accusations made by Senator Joseph R. McCarthy in the early 1950s.

4. Even though a lot of people will disagree, I think that prayer is okay in public schools.

5. By encouraging managers in some U.S. corporations to play with a matchbox, some string, and a candle, cognitive psychologists are passing on important lessons in creative problem solving.

6. The United States government should retaliate quickly against terrorism.

7. Achieving competency in a foreign language is among the highest rewards of education.

8. Women should not always be awarded custody of children in divorce settlements.

EXERCISE 1.6 ❯ Thesis statements

Write a thesis statement about your topic. Revise it as often as necessary to achieve a clear statement of the topic, your opinion on it, and any necessary qualifications. Consider carefully your role, your readers, and your purpose, and establish an appropriate tone.

Planning on the word processor

After you have tried a number of the planning strategies in this chapter, start a file in which you record the guiding questions or categories of those that work best for you. For example, record the following:

the list of ways to think of topics (pages 4–5)

the questions used to narrow topics (pages 20–21)

the categories for classifying information (pages 16–20)

the questions journalists use to anticipate their readers' questions (pages 10–11)

the key concepts and questions useful for analyzing your role, audience, and purpose (pages 21–24)

the categories for evaluating your thesis (pages 25–28)

Include any additional comments, questions, or strategies that you have developed on your own. Separate each strategy with a page break and mark it with a key word as a heading so that you can use the "search" function to find quickly the material you need.

When planning a piece of writing, call up your file of planning strategies into a window or second screen and use its contents as prompts for varying your approach to your topic. Or "block" and "copy" a specific set of planning prompts to a separate file devoted to your topic and expand them with relevant notes — examples, facts, questions, possible sources, and so on.

As you continue to write, you will develop new strategies and modify old ones. Update your planning file from time to time to take advantage of your increasing experience.

---

2 Drafting

Even during early stages of planning, most writers begin to think about ways to express their ideas. They think about structural patterns for the entire paper, but also about paragraph patterns, sentences, phrases, or even word choices. No matter what form or how long their planning takes, writers must at some point stop planning and sit down at a desk or keyboard to begin work on a rough draft.

Quick Reference

Drafting is an opportunity for you to experiment with ways to express your ideas, knowing that you can revise the work later. As you draft your paper, keep these principles in mind:

❯ *Use the broad organizational pattern that emerges most naturally from your planning.*

❯ *Use outlining to help you achieve a logical structure for your ideas, but do not let the outline dictate your draft. Revise the outline when necessary.*

❯ *Use drafting to get ideas on paper in a reasonably coherent form without pausing too much over the exact expression or striving for technical correctness.*

❯ *Experiment with various techniques for introducing a paper that interests readers and concluding a paper that satisfies them.*

Writing a rough draft is a rehearsal, an opportunity to explore possibilities for the arrangement and expression of ideas. In the drafting stage, writers organize ideas from their planning materials and explore ways to express them in sentences, paragraphs, and ultimately a complete, though not yet final, paper. Drafting a paper is rarely a neat and easy matter of writing up available notes, however. Writers must be flexible and open to new ideas that occur as they write, filling gaps and making new connections. Drafting begins the process of transferring ideas into sentences.

| 2a | > | **Organize your materials and continue to seek new ideas.** |

Examine the materials you wrote during planning. Look for emerging patterns among ideas and for ideas that seem especially important or that illustrate your thesis especially well. Your planning materials generally will suggest a natural pattern for organizing your paper. Some common organizational arrangements are **chronological, spatial,** and **topical.**

Chronological Arrangement

Chronological arrangement presents information in sequence, explaining what happened first, second, third, and so on. Personal narratives, such as a description of your first day at a new job, and narratives of events, such as a political debate, make good use of a chronological arrangement.

Spatial Arrangement

Spatial arrangement recreates the physical features of a subject. For instance, a writer might describe a town by "leading" readers from a residential area in the north to a commercial or industrial area in the south. Spatial arrangement has limited application; but when physical features are important, it can convey insights more effectively than any other arrangement.

Topical Arrangement

Topical arrangement, a pattern often used in writing arguments, organizes supporting ideas to present the thesis with the greatest possible emphasis. Topical arrangement can follow a number of patterns according to your purpose — from most important point to least important, for instance, or from simplest to most complex. Sometimes a mixed pattern works best. For example, present your second most important point first, interesting readers with strong material, and then sandwich in lesser points to fill out the discussion; use your most important point last, thus closing with especially convincing evidence.

Other Methods of Arrangement

The organizational patterns used to arrange the ideas in paragraphs can also be used to organize full-length papers. Your planning materials, for example, may suggest one of these common patterns: analogy, cause and effect, process, classification, and definition. Jacob's planning materials reveal an emerging comparison and contrast pattern. The principles discussed in Chapter 4, "Paragraphs," can be expanded so that you use full paragraphs to develop each of your ideas within the overall organizational pattern.

EXERCISE 2.1 ❯ *Organizing materials*

Review your thesis and planning materials from Chapter 1 and experiment with each of the organizational patterns described above. (For more information on alternate patterns, see section 4d.) Choose one pattern and then organize your planning materials according to the arrangement suggested by the pattern.

| 2b | > | **Outline your paper.** |

Having selected a pattern of arrangement, prepare an **outline,** a structural plan using headings and subdivisions to clarify the main features of your paper and the interrelationships among them. Some writers create loosely structured, informal outlines; other writers prefer to create highly systematic, formal outlines. Many writers use both kinds, benefiting at different stages of their writing from the simplicity and freedom of informal outlines and the clarity and completeness of formal outlines. In the earliest stages of drafting — when writers are deciding what should come first, second, third, and so on — informal outlines seem to work best. At later stages, writers often use formal outlining to analyze their work for consistency, completeness, and logic. Experiment to discover when and what form of outlining works best for you. **》》** *When classroom work or other specialized writing requires you to produce a formal outline, follow the procedures discussed on pages 36–37.* **《《** Remember, informal and formal outlines are plans, not descriptions of what you must do. Sometimes plans do not work because they are flawed or incomplete. If your plan is not working, do not frustrate yourself by trying to make it work. Instead, decide why it does not work and make appropriate changes.

Informal Outlines

Informal outlines, intended for the *writer's* use only, may be simple lists marked with numbers, arrows, dots, dashes, or any other convenient symbol to indicate relative importance among ideas. Because they are not systematically composed, arranged, and labeled, informal outlines can be completed more easily and quickly than formal outlines. And because they seem less final, writers feel freer to modify them.

Below is Jacob's brief, informal outline.

Plots

⟶ *Novels: complicated situations*

⟶ *Films: simplified situations*

Characterization

⟶ *Novels: variety of relationships*

⟶ *Films: smaller number of relationships*

Theme

⟶ *Novels: multiple themes*

⟶ *Films: primary theme*

Because they make it possible to move items easily without retyping, word-processing programs are ideal tools for informal outlining. Prepare and then print a first version of your informal outline. Evaluate the outline, marking the printed copy with changes. Use the "block" and "move" functions on your computer to execute the changes, and then print a clean version of the outline. A clean printed version of your informal outline is easier to work from than one with scribbled changes.

EXERCISE 2.2 ❯ *Informal outlining*

Compose an informal outline that arranges the large elements from your planning materials. Add missing details and examples as you continue to draft your paper.

Formal Outlines

When an outline is intended for *readers,* **formal outlines** are used because they adhere to a commonly accepted and understood system. Writers often develop an informal outline and then, as ideas and explanations take shape, a formal outline.

Note the following conventions of formal outlines:

Indicate *major topics* with upper-case roman numerals (*I, II, III*). Each of these entries represents one or more whole paragraphs.

Indicate *subdivisions* of topics with upper-case letters (*A, B, C*). Each of these generally represents a cluster of sentences within a paragraph.

Indicate *clarifications* of subdivisions (examples, supporting facts, and so on) with arabic numbers (*1, 2, 3*). Each of these generally represents a sentence.

Indicate *details* in sentences with lower-case letters (*a, b, c*).

In addition, the following conventions are also observed:

Use parallel forms throughout. Use phrases and words in a **topic outline** and full sentences in a **sentence outline.** An outline may use topic sentences for major topics and phrases in subdivisions of topics (a **mixed outline**) but should do so consistently.

Include only one idea in each entry. Subdivide entries that contain more than one idea.

Include at least two entries at each sublevel.

Indicate the inclusion of introductions and conclusions, but do not outline their content.

Align headings of the same level at the same margin.

> **!** Many word-processing programs offer easy-to-use outlining
> features. These generally position automatically the roman
> numeral, capital letter, and other division indicators and
> correctly align the text that you supply for each level. If your
> word processor has these features, learn to use them. They
> will save you time and effort.

The formal outline below organizes Jacob's materials. It is a
mixed outline, using sentences at the roman numeral, or paragraph, level and phrases for the topics within paragraphs.

INTRODUCTION

*Thesis statement: Although film adaptations of novels may seem to
distort original works, the adaptations often create worthy counterparts to the originals.*

   *I. Although plots are simplified for films, films retain the primary
      focus of the original work.*

      A. Huckleberry Finn (Mark Twain): 1885

         1. Forty-three chapters, over three hundred pages

         2. Hundreds of episodes included

      *B. Huckleberry Finn (Joseph Mankiewicz film, with Mickey
         Rooney): 1939*

         1. Eighty-eight minutes

         2. Focuses on five primary episodes

  *II. Films selectively develop characters, necessarily omitting some
      details from the novels.*

      *A. Out of Africa and Shadows on the Grass (Isak Dinesen):
         1938 and 1960, respectively*

      1. *Character of first-person narrator introduced through description of life around her*

      2. *Character developed through cumulative effect of many episodes*

    B. *Out of Africa (Sidney Pollack film, with Meryl Streep): 1986*

      1. *Character revealed through narrative voice-overs*

      2. *Exploration limited to five selected episodes*

  III. *Because of their nature, films often highlight a crucial theme rather than including the multiple themes found in novels.*

    A. *The Grapes of Wrath (John Steinbeck): 1939*

      1. *Thirty chapters, over six hundred pages*

      2. *Interwoven fiction and essays on social problems*

      3. *Multiple themes*

    B. *The Grapes of Wrath (Darryl Zanuck film, with Henry Fonda): 1940*

      1. *129 minutes*

      2. *Three-part narrative*

      3. *Three major themes retained*

CONCLUSION

Use the computer to revise your informal outline into a formal outline. Insert roman numerals and upper-case letters to mark major divisions and then move elements to align them correctly. Insert arabic numerals and lower-case letters, plus additional clarifying materials, to show the degree of detail that your paper will include. Use the word processor's abilities to insert and reformat without retyping existing materials.

EXERCISE 2.3 ❱ *Formal outlining*

Using your informal outline from Exercise 2.2 as a starting point, complete a formal outline, providing necessary elaboration. Create either a mixed outline or a sentence outline, labeling it appropriately. Double-check your work against the guidelines for outlining given on page 36.

2c	❱	**Write a rough draft of your paper.**

The **rough draft** is the first full-length, written form of a paper. It is usually very messy and unfocused. Some parts develop clearly and smoothly from your planning materials, but others develop only after three or four tries. That pattern is typical because writing a rough draft is a shifting process that requires thinking, planning, writing, rethinking, rewriting, replanning, and rewriting again.

Every rough draft has different requirements, varying from paper to paper even for the same writer. Most writers begin their rough drafts by working on the body paragraphs, postponing work on opening and closing paragraphs. They do, however, write with their thesis statements clearly in mind. These additional general strategies are helpful for most writers:

Gather all your materials together. Your work can proceed with relatively few interruptions if all your planning materials and writing supplies are nearby.

Work from your outline. Write one paragraph at a time, in any order, postponing work on troublesome sections until you have gained momentum.

Remember the purpose of your paper. As you write, concentrate on arranging and developing only the ideas presented in your outline or closely related ideas that occur to you.

Use only ideas and details that support your thesis statement. Resist any tendency to drift from your point or to provide interesting but extraneous details.

Remember your readers' needs. Include all information and explanations that readers will need to understand your discussion.

Do not worry about technical matters. Concentrate on getting your ideas down on paper. You can attend to punctuation, mechanics, spelling, and neatness later.

Rethink and modify troublesome sections. If your outline is not working, if an example seems weak or the order of the paragraphs no longer seems logical, change it.

Reread sections as you write. Rereading earlier sections as you write will help you to maintain a reasonably consistent tone.

Write alternative versions of troublesome sections. When you come to a problematic section, write multiple versions of it and then choose the one that works best.

Periodically give yourself a break from writing. Interrupting your writing too often creates problems with consistency of style or tone, but occasionally getting away from it will help you to maintain a fresh perspective and attain objectivity.

Drafting on the word processor

Composing at the computer can be fluid and productive. With the help of the "add," "delete," "move," and "reformat" features in your word-processing program, you will be able to generate a rough draft with relative ease, knowing that you can make both small and large changes without substantial retyping. Using a word processor now will enable you to do the following easily later:

Move words, phrases, sentences, and paragraphs.

Check spelling.

Check format and spacing.

Count the number of words.

Complete "search" and "replace" procedures to change words and phrases.

Begin by copying your outline to a new file, renaming it, and proceeding to compose and type sentences that explain and expand its divisions. Set the line spacing at double-space for good readability; later, when you are ready to print your draft, set the line spacing at triple-space to provide extra room for making changes during revision.

Draft freely, without worrying about missing details, exact wording, or technical correctness. Devise your own system of symbols or key words to mark places in the draft to which you would like to return. Keep your system simple and use it consistently so that it becomes part of your drafting technique and does not interfere with it. The following are helpful strategies:

Use symbols unlikely to appear in your writing (such as *, #, >, +, or ~) or double end punctuation marks. You might use + to mark places needing development or additional details, !! to mark places needing examples, or ?? to mark places at which you are unsure of your information or opinions.

Use brackets or boldface to include alternate word choices or versions of sentences or longer passages.

Use abbreviations or distinctive symbols in place of frequently used long phrases or difficult to spell words and names.

Symbols, abbreviations, and key words can be located using the "search" function. Make your changes and then delete the symbol and unwanted material, or use the "replace" feature to substitute the full form for any abbreviated form.

Until you have completed your final draft, use the "move" function to save material you are tempted to delete. Alternate versions, digressions, examples, and so on, can be moved to the end of the draft, where they will be available for review and possible retrieval. Insert a page break and a heading, such as "Scrap" or "Discard," and hold this material separate from your draft but convenient to it.

For many writers, the process of drafting creates a flood of ideas, not all of them relevant to the project at hand. If that is the case for you, use the capabilities of your word processor to capture these ideas before they escape you. Open a second file in a window or second screen or use your program's "notepad" feature to record ideas, images, questions, reminders, and so on for future use.

Remember to give your draft a clear, logical, recognizable file name; note the date at the beginning of the draft and the name at the end.

EXERCISE 2.4 ❯ *Rough draft*

Write a rough draft of your paper, using the guidelines given above. Work from your outline to ensure that your ideas are supported by adequate detail.

2d

Plan your title and introductory and concluding paragraphs.

The title and the beginning and ending paragraphs of a paper are important because first and final impressions are important. The best time to plan and write these special parts of a paper varies from one paper to the next. They can be developed, written, and rewritten at any time during your planning, drafting, or revising.

Titles

A good **title** is at once descriptive, letting readers know what the paper is about, and imaginative, sparking readers' interest. To achieve these ends, try one or more of these strategies:

Use words or phrases that explicitly identify your topic. Search your draft for expressions that are clear and brief.

Play with language. Consider variations of well-known expressions. Use **alliteration** (repetition of the initial sounds of words) or **assonance** (repetition of internal vowel sounds of words).

Consider two-part titles, the first part imaginative, the second part descriptive. Separate the two parts with a colon.

Match the tone of the title to the tone of the paper. Use serious titles for serious papers, ironic titles for ironic papers, factual titles for factual papers, and so on.

Keep an open mind as you write titles; write as many as you can and select the one that best clarifies your topic for your readers and piques their interest.

Jacob began his search for an effective title by describing his topic in a phrase: "Novels and their film adaptations." Although the phrase labeled his paper clearly, it would not create any special interest among readers. He tried playing with language and considered "A Moving Picture Can Be Worth a Thousand Words" (a variation of a well-known proverb) and "First There Was Fiction, Then There Was Film" (an experiment with alliteration and assonance). Jacob also tried combining his descriptive title with a phrase from his paper to create a two-part title: "From Page to Screen: Novels and Their Film Adaptations." He eventually chose his combined title.

Introductions

The **introduction** to a paper creates interest and clarifies your subject and your opinion for your readers. Depending on the length of the paper, an introduction may be one or several paragraphs long.

Writers generally prepare drafts of alternate introductions, keeping these general goals in mind:

Adjust the length of the introduction to the length of the writing. A brief paper needs a proportionately brief introduction.

Match the tone of the introduction to the tone of the paper. A casual, personal paper needs an informal introduction, whereas a serious, academic paper requires a formal introduction.

The introduction must draw readers into the discussion. It must create interest, suggest the direction the paper will take, and indicate the paper's development.

Although writers use many types of introduction, most openings begin with one or more of the following general strategies and end by presenting a specific thesis statement.

general strategy

specific thesis statement

Below are descriptions of ten of the most commonly used strategies for introductions, with examples.

Allusion

Refer to a work of art, music, literature, film, and so on, or to a mythical, religious, or historical person or event.

> Pity-and-terror, the classically prescribed emotional response to tragic representation, was narrowly restricted to drama by the ancient authorities. In my view, tragedy has a wider reference by far, and pity-and-terror is aroused in me by works of art immeasurably less grand than those which unfold the cosmic undoings of Oedipus and Agamemnon, Antigone, Medea, and the women of Troy. The standard Civil War memorial, for example, is artistically banal by almost any criterion, and yet I am subject to pity-and-terror whenever I reflect upon the dense ironies it embodies. — Arthur C. Danto, "Gettysburg"

Analogy

Make a comparison that is interesting, helpful, and relevant to the topic.

> Were it announced tomorrow that anyone who fancied it might, without risk of reprisals or recriminations, stand at a fourth-storey window, dangle out of it a length of string with a meal (labelled "Free") on the end, wait till a chance passer-by took a bite and then, having entangled his cheek or gullet on a hook hidden in the food, haul him up to the fourth floor and there batter him to death with a knobkerry, I do not think there would be many takers. — Brigid Brophy, "The Rights of Animals"

Anecdote

Begin with a short description of a relevant incident.

> One summer day in 1923 I was taken with two small cousins by trolley westward over the Queensborough Bridge. We were making an ex-

cursion to a matinee at Roxy's. To our left as we clanged across the great web of the bridge I had my first full view of Manhattan, the buildings in their dreamy altitudes piling up down the island around the tallest of all, the Woolworth tower. A heat haze enriched light and shadow on the distant masses. Here and there small plumes of vapor appeared. As the vista slowly shifted, I felt the wonder expected of me as a visiting twelve-year-old from the Midwest. The city already belonged to myth, standing like Asgard beyond the East River water, more of the sky than of the earth. I felt, even so, some formless question stirring at the edge of my mind as to what sense of life that skyline honored or expressed. There was as yet nothing like it in the world. — Robert Fitzgerald, "When the Cockroach Stood by the Mickle Wood"

Definition

Define a term central to your topic. Avoid defining terms already understood, unless such a definition serves a special purpose.

One of the most interesting and characteristic features of democracy is, of course, the difficulty of defining it. And this difficulty has been compounded in the United States, where we have been giving new meanings to almost everything. It is, therefore, especially easy for anyone to say that democracy in America has failed.

"Democracy," according to political scientists, usually describes a form of government by the people, either directly or through their elected representatives. But I prefer to describe a democratic society as one which is governed by a spirit of equality and dominated by the desire to equalize, to give everything to everybody. In the United States the characteristic wealth and skills and know-how and optimism of our country have dominated this quest. — Daniel J. Boorstin, "Technology and Democracy"

Description

Use a description of a scene, person, or event to establish context or mood for your topic.

A single knoll rises out of the plain in Oklahoma, north and west of the Wichita Range. For my people, the Kiowas, it is an old landmark; and they gave it the name Rainy Mountain. The hardest weather in the world is there. Winter brings blizzards, hot tornadic winds arise in the spring, and in summer the prairie is an anvil's edge. The grass turns brittle and brown, and it cracks beneath your feet. There are green belts along the rivers and creeks, linear groves of hickory and pecan, willow and witch hazel. At a distance in July or August the steaming foliage seems almost to writhe in fire. Great green and yellow grasshoppers are everywhere in the tall grass, popping up like corn to sting the flesh, and tortoises crawl about on the red earth, going nowhere in the plenty of time. Loneliness is an aspect of the land. All things in the plain are isolate; there is no confusion of objects in the eye, but *one* hill or *one* tree or *one* man. To look upon that landscape in the early morning, with the sun at your back, is to lose the sense of proportion. Your imagination comes to life, and this, you think, is where Creation was begun. — N. Scott Momaday, "The Way to Rainy Mountain"

Facts and Figures

Begin with specific, interesting, useful information or statistics.

Molokai lies just twenty-six miles from Oahu across the Kaiwi Channel, but the two islands are worlds apart in terms of mood, style and pace. While Honolulu wrestles with traffic, pollution and all the other problems of urbanization, Molokai is relishing its peaceful, rural existence. It has no freeways, stoplights, movie theatres, bowling alleys, elevators, nightclubs, shopping centers, supermarket chains or fast-food outlets. None of its buildings stands more than three stories high. Newcomers may regard Molokai as being unsophisticated, perhaps even backward, but those who know it best recognize the magic in its simplicity. — Cheryl Chee Tsutsumi, "Molokai: One of the Last Hawaiian Outposts"

New Discussion of an Old Subject

Explain why a topic that may be "old hat" is worth examining again.

That the world is mad has been the judgment of self-denominated sane philosophers from the Greeks to the present day. It is not a discovery of our own age that both the public and private lives of human beings are dominated by folly and stupidity. Philosophers pressing the point have brought such charges not against human nature only — that is, the world of human relations — but against that larger universe in which the world of human relations is set. As far back as the Book of Job and probably much further back, for there must have been at least gruntingly articulate Jobs in prehistory, it is not only men who have been declared mad: by any standards of rationality the universe itself has been called irrational, pointless, meaningless, with incidental, unintended overtones of cruelty and injustice.

With the provincialism of each generation, ours imagines that the causes of cynicism and despair are new in our time. There have, of course, been modern improvements and refinements of stupidity and folly. No previous generation has been by way of organizing itself with insane efficiency for blowing the whole race to smithereens. It does not take a particularly logical mind at the present moment to discover that the world is quite mad, though a great many critics apparently think that the cruel absurdity of technical efficiency combined with moral bankruptcy is a discovery that it took great wit on their part to turn up. — Irwin Edman, "A Reasonable Life in a Mad World"

Question

Use a question or a series of questions to provoke readers to think about your subject.

Motherhood is in trouble, and it ought to be. A rude question is long overdue: Who needs it? The answer used to be (1) society and (2) women. But now, with the impending horrors of overpopulation, society desperately *doesn't* need it. And women don't need it either. Thanks to the Motherhood Myth — the idea that having babies is something that all normal women instinctively want and need and will enjoy doing — they just *think* they do. — Betty Rollin, "Motherhood: Who Needs It?"

Quotation

Use what someone else has said or written in a poem, short story,
book, article, or interview.

"We began to sail up the narrow strait lamenting," narrates Odysseus.
"For on the one hand lay Scylla, with twelve feet all dangling down;
and six necks exceeding long, and on each a hideous head, and there-
in three rows of teeth set thick and close, full of black death. And on
the other mighty Charybdis sucked down the salt sea water. As often
as she belched it forth, like a cauldron on a great fire she would seethe
up through all her troubled deeps." Odysseus managed to swerve
around Charybdis, but Scylla grabbed six of his finest men and de-
voured them in his sight — "the most pitiful thing mine eyes have seen
of all my travail in searching out the paths of the sea."

False lures and dangers often come in pairs in our legends and metaphors — consider the frying pan and the fire, or the devil and the deep
blue sea. Prescriptions for avoidance either emphasize a dogged
steadiness — the straight and narrow of Christian evangelists — or an
averaging between unpleasant alternatives — the golden mean of
Aristotle. The idea of steering a course between undesirable extremes
emerges as a central prescription for a sensible life. — Stephen Jay
Gould, "Darwin's Middle Road"

Startling Statement

Use an arresting statement to get readers' attention and arouse
their interest.

Young people should have the right to control and direct their own
learning, that is, to decide what they want to learn, and when, where,
how, how much, how fast, and with what help they want to learn it. To
be still more specific, I want them to have the right to decide if, when,
how much, and by whom they want to be *taught* and the right to decide whether they want to learn in a school and if so which one and for
how much of the time.

No human right, except the right to life itself, is more fundamental than this. A person's freedom of learning is part of his freedom of thought, even more basic than his freedom of speech. — John Holt, "The Right to Control One's Own Learning"

> Write sample introductions at the computer, where you can easily copy and revise them. Decide on a number of strategies and quickly type out a draft of each, incorporating your thesis statement by using the "block" and "copy" commands to save typing time. Then print copies.
> Rereading the draft introductions in printed form is easy and gives you a clear sense of their length. Decide which introduction seems most effective, and move it to the beginning of the draft of your paper. You can always move it again and try another. Save all versions until you have completed your final draft; they may provide you with good ideas later.

Jacob considered a number of introductions for his paper, trying to find one that would interest his readers as well as clarify his topic:

Anecdote
   Tell about Todd and me at the video store.

Facts and figures
   Discuss details of making of The Birth of a Nation, the first major film adaptation of a novel.

Allusion
   Discuss the wide variety of books adapted into film: The Scarlet Letter, Of Human Bondage, Gone with the Wind, Great Expectations, and so on.

Jacob considered the anecdote but decided that its personal, informal tone did not match his purpose for the paper, which was to

be informative. The facts about *The Birth of a Nation,* though interesting, if arranged as an anecdote, might not clearly relate to his
thesis. A list of allusions might seem superficial. Jacob decided to
combine facts and figures with allusions to create interest, connect with readers' experiences, and suggest the wide range of his
topic.

EXERCISE 2.5 ❯ *Title and introductory paragraphs*

*Write several titles for your paper and select the most effective one.
Then write two draft versions of the introduction, using the guidelines
given above. Make sure that your strategies both create interest and
clearly and appropriately introduce your topic.*

Conclusions

A **conclusion** reemphasizes the writer's point and provides an
opportunity to create a desired final impression. Most conclusions
begin with a brief but specific summary and then use a concluding
strategy to present a general observation.

Some introductory strategies — such as allusion, analogy,
anecdote, description, and quotation — can also be useful concluding strategies. The following strategies are particularly appropriate for conclusions.

Challenge

Ask readers to reconsider and change their behavior or ideas or to consider new behavior and ideas.

> These arguments give me reason to think that in setting out the finds from the Phylakopi Sanctuary in sometimes almost exhaustive detail we are not presenting the trivial minutiae of something that might better be relegated to an unregarded data archive. One can readily sense that there still remain possibilities within these data, as yet unexploited by us, for much broader and more illuminating interpretations. These will be difficult to develop effectively until we have the materials from other Aegean sanctuaries available to us with a comparable degree of detail. When we do, I believe that we shall begin to see our way of tackling more effectively some of the really big questions concerning the early development of Aegean life and culture. — Colin Renfrew, *The Archaeology of Cult*

Framing Pattern

Frame your essay by modifying some central words, phrases, or images used in the introduction to reflect the progress in thought made in the paper. When appropriate, the introductory strategy may be repeated as the concluding strategy, intensifying the framing effect, as in the following example using description. (The corresponding introduction appears on page 46.)

> The next morning I awoke at dawn and went out on the dirt road to Rainy Mountain. It was already hot, and the grasshoppers began to fill the air. Still, it was early in the morning, and the birds sang out of the shadows. The long yellow grass on the mountain shone in the bright light, and a scissortail hied above the land. There, where it ought to be, at the end of a long and legendary way, was my grandmother's grave. Here and there on the dark stones were ancestral names. Looking back once, I saw the mountain and came away. — N. Scott Momaday, "The Way to Rainy Mountain"

Summary

Summarize, restate, or evaluate the major points you presented in your paper. This strategy must be used carefully and thoughtfully to avoid becoming mere repetition.

> True as it is that the essential function of art for a class destined to change the world is not that of *making magic* but of *enlightening* and *stimulating action,* it is equally true that a magical residue in art cannot be entirely eliminated, for without that minute residue of its original nature, art ceases to be art.
>
> In all the forms of its development, in dignity and fun, persuasion and exaggeration, sense and nonsense, fantasy and reality, art always has a little to do with magic.
>
> Art is necessary in order that man should be able to recognize and change the world. But art is also necessary by virtue of the magic inherent in it. — Ernst Fischer, "The Function of Art"

Visualization of the Future

Predict what the nature or condition of your topic will be like in the near or distant future. Be realistic.

> Ultimately a new breed of pioneer will colonize space, just as last century's pioneers settled the western frontier of this country. Once the rockets are flying, the labs are orbiting, and the external tanks are converted into habitable environments, workers who can't find jobs on Earth will relocate to space, where industry will be as rich and multifarious as industry on Earth. "The next billionaires will be made in space," says Amroc's Koopman. "The skies are paved with gold."
> — Beth Karlin, "Starship Enterprise"

> Work at the keyboard to produce a draft of your conclusion. Work quickly, emphasizing important connections among ideas in the body paragraphs. Remember that you will be able to revise your work later.

Jacob, though aware that his plans might change as he wrote his paper, considered several conclusion strategies:

Use a quotation from E. D. Hirsch stating that people sometimes know about novels they have not read from seeing film adaptations.

Challenge readers to read a novel whose film adaptation they have seen (or to see the film version of a novel they have read) and then to compare the two experiences.

As in introduction, allude to specific films, varying the list, and suggest that readers take the opportunity to read the corresponding novels.

Jacob ultimately decided to combine quotation and challenge.

EXERCISE 2.6 ❯   *Concluding paragraphs*

Write two draft versions of your conclusion. Make sure that your strategies are closely connected to the tone and topic of your paper.

3 Revising

Few writers produce a clear, consistent, complete, and correct piece of writing with their first draft — and few expect to. Rather, writers work knowing that they will have the chance to go back to their drafts and reread and revise them. **Revision,** which means "to see again," provides an opportunity for writers to rethink, reorganize, rephrase, refine, and redirect their work. It allows writers to polish their work, preparing it for readers by putting it into the best possible form.

Quick Reference

Revising is much more than proofreading and correcting technical errors. It is a rich opportunity to refine, clarify, and, if necessary, reconceive the paper, from its large to its small features.

> ❯ *Evaluate your content critically and delete or replace anything that does not effectively support your main idea.*

> ❯ *Improve the style of your paper by reworking sentences to make them varied, emphatic, and clear.*

> ❯ *Eliminate technical errors. These interfere with easy reading and draw attention away from your ideas.*

> ❯ *Use peer review for an unbiased response to your specific questions and an assessment of the strengths and weaknesses of the paper as a whole.*

> ❯ *Prepare the final copy of your paper, making any additional changes necessary and following accepted guidelines for manuscript preparation.*

Experienced writers often revise by rereading their writing and making simultaneous changes in content, sentence structure, word choice, punctuation, and mechanics; such single-stage reworking is often called a **global revision.** When you have sufficient experience with writing, you too will be able to make global revisions. For now, it will be easier for you to revise in the three stages described in this chapter: **content revision, style revision,** and **technical revision.**

A Revision Sequence

Set aside the rough draft.

Reread the draft.

Revise content.

Revise style.

Revise technical errors.

Consult a peer editor.

Make final changes.

Prepare a final copy to submit.

3a ⟩ **Set aside your rough draft for as long as possible.**

After finishing your draft, take a break from your writing. At this point in the process, many writers are tired or even frustrated, and most cannot see their own work clearly. Absorbed in thinking about their topics, they sometimes assume that their drafts are clearer or more complete than they really are. Knowing this, most writers interrupt their work to relax briefly and to gain or regain objectivity about their drafts before they begin revision.

To begin your revision with objectivity, set your rough draft aside for as long as possible. Several days would be best, but if that is not possible, then stop working on the paper for at least several hours. Telephone a friend, listen to music, take a walk, or study for another course. Do *anything* that will rest and refresh your mind for writing and allow you to look at your work critically and with detachment.

| 3b | > | **Revise the content of your paper.** |

When you return to your paper, examine its content for clarity, coherence, and completeness. To guide your revision, consider the following questions:

Are the title and the introductory strategy interesting, clear, and appropriate in tone?

Does the thesis statement clearly present the topic and your opinion about it?

Do the topics of the paragraphs support the thesis statement? Are they clearly stated?

Are the topics presented in a clear, emphatic order?

Are the paragraphs adequately developed? Is there enough detail? Are there enough examples? Does information in each paragraph relate to the thesis statement?

Are the summary and concluding strategy effective?

When you have many content revisions, do more than one revised draft.

!   ***Word processing and content revision***

Revising papers written on a word processor can be relatively easy. Two basic approaches to computer revision are possible; the choice between them depends on how comfortable you feel working at the keyboard. Each is presented below.

"Hard-Copy" Revision

Working from a printed copy of the rough draft is best for writers who have limited experience with word processors or who are uncomfortable with computers.

Triple-space the draft; leave extra-wide margins.

"Hard-copy" revision allows you to evaluate several pages simultaneously, making it a good method for evaluating and correcting organizational and other large-scale problems.

Once you produce revision notes and rewritten portions of the draft, transfer them to the computer file, first making a back-up copy of the original and giving it a different file name. This transfer stage makes "hard-copy" revision somewhat slower than "on-screen" revision.

"Hard-copy" revision works best for complex or extensive revisions, such as remedying problems with logical coherence and transitions.

Advice: Avoid the urge to "respect" a printed version just because it looks finished; it may still require major reworking.

"On-Screen" Revision

"On-screen" revision works best for writers familiar and comfortable with computers and word-processing programs.

Keep a back-up copy of the original draft, giving it a different file name.

Work one screen at a time, evaluating each phrase, sentence, and paragraph and typing changes as you think of them.

Working "on screen" can be quicker than working on a "hard copy."

"On-screen" revision works best for simple revisions: additions, deletions, and limited rearranging of material.

Use whichever approach best matches your needs and experience with computers. Remember that each approach will help you to incorporate content revisions without completely retyping or rewriting the paper.

Figure 1 shows the content revisions that Jacob made in the rough draft of his first body paragraph: (1) he clarified several sentences; (2) he added important information about the film that he had inadvertently omitted; (3) he deleted an example that he had mistakenly thought was in the film; and (4) he added a sentence explicitly connecting the example to his thesis statement.

Figure 1

and selectively
Because of time limits films necessarally omit parts of a novel to fit
to 3
a 2 hour format. The filmmaker must choose the primary elements of
The Adventures of Huckleberry Finn (1885)
the plot to include. A good example is Twain's ~~Huck Finn~~*. It is 43*

chapters, it is 300+ pages, and it includes many episodes. Such a
in full form
long work could not be brought to the screen, so the 1939 film ver-
produced by J. Mankiewicz and starring Mickey Rooney
sion includes portions of Twains work, the the most important plot
the trip down the Mississippi river,
elements in abbreviated form. Huck and Jim's escape, the Duke
and Daulphin
episode, ~~the Sarah Mary Williams episode,~~ and the Grangerferd

feud are brought from the page to the screen, showing the the

most important of Huck's adventures, even though many secondary
seens are left out. Elements of novels must be cut. Most often filmakers
keep the important elements to capture the spirit of the original novel.

EXERCISE 3.1 ❯ Content revision

Reread your draft and respond to the questions on page 57. Unless
you can answer each question with an unequivocal yes, *revise your*
draft until the content is clear, coherent, and complete.

| 3c | ⟩ | **Revise the style of your paper.** |

Achieving clear, adequately developed content is the first step in
revision. The second step is achieving a clear and compelling
presentation of that content.

When you have developed strong content in your paper, refine
the style, using these questions as a guide:

Do the lengths and types of sentences vary?

Do sentences clearly and concisely express their meaning?

Are word choices vivid, accurate, and appropriate?

Word processing and style revision

Style revision can be effectively done on the computer because you can add to, delete from, and combine or separate your sentences without completely retyping the text. Some specific guidelines follow:

Check sentence length. Have your word-processing program locate periods (most will end sentences) using the "search" commands. As the program executes the search, notice the approximate number of lines the cursor skips. If it is pausing frequently within lines or on every line, some sentences are probably too short. If the cursor often skips three or more lines, some sentences may be too long.

Check for repeated expressions. Use the "search" commands to locate words that you suspect you use too often. Especially look for slang, jargon, and technical terms, intensifiers like *very,* and proper names, all of which can be distracting if overused. Then change some of them.

Check for passive constructions. Search for forms of the verb *to be,* the auxiliary forms used to create passive sentences. When the search finds one of these verbs, reread the sentence, check for passive voice, and rephrase the sentence if necessary.

Do most sentences use the active voice?

Do transitions adequately relate ideas?

To get a sense of how your paper flows, read it aloud, with or without an audience, noting where word choices are awkward or

where phrases are difficult to follow. Your hesitations while reading orally will help you pinpoint areas that require reworking.

After revising the content of his paper, Jacob considered the
effectiveness of its style. He decided to make a number of major
and minor changes: (1) he altered his word choices throughout
the paragraph, making them more vivid; (2) he added transitions;
and (3) he combined some short, choppy sentences to improve
the flow of the paragraph. Jacob's content revisions are shown in
Figure 2.

Figure 2

constraints adaptations must distill
Because of time limits films necessarally and selectively omit parts
                                                 , as a result, select
of a novel to fit a 2 to 3 hour format. The filmaker must choose the
                                  For example, Mark
primary elements of the plot to include. A good example is Twain's
                                  a lengthy novel of   presented in
The Adventures of Huckleberry Finn (1885). It is 43 chapters, it is
approximately 300 pages.   *Its*   *would make it impossible to*
300+ pages, and it includes many episodes. Such a long work
bring the novel to film in its   ⊙   *Consequently,*
could not be brought in full form to the screen, so the 1939 film
                       Joseph
version produced by J. Mankiewicz and starring Mickey Rooney
             only the most pivatal   presenting an abbreviated
includes portions of Twains work, the the most important plot ele-
   version of the novel.
ments in abbreviated form. Huck and Jim's escape, the trip down

the Mississippi river, the Duke and Daulphin episode, and the
                                transposed
Grangerferd feud are brought from the page to the screen, show-
   presenting only   ^   ⊙ *Although*
ing the the most important of Huck's adventures, even though
                                       e   *like Huckleberry Finn*
many secondary seens are left out. Elements of novels must be
                                typically retain core   *of the plot*
cut. Most often filmakers keep the important elements to capture

the spirit of the original novel.

EXERCISE 3.2 ❭   *Style revision*

Revise the style of your paper by answering the questions on pages 60–61.

3d	❭	**Eliminate technical errors and inconsistencies.**

Technical revision focuses on grammar, punctuation, mechanics, spelling, and manuscript form. After eliminating major problems with content and style, consider the technical revisions that will make your paper correct and precise.

Ask yourself the following general questions and also watch for technical errors that you know you make frequently.

Are all words correctly spelled? (When in doubt, always look up the correct spelling in your dictionary.)

Are any necessary words omitted? Are any words unnecessarily repeated?

Is punctuation accurate? (See "Punctuation," starting on page NO TAG.)

Are elements of mechanics properly used? (See "Mechanics," starting on page 380.)

Are all sentences complete?

Do nouns and pronouns and subjects and verbs agree in number and gender as appropriate?

Are all pronoun antecedents clear?

Are all modifiers logically positioned?

Make technical revisions slowly and carefully, giving particular attention to the kinds of errors that you have made in the past. If you

Word processing and technical revision

Use word-processing capabilities to help you check for potential problems and make some technical revisions.

Check spelling. A spelling program (a standard feature of many word-processing programs) will search your manuscript for words not found in its dictionary. When the spelling program highlights a word that is suspect, consider the word carefully. It may be spelled incorrectly, or it may be a technical term or a proper name not found in the program's dictionary. Look up suspect words in a standard college dictionary. Spelling programs will also highlight words typed twice in succession.

▶▶▶ *Remember that spelling checkers will not highlight a misspelled word that happens to be another word correctly spelled (for example,* hale *instead of* half *) nor a correctly spelled word used in the wrong context (for example,* their *instead of* there *). Always carefully proofread the spelling of your papers.* **◀◀◀**

Check for specialized punctuation. Because some marks of punctuation — semicolons, colons, dashes, and parentheses — must be used with special care, use the "search" commands to locate them in your manuscript; then double-check their use. For example, search for colons and then check to see that they are preceded by full sentences.

Check pronoun usage. Use the "search" commands to find uses of pronouns (*he, she, they,* and others). Note whether each pronoun has a clear and correct antecedent (the word it refers to), and correct any unclear or inaccurate references.

are uncertain whether you have made an error, look up the applicable rule in this book.

After making his content and style revisions, Jacob made his technical revisions: (1) he corrected spelling errors; (2) he inserted necessary italics; (3) he corrected his use of numbers; (4) he eliminated words inadvertently repeated; (5) he corrected his punctuation. Jacob's style revisions are shown in Figure 3.

Figure 3

Because of time constraints, film adaptations must distill a novel to fit a ~~2 to 3 hour~~ two-to-three-hour format. ~~The filmaker~~ Filmmakers must, as a result, select primary elements of the plot to include. For example, Mark Twain's ~~The Adventures of Huckleberry Finn~~ The Adventures of Huckleberry Finn (1885) is a lengthy novel of ~~43~~ forty-three chapters, presented in approximately ~~300~~ three hundred pages. Its many episodes would make it impossible to bring the novel to film in its full form. Consequently, the 1939 film version, produced by Joseph Mankiewicz and starring Mickey Rooney, includes only the most ~~pivatal~~ pivotal portions of ~~Twains~~ Twain's work, presenting an abbreviated version of the novel. Huck and Jim's escape, the trip down the Mississippi ~~river~~ River, the Duke and ~~Daulphin~~ Dauphin episode, and the ~~Granger-ferd~~ Grangerford feud are transposed from the page to the screen; the film presents ~~, presenting~~ only the most important of Huck's adventures. Although elements of novels like ~~Huckleberry Finn~~ Huckleberry Finn must be cut, ~~filmakers~~ filmmakers typically retain core elements of the plot to capture the spirit of the original novel.

EXERCISE 3.3 ❱ *Technical revision*

Return to your paper and examine it for technical errors, revising to eliminate them as you work. Work slowly and carefully, using Parts 4, 5, and 6 of this handbook to review rules of grammar, punctuation, and mechanics.

3e ⟩ **Use peer editing to help you revise.**

A peer editor, often another student in the course for which you are writing, will read your paper and evaluate its content, style, and technical correctness. In many composition classes, sessions are set aside for peer reviews; but when they are not (or for other courses), ask another writer to read and respond to your paper — not to rework it for you but to point out anything incomplete, unclear, inconsistent, or incorrect.

If your instructor does not provide specific guidance for peer editing, consider these basic approaches:

Find a peer editor with writing experience and standards that are similar to yours. Ideally, your peer editor should be from your class because then you and he or she are likely to share similar expectations about audience, purpose, and requirements for the paper.

Ask a peer editor specific questions, focusing on issues of particular importance to you. If, for instance, you are concerned about the organization of your paper, ask for an assessment of the order of the information or paragraphs. If you have difficulties with subject-verb agreement, ask the peer editor to check agreement. Don't simply ask for an editor to read and praise the paper, for such an undirected review will not help you to revise. Rather, ask for specific comments matched to your needs and expect criticism as well as praise.

Ask th... peer editor to point out problems but to refrain from
alt... your paper. A good peer editor would note, for in-
...that your introductory strategy does not reflect the tone
...pose of your paper but would leave it to you to recon-
...nd revise the strategy — if you agreed with his or her as-
...ent. Don't expect the editor to rewrite your paper for you.

...sider carefully the comments and queries of your peer edi-
...but also trust your own judgment. Notes about confusing,
...mplete, or incorrect passages will always require attention.
... on matters of judgment or personal taste — specific word
choices, titles, and so on — consider your editor's notations
carefully but remember that the paper is *yours*. Make no subjective changes that do not seem right and necessary to you.

Peer editing will not substitute for your own careful evaluation
and revision of your paper, and it will not eliminate all problems.
It will elicit useful responses to your work before you prepare the
final copy.

EXERCISE 3.4 ❯ *Peer editing*

*Prepare for peer editing by listing four to six features that you would
like an editor to check. They may relate to any aspect of the content,
style, or technical correctness of your paper. Using your list of specific
concerns and the following list of editing questions, ask a peer editor
to evaluate your revised paper.*

Introduction

Do the title and introductory strategy create interest? Are they appropriate?

Is the thesis statement appropriately positioned? Does it express a
clear topic and opinion? Does it include any necessary qualifications
and clarifications?

Body paragraphs

Is the order of the paragraphs appropriate? Would another ~~arrange~~-ment work better?

Does the topic of each paragraph clearly relate to the thesis state~~ment?~~
Are topics developed sufficiently?

Are transitions smoothly made between sentences within paragra~~phs~~ and between paragraphs?

Conclusion

Does the conclusion effectively draw together and summarize the paper?

Is the concluding strategy appropriate?

Style

Are the sentences varied, coherent, forceful, and smooth?
Are the word choices vivid, accurate, and appropriate?

Technical matters

Are the sentences grammatical?
Is the usage standard?
Are punctuation and mechanics correct?

Word processing and personal revision guidelines

Use the guidelines for revising content, style, and technical matters on pages 57, 60–61, and 63–64 as the basis for a personal file of revision guidelines. Type the questions listed, or as many of them as you regularly find useful in your college writing, into a separate file. Add to the file reminders about frequent or recurring problems in your drafts and useful suggestions for improving your writing made by peer editors and teachers. Add a list of words you most frequently misspell.

Print a copy of the file to use when reviewing drafts, or use it on-screen, in a second screen or a window, as a personal revision checklist.

| **3f** > | **Prepare a final copy of your paper.** |

Most papers should be not handwritten but neatly and cleanly typewritten or printed on a computer printer, following the general manuscript guidelines that appear in Appendix A, "Manuscript Form." Your instructor will let you know of any specific requirements for preparing a final manuscript.

EXERCISE 3.5 ❯ *A final copy*

Prepare the final copy of your paper. Work carefully, proofreading each page before you remove it from the typewriter. As a safeguard, photocopy the final manuscript. Submit the original typed copy of your paper — on time.

Word processing and preparing a final manuscript

If you have been working on the computer, preparing the final copy will be easy.

Make final changes. Having made most of your substantive changes during content, style, and technical revision, in all probability you will need to make only small changes — for example, final adjustments in word choice.

Insert paging codes. For your final copy, include your name and the page number in the upper right corner of each page. Using the program's "menu," usually with the designation *heads* or *running heads,* insert the codes to print name and page number. One code will then run throughout the paper, and paging will be done automatically.

Print a draft-quality copy for yourself. Using the draft mode, prepare a copy of the final paper to keep for yourself. Double-check to make sure that the manuscript format is accurate; if it is not, make necessary changes.

Print a high-quality copy to submit. Use a letter-quality printer, if possible, to produce a manuscript that looks typed. If one is not available, use the correspondence-quality mode of the available printer.

3g > **A sample paper.**

Jacob Westgard   Westgard 1

Ms. Chiu

English 105

7 January 1990

                        From the Page to the Screen:

                    Novels and Their Film Adaptations

        In 1915, just two decades after the first film was

shown publicly, The Birth of a Nation premiered in New

York. This major work by D. W. Griffith is a landmark

film for a number of reasons, not the least of which is

that it was the first full-length film adaptation of a

novel, Thomas Dixon's The Clansman. In the decades which
followed, other adaptations of novels--The Hunchback of
Notre Dame, The Phantom of the Opera, The Scarlet Letter,
Anna Karenina, and Mutiny on the Bounty, to name but a
few--introduced works of literature to viewing audiences.
The legacy of adaptations continues to our times, although some critics skeptically note that these are
"Hollywood" versions, bastardizations of the novels that
inspired them. But such films deserve our attention.
Although film adaptations of novels may seem to distort
original works, the adaptations often create worthy
counterparts to the originals.

Because of time constraints, film adaptations must
distill a novel to fit a two-to-three-hour format.
Filmmakers must, as a result, select primary elements of
the plot to include. For example, Mark Twain's The
Adventures of Huckleberry Finn (1885) is a lengthy novel
of forty-three chapters, presented in approximately three
hundred pages. Its many episodes would make it impossible to bring the novel to film in its full form. Consequently, the 1939 film version, produced by Joseph
Mankiewicz and starring Mickey Rooney, includes only the
most pivotal portions of Twain's work, presenting an
abbreviated version of the novel. Huck and Jim's escape,
the trip down the Mississippi River, the Duke and Dauphin

episode, and the Grangerford feud are transposed from the page to the screen; the film presents only the most important of Huck's adventures. Although elements of novels like <u>Huckleberry Finn</u> must be cut, filmmakers typically retain core elements of the plot to capture the spirit of the original novel.

Filmmakers also elliptically develop characters to create the essence of their novelistic counterparts. In Isak Dinesen's essay-novels <u>Out of Africa</u> (1938) and <u>Shadows on the Grass</u> (1960), the character Karen Blixen emerges through her descriptions of other characters and incidents. It is a cumulative characterization, not one described--for the character Karen Blixen is a self-portrait. In the 1985 film <u>Out of Africa</u>, produced by Sidney Pollack, Meryl Streep creates the crucial impressions of Karen Blixen in several important ways. She narrates the opening and several key portions of the film, helping to recreate the emotional distance Dinesen established in her work. And a few wisely selected episodes from the novels show Blixen's stoicism, independence, and temerity: her marriage of convenience, her response to contracting syphilis from her husband, her schooling of the Kikuyu children, her openly taking a lover. These episodes become visual symbols representing the character of Karen Blixen and capture the spirit of

the novels. All complexities of characterization are not
and cannot be included in <u>Out of Africa</u> and in other
adaptations, but because of similar selective portrayals,
films can offer representative and satisfying characterizations.

Because films must compress their messages into
restricted time frames, filmmakers must also reduce the
thematic complexities of novels when they are adapted for
the screen. When filmmakers select central themes to
concentrate upon, omitting minor ones, something of the
intricacy of the novel is lost, of course, but the major
emphasis remains. John Steinbeck's <u>The Grapes of Wrath</u>
(1939), for example, contains thirty chapters covering
over six hundred pages. In a work so long. myriad themes
emerge that could not possibly be treated in a two-to-
three-hour film. Yet in the 1940 film adaptation, produced by Darryl Zanuck and starring Henry Fonda, the most
powerful themes--humanity's powerlessness against nature,
people's exploitation of other people, and the tantaliz-
ing nature of socialist reform--all come through. Secondary themes from the sweeping novel do not make their
way to the screen, but the most important ones do.
Filmmakers like Zanuck cannot hope to imbue their films
with the multiple themes found in many novels, but
through careful selection they reduce the number of

themes and concentrate upon giving them the dramatic, visual impact that films can offer.

Novels and films are distinct genres, each with its strengths and appeals. Film adaptations--though necessarily simpler in terms of plot, character, and theme than the novels on which they are based--do represent the complexities of the printed works. E. D. Hirsch has noted, "The American conception of Sherlock Holmes has been formed more by the acting of Basil Rathbone than by the writing of Conan Doyle. Judy Garland and Bert Lahr have fixed our conception of The Wizard of Oz more vividly than Frank Baum" (147). What we must remember is that reading novels and seeing film adaptations do not have to be mutually exclusive activities. Instead, there is insight to be gained and enjoyment to be found in examining the ways that filmmakers take a novel from the page to the screen.

Work Cited

Hirsch, E. D. Cultural Literacy: What Every American Needs to Know. Boston: Houghton, 1987.

4 Paragraphs

Paragraphs focus on single facets of a subject. A single paragraph describes or explains one idea; as part of a series of paragraphs in a paper, a single paragraph develops one aspect of the paper's thesis. Paragraph length varies with the writer's purpose, the nature of the material in the paragraph, and the function of the paragraph. To present ideas effectively, all paragraphs, short or long, must be unified, coherent, complete, and developed.

Quick Reference

Paragraphs, the building blocks of papers, must be focused, structured, and developed.

> *Write paragraphs that develop single ideas, using topic sentences, when appropriate, to clarify your focus for readers.*

> *Use the stylistic techniques of transition and repetition to link ideas within and between paragraphs.*

> *Use varied methods of paragraph development, selecting patterns appropriate to the ideas that you generated during planning.*

4a ▷ Develop unified paragraphs.

A **unified paragraph** includes information pertinent to the main idea and excludes information that is not pertinent. Often a topic

---

Note: Many of the exercises in this chapter will take you through the steps of writing paragraphs. Keep the work from each exercise to use in later exercises.

sentence states the main idea explicitly and indicates by its phrasing the pattern of development that the paragraph follows.

Lack of unity is a common problem in early drafts. You can
avoid blurring the focus of a paragraph by keeping the following
points in mind.

Focus on One Topic

A unified paragraph develops one main idea only; it does not include information that is loosely related to the main idea or that
constitutes an additional main idea. The following paragraph is
not unified because it describes two museums (two topics) without establishing a connection between them.

> The Metropolitan Museum of Art in New York City is an impressive
> example of nineteenth-century architecture. Made of stone with mas-
> sive columns and elaborately carved scrollwork, it is institutional ar-
> chitecture of the sort we expect in public buildings. Farther up Fifth
> Avenue, the Guggenheim Museum of Modern Art is built of reinforced
> concrete. This museum forms a spatial helix, a continuous spiral that
> expands as it rises; each level is marked by a narrow band of windows.
> Its design is severe and unusual.

Without any suggestion that the museums are being contrasted,
the writer creates an unnecessary shift in topic as the discussion
moves from one museum to the other. The writer could add a
topic sentence to show the relationship between the Guggenheim
and the Metropolitan Museum of Art or treat each museum in a
separate, focused paragraph.

> The Metropolitan Museum of Art in New York City is a typical example
> of nineteenth-century public architecture. Made of stone, with mas-
> sive columns, tall casement windows, and an elaborately carved enta-
> blature, it is institutional architecture that conveys the dignity we ex-
> pect in great public museum buildings. It is reminiscent of the Louvre
> in Paris, the British Museum in London, and the National Gallery in
> Washington. Familiar yet impressive, it suggests a grand purpose.

Farther up Fifth Avenue, the Guggenheim Museum of Modern Art offers a contrasting, twentieth-century view of museum architecture. Built of reinforced concrete in the form of a spatial helix, a continuous spiral that expands as it rises, it is adorned only by a continuous band of simple windows. In 1937, when it was designed by Frank Lloyd Wright, the building's severity made it seem very modern, very alien, and austere rather than august. Yet it changed the way Americans perceived institutional architecture, and we now find similar designs in a range of public buildings from libraries to high schools.

Include Relevant Details Only

In trying to be specific, writers sometimes include a number of interesting details, some of which are marginally related or irrelevant to the topic. Unrelated information takes a paragraph in too many directions and destroys unity, as in this paragraph:

(1) Hurricanes are cyclones that develop in the tropical waters of the Atlantic Ocean. (2) Forming large circles or ovals, they have winds of 75 miles per hour or more and can measure 500 miles across. (3) Years ago, hurricanes were named after women — Irene, Sarah, Becky, for example — but now they are also named after men. (4) They usually form hundreds of miles from land and then move slowly to the northwest at about 10 miles per hour. (5) For reasons unknown, they pick up speed rapidly when they reach the twenty-fifth parallel. (6) That means, in very practical terms, that they reach peak speed and destructive power by the time they hit North American coastlines. (7) Hurricanes that form in the Pacific Ocean are commonly called typhoons.

Here, all the material relates to hurricanes, but some of it only loosely. Sentences 1, 2, 4, 5, and 6 are factual descriptions of how the storms form and move. Sentences 3 and 7 include interesting but only marginally relevant information. The unity of the paragraph would be improved by omitting the unrelated material, which might fit into another paragraph.

Use Topic Sentences

A **topic sentence** presents a paragraph's main idea and indicates the writer's opinion about it. As succinct statements of the writer's idea and intended development of that idea, topic sentences unify the paragraphs in which they appear. In long papers, the topic sentences of all body paragraphs, taken together, constitute the ideas and major illustrations that support the paper's thesis.

A topic sentence at the beginning of a paragraph works like a map, providing an overview that guides readers through the writing. A topic sentence at the end of a paragraph summarizes its ideas. Sometimes, especially in descriptive paragraphs, a topic sentence is unnecessary; readers will be able to infer the writer's point from the paragraph as a whole. Writers sometimes feel that including a topic sentence in every paragraph makes writing mechanical and predictable. If you decide to omit a topic sentence from one of your paragraphs, remember that its absence may be confusing to your readers, who may not fully understand or may misinterpret your point.

Topic sentence at the beginning

Euphemisms thus serve as verbal placebos; they are particularly frequent when the ill-timed provocation could expose one to instant retaliation. Sports figures are always careful to speak with respect, even admiration, of their upcoming opponents, however inept. Precautionary and placatory euphemisms include variations on the theme, "They're a much better team than their record shows," and that minimal, thread-bare uncompliment, "They never give up." Everywhere except in politics (where it's accepted practice to toot one's own horn as loudly as possible), false modesty is useful protection against overconfidence on one's own part and provocation of the opponent. — Robert M. Adams, "Soft Soap and the Nitty-Gritty"

Topic sentence at the end

When we think of providing substance, we are perhaps tempted first to find some way of filling students' minds with a goodly store of general ideas, available on demand. This temptation is not necessarily a bad one. After all, if we think of adult writers who interest us, most of them have such a store; they have read and thought about man's major problems, and they have opinions and arguments ready at hand about how men ought to live, how society ought to be run, how literature ought to be written. Edmund Wilson, for example, one of the most consistently interesting men alive, seems to have an inexhaustible flow of reasoned opinions on any subject that comes before him. **Obviously our students are not going to interest us until they too have some ideas.** — Wayne C. Booth, "Boring from Within"

No topic sentence

Whenever I had nothing better to do in San Salvador I would walk up in the leafy stillness of the San Benito and Escalón districts, where the hush at midday is broken only by the occasional crackle of a walkie-talkie, the click of metal moving on a weapon. I recall a day in San Benito when I opened my bag to check an address, and heard the clicking of metal on metal all up and down the street. On the whole no one walks up here, and pools of blossoms lie undisturbed on the sidewalks. Most of the houses in San Benito are more recent than those in Escalón, less idiosyncratic and probably smarter, but the most striking architectural features in both districts are not the houses but their walls, walls built upon walls, walls stripped of the copa de oro and bougainvillea, walls that reflect successive generations of violence: the original stone, the additional five or six or ten feet of brick, and finally the barbed wire, sometimes concertina, sometimes electrified; walls with watch towers, gun ports, closed-circuit television cameras, walls now reaching twenty and thirty feet. — Joan Didion, "Salvador"

Use the computer's capabilities to block and move materials to reposition your topic sentences, experimenting with different ways to create emphasis. Print copies of different versions and read and evaluate them, noting their relative effectiveness. Choose the version that best suits your purpose and tone to use in your draft.

EXERCISE 4.1 ❯ *Topic sentences*

 The following paragraph lacks unity because it has a poor topic sentence. Revise the topic sentence to give the paragraph a clearer focus and then strike out any irrelevant material.

In the early days of television, children in major roles were represented as middle class and stereotypically good looking and childlike. Timmy, the boy on *Lassie,* had well-cut blond hair, sparkling eyes, a straight-toothed smile. He even had dimples. He was naive in a way children were only when portrayed in early television. He ignored warnings, got into trouble, was rescued by his dog, and learned a new lesson each week — and the lesson always had to do with following adults' rules. Timmy, in an idealized way, always learned to like adult rules. Nobody on today's programs is like that. Certainly Kevin, the cute boy on *The Wonder Years,* isn't so attuned to adult expectations. Like Timmy, Kevin is adorable, has a good haircut, wears nice clothes, and has a winning smile. But unlike Timmy, Kevin doesn't learn simple and positive lessons about adult rules. In fact, Kevin often learns to accept the stupidity but inevitability of adult rules with a wry and cynical maturity beyond his years. He and Timmy may both be adorable, but Kevin shows that television's portrayals of children have become more realistic in at least one way.

EXERCISE 4.2 ❯ *Topic sentences*

Using four of the subjects listed below, write topic sentences. Make sure that your topic sentences clearly identify the subject and indicate how you will discuss it.

Example

Subject: lawyers
Topic sentence: Lawyers sometimes act more as legal interpreters than as advocates.

1. Book censorship

2. Sibling rivalry

3. Nationalized medical insurance

4. The Olympic Games

5. Religious prejudice

6. Standardized achievement tests

7. National parks

8. Political debates

9. Holiday celebrations

10. Water conservation

| 4b | Create coherent paragraphs. |

To allow readers to proceed smoothly through paragraphs, writers must make the necessary effort to think clearly, to be thorough, and to explain ideas and the connections between ideas. When sentences fit together well, the paragraph is coherent and readers are able to concentrate on what the writer is saying. The strategies used to achieve coherence are *transition* and *repetition*.

Transitional Words and Phrases

Transition is movement from one facet of a subject to another. Transitional words and phrases facilitate these shifts in focus. The English language is rich in such words and phrases. Coordinating conjunctions (*and, but,* and others), subordinating conjunctions (*although, since,* and others), and correlative conjunctions (*either . . . or, not only . . . but also,* and others) are the most commonly used transitional words and phrases. Use transitional words and phrases to establish relationships within sentences, between paragraphs, or among the parts of a paper. The following lists indicate some of the relationships you can establish by using transitional words and phrases and give examples of words and phrases that produce each relationship.

Addition

also	furthermore
and	in addition
besides	moreover
equally	next
further	too

Similarity

also	moreover
likewise	similarly

Difference

but	in contrast
however	nevertheless
on the contrary	yet
on the other hand	

Examples

for example	specifically
for instance	to illustrate
in fact	

Restatements or summaries

finally	in summary
in brief	on the whole
in conclusion	that is
in other words	therefore
in short	to sum up

Result

accordingly	so
as a result	therefore
consequently	thereupon
for this reason	thus

Chronology

after	earlier
afterward	finally
before	first
during	immediately
in the meantime	soon
later	still
meanwhile	then
next	third
second	when
simultaneously	while

Location

above	opposite
below	there
beyond	to the left
farther	to the right
here	under
nearby	

The following paragraph makes use of a number of transitional words and phrases, each marked with italics, to emphasize the relationships among ideas.

> *In recent years,* some doctors have begun diagnosing allergies by combining blood droplets with different allergens to determine a sensitivity. [Allergy specialist] Lieberman warns, *however,* that this method is less accurate, more expensive and takes longer to get answers than skin testing. *Generally,* doctors recommend the blood test when it might be dangerous to use the allergen directly on the skin — as might be the case in someone hypersensitive to bee venom, *for example* — or if a skin disease *such as* eczema makes it difficult to see the results of a skin test. — Cynthia Green, "Sneezy and Grumpy? See Doc"

Repeat Words and Phrases

Selective **repetition** of words and phrases can make writing unified and effective. To avoid monotony, use variations of key words or phrases, synonyms (words with the same meaning), and pronouns to create variety as you create unity. The following paragraph uses all three.

> *Laughter* is surely one of humanity's greatest gifts, for the ability to *laugh* — to appreciate the pleasure or *absurdity* in daily activities — allows people, young and old alike, to keep problems in perspective. Children are natural *laughers.* In situations, both appropriate

and inappropriate, the *chuckles, giggles,* and outright *peals of laughter* of children can emphasize their innocence, their joyful ignorance of the problems of the world. *Levity* among adults is, unfortunately, far less common, but *it* is equally welcome. How fortunate are the adults who can react to potentially frustrating situations — a collapsed tent, a split seam in a pair of pants, a surprise guest — and see the sheer *absurdity* of their attempts to maintain absolute control. *Laughter* expresses pleasure, eases tension, and lifts the spirit. *It* is a gift we should all share more often.

Repeat Sentence Structures

The repetition of sentence structures creates unity within a paragraph by presenting similar ideas in similar ways. If you strive for variety in most sentences, then selectively repeated patterns will stand out. The following excerpt from a lengthy paragraph uses repeated sentence structures (all italicized) to focus attention on similar activities.

But though I was initially disappointed at being categorized as an extremist, as I continued to think about the matter I gradually gained a measure of satisfaction from the label. *Was not Jesus an extremist for love:* "Love your enemies, bless them that curse you, do good to them that hate you, and pray for them which despitefully use you and persecute you." *Was not Amos an extremist for justice:* "Let justice roll down like waters and righteousness like an ever-flowing stream." *Was not Paul an extremist for the Christian gospel:* "I bear in my body the marks of the Lord Jesus." *Was not Martin Luther an extremist:* "Here I stand; I cannot do otherwise, so help me God." *And John Bunyan:* "I will stay in jail to the end of my days before I make a butchery of my conscience." *And Abraham Lincoln:* "This nation cannot survive half slave and half free." *And Thomas Jefferson:* "We hold these truths to be self-evident, that all men are created equal . . . " So the question is not whether we will be extremists, but what kind of extremists we will be. — Martin Luther King, Jr., "Letter from Birmingham Jail"

 Use the word processor to add transitions to your paragraphs. The program will automatically reformat your paragraphs without retyping. Copy your paragraphs and experiment freely with repeating words, phrases, and sentence structures. You can always return to your original version or try another. Print out your paragraphs and mark the transitional words and phrases, as in the example on page 84, to check for consistency of pronoun and other references and for excessive repetition.

EXERCISE 4.3 ❯ *Transitions and repeated sentence elements*

Notice the use of transitional words and phrases and repetition in the following paragraphs, and comment on the purpose and effectiveness of each use.

One great difficulty in getting straightforward answers is that so many of the diseases in question have unpredictable courses, and some of them have a substantial tendency toward spontaneous remission. In rheumatoid arthritis, for instance, when such widely disparate therapeutic measures as copper bracelets, a move to Arizona, diets low in sugar or salt or meat or whatever, and even an inspirational book have been accepted by patients as useful, the trouble in evaluation is that approximately 35 percent of patients with this diagnosis are bound to recover no matter what they do. But if you actually have rheumatoid arthritis or, for that matter, schizophrenia, and then get over it, or if you are a doctor and observe this happen, it is hard to be persuaded that it wasn't *something* you did that was responsible. Hence you need very large numbers of patients and lots of time, and a cool head.

Magic is back again, and in full force. Laetrile cures cancer, acupuncture is useful for deafness and low-back pain, vitamins are good for anything, and meditation, yoga, dancing, biofeedback, and shouting one another down in crowded rooms over weekends are specifics for the human condition. Running, a good thing to be doing for its own sake, has acquired the medicinal value formerly attributed to rare herbs from Indonesia. — Lewis Thomas, "On Magic in Medicine"

EXERCISE 4.4 ❯ Transitions and repeated sentence elements

Revise one of your paragraphs to make effective use of transitional words and phrases and repeated words, phrases, and sentence structures.

| 4c | ❯ | **Write complete paragraphs.** |

Paragraphs vary in length. Short paragraphs can be emphatic and useful for presenting simple ideas, but too many in succession may seem choppy and leave ideas undeveloped. Long paragraphs are useful for presenting complex ideas, but too many in succession may seem tiring and the ideas too concentrated. The best general rule about paragraph length is to make paragraphs long enough to explain ideas fully and to serve their purpose in a paper — and no longer. Look at the following paragraphs, which vary considerably in length.

Brief paragraph

The drama begins to unfold with the arrival of the corpse at the mortuary. — Jessica Mitford, "Behind the Formaldehyde Curtain"   (This one-sentence paragraph creates an emphatic transition to a lengthy technical discussion of embalming procedures used by morticians.)

Moderate paragraph

Thus one can conclude that Chicano literature is, in essence, decidedly optimistic, even when it is set in what appears to be a hostile environment. Similarly, the Chicano self-image now emerging is a positive one, the antithesis of caricatures born of Anglo writers. Chicano writers are trying to paint a truer and more representative picture of themselves and their circumstances, of their present and past, while at the same time they are calling for conflict, action. But most important, Chicano writers are recording their own history, a history that never before has been written. — Luis Leal and Pepe Barron, "Chicano Literature: An Overview"   (This moderate-length paragraph uses four sentences to assess current attitudes among Chicano writers. It summarizes points already made and, through emphatic expression, creates interest in material to follow.)

Long paragraph

Poor Columbus! He is a minor character now, a walk-on in the middle of American history. Even those books that have not replaced his picture with a Mayan temple or an Iroquois mask do not credit him with discovering America — even for the Europeans. The Vikings, they say, preceded him to the New World, and after that the Europeans, having lost or forgotten their maps, simply neglected to cross the ocean again for five hundred years. Columbus is far from being the only personage to have suffered from time and revision. Captain John Smith, Daniel Boone, and Wild Bill Hickok — the great self-promoters of American history — have all but disappeared, taking with them a good deal of the romance of the American frontier. General Custer has given way to Chief Crazy Horse; General Eisenhower no longer liberates Europe single-handed; and indeed, most generals, even to Washington and Lee, have faded away, as old soldiers do, giving place to social reformers such as William Lloyd Garrison and Jacob Riis. A number of black Americans have risen to prominence: not only George Washington Carver but Frederick Douglass and Martin Luther King, Jr. W. E. B. Du Bois now invariably accompanies Booker T. Washington. In addition, there is a mystery man called Crispus Attucks, a fugitive slave about whom nothing seems to be known for certain except that he was a victim of the Boston Massacre and thus became one of the first casualties of the American Revolution. Thaddeus Stevens has been reconstructed — his character changed, as it were, from black to white, from cruel and vindictive to persistent and sincere. As for Teddy Roosevelt, he now champions the issue of conservation instead of charging up San Juan Hill. No single President really stands out as a hero, but all Presidents — except certain unmentionables in the second half of the nineteenth century — seem to have done as well as could be expected; given difficult circumstances — Frances FitzGerald, "Rewriting American History"   (In this lengthy paragraph near the beginning of her essay, FitzGerald uses a series of examples to establish the scope of the essay.)

A complete paragraph presents the writer's ideas clearly, along with enough supporting detail to satisfy readers. Although supporting detail will vary from paragraph to paragraph, depending on purpose and length, complete paragraphs are usually developed through the use of specific examples, facts, and description, as described in section 4d.

EXERCISE 4.5 ❱ *Complete paragraphs*

Use one topic sentence from Exercise 4.2 to construct a paragraph that elaborates on your central idea.

EXERCISE 4.6 ❱ *Complete paragraphs*

 Use the topic sentence that follows and the accompanying examples (or others of your choosing) to construct a paragraph that is complete enough to satisfy a reader's expectations.

Topic sentence

In recent years, presidents' wives have provided a useful focus on national issues.

Examples

Eleanor Roosevelt: supporter of minority and women's rights and international cooperation. Jacqueline Kennedy: supporter of historical preservation and the fine arts. Lady Bird Johnson: supporter of environmental protection, forestation, and parks preservation. Betty Ford: supporter of substance-abuse programs and the arts. Nancy Reagan: supporter of substance-abuse programs and foster-child programs. Barbara Bush: supporter of substance-abuse programs and literacy programs.

| 4d | > | **Vary the organization and development of paragraphs.** |

Organize Paragraphs in Alternative Ways

Deductive Structure

A **deductive paragraph** begins with a topic sentence and continues with supporting descriptions, examples, and facts. Writers use this structure frequently because it offers a sure way to make their meaning clear. This paragraph has a deductive structure:

> The champions of applied science arose among the middle class. Scientific American ("The Advocate of Industry & Enterprise") was founded by a religious cultist named Rufus Porter in 1845, but it was sold the next year to a group of businessmen. The new owners linked it to a patent preparation service, aimed it at "Every Manufacturer, Mechanic, Inventor and Artisan," and spent the rest of the century gleefully promoting inventions, saluting technological progress and largely ignoring pure research. — Bob Coleman, "Science Writing: Too Good To Be True?"

Inductive Structure

The inverse of the deductive paragraph, an **inductive paragraph** begins with descriptions, examples, and facts and ends with the topic sentence. This structure builds suspense, heightens interest, and emphasizes details over generalization. Despite these advantages, the inductive structure should be used selectively to avoid dulling its effect or frustrating readers by asking them too often to wait for the main idea. This paragraph has an inductive structure:

> On that particular day [4 September 1893] Beatrix Potter decided to write a letter, which was to become famous. It was to five-year-old Noel Moore, the youngest son of her ex-governess Annie Moore, a delicate boy who was often ill and who found great comfort in the generously illustrated letters that arrived regularly from 'Yours affectionately, Beatrix Potter'. This particular letter began: 'My dear Noel, I

don't know what to write to you, so I shall tell you a story about four little rabbits whose names were Flopsy, Mopsy, Cottontail and Peter. They lived with their mother in a sand bank under the root of a big fir tree. . .' The letter continued with the whole of the now famous story of Peter Rabbit. — Judy Taylor, "The Tale of Beatrix Potter"

EXERCISE 4.7 ❱ *Deductive and inductive structure*

Using two of the topic sentences you wrote for Exercise 4.2, write one deductive and one inductive paragraph. Underline the topic sentence in each and number the details in the margin of the paper. Be ready to explain why you chose the paragraph structure you did for developing each topic sentence.

Develop Your Paragraphs

Purpose

Let purpose determine the development of your paragraphs. Although it is possible first to select an appropriate pattern of development and then to fit information to the pattern, the result is often awkward or mechanical. A better strategy is to complete some planning activities, decide on a general purpose and thesis for the whole paper, outline the information, and then write the first draft, letting the patterns of the paragraphs develop naturally. In this way, each paragraph extends and strengthens a paper's purpose.

For example, in her brief essay "In Bed," Joan Didion narrates her history of ignoring, fighting, and finally learning to live with migraine headaches. In the course of eight paragraphs, Didion vividly describes and provides facts on the effects, course, and treatment of this illness; she narrates her own experience from childhood; and, ultimately, she persuades readers that such afflictions can be beneficial when they remind us of the beauty and serenity of life.

Descriptions

All writing benefits from apt and vivid details that evoke the five senses. In your writing, search for words that describe your subject's sights (*mauve* wallpaper, *glistening* chrome), sounds (*faint* tapping, *shrill* laughter), touch (*satiny* varnish, *leathery* skin), tastes (*salty* crackers, *sour* apples), and smells (*fishy* smell, *lavender* scent). Be specific, and try for both originality and accuracy.

> To new arrivals in London, it seemed pitch black out of doors, too, but not, by 1943, to Londoners. People had become conscious again of the phases of the moon, the light from the stars. They had regained their country eyes. The darkness was full of noises, the echo of footsteps, of people talking, the cries for taxis. Sound itself seemed amplified and dependable in the half-blindness of the street. The smell was of dust, of damp plaster in the air, and of the formaldehyde scent of the smoke from the dirty coal that lodged in the yellow fog. The stained sandbags, the rust, the dull, peeling paint, damp that made great dark lines down the walls, made London seem like a long-neglected, leaky attic.
> — Mary Lee Settle, "London — 1944"

Examples

One of the most effective methods for developing a paragraph is through the use of specific, appropriate examples. Be precise; name names. Don't write "a comedy program"; write "*Cheers.*" Don't write "a school on the west coast"; write "Stanford." To be convincing, examples need to be precise, but also representative. Do not use extremely positive or negative examples that will seem to readers exceptional rather than typical. Often, presenting a single extended example will best show readers how you reached your conclusion. One useful way to present examples fully is to answer the journalists' questions: *who, what, when, where, how,* and *why.*

> Gold also remains an integral part of social and religious customs in many nations. From Morocco through the Middle East and on to India

the status of a bride is still judged by the amount of gold in her dowry. The typical Saudi Arabian adornment for women includes 12 bangles for each wrist, a belt, a necklace, earrings and ring all in 21-karat gold. This endowment may weigh over a kilo (32.5 troy ounces). Many Saudi brides are also decked out with *duru,* a lace-like embroidery of gold chains interwoven with small coins that often weighs two or three kilos (the gold worth over $70,000) that draped the bride from her neck to her knees like a cascade of armor. The normal American wedding ring containing four or five grams of 14-karat gold hardly bears comparison. — Timothy Green, "All That Glitters"

Facts

Using facts and technical and statistical information effectively demonstrates how and why you reached your conclusion. Be as specific as possible. Don't write that a car costs "a lot"; write "$54,000." Don't write that tuition has "increased dramatically" in the last decade; write "26 percent." If you use facts that you have gathered yourself, simply incorporate them in your writing. If your facts come from research, be sure to include full documentation (see pages 536–42 for guidelines).

In 1955 state psychiatric hospitals had 559,000 patients. Today there are about 130,000, a decline of 75 percent. Now the incidence of severe mental illness has not changed. (Schizophrenia, for example, afflicts about one percent of the population.) Nor have drugs and modern treatment yielded a cure rate of 75 percent. Many of the 75 percent discharged from the state hospitals have simply been abandoned. They have become an army of grate-dwellers. — Charles Krauthammer, "How to Save the Homeless Mentally Ill"

Comparison and Contrast

Comparison and contrast bring together two subjects in order to analyze their respective similarities and differences. Use this technique to explain the unfamiliar in terms of the familiar or use it to explore the features or qualities of your subjects. Your topic sentence should offer a clear synthesis of the compared or contrasted elements.

Comparison and contrast paragraphs can be structured in two ways: whole-to-whole and part-to-part. **Whole-to-whole,** or divided, **development** fully discusses first one subject and then the other. The topic sentence of a paragraph with this pattern generally emphasizes the two subjects, subordinating features or qualities.

In the waning years of the nineteenth century, two remarkable women, exact contemporaries living at opposite ends of the immense American diversity, dissented from the cultural shibboleths and popular taste of their time in the way they wrote about the life they knew best. Kate Chopin (1851–1904) was consciously defiant of the decencies and sexual prudery of the late 1890s, and sought to uncover the sensuality and discontent of women which the stultifying conventions of the age refused to acknowledge. Sarah Orne Jewett (1849–1909) preferred to look back rather than forward to the emancipated future envisioned by Mrs. Chopin; her sensibility and values were deeply anchored in the past of a rural New England that was rapidly disappearing in her lifetime, but she, too, shunned the idealized versions of actuality which a culture dedicated to gentility demanded of its literature. — Pearl K. Bell, "Kate Chopin and Sarah Orne Jewett"

The second pattern for comparison and contrast, **part-to-part,** or alternating, **development** provides a point-by-point, alternating comparison between two subjects. The topic sentences generally emphasize qualities, features, or, as in the next example, the specific consequences following from the topic.

Ethically, most Americans are simultaneously egalitarians and capitalists. This set of beliefs leads to an alarming chain reaction. A new and expensive treatment is developed. Since, as capitalists, Americans believe that individuals should be allowed to spend their money on whatever they wish, the wealthy are allowed to buy the treatment privately. People who cannot afford the treatment start to demand it. Being egalitarians, Americans do not have the political ability to say "no" to any person dying from a treatable disease, and so ways are found to pay for the treatment through private or public health insurance. As egalitarians, we feel we have to provide the treatment to everyone or deny it to everyone; as capitalists, we cannot deny it to those who can afford it. But since resources are limited, we cannot afford to give it to everyone. — Lester C. Thurow, "The Ethical Costs of Health Care"

Extended Analogy

An analogy illuminates a subject by pointing to an unexpected connection between dissimilar things. This quality of the unexpected can make writing vivid, but be sure to select or construct analogies in which the connections are reasonable and clear. The following example contains three analogies.

All guardians of the language resemble a little the village idiot in the *shtetl* of Frampol who was given the job of standing at the village gates in wait for the coming of the Messiah. The pay is not high, he was told, but he didn't have to worry about running out of work. The guardians of the language need similarly never worry about running out of work. Like Heraclitus's famous river — 'Upon those who step into the same river different and ever different waters flow down" — the river of language continues to flow along, never remaining the same, changing every foot of the way. Heraclitus spoke of his river being in perpetual flux but never of its muddying, whereas in the river of language flux frequently does issue in mud, garbage, and other detritus. To change classical references, the task of the guardian of the language can be likened to cleaning out the Augean stables with the horses still in them. This, for reasons needing no explanation, is not everybody's idea of a good time. — Joseph Epstein, "What's the Usage?"

Cause and Effect

Analyzing an event or condition often involves asking why it happened or how it came to be — that is, inquiring into its known or likely causes. Remember that a single cause may have multiple effects, and a single effect multiple causes. Remember, too, that a cause and effect relationship is not established by mere association. It is not necessary to document the relation in your paragraph, but if you are speculating, make that clear to your readers.

Nonetheless, in 1917 fishermen and fox farmers convinced the Alaska Territorial Legislature that the eagles' appetite for salmon and small mammals should reduce them to varmint status. A bounty was posted — $1 per pair of talons, later raised to $2. By the time experts realized that foul play had been exaggerated, 128,000 eagles had been shot. The Bald Eagle Protection Act of 1940 made killing an eagle a federal offense. — Jessica Maxwell, "The Eagles Have Landed"

Process Analysis

To describe how something is done or made or how something happens, you need to describe accurately and completely the series of steps involved. A paragraph describing a process can be organized *spatially,* as when a writer describes the spreading consequences of the destruction of a rain forest by beginning with the cutting of one tree, or *chronologically,* as in this example.

A homemade *sorbetto* [Italian sorbet] uses a sugar syrup, which is one part sugar and one part water boiled together for five minutes and then cooled. Two parts fruit puree or juice are added to the syrup, and the mixture is frozen. You can freeze the mixture in an ice-cream maker, which continuously beats air into it as it freezes, but you're almost as well off putting it into an ice tray with the dividers removed or into a cake pan, and transferring it to a chilled bowl to beat it twice — after it turns to slush and before it freezes completely. The whole freezing process takes between three and five hours. After the *sorbetto* is frozen hard, you should put it in the refrigerator for an hour or so to temper it before serving. — Corby Kummer, "Summer Ices"

Classification

A large subject can be examined by dividing it into its parts or sub-groups. You must establish meaningful, consistent criteria for your division, supplying readers with the information they need to distinguish among the classes. Subgroups should not overlap.

For present purposes, it will be useful to distinguish four degrees of poverty: *destitution,* which is lack of income sufficient to assure physical survival and to prevent suffering from hunger, exposure, or remediable or preventable illness; *want,* which is a lack of enough income to support "essential welfare" (as distinguished from comfort and convenience); *hardship,* which is lack of enough to prevent acute, persistent discomfort or inconvenience; and *relative deprivation,* which is lack of enough to prevent one from feeling poor by comparison with others. — Edward C. Banfield, "Several Kinds of Poverty"

Definition

Definitions clarify your thinking and your writing, explaining terms and concepts to your readers. A formal definition, such as those in dictionaries, places the subject in a class and then distinguishes it from other items in the same class.

Some dunes, enormous, dwarf a three-story house. Lying between them are the *wadis, old water courses dry most of the year.* — Russell Fraser, "Wadi-Bashing in Arabia Deserta"

An informal or extended definition may describe the subject, provide examples of it, or compare or contrast it with some other thing. The following paragraph contains examples of both types of definition.

Gardeners have long squabbled over what wildflowers are. Purists insist that they are native plants that grew before the arrival of the Europeans. Others include naturalized plants in the classification — those introduced from other parts of the world that reproduce freely in their nonnative habitat. Opinion these days favors the definition that includes both native and naturalized plants. Weeds, incidentally, are just wildflowers that grow when they are not wanted. Noxious weeds are plants that the authorities have determined threaten human health or agricultural practices. Some common attractive weeds are Queen Anne's lace (*Daucus carota*), chicory (*Cichorium intybus*) and even oxeye daisy (*Chrysanthemum leucanthemum*). — Eva Hoepfner, "Wildflower Meadows"

EXERCISE 4.8 ❯ *Paragraph development*

Write a paragraph using one of the following methods of development. Use one of the topics provided, or select one of your own.

Description: an incident of prejudice, a scene showing family support, a situation in which trust was crucial, a depiction of a smoothly run business

Examples: the need for urban planning, the importance of energy conservation, the practical value of hobbies, the growing dependence on computers

Facts: high costs of education, everyday uses of mathematics, basic equipment necessary for cooking, questionable recruitment procedures in college athletics

Comparison and contrast: seeing a horror film on television and at a theater, celebrations in different cultures, two specialized magazines, your language patterns with close friends and with parents

Analogy: preparing for a date and for a religious ritual, political ads and soft-drink ads, a college campus and a city, marriage and a corporate merger

Cause and effect: a death in the family, the farming crisis in the United States, a major industry closing in your city, personal financial difficulties

Process: preparing a speech, analyzing a work of literature, buying a stereo, applying for college

Definition: music videos, patriotism, a good parent-child relationship, luck

Classification: types of museums, kinds of cartoon strips, types of radio stations, kinds of football fans

5 Critical Thinking and Writing

Human beings from a very young age continually think. Consciously or unconsciously, through every waking hour, we reflect, respond, react, infer, deduce, and intuit. Remembering and anticipating are further examples of ways we think about and try to understand our world. Trying to communicate that understanding to others, however, requires critical thinking skills.

All purposeful verbal communication — whether speaking, listening, reading, or writing — requires critical thinking, an active, focused engagement with the topic. When people speak or write, they first synthesize ideas and experiences and then communicate their insights or observations to others. Conversely, when people listen or read, they actively seek to comprehend the insights and observations of others, thus completing the speaker's or writer's intended communication.

Quick Reference

By thinking critically when you read and write, you will improve your understanding of others' writing and their understanding of yours.

> *Think critically, actively focusing on the topic and its development.*

> *Support different kinds of assertions with the appropriate kinds of evidence.*

> *Evaluate discussions to determine whether supporting evidence is adequate.*

> *Recognize patterns of fallacious reasoning. Challenge them in what you read and avoid them in what you write.*

Some people possess an apparently innate ability to think critically, to sort through information, to respond to experiences, and to articulate ideas with clarity and precision. Others gain these skills by studying and practicing the techniques of critical thinking and writing. The systematic study and practice of critical thinking and writing, whatever a person's innate ability, improves all forms of communication by fostering substantive, precise, and thorough analysis, expression, and response.

This chapter explores the techniques of critical thinking as they apply to both reading and writing.

5a Think critically, actively focusing on the topic and its development.

Critical thinking involves active, focused, systematic engagement with the topic. The method and intensity of applying critical thinking skills varies with the topic and with the reader's and writer's purpose.

Critical thinking, required in most college work, involves systematic, objective, and rigorous scrutiny and evaluation of ideas — both in what you read and in what you write. When you read a paper, article, report, or book that argues a position, think about it critically, actively examining and evaluating its purpose, assumptions, evidence, and development. Ultimately, you must decide whether it has succeeded in establishing the validity of its position.

To work as a writer, you must use your critical thinking skills to clarify and support your own purposes, assumptions, evidence, and development. Your general goal in thinking critically when you write is to make certain that you demonstrate the validity of your position.

Critical thinking, then, can be used as you read, to deconstruct someone's thought processes, and as you write, to construct a presentation that will effectively convey your ideas.

In thinking critically, readers and writers use three patterns of reasoning: inductive, deductive, and warrant-based reasoning. These methods organize ideas and evidence in different ways that reflect differences in the type of evidence, in the writer's emphasis, and in the source of the main idea.

Inductive Reasoning

Writers use **induction** when they first compile a set of specific observations (examples, facts, testimony, and so on) and then, on the basis of the interpretation of those observations, derive a conclusion or generalization. The validity of inductive reasoning depends on both the representativeness of the observations and the accuracy of the interpretation.

Consider, for example, this circumstance. You discover through discussions that ten students in your writing class are on scholarships. You learn through conversations that many of your friends in other classes also have student loans and grants. You read a newspaper article that notes that college expenses have risen beyond the means of many parents. On the basis of these observations, you reasonably conclude by induction that many students at your college receive financial aid.

Deductive Reasoning

Writers use **deduction** when they reason from a general, accepted premise to a specific, related conclusion. In deductive reasoning, the writer provides support for or extends the original generalization using additional information (sometimes called a *minor premise*). The validity of a deductive pattern depends on the validity of the original premise and of the reasoning used to reach the conclusion.

A traditional form of the deductive argument is the **syllogism,** which consists of a *major premise,* a broad conclusion or generalization; a *minor premise,* a statement related to but more specific than the major premise; and a *conclusion,* the logical consequence of the major premise in light of the minor premise.

Major premise
Gasoline prices increase when OPEC raises its per-barrel price of crude oil.

Minor premise
OPEC has raised the price of crude oil.

Conclusion
Gasoline prices will rise.

Warrant-based Reasoning

Warrant-based reasoning is a process somewhat like the writing process. Beginning with an idea expressed as a thesis or an assertion, the writer accumulates necessary supporting evidence through research or other forms of planning. The writer's values and perspective emerge most clearly in the underlying warrant, the sometimes unstated or implicit connection that the writer makes between the assertion and the evidence. Although the writer's reasoning must be sound, it will not have the inevitability of deductive or inductive reasoning. Thus, in order for the writer to convince readers of the validity of the assertion, the evidence offered must be convincing and complete.

Assertion
Mr. Lidstrom will be an effective district attorney.

Evidence
Mr. Lidstrom has worked for ten years as an assistant district attorney.

Warrant

Ten years as assistant district attorney has provided Mr. Lidstrom with the range of experiences and the contacts and credibility he needs to do his new job well.

This kind of argument cannot be conducted according to deductive or inductive reasoning because there is an inevitable subjective element in deciding what makes a good district attorney. One writer's position is that length of service, rather than education or a particular kind of experience, such as prosecuting crime bosses or drug dealers, will help Lidstrom do a good job. Depending on the audience and the issue, the writer may want to offer more, and more varied, evidence. **》》》** *Be sure to think through your implicit warrants. An invalid warrant, even if unstated, can lead to invalid conclusions.*

Because college admissions tests are administered nationwide, they are an effective measure of student potential.   (The implicit warrant is that widely used tests are effective. Because this notion is questionable, the conclusion is questionable as well.) **《《《**

EXERCISE 5.1 **》** *Patterns of critical thinking*

Complete the following arguments; then, using the guidelines given above, compose an inductive, a deductive, and a warrant-based argument.

Inductive argument

Evidence

_____

_____

Conclusion

College students contribute to and are responsible members of society and should be treated accordingly.

Deductive argument

Major premise

Children require good nutrition in order to concentrate and learn in school.

Minor premise

Schools have a responsibility and public mandate to ensure that students concentrate and learn.

Conclusion

_____

_____

Warrant-based argument

Assertion

Capital punishment is immoral and should be illegal.

Evidence

Executions do not deter others from similar crimes and encourage barbaric public displays in a carnival atmosphere.

Warrant

_____

_____

EXERCISE 5.2 ❯ Warrants

Identify the warrants, both implicit and explicit, in the following paragraph.

Low wages and lack of job security create frustration, however. This leads to a 40 percent turnover rate among congressional staffers.

There is something to be said for new blood, but not when a complete transfusion is taking place about every two years. The result is not only a less efficient staff but in the long run a less effective Congress. Without experienced staff, there is no institutional memory — those who will recall what happened on an issue four years before. Without them, in fact, Congress becomes more vulnerable to criticism even from the people it most benefits. — Jonathan Yates, " 'Reality' on Capitol Hill"

5b	⟩	**Analyze purpose, audience, and content.**

To read and write effectively, you must analyze the roles of purpose, audience, and content in ensuring communication. See section 1d for more information on audience and purpose.

Evaluate Purpose

To think critically about a piece of writing — one that you are reading or one that you are writing — you must evaluate its general purpose. Different kinds of writing require different kinds of development. The following four types apply to both spoken and written communication.

Purposes of Writing

In **expressive writing,** writers share perceptions and experiences, generally those gathered from personal observations. Personal essays and letters, poetry, and fiction are examples of expressive writing.

In **referential writing,** writers share information and ideas, generally those gathered through systematic research. Reports, research papers, memoranda, and informational articles in newspapers and magazines are examples of referential writing.

In **persuasive writing,** writers present information and observations with the specific intent of convincing readers to alter their perceptions or to take action. Letters to newspaper editors, requests, petitions, arguments in law courts, and advertisements are examples of persuasive writing.

In **argumentative writing,** writers present ideas, information, experiences, and insights to articulate an opinion about an arguable topic. The writer's goal is to state an opinion and to illuminate the topic. Debates, political and other speeches and articles, newspaper editorials, articles and essays of criticism and analysis are examples of argumentative writing.

Recognizing the different purposes that expressive, referential, persuasive, and argumentative writing serve will help you to test the validity of a paper's assumptions and presentation. For instance, a single apt, well-written example may effectively illustrate a point in an expressive paper but be inadequate support to convince readers in a persuasive paper on the same topic. The different reasons for writing establish different expectations for development.

Understanding an Audience

Effective writing always accommodates itself to the needs of its readers. Persuasive and argumentative writing, however, must do so even more thoroughly and systematically than other kinds of writing.

As a critical reader and writer, you can examine and evaluate the needs of a reading audience and assess how effectively the writing meets those needs.

Questions about Readers

- How much will they already know about the topic?

- How skeptical might they be about the assertion?

- What preconceptions or misconceptions might they have?

- What kinds of evidence will they require?
- What kinds of objections will they raise?
- What needs will they bring to the reading?

Because your position will be arguable, consider how your opposition will think about the topic. In a simulated debate, consider how your opposition might refute your claims. Similarly, how might you refute theirs? Consider ways you might reconcile these opposing views. A consideration of opposing views, especially in written form, will prepare you to write a balanced, knowledgeable paper.

For instance, you might freewrite to explore the opposition's objections to your views and then highlight the primary objections with a marker for consideration and incorporation in your paper. Or use two columns, listing your most important evidence on the left and an opponent's response on the right.

It is not always possible to accommodate all potential readers — their diversity is too great — but thoughtful writers who expect to have critical readers in their audience try to anticipate their needs and expectations.

Use the word processor to generate and organize thoughts about your audience. ■ Use freewriting to describe your audience. Turn off or dim your computer monitor and freewrite about your audience, using the questions listed above as guidelines. Assess your audience fairly, respecting opposing views. Record your thoughts quickly.

■ Organize your thoughts about your audience. Using the audience description you have generated, group ideas and assess your audience's general needs.

■ Brainstorm for objections to your position. If your topic is controversial, some members of your audience will disagree with your assertion. Use the computer to construct a brainstorming list of objections; then supply the counterarguments.

Summarize General Content

Reading is an active process of decoding written symbols (words) to reveal a writer's meaning or content. As a reader, you must first decide what is being said before you can evaluate its effectiveness or validity. The simplest technique for articulating a writer's content is to summarize it, in your head or on paper.

A **summary** is a brief, objective restatement in your own words of the central idea presented in a short written work or in a portion of a longer work. For brief texts of only a few paragraphs, a summary may be a single sentence; for longer texts, a complete summary may be several sentences or a paragraph.

Strategies for Writing Summaries

- Look for the writer's thesis statement or topic sentence. It will present the most direct, comprehensive statement of the central idea.

- Read the text carefully and then put it aside; do not look at the text while writing your summary.

- Select and restate the central idea(s) only.

- Omit details, explanations, examples, and clarifications.

- Express the text's main idea(s) in your own words, not in the writer's.

- Name the author or source explicitly in the summary, and provide a page citation.

Learning to write a summary takes practice, but the skill is valuable for your reading and your writing. Expect to revise a summary several times to make it brief, accurate, objective, and complete.

To demonstrate how summaries work, first read the following passage from an article in the *State Department Bulletin* on international trade competition and trade deficits:

What are the sources of competitive pressure on U.S. industry? Some competitive pressures result, in the normal course of events in a dynamic world economy, from shifting patterns of comparative advantage. As countries develop and mature they move into new lines of production and exports. The accumulation of capital, new technologies, and product innovations abroad may make nations internationally competitive in a new product line, and their exports can put pressure on existing producers elsewhere. While we may wish to protect ourselves from disruptive import surges, it is in our longrun interest to adjust to these changing conditions by either increasing our own competitiveness in these product lines or moving resources into other areas where our comparative advantage resides. While such adjustment is painful for the affected industries in the short run, the process is the mechanism through which the benefits of economic advance in one country are shared internationally. Certain U.S. industries are finding this adjustment very difficult and painful, but we should not confuse their plight with the problem of the overall trade deficit. — Elinor G. Constable, "International Competition, Trade Deficits, and National Policy"

A clear, concise, and complete summary of Constable's paragraph requires several drafts:

First attempt

Trade competition arises for a number of reasons.   (Though concise, this summary is too simplistic.)

Second attempt

Trade competition arises as foreign countries develop their technologies and enter world markets.   (Although this summary is clearer than the first, it presents only part of Constable's point. It needs further elaboration.)

Third attempt

When trade competition arises because foreign countries develop their technologies and enter world markets, American companies must improve their own technologies or shift to other areas of trade. (This summary presents the major points of Constable's paragraph.)

Fourth attempt

Elinor G. Constable, in "International Competition, Trade Deficits, and National Policy," notes that when trade competition arises because foreign countries develop their technologies and enter world markets, American companies must either improve their own technologies or shift to other areas of trade (60).   (Citing the author, title, and page number completes the summary.)

》》》 When including a summary as part of a paper, include a full citation of the source on your works cited page. **《《《**

Use a word processor to help you create and revise a clear and concise summary. ▪   Draft the summary. Working at the keyboard, type out the first version of your summary. ▪   Refine the summary. Use the add and delete capabilities of a word processor to incorporate overlooked central ideas and to eliminate extraneous details. ▪   Add clarifying information. Incorporate the author, title, and page number of the original work.

EXERCISE 5.3 **》** *Summaries*

Write a summary of each of the following paragraphs.

A.   The tropical rain forest north of Manaus, like that in many other parts of the Amazon basin, is being clear-cut from the edge inward. It is being lifted up from the ground entire like a carpet rolled off a bare floor, leaving behind vast stretches of cattle range and cropland that need artificial fertilization to sustain even marginal productivity for more than two or three years. A rain forest in Brazil differs fundamentally from a deciduous woodland in Pennsylvania or Germany in the way its key resources are distributed. A much greater fraction of organic matter is bound up in the tissues of the standing trees, so that the leaf litter and humus are only a few inches deep. When the forest is felled and burned, the hard equato-

rial downpours quickly wash away the thin blanket of top soil.
— Edward O. Wilson, "The Superorganism"

B.   When we look back in time and study old cultures and people, we
are impressed that death has always been distasteful to man and will
probably always be. From a psychiatrist's point of view this is very under-
standable and can perhaps be best explained by our basic knowledge
that, in our unconscious, death is never possible in regard to ourselves. It
is inconceivable for our unconscious to imagine an actual ending of our
own life here on earth, and if this life of ours has to end, the ending is
always attributed to a malicious intervention from the outside by someone else. In simple terms, in our unconscious mind we can only be killed;
it is inconceivable to die of a natural cause or of old age. Therefore death
in itself is associated with a bad act, a frightening happening, something
that in itself calls for retribution and punishment.   — Elisabeth
Kübler-Ross, "On the Fear of Death"

C.   In social organizations which embody a strong class system, such
as military units and large business concerns, there are many territorial
rules, often unspoken, which interfere with the official hierarchy.
High-status individuals, such as officers or managers, could in theory enter any of the regions occupied by the lower levels in the peck order, but
they limit this power in a striking way. An officer seldom enters a ser-
geant's mess or a barrack room unless it's for a formal inspection. He re-
spects those regions as alien territories even though he has the power to
go there by virtue of his dominant role. And in businesses, part of the
appeal of unions, over and above their obvious functions, is that with
their officials, headquarters, and meetings they add a sense of territorial
power for the staff workers. It is almost as if each military organization
and business concern consists of two warring tribes: the officers versus
the other ranks, and management versus the workers. Each has its special
home base within the system, and the territorial defense pattern thrusts
itself into what, on the surface, is a pure social hierarchy. Negotiations
between managements and unions are tribal battles fought out over the
neutral ground of a boardroom table, and are as much concerned with
territorial display as they are with resolving problems of wages and conditions. Indeed, if one side gives in too quickly and accepts the other's
demands, the victors feel strangely cheated and deeply suspicious that it
may be a trick. What they are missing is the protracted sequence of ritual

and counter-ritual that keeps alive their group territorial identity.
— Desmond Morris, "Territorial Behavior"

| 5c | > | **Evaluate assertions.** |

Assertions positively state ideas or information. Critical thinkers, whether in writing or when responding to reading, require appropriate, clearly expressed assertions.

Every written work contains many assertions. The most important assertion is the thesis statement, but that controlling idea will be supported by a number of other assertions, notably the topic sentences in supporting paragraphs. Assertions can take three forms, each requiring different substantiation and development.

Assertions

Facts

Assertions of fact state verifiable, objective information. Facts need not necessarily be verified in your paper, though facts not considered common knowledge must be documented (see section 33g).

Facts generally cannot provide, but only support, a thesis, since they are not themselves arguable. The assertion, for instance, that *The Phantom of the Opera* (1917) was the first colorized film may support a thesis about technical innovations in early films, but it cannot be the thesis of a developed paper. Facts, because they can be verified by referring to a reliable reference, cannot be the basis of formal arguments. Once a fact is verified, there is no debate.

Beliefs

Assertions of belief express nonverifiable, subjective ideas. Beliefs may be used to support a thesis, but they cannot be the basis for a thesis because they are not arguable. Someone might assert, for example, that Tchaikovsky's symphonies are overrated, but such an assertion is based on aesthetic taste rather than on objective evidence that can be substantiated. Other sources of belief are religious faith, cultural and social environment and prejudice. Assertions of belief, appropriately used and strongly and knowledgeably expressed, can produce writing that persuades readers to agree.

Opinion

Assertions of opinion state conclusions that are logically inferred from facts. To assert, as Constable does (page 109), that tariffs harm rather than help a nation's economy is an assertion of an opinion formed after consideration of the data. Opinions can provide a thesis because they are arguable; writers reach different judgments even when they consider the same information because they approach facts, examples, testimony, and so on from their individual perspectives.

Supporting Assertions

The ability to recognize different kinds of assertions will prove helpful in your critical reading — and especially in researching. Assertions based on facts are often illustrated and verified by useful, detailed technical information. Assertions based on belief or opinion are almost always substantiated with extended explanations, facts, statistics, examples, and expert testimony — providing fully developed discussions of the topic. Knowing that assertions signal such development will help you to think critically and respond appropriately as you read, evaluate, and use materials. In your own writing, consider whether you have used assertions effectively and appropriately and supported them where necessary to enhance your credibility and communication with your readers.

EXERCISE 5.4 〉 *Assertions*

Identify the following assertions, all from George F. Will's essay "Grandmother Was Right," as assertions of fact, belief, or opinion. Then describe the kind of verification you would expect to find for each one.

1. Americans do have a heightened interest in health, thanks in part to Dr. Kenneth H. Cooper.

2. Cooper's clinic has conducted 100,000 physical examinations, generating an invaluable data base for the study of preventative and rehabilitative behavior.

3. There is something sick about some contemporary thinking about health.

4. The modern refusal to accept material and social limits has enabled mankind to live better, materially and morally, than premodern peasants.

5. Many values of modernity conflict with another value, grace in the face of the fact of death.

5d 〉 **Evaluate evidence.**

Evidence, material used to support an assertion, must be pertinent, verifiable, and reliable. Useful for assertions based on both beliefs and opinions, evidence can be classified as facts and statistics, examples, and expert testimony.

Facts and Statistics

A **fact** is objectively verifiable information; **statistics** are mathematical data. Familiar examples of facts and statistics include dates, percentages, and quantities. It is a verifiable fact that 58,135 American soldiers died in the Vietnam War. It is a verifiable statistic that roughly 65 percent of those killed were in the U.S. Army.

Facts and statistics, when relevant and accurate, are effective tools with which to support formal arguments. **>>>** *When facts are not common knowledge, they must be fully documented. See section 33g for a full discussion.* **<<<**

Examples

Examples are individual cases illustrating assertions of belief or opinion. Examples drawn from personal experience are considered **primary evidence** and are usually incorporated in expressive and persuasive papers. Examples drawn from other people's writing are considered **secondary evidence** and are most often used in referential, persuasive, and argumentative papers. To be effective, examples must be relevant, representative, and complete.

Relevant Examples

Relevant examples clearly illustrate the topic at hand. In supporting a paper asserting that film censorship today is ineffective, D. W. Griffith's *Intolerance* (1918) would not be a relevant example because the issues it raised — by its depiction of adultery, for example — are less controversial today than they were when the picture was made and are unlikely to be censored. The use of a more recent example, such as Martin Scorsese's *The Last Temptation of Christ* (1988), would allow a writer to discuss current censorship issues.

Representative Examples

Representative examples are neither extremely positive nor extremely negative. Extreme examples are exceptions, and thoughtful readers are likely to find them unconvincing. In a paper on the negative effects of state lotteries on family finances, for instance, a five-million-dollar winner would not be representative, nor would a person who spent the family's food money on lottery tickets. Representing extremes, neither example would convincingly support the assertion.

Complete Examples

Complete examples allow readers to see how the examples work as evidence. Incorporating responses to the journalists' questions (*who, what, when, where, how,* and *why*) is one useful way to guarantee completeness. Adding a summary can further clarify important connections.

Expert Testimony

Expert testimony in an argument, like expert testimony in court trials, is a statement of opinion or a judgment made by an expert or authority in a field. To support an assertion about sexual discrimination in government hiring, a specialist in labor practices or a statistician working with government hiring data could speak authoritatively. A feminist critic of literature would not have necessary expertise, even though he or she might have an informed opinion on discriminatory hiring practices.

Appeals

Critical thinking and writing involve more than assessing the reasoning in a paper. Writers use **appeals** to reach and convince their audiences, and critical readers learn to identify them. The three kinds of appeals are **logical, ethical,** and **emotional**.

Logical Appeals

Logical appeals emphasize the topic, stressing the central issues and supplying necessary evidence. The following paragraph uses a logical appeal, offering facts and statistics to support its position that chemical poisoning is gradually decreasing.

> It took the social activism of the 1960s and early 1970s to bring about controls. The Lead-based Paint Poisoning Prevention Act banned the manufacture and sale of leaded paint and directed the Department of Housing and Urban Development (HUD) to develop a strategy for re-

moving old paint from old housing. In the mid-1970s the Food and Drug Administration (FDA) pressured the food industry to remove lead solder from the seams of baby-food and baby-formula cans. According to the EPA, more than 161,000 metric tons of lead tainted the air in 1975. In an effort to lower this atmospheric pollution the agency ordered oil companies to start phasing out lead additives in gasoline beginning in 1977. By 1984 the count had fallen by 75 percent, to 39,000 metric tons. Each year since, the levels have continued to fall. — Michael Weisskopf, "Lead Astray: The Poisoning of America"

Ethical Appeals

Ethical appeals emphasize the writer, stressing his or her trustworthiness, honesty, clarity, and directness. Note that the ethical appeal refers not to the ethicalness of the writer's position but to the way in which the position is described. The writer of the following paragraph uses an ethical appeal by establishing his knowledge of and fairness to opposing views and by carefully qualifying his statements.

In the great debate over legalizing recreational drugs, the least convincing assertion of the pro-legalizers is that drug use might not even increase as a result. I can state for certain that drug use would increase. I don't use drugs now. If they were legal, I would use them. Or, rather, if marijuana were legal, I would use it occasionally instead of the legal drug I now use regularly, alcohol. To be sure, increased respect for the law is not the only reason so many middle-class, middle-age people have abandoned marijuana: you're also no longer so carefree about where your mind might take you on automatic pilot, especially in public. But society's official disapproval is a substantial deterrent. Without it, many of us would sneak the odd toke or two. — Michael Kinsley, "Glass Houses and Getting Stoned"

Emotional Appeals

Emotional appeals emphasize readers, stressing their needs, desires, hopes, and expectations. The following paragraph makes emotional appeals to readers' sympathy and self-interest.

Obviously the decisions that must be made when an elderly patient faces a medical crisis are difficult ones for everyone — patient, loved ones, doctors, hospitals and health-care personnel alike. When a satisfying, although perhaps restricted, life is possible if treatment is successful, the decisions are easy: You do everything you can. But when someone has had a medical crisis and is in failing health with little hope of recovery; when all the painful, costly, possibly degrading though heroic measures may gain no more than a few extra days or weeks or, maybe, months for a patient who is probably miserable and often unconscious, the decisions are more difficult and individuals may vary widely in their preferences — if, indeed, they are given a choice. — Roy Hoopes, "Turning Out the Light"

》》》 *Use emotional appeals cautiously. Although some highly charged topics require acknowledgment of their emotional aspect, and almost any topic may have an emotional aspect to those most intimately involved with it, readers may react with suspicion if the emotional appeal seems inappropriate or overdone.* **《《《**

EXERCISE 5.5 **》** *Evidence*

Identify the kinds of evidence used in the following paragraphs. Discuss why this evidence is effective and consider alternative ways to support the assertions in the paragraphs.

Spurred by a scientific consensus that significant greenhouse-effect warming will occur in the early decades of the next century, delegates from 46 countries at a Conference on the Changing Atmosphere held in Toronto have called for an urgent action plan. The conferees, who included scientists and policymakers (but no senior U.S. Government official), recommended that governments initially reduce emissions of carbon dioxide — thought to play a major role in greenhouse warming — by 20 percent before the year 2005.

Some workers maintain that greenhouse warming, which results when trace gases prevent infrared radiation from the earth's surface from escaping to space, has already set in; indeed, a scientist at the National Aeronautics and Space Administration (NASA) is searching for a greenhouse "fingerprint" in existing data. The four warmest years in a century of instrumental records have fallen within the 1980's, and the first five months of 1988 were the hottest five-month period ever recorded.

One climate analyst, James E. Hansen of NASA's Goddard Institute for Space Studies, told a Senate subcommittee in Washington just before the Toronto conference that the recent warming could be ascribed "with a high degree of confidence" to the greenhouse effect. At Toronto the delegates kept an open mind about whether the greenhouse effect has contributed to the warmth of the 1980's. They agreed, however, that past emissions of greenhouse gases make significant warming inevitable. Indeed the most recent computer models predict that accumulating trace gases will harm the lower atmosphere sooner than expected.

Carbon dioxide, which is increasing by .4 percent each year because of combustion of fossil fuels and the destruction of tropical forests, accounts for half of the predicted warming. Other greenhouse gases include methane, which is increasing at an even faster rate, and the synthetic refrigerants and solvents called chlorofluorocarbons (CFC's).

The consensus view was that a global warming of between three and nine degrees Fahrenheit is likely to occur by the middle of the next century if emissions are not curtailed. It is impossible to say what the climatic consequence for particular regions would be — the current U.S. drought, for example, cannot necessarily be blamed on the greenhouse effect. Nevertheless, some studies suggest that continental interiors will become dryer as greenhouse warming occurs. The sea level is expected to rise by at least 30 centimeters over the next 50 to 100 years. — Tim Beardsley, "Winds of Change"

5e	Avoid logical fallacies.

Logical fallacies are errors in thinking and writing that result from faulty logic. The ability to identify logical fallacies will help you in two ways. First, you will be able to evaluate the accuracy of presentation in the materials you read. Second, you will be able to avoid logical fallacies in your own writing.

Hasty Generalization

A **hasty generalization** is a conclusion based on too little evidence. This fallacy suggests that a writer has reached a conclusion too quickly, without thoroughly investigating an issue, and seems to assume that readers will not challenge his or her assumptions.

Be especially careful not to generalize on the basis of a single example. That is the fault in the following example and the most common cause of hasty generalizations.

> The Bedderman Street Housing Project cost hundreds of thousands of dollars and is now a shambles. Federally subsidized housing is a waste of taxpayers' money.   (One failed housing project is not enough evidence to support the assertion that the whole system of subsidized housing has failed. A larger sampling is necessary to justify such a sweeping claim.)

Oversimplification

Oversimplification ignores the complexities, variations, and exceptions relevant to an issue.

> The influx of foreign cars almost destroyed the American automobile industry   (Imported cars caused some problems for the industry, but so did high prices, overly large cars with poor designs, dated technology, poor gas mileage, and other factors.)

Carefully consider exceptions before you reach a conclusion, and include in your writing the necessary qualifications.

Either/Or

The **either/or fallacy** suggests that only two choices exist when, in fact, there are more than two. This type of thinking is not only illogical (because multiple alternatives are almost always available) but also unfair (because ignoring complexities and choices distorts a discussion).

For the sake of learning, we must maintain the firmest kind of discipline, including corporal punishment, in our public schools, or we can expect chaos, disorder, and the disintegration of education as we know it.   (The two alternatives presented are extremes: firm discipline resulting in order versus relaxed discipline resulting in chaos. The statement at once ignores moderate methods of maintaining discipline and asserts that without firm discipline the worst will happen. It is highly manipulative.)

Begging the Question

Begging the question is a type of circular reasoning used to slant an issue. When writers beg the question, they include in their writing an idea that requires proof, but they offer no proof. Instead, they present the idea as if it were a fact or a foregone conclusion needing no support or explanation. Writers who beg the question undercut their credibility by implying knowledge that they do not demonstrate.

> Since Senator Hillard is a pawn of major corporations, we can expect him to support their interests instead of ours.   (The writer provides no evidence that Hillard is controlled by corporations. The statement attempts to mislead readers by asserting that an affiliation exists rather than proving that it does.)

Sometimes begging the question is done very subtly, through word choice.

> The antiwar demonstrators of the 1970s should be remembered as the cowards that they were.   (The writer uses the word *cowards* to define the group without making any attempt to prove the implicit warrant that protesting is cowardly.)

Association

Fallacies of association suggest that ideas or actions are acceptable or unacceptable because of the people who are associated with them. Such a fallacy ignores that ideas or actions should be evaluated on their own merits.

> The hijackers were Lebanese, so obviously the Lebanese people support terrorism. (This assertion links all people in Lebanon with a small group of terrorists. Such reasoning ignores that terrorists often act on their own or in groups and do not necessarily represent a country's people.)

Non Sequitur

Non sequitur is a Latin expression meaning "it does not follow." A non sequitur is a conclusion that is not the logical result of the premises or evidence that precedes it.

> Japanese children spend forty percent more time in the classroom than, and outperform, American children. American parents should take more interest in their children's schooling. (Both statements may be true, but the writer does not establish any logical connection between them.)

Bandwagon

The **bandwagon** fallacy suggests that if a majority of people express a belief or take an action that everyone should think or do the same. Such arguments give the weight of truth or inevitability to the judgments of the majority, which may not be justified and which may, in fact, be only a passing fashion or fascination.

> Over 70 percent of Americans favor tariffs on imports from Japan, and you should, too. (The argument falsely implies that the force of public opinion alone should sway undecided opinion. Such arguments are often bolstered by statistics from studies or surveys, but the use of numbers alone does not sufficiently support the writer's position. The advisability of tariffs should be decided on the basis of their effect on national and international interests, not on possibly uninformed or self-interested and emotional opinions.)

Red Herring

A **red herring** is an irrelevant issue introduced into an argument to draw attention from the central issue.

> This School Board should not vote to spend money for education in art and music when so many of our children fail to read at their grade levels. (Deplorable as the children's poor preparation in reading may be, it has no bearing on the quality or benefit to students of arts education programs.)

Post Hoc, Ergo Propter Hoc

Post hoc, ergo propter hoc is a Latin expression meaning "after this, therefore because of this." Post hoc reasoning asserts a cause and effect relationship between two actions even though one action simply preceded the other.

> Since Charles Braddock became mayor, housing prices have risen in our town. Clearly, Braddock's administration has been bad for prospective homeowners. (Although prices rose after Braddock became mayor, there is no necessary connection between the events.)

A cause must come before an effect, but not everything that occurs first is a cause of what follows. To avoid post hoc reasoning, take time to establish that the effects you note can be clearly and systematically linked to the causes you identify.

Ad Hominem

Ad hominem is a Latin expression meaning "to the man." Ad hominem reasoning occurs when writers attack the people involved with an issue rather than the issue itself. By shifting the focus from the idea to people, writers fail to address the real issues.

> Universities should not grant honorary degrees. After all, Walter Hale, who received a degree from Lawrence Institute, is supposedly linked

to organized crime.   (The main issue should not be Hale but rather honorary degrees. The mention of Hale inappropriately sidetracks the discussion and fails to make any case against the degrees themselves.)

False Analogy

A **false analogy** is a comparison that is not based on relevant points of similarity. For an analogy to be logical, the subjects must be similar in several important, not superficial, ways.

If eighteen-year-olds are old enough to get married, vote, and serve in the military, they are old enough to drink alcohol.   (This analogy falsely suggests that activities performed when under complete control have a bearing on an activity that often results in lack of control. The comparison is based on strained similarities.)

EXERCISE 5.6 ❯ *Logical fallacies*

Identify and explain the logical fallacies in the following sentences. Rewrite the sentences to qualify the statements and avoid the fallacies.

1. Ernest Hemingway's novels should not be regarded so highly. After all, he was clearly sexist.

2. Many Nobel Prize winners in science used animals in their experiments, so using animals in research must be acceptable.

3. I saw a woman at the grocery store use food stamps to buy steaks, artichokes, and hand-packed ice cream. Food stamps allow the unemployed to eat very well.

4. If secondary schools require four years of English, writing skills will no doubt improve.

5. If business people can deduct expenses for lunches, then factory workers should have the same privilege.

6. To reduce the trade deficit, all we need to do is increase taxes.

7. Unless we imprison industrial spies, all our technological secrets will end up in the hands of the Russians.

8. Atlanta is the home of both the Turner Broadcasting System and the Braves. It is a great place to raise a family.

9. If an actress lives long enough, she is sure to win an Academy Award.

10. Since smoking marijuana is immoral, we should punish anyone caught using it.

| 5f | > | **A sample argument.** |

The following article appeared in the "My Turn" section of *Newsweek* magazine, 16 January 1989. Numbered annotations listed on pages 128–30 identify important features and strategies.

You Get What You Pay For
by Norman Ornstein

1. There are few things that unite Americans more than the antipathy we feel toward government officials when pay raises come up.

2. We may divide over aid to the Nicaraguan contras, the Strategic Defense Initiative and nuclear power, but we join together powerfully when a blue-ribbon commission proposes increasing the pay of lawmakers, government executives and judges. Talk-radio telephone lines haven't stopped lighting up since the Quadrennial Commission on Executive, Legislative and Judicial Salaries issued its recommendations in December [1988], including raising congressional pay

3. from its current $89,500 to $135,000. (Pay of judges and top federal

executives, tied to congressional salaries, would go up correspond-
ingly.)

     I suppose it should be heartening to find at least one policy area
that brings Americans together. It would be — if they weren't wrong

4. about it. I live in Washington; while I'm not a part of government, I
interact daily with congressmen, federal executives and judges and
their counterparts in the private sector. My conclusion: in govern-

5. ment, as in any other area, you get what you pay for. Without a size-
able salary increase (combined, sensibly, with the elimination of
honorariums for speeches called for by the commission), we will
end up with fewer and fewer competent and experienced lawmakers and judges — and more and more millionaires, charlatans and
ideologues.

6.   This argument does not play well, to put it delicately, with critics
of a pay raise. To Pat Buchanan, now living comfortably after his
government service on a half million dollars a year as a commentator, and to bachelor Ralph Nader, who has no kids to put through
college and believes that everyone ought to live like Mother Teresa,
$89,500 a year is enough for anybody to live on. To the assem-
bly-line worker trying to get by on $25,000 in Wichita, the notion of
needing more than $100,000 is nothing short of absurd.

     It does no good to note that exactly the same arguments have
been put forth by outraged citizens for 200 years, since our legislature tried to go from $6 per day to $7 a day. Whatever the size of the
increase, raising the pay of public officials touches a deep and sensitive cultural nerve in our citizenry — one that reinforces our suspi-
cions about venal and selfish politicians robbing the rest of us for
their own personal gain, and that goes against our predispositions
for "citizen-politicians" who labor for the public interest without regard to their own concerns.

     For centuries, Congress has struggled with the dilemma of voting
on its own compensation, along with that of presidents, Supreme
Court judges and other federal officials. To justify its pay and to blunt
the charge that lawmakers are unfairly feathering their nests,

7. Congress and the president created the blue-ribbon commission that meets every four years to examine the state of federal pay. But the firestorm over government pay increases turns out to have little to do with who proposes them.

It also has little to do with the amount of increase. Nevertheless, this year a raise from $89,500 to $135,000 has made it nearly impossible to even discuss with voters the reasons behind the increase. Most Americans get COLA's, raises or promotions every year or two, but federal pay is adjusted only every few years. In 1970 congressional pay went up from $30,000 to $42,500 (incidentally, provoking the same outraged reaction as now). In the years since, private-sector white-collar pay has gone up more than 200 percent and blue-collar pay almost as much. Social-security recipients have seen their sti-
8. pends go up 232 percent. The consumer price index has risen 219 percent. Congressional pay, however, has gone up 109.6 percent — barely more than half of the cost of living and half the increase in the private sector.

The numbers, though, are not nearly as important as the basic reality of the cost of living in Washington, and the realities of balancing an existence as a public official and a family breadwinner. A
9. reasonable, four-bedroom house in a decent but not posh neighborhood in Wichita probably would run around $100,000. Try to find something comparable in Washington or a close-in suburb for under $300,000. Add to that the astronomical costs of everything from food to insurance, and living a decent middle-class life in Washington simply doesn't compare in cost to the same lifestyle in Cleveland or Seattle, much less Wichita.

We all have crushing burdens, and for many of us, who work two jobs or have to leave children in costly childcare, using our tax dollars to cushion the burden for public servants, with all their perks and status, is too much to bear. But if we could get past the emotion, we would see the grim bottom line: the rewards for public officials have rarely been lower, the drawbacks higher. Increasingly, we are having difficulty finding top-flight people to run for Congress, to work on medical research or to serve as judges. Do we really want the satisfaction of slapping down congressmen, if it means, as

10. Anthony Fauci, head of the federal government's AIDS program, told the commission, that he cannot recruit a single senior researcher to try to find a cure for the disease because of poor federal pay and benefits? Who do we really want running our defenses or overseeing $1.2 trillion in federal spending each year?

11. The fact is that to deal with the unbelievably complex and challenging problems facing us as a nation, we need to attract good people to government at all levels, and we need to keep many of them long enough to provide some maturity and some institutional memory. To do that, we need not pay what investment bankers or Wall Street lawyers make — but we do need to pay enough that government employees can live reasonable middle-class existences, comparable to top professionals at least in non-profit areas like higher education and the foundations. That is what the Quad Commission has recommended. If we reject it, we'll continue to play with fire, hoping we can get a better government than we are willing to pay for.

Annotations

1. Ornstein's introductory paragraph is deductive, leading with a topic sentence that clearly states the premise and following with illustrative details.

2. By using *we,* Ornstein skillfully makes an emotional appeal in order to establish a bond with his readers.

3. Ornstein ends the first paragraph by specifying the salaries at issue. Throughout the essay, Ornstein skillfully uses facts to help make his point.

4. In the second paragraph, Ornstein states that he is a resident of Washington and has daily contact with politicians.

Establishing this firsthand knowledge of politics constitutes an ethical appeal.

5. The second paragraph ends with Ornstein's thesis, which contains an implicit warrant. What Ornstein leaves unstated are his beliefs and opinions that (1) good people require good salaries, (2) we do not pay our political leaders good salaries, and (3) good salaries attract good people to politics. The use of an implicit warrant allows Ornstein to proceed with his discussion without immediately alienating readers who might disagree with him.

6. Ornstein uses an emotional appeal in the third paragraph. He cites opponents of salary increases but carefully chooses his words to make their objections seem untenable, and he creates a hypothetical worker in Wichita with whom he hopes readers will identify.

7. The fifth paragraph is inductive, leading readers through historical details to Ornstein's point that objections to pay raises arise no matter who proposes them.

8. Facts and statistics, salaries and percentages, create a specific context. Salaries alone, however, would not illustrate Ornstein's point, since they are higher than those earned by many average citizens. The use of percentages, as a result, becomes crucial to his argument.

9. Ornstein uses a four-bedroom home as an example, noting that comparable homes in Wichita and Washington would cost radically different amounts.

10. In an extended analogy (poor salaries in science have the same results as poor salaries in politics), Ornstein incorporates expert testimony from Anthony Fauci. Although testimony from an expert in political science might have

seemed a more logical choice, the conditions Fauci describes clearly apply to politics as well as to medical research.

11. Ornstein closes his essay with a paragraph that explicitly states the warrant of his argument. Each sentence (and sometimes each clause) presents a premise that, if accepted, leads directly to the next. To conclude his essay and effectively underscore his thesis, Ornstein's position and reasoning must be very clear, and the use of explicitly stated warrants achieves that end.

EFFECTIVE SENTENCES

6 Understanding Parts of Speech

Sentences consist of words used in specific ways according to their parts of speech. Words combined into phrases, clauses, and sentences create meaning.

This chapter explores parts of speech so that you will be able to use each of them flexibly and precisely to compose effective sentences.

Quick Reference

Learning about the parts of speech is a means to an end: technical knowledge of sentence elements allows you to analyze and improve your sentences.

> *Use the most specific nouns that suit the meaning of your sentence.*

> *Use only pronouns that have clear antecedents.*

> *Use verbs whose tenses create the time distinctions you intend.*

> *Use coordinating conjunctions to join equivalent elements; use subordinating conjunctions to join subordinate and independent clauses; use correlative conjunctions in pairs.*

English has eight parts of speech: **nouns, pronouns, verbs, adjectives, adverbs, conjunctions, prepositions,** and **interjections.** Learning to identify parts of speech in sentences is not an end in itself but a means to understanding how words work together in sentences. Knowing this, you can analyze your writing, identifying and eliminating grammatical inconsistencies and building sentences that express your exact meaning.

When analyzing the parts of speech in a sentence, note carefully how the words function. Remember that the same word can be used in different ways in different sentences. In the following sentences, *stain* appears as a noun, a verb, and an adjective.

Noun
The oriental carpet in the foyer had a large *stain* in the center, the result of an accident long since forgotten.

Verb
Grape juice will *stain* skin, fabric, wood, and almost anything else it touches.

Adjective
Many common substances — such as milk, baking soda, and vinegar — are effective *stain* removers.

6a ⟩ Nouns

A **noun** names a person, place, thing, idea, quality, or condition and can be proper, common, collective, abstract, or concrete.

Proper Nouns

Proper nouns name specific people, places, and things: *Julia Child, Stockholm, Corvette*. They are always capitalized.

Roger lost his *Minolta X700* while vacationing in *Spain*.

Common Nouns

Common nouns name people, places, and things by general type: *chef, city, sports car*. They are not capitalized.

My *friend* lost his thirty-five-millimeter *camera* while vacationing in a foreign *country*.

Collective Nouns

Collective nouns name groups of people or things; although each group includes two or more members, it is usually considered *one* group: *team, class, group, audience.*

> The *congregation* at St. Mary's has raised four thousand dollars for the *hungry* in Africa.

Abstract Nouns

Abstract nouns name ideas, qualities, and conditions: *freedom, honesty, shyness.*

Concrete Nouns

Concrete nouns name things or qualities perceptible by the senses: *chair, salt, warmth, noise.*

| 6b | > | Pronouns |

Pronouns substitute for nouns. Generally, a pronoun refers to a previously stated noun, called an **antecedent.**

> The movers dropped the desk while carrying *it* up the stairs. *They* immediately filled out a damage report, *which* required John's signature. (*It, they,* and *which* are the pronouns; *desk, movers,* and *report* are the antecedents.)

Pronouns are classified as **personal, possessive, reflexive, interrogative, demonstrative, indefinite,** and **relative,** depending on their function in a sentence.

Personal Pronouns

Personal pronouns substitute for nouns that name people or things. The form of the pronoun depends on the gender and number of the antecedent and whether the pronoun is a subject or an object (see pages 179 and 183–84).

Subject		Object	
Singular	*Plural*	*Singular*	*Plural*
I	we	me	us
you	you	you	you
he		him	
she	they	her	them
it		it	

The archer was distracted by noisy people in the crowd, so *she* delayed the shot until the referee had quieted *them*.   (*She* and *them* are the pronouns; *archer* and *people* are the antecedents.)

Possessive Pronouns

Possessive pronouns show ownership.

Singular	*Plural*
my, mine	our, ours
your, yours	your, yours
his, his	
her, hers	their, theirs
its, its	

Use the first form, often called a **pronoun-adjective,** with a noun; use the second form if the pronoun stands alone in place of a noun.

> Matt, *your* solution is more idealistic than *mine.*   (*Your,* a pronoun-adjective, modifies the noun *solution; mine* stands alone but also implies reference to the same antecedent, *solution.*)

》》》   *Do not confuse* its, *the possessive pronoun, with* it's, *the contraction for* it is. **《《《**

Reflexive Pronouns

Reflexive pronouns show that someone or something in the sentence is acting for or on itself; if used to show emphasis, they are sometimes called **intensive pronouns.**

Singular	*Plural*
myself	ourselves
yourself	yourselves
himself	
herself	themselves
itself	

Self-related action

The state senators voted *themselves* a raise for the third time in a decade.   (*Themselves* shows that the senators raised their own wages.)

Emphasis

Although his friends offered to help paint the apartment, Russell preferred to do it himself.   (*Himself* emphasizes that Russell wanted no help.)

Reflexive pronouns require antecedents within the same sentence and, as a result, should not be used as subjects.

Faulty

Joan and *myself* renovated the cabin.   (*Myself* cannot function as the subject of the sentence.)

Correct

Joan and *I* renovated the cabin *ourselves*.   (*I* is a suitable subject pronoun; *ourselves*, with *Joan and I* as the antecedents, is correctly used to show emphasis.)

Interrogative Pronouns

Interrogative pronouns are used to ask questions.

Subject	*Object*
who	whom
whoever	whomever
Other interrogative pronouns	
what	whose
which	

Who won the Nobel Peace Prize this year?

To *whom* should I send the application?

Which musical had the longer Broadway run, *Evita* or *Cats?*

Demonstrative Pronouns

Demonstrative pronouns are used alone to substitute for specific nouns.

Singular	*Plural*
this	these
that	those

Used with nouns, these four words function as **demonstrative adjectives.** If the antecedent of the demonstrative pronoun is unclear, use the demonstrative adjective with the noun.

Confusing

Vonin hesitated before speaking. That helped her to control her emotions.   (Did *that* refer to hesitating or speaking or both?)

Clear

Vonin hesitated before speaking. That pause helped her to control her emotions.

Indefinite Pronouns

Indefinite pronouns, pronouns without specific antecedents, serve as general subjects or objects in sentences. When using an indefinite pronoun as a subject, remember that some are singular and some are plural and choose the verb that agrees with the indefinite pronoun you are using.

Common Indefinite Pronouns

Singular

another	either	nobody
any	everybody	no one
anybody	everyone	one
anyone	everything	somebody
each	neither	someone

Plural

all	few	several
both	many	some

When used alone, these words are pronouns. Some of these words — *someone's* passport, *anybody's* guess, *several* women — can also modify nouns and thus serve as pronoun-adjectives.

Someone is sure to discover that the dates in the chart are inaccurate. (Singular pronoun is the subject of the sentence.)

Several are available on the table at the back of the lecture hall. (Plural pronoun is the subject of the sentence.)

Both archaeologists agree that their earlier finds were misleading. (Pronoun-adjective modifies *archaeologists*.)

Relative Pronouns

Relative pronouns substitute for nouns already mentioned in the sentence and are used to introduce adjective or noun clauses.

To refer to people	
who	whoever
whom	whomever

To refer to things		
that	what	which

To refer to people or things

that (generally for things)

whose (generally for people)

Novelists *who* achieve notoriety quickly often fade from view just as quickly.

Anger *that* is not expressed is often the most damaging.

People *whose* children attend private schools pay for education twice, through taxes and through tuition.

Sometimes the relative pronoun *that* can be left out (understood) in a sentence where the noun-clause relationship is clear without it. As a general rule, use *that* to introduce essential information, but use *which* to introduce information that can be omitted.

An object *that is over one hundred years old* is considered an antique. (The clause is essential to the meaning of the sentence.)

The steamer trunk, *which we found in Aunt Melissa's attic,* belonged to my great grandfather.   (The clause can be omitted without altering the meaning of the sentence.)

> **!** Although relative pronouns allow writers to embed informa-
> tion in sentences, too much embedded material can make
> sentences difficult to read. Use the "search" codes with your
> word processing program to locate uses of relative pro-
> nouns. Decide whether sentences with several pronouns
> might be more effective if separated.

EXERCISE 6.1 ❯ *Nouns and pronouns*

Underline the nouns and pronouns in each of the following sentences and label each according to type.

1. Acupuncture, a medical treatment, developed centuries ago in China.

2. The acupuncturist uses extremely thin gold needles to pierce the patient's skin.

3. Patients frequently receive sedation before the treatment begins and the needles are implanted.

4. The areas where the needles are inserted do not correspond to the areas of discomfort or pain.

5. Those who have been helped by acupuncture advocate the treatment most strongly.

6. Why should those of us who have not tried acupuncture question their satisfaction?

7. Teams of Western scientists have studied acupuncture and found no physiological explanations for its success.

8. Yet success rates for patients who have faith in the procedure suggest that we can learn more than we already know about the psychological effects of medical treatments.

9. Ironically, while acupuncture has been attracting attention in Europe and America in recent years, its use in China has declined.

10. Some say acupuncture is merely a medical hoax, but others continue to search for scientific explanations for its apparent success.

EXERCISE 6.2 ❯   *Nouns and pronouns*

Revise the following paragraph, replacing some nouns with pronouns to achieve a smoother style.

Theodore Roosevelt, the twenty-fifth president of the United States, was an individualist. Nonetheless, Roosevelt served the public well. Roosevelt's individualistic tendencies were illustrated first by Roosevelt's attempts at boxing, an uncommon activity for an upper-class gentleman at Harvard. After Roosevelt's graduation, Roosevelt made a trip west, where Roosevelt experimented briefly with ranching and cowboy life. Roosevelt returned to the East to serve in the government, but in 1898 Roosevelt resigned Roosevelt's post as secretary of the navy to organize the Rough Riders, a regiment formed to fight in the Spanish-American War. The Rough Riders found Roosevelt to be an able leader, and though the Rough Riders did not follow Roosevelt up San Juan Hill as legend has it, the Rough Riders did fight with Roosevelt in Cuba. Roosevelt returned to the United States a hero; Roosevelt's notoriety helped Roosevelt to win the mayoral race of New York. Two years later, Roosevelt was elected vice-president in spite of opposition from political bosses and industrial leaders. Political bosses and industrial leaders must have found Roosevelt's freewheeling individualism unsettling and certainly unpredictable. The political bosses and industrial leaders fought Roosevelt in Roosevelt's antitrust actions when Roosevelt became president after McKinley's assassination. Throughout Roosevelt's presidency and the rest of Roosevelt's life, Roosevelt continued to act as an individual but with the public good in mind.

6c ❯ Verbs

A **verb** expresses action (*organize* or *sing*) or state of being (*seem* or *was*). Grammatically complete sentences contain at least one verb, and effectively chosen verbs make writing clear, exact, and interesting.

Types of Verbs

The three types of verbs are **action, linking,** and **auxiliary.**

Action Verbs

Action verbs express both physical and mental activities.

> *action verb*
> Angela *parked* her car on a designated snow route.

> *action verb*
> She *thought* the snow would stop.

Action verbs are either intransitive or transitive. **Intransitive verbs** do not need direct objects (a person or thing that receives the action of the verb, like *car* in the first example above) to complete their meaning.

> *subj. intrans. verb*
> The negative ad *campaign backfired.*   (Without a direct object, the sentence is still clear.)

Transitive verbs require direct objects to complete their meaning.

> *subj. trans. verb   d.o.*
> At last, *Bernie earned* her *respect.*   (Without the direct object *respect,* the sentence's meaning would be unclear.)

> *subj.*   *trans. verb*   *d.o.*
> *Leonardo da Vinci painted* very few *works*.   (*Painted* could be either
> intransitive or transitive, depending on the meaning of the sentence.)

Linking Verbs

Linking verbs express either a state of being or a condition.

Common Linking Verbs			
Forms of **to be**			
is	be	being	been
am	are	was	were
Other linking verbs				
appear	feel	look	seem	sound
become	grow	make	smell	taste

Forms of *to be* join the subject of a sentence or clause with a complement (either a predicate noun or a predicate adjective), creating a parallel relationship.

With predicate nouns

> linking verb
> Rachel *is* the best player on the volleyball team.   (*Rachel* [subject] =
> *player* [predicate noun]. The predicate noun further identifies Rachel.)

With predicate adjectives

                linking verb
                    |

Woodrow Wilson *was* enthusiastic about the League of Nations. (*Woodrow Wilson* [subject] = *enthusiastic* [predicate adjective]. The predicate adjective describes Wilson.)

Auxiliary Verbs

Auxiliary, or **helping, verbs** work with other verbs to create verb tenses or to form questions.

Common Auxiliary Verbs				
Forms of **to be**				
am	is	were	being	
are	was	been		
Other auxiliary verbs				
will	do	did	may	must
could	should	would	might	

      aux. verb   verb
           | |

Ophelia *will enter* from stage right.

        aux. verb   verb
             | |

Greenpeace *must oppose* chemical dumping in our waterways.

When modifiers are used, they often separate the auxiliary from the main verb. In forming questions, the auxiliary usually precedes the subject. Auxiliary verbs always precede main verbs.

     aux. verb mod.   verb
        | | |
Ophelia *will* probably *enter* from stage right.

 aux. verb   verb
   | |
Must Greenpeace *oppose* chemical dumping in our waterways?

EXERCISE 6.3 ❭ *Verbs*

Underline and label the verbs in the following sentences.

1. Stoics are people who accept their fate without question.

2. They have learned not to concern themselves with what they will be unable to change or to waste time worrying about what is past.

3. Modern stoics have as their model, though they may not know it, a fourth-century Greek philosopher.

4. Zeno and his followers believed that the Fates (goddesses in Greek mythology) determine people's destinies.

5. Modern-day stoics, however, must grapple with Judeo-Christian beliefs that teach us that we have free will.

Forms of Verbs

In English, verbs have three principal parts or forms: the **infinitive,** the **past tense,** and the **past participle.** The infinitive is a verb's primary form (*work, cope*); it is often used with *to*. For regular verbs, the past tense and past participle are formed by adding *-ed* or *-d* to the infinitive (*worked, coped*).

Principal Parts of Regular Verbs

Infinitive	Past tense	Past participle
select	selected	selected
inform	informed	informed
cook	cooked	cooked

Many common English verbs are irregular and form the past tense and past participles in a variety of ways. Because there is no predictable pattern for these verbs, it is helpful to become familiar with the principal parts of common irregular verbs.

Principal Parts of Common Irregular Verbs

Infinitive	Past tense	Past participle
arise	arose	arisen
awake	awoke, awakened	awakened
be	was/were	been
beat	beat	beaten, beat
begin	began	begun
bend	bent	bent
bite	bit	bitten
blow	blew	blown
break	broke	broken
bring	brought	brought
build	built	built

Infinitive	*Past tense*	*Past participle*
burst	burst	burst
catch	caught	caught
choose	chose	chosen
come	came	come
cost	cost	cost
creep	crept	crept
deal	dealt	dealt
dig	dug	dug
dive	dived, dove	dived
do	did	done
drag	dragged	dragged
draw	drew	drawn
dream	dreamed, dreamt	dreamed, dreamt
drink	drank	drunk
drive	drove	driven
eat	ate	eaten
fall	fell	fallen
fight	fought	fought
find	found	found
fly	flew	flown
forbid	forbade, forbad	forbidden
forget	forgot	forgotten, forgot
freeze	froze	frozen
get	got	got, gotten

Infinitive	Past tense	Past participle
give	gave	given
go	went	gone
grow	grew	grown
hang	hung	hung
hang (to execute)	hanged	hanged
have	had	had
hear	heard	heard
hurt	hurt	hurt
keep	kept	kept
know	knew	known
lay (to put)	laid	laid
lead	led	led
lend	lent	lent
let	let	let
lie (to recline)	lay	lain
lie (to tell an untruth)	lied	lied
lose	lost	lost
make	made	made
read	read	read
ride	rode	ridden
ring	rang	rung
rise	rose	risen
run	ran	run

Infinitive	*Past tense*	*Past participle*
say	said	said
see	saw	seen
send	sent	sent
set (to put)	set	set
shake	shook	shaken
shine	shone, shined	shone, shined
shoot	shot	shot
shrink	shrank, shrunk	shrunk, shrunken
sing	sang	sung
sink	sank	sunk
sit (to take a seat)	sat	sat
slay	slew	slain
sleep	slept	slept
speak	spoke	spoken
spin	spun	spun
spring	sprang	sprung
stand	stood	stood
steal	stole	stolen
sting	stung	stung
strike	struck	struck, stricken
strive	strove	striven
swear	swore	sworn
swim	swam	swum
swing	swung	swung

dead? (handwritten note)

Infinitive	Past tense	Past participle
take	took	taken
teach	taught	taught
tear	tore	torn
throw	threw	thrown
wake (to wake up)	woke, waked	waked, woken
waken (to rouse)	wakened	wakened
wear	wore	worn
wring	wrung	wrung
write	wrote	written

Verb Tenses

English has three simple tenses (**present, past,** and **future**); three perfect tenses (**present perfect, past perfect,** and **future perfect**); and six progressive tenses, one corresponding to each simple and each perfect tense.

Distinguishing among verb tenses will enable you to understand in reading and use in writing the clear, precise time distinctions they express.

Present Tense

The **present tense** indicates an existing condition or state, something occurring at the present time, or a habitual action.

The plums *are* ripe.   (existing condition)

I *hear* a baby crying.   (occurring at the present time)

Marla *plays* the viola.   (habitual action)

Past Tense

The **past tense** indicates that something has already occurred and is in the past.

The architectural plans *arrived* last week.

Future Tense

The **future tense** indicates that something will happen in the future. Form the future tense by adding the auxiliary *will* to the infinitive. (*Shall,* an alternative auxiliary, is rarely used in current American writing.)

Sasha's poem *will appear* in next month's issue of the magazine.

Present Perfect Tense

The **present perfect tense** indicates that something began in the past and continues into the present or that it occurred at an unspecified time in the past. Form the present perfect tense by using the auxiliary *has* or *have* plus the past participle of the verb.

Marcus *has accepted* a football scholarship for next year.   (beginning in the past, continuing to the present)

Inclement weather *has* always *created* problems for farmers.   (unspecified time)

Past Perfect Tense

The **past perfect tense** indicates that an action was completed before some time in the past. Form the past perfect tense by adding the auxiliary *had* to the past participle.

Great cities *had flourished* in the Western Hemisphere long before Spanish explorers reached North and South America.

Future Perfect Tense

The **future perfect tense** indicates that an action will be completed before a certain time in the future. Form the future perfect tense by adding the auxiliaries *will have* (or *shall have*) to the past participle.

> By the turn of the century, we *will have depleted* many of the earth's natural resources.

Progressive Tenses

For every basic tense, an equivalent **progressive tense** exists that indicates continuing action. Form the progressive tenses by using a form of the verb *to be* (*is, was, will be, have been, had been,* or *will have been*) and the present participle (*-ing*) form of the verb.

Progressive Tenses

Present progressive	*is playing*
Past progressive	*was playing*
Future progressive	*will be playing*
Present perfect progressive	*has been playing*
Past perfect progressive	*had been playing*
Future perfect progressive	*will have been playing*

EXERCISE 6.4 ❯ *Verb tenses*

Underline the verbs in the following sentences and label each verb with its tense.

1. In 1947, Kenneth Arnold, a pilot, described saucer-shaped objects that he saw traveling at great speeds.

2. Since then, thousands of people around the world have reported similar incidents of seeing "unidentified flying objects" (UFOs).

3. During the 1950s and 1960s, Project Bluebook, a division of the U.S. Air Force, attempted to explain these sightings and found that most were misinterpreted observations of natural phenomena.

4. By the late 1960s, Project Bluebook had served its purpose — to reassure military and civilian populations that the earth was not being watched or attacked — and was consequently disbanded.

5. Today, some people still claim to see bright, formless objects traveling at great speeds through our skies — and no doubt such claims will continue.

EXERCISE 6.5 ❯ *Verbs*

The following passage from Benjamin Franklin's letter describing how to reproduce his electrical experiments is written primarily in the present tense. Reconstruct the passage as though Franklin had written a narrative of his procedure. Make appropriate changes in the verbs. (Hint: Many verbs will be in the past tense.)

Make a small cross of two light strips of cedar, the arms so long as to reach to the four corners of a large thin silk handkerchief when extended; tie the corners of the handkerchief to the extremities of the cross, so you have the body of a kite; which being properly accommodated with a tail, loop, and string, will rise into the air, like those made of paper; but this being silk, is fitter to bear the wet and wind of a thunder-gust. To the top of the upright stick of the cross is to be fixed a very sharp-pointed wire, rising a foot or more above the wood. To the end of the twine, next the hand, is to be tied a silk ribbon, and where the silk and the tie join, a key may be fastened. This kite is to be raised when a thunder-gust appears to be coming on, and the person who holds the string must stand within a door or window, or under some cover, so that the silk ribbon may not be wet; and care must be taken that the twine does not touch the frame of the door or window. . . . And when the rain has wet the kite and twine, so that it can conduct the electrical fire freely, you will find it stream out plentifully from the key on the approach of your knuckle. — Benjamin Franklin, "Letter to Peter Collinson"

6d Adjectives

An **adjective** modifies or limits a noun or pronoun. Adjectives come in three forms: **positive, comparative,** and **superlative.**

Forms of Adjectives

Positive Adjectives

A **positive adjective** modifies a noun or pronoun without suggesting any comparisons.

These are *clear* instructions.

Comparative Adjectives

A **comparative adjective** compares two people, places, things, ideas, qualities, conditions, or actions.

These are *clearer* instructions than those we had last time.

Superlative Adjectives

A **superlative adjective** compares three or more items.

These are the *clearest* instructions I've ever seen

Questions Adjectives Answer

What kind?	*auburn* hair
Which one?	the *fourth* presentation
How many?	*sixteen* guests
Whose?	*Jeffrey's* assessment

Kinds of Adjectives

Regular Adjectives

A **regular adjective** precedes the word it modifies. Several adjectives can modify the same word.

$$\text{adj.} \quad \text{adj.} \quad \text{noun} \qquad\qquad \text{adj.} \quad \text{adj.} \quad \text{noun}$$

There is a *mauve velvet jacket* hanging in *Shirley's hall closet*. (*Mauve* jacket, *velvet* jacket; *Shirley's* closet, *hall* closet.)

▶▶▶ *When adjectives in a series function together as one modifier — when each word alone cannot modify the noun or pronoun — hyphenate the series of words.*

In 1982, American car manufacturers reintroduced *two-tone* cars. (not *two* cars or *tone* cars but *two-tone* cars; on the other hand, *American* manufacturers or *car* manufacturers, not *American-car manufacturers*) **◀◀◀**

Predicate Adjectives

A **predicate adjective** follows a linking verb but modifies the subject of the sentence or clause.

$$\text{pred. adj.}$$

The sleeping child was obviously *content*.

>>>   *When adjectives in a series work as a unit but are in the predicate-adjective position, do not hyphenate them.*

Toni's comments were *off the cuff,* but they were sensible.   **<<<**

Articles and Demonstrative Adjectives

The **articles** — *a, an,* and *the* — and the **demonstrative adjectives** — *this, that, these,* and *those* — also function as adjectives.

The shortest distance between two points is *a* straight line.

Those forms go in *this* folder.

| 6e | > | **Adverbs** |

Adverbs modify verbs, adjectives, other adverbs, phrases, clauses, or entire sentences. Adverbs come in three forms: **positive, comparative,** and **superlative.**

Positive Adverbs

A **positive adverb** modifies a verb, an adjective, another adverb, a phrase, a clause, or an entire sentence but does not suggest a comparison.

Erica runs *quickly.*   (modifies the verb *runs*)

Erica runs *very* quickly.   (modifies the adverb *quickly*)

Comparative Adverbs

A **comparative adverb** compares two actions or conditions.

Erica runs *more quickly* than I do.   (modifies *runs,* comparing the two running speeds)

Superlative Adverbs

A **superlative adverb** compares three or more actions or conditions.

Of all the members of the relay team, Erica runs the *most quickly.*
(modifies *runs,* comparing the running speeds of Erica and the group)

Questions Adverbs Answer

How?	*slowly* approached
When?	laughed *first*
Where?	searched *everywhere*
How often?	praised *repeatedly*
To what extent?	*thoroughly* disliked

>>> *Although many adverbs end in* -ly, *many do not, and many words ending in* -ly *are not adverbs. Use an* -ly *ending as a guide, but identify adverbs by their function in sentences.*

The lonely widower was treated well by his neighbors.   *(Lonely* is an adjective; *well* is an adverb.)   **<<<**

EXERCISE 6.6 **>** *Adjectives and adverbs*

Underline the adjectives and adverbs in the following sentences and draw arrows to show the word or group of words that each modifies.

1. American folklore has created a number of important national heroes, among them Abraham Lincoln.

2. Lincoln, the sixteenth president of the United States, was a man destined to become a legend.

3. His solemn, idiosyncratic appearance made him an easily recognizable figure, and his pivotal role during the Civil War clearly made him an important historical character.

4. Yet the reverential anecdotes and the blatant fabrications about him must surely seem questionable.

5. Lincoln's early life, though austere, was not backward, yet the rail-splitting Abe of the rustic log cabin in New Salem far overshadows the sophisticated lawyer that Lincoln clearly was in Springfield.

6. Lincoln belonged to no Christian church, yet he was often depicted in Christ-like terms as an always suffering, always kind, and always patient man.

7. Folklore has undoubtedly skewed the biographical facts of Lincoln's life, but it has created a fascinating — albeit false — vision of a man.

EXERCISE 6.7 ❯ *Adjectives and adverbs*

Underline the adjectives and adverbs in the following paragraph and indicate with an arrow the word or group of words that each modifies.

My favorite spot at Aunt Ruth and Uncle Dan's house is the small, secluded patio just outside their bedroom. Every time I quietly open the sliding doors and step outside, I know I will feel more peaceful. The 8-by-8-foot patio is brick, meticulously set in a herringbone design. A comfortable, well-padded lounge chair provides a place to sit, and a small redwood table is a convenient spot to place my usual drink, a tall glass of Aunt Ruth's lightly spiced tea. Once comfortably seated, I always enjoy the various flowers, my favorite feature. Close to the front edge of the patio are pink, plum, red, and yellow moss roses, gently trailing their waxy green stems onto the dull red bricks. Slightly back, radiating away from the patio, are miniature yellow and orange marigolds, with their dense, round flowers set against dark green, sharp-edged leaves. Close behind those are Aunt Ruth and Uncle Dan's prize roses — white, pink, red, and yellow tea roses that are carefully pruned. The small buds, usually a darker color, contrast noticeably with the large open blossoms that always remind me of fine damask. I always love to escape from the cheerful but noisy family activities to this secluded spot where the flowers are so beautiful. Inevitably, a visit to this floral oasis makes me feel more tranquil than before.

6f ⟩ Conjunctions

Conjunctions link words, phrases, or clauses. They show relationships of equivalence, contrast, alternatives, chronology, and cause and effect. Conjunctions may be **coordinating, subordinating,** or **correlative. Conjunctive adverbs,** used only in independent clauses, function similarly to conjunctions.

Coordinating Conjunctions

Coordinating conjunctions link equivalent sentence parts. They are the most commonly used conjunctions.

Coordinating Conjunctions			
and	for	or	yet
but	nor	so	

In a desk drawer in his office, Todd always keeps a needle *and* thread. (joining nouns)

Struggling for modernity *but* ruling in the old style, Peter the Great imposed a tax on beards.   (joining phrases)

Subordinating Conjunctions

Subordinating conjunctions introduce subordinate clauses (those that cannot stand alone as sentences) and link them to independent clauses (those that can stand alone as sentences).

Common Subordinating Conjunctions

after	because	since	until
although	before	so that	when
as if	even if	that	wherever
as long as	if	unless	while

---

subordinate clause

While Gilbert was stationed in the Philippines, he returned home once.

subordinate clause

Interest rates will rise *as long as* the national debt grows.

Correlative Conjunctions

Correlative conjunctions always work in pairs and give additional emphasis to parts of sentences. The words, phrases, or clauses joined by these correlative constructions must be in parallel form.

Correlative Conjunctions

both . . . and	neither . . . nor
either . . . or	not only . . . but also

Both Mobil *and* Atlantic Richfield underwrite programs for the Public Broadcasting Service.

A successful gardener *not only* selects plants carefully *but also* attends to them painstakingly.

Conjunctive Adverbs

Conjunctive adverbs connect ideas in independent clauses or sentences. Like other adverbs, conjunctive adverbs can appear in any position in a sentence. (See sections 22c and 22d for information on punctuating conjunctive adverbs.)

Common Conjunctive Adverbs

accordingly	however	next
also	incidentally	nonetheless
besides	indeed	otherwise
consequently	instead	similarly
finally	likewise	still
further	meanwhile	then
furthermore	moreover	therefore
hence	nevertheless	thus

Conjunctive adverbs show relationships similar to but with a slight shift in focus or emphasis from those shown by conjunctions. For example, the coordinating conjunctions *but* and *yet* signal a simple contrast between balanced clauses; the subordinating conjunctions *although, even though,* and *though* signal contrast but emphasize one clause over the other; the conjunctive adverb *however* signals contrast but keeps the clauses separate.

Coordinating conjunction

Children learn to use computers with ease, *but* most adults learn with some difficulty.

Subordinating conjunction

Although children learn to use computers with ease, most adults learn with some difficulty.

Conjunctive adverb

Children learn to use computers with ease. Most adults, *however*, learn with some difficulty.

》》》 *Since they are punctuated differently (see section 22c), it is important to distinguish between short conjunctive adverbs and other short conjunctions. A simple method is to count the letters in the word: all conjunctive adverbs contain at least four letters, while coordinating conjunctions contain either two or three letters.* **《《《**

EXERCISE 6.8 ❯ *Conjunctions*

Use conjunctions to combine the following sets of sentences. Some rewording will be necessary.

1. Geography is the study of land masses. It includes the study of territorial divisions. It includes the study of bodies of water.

2. Geography was once studied as a separate course in public schools. It has now been subsumed by the social studies curriculum in most schools.

3. American students today are not receiving sufficient instruction in geography. They are not making the effort to learn the material.

4. College students in 1950 took a geography test sponsored by the *New York Times*. College students in 1984 took the same test. The comparative scores were startling.

5. Scores in some areas dropped 50 percent. That is not surprising. Seventy-two percent of the 1984 sample group said they had received little instruction in geography.

6g ▷ Prepositions

Prepositions link words in sentences. **Prepositional phrases** consist of a preposition, a noun or pronoun (the object of the preposition), and, frequently, modifiers.

                                         prep.   obj.
We seem to be losing the fight *against crime.*

          pron.
prep.   adj.   adj.   obj.
   | | | |
Because of his heretical views, Galileo was excommunicated.

Common Prepositions

Single–word prepositions

about	along	behind
above	among	below
across	around	beneath
after	at	beside
against	before	besides

Single-word prepositions

between	into	throughout
beyond	like	till
but	near	to
by	of	toward
concerning	off	under
despite	on	underneath
down	onto	until
during	out	up
except	outside	upon
for	over	with
from	past	within
in	since	without
inside	through	

Multiple-word prepositions

according to	in addition to	in spite of
ahead of	in case of	in side of
as well as	in front of	instead of
because of	in place of	rather than

Prepositional phrases modify specific words or phrases, functioning sometimes like adverbs (answering questions like *when, where,* or *how often*) and sometimes like adjectives (answering questions like *what kind* or *whose*).

             prep.   *obj.*   *prep.*   *obj.*
Our flight landed *in Montreal ahead of schedule.*   (Adverbial functions: Where did it land? When did it land?)

              prep.   *obj.*   *prep.*   *obj.*

Novels *about families* often describe conflicts *between parents*

              obj.

and their children.   (Adjective functions: What kinds of novels? What kinds of conflict?)

EXERCISE 6.9 ❯ *Prepositions*

Underline the prepositional phrases in the following paragraph and label the preposition and object in each phrase.

The dog has got more fun out of Man than Man has got out of the dog, for the clearly demonstrable reason that Man is the more laughable of the two animals. The dog has long been bemused by the singular activities and the curious practices of men, cocking his head inquiringly to one side, intently watching and listening to the strangest goings-on in the world. He has seen men sing together and fight one another in the same evening. He has watched them go to bed when it is time to get up, and get up when it is time to go to bed. He has observed them destroying the soil in vast areas, and nurturing it in small patches. He has stood by while men built strong and solid houses for rest and quiet, and then filled them with lights and bells and machinery. His sensitive nose, which can detect what's cooking in the next township, has caught at one and the same time the bewildering smells of the hospital and the munitions factory. He has seen men raise up great cities to heaven and then blow them to hell. — James Thurber, "A Dog's Eye View of Man"

| 6h | ❯ | **Interjections** |

Interjections express surprise or another emotion or provide transitions in sentences.

Okay, I'll try the steamed oysters if you insist.

Oh no! You didn't use aluminum foil in the microwave oven?

Strong interjections may be punctuated like a sentence, with a period or an exclamation point; milder interjections are joined to a sentence with a comma. Because most interjections are conversational and generally do not clarify a sentence's meaning, use them sparingly in formal writing.

EXERCISE 6.10 ❯ Parts of speech

Indicate the part of speech of the numbered words and phrases in the following paragraphs. For verbs, name the specific tense.

In the (1) *old* days, when I (2) *was writing* a great deal of (3) *fiction,* there would come, once in a while, moments when I was (4) *stymied.* (5) *Suddenly,* I would find I (6) *had written* (7) *myself* (8) *into* a hole and could see no way out. To take care of that, (9) *I* developed a (10) *technique* which (11) *invariably* worked.

It was simply this — I (12) *went* (13) *to* the movies. Not just any movie. I had to pick a movie which was loaded with action (14) *but* (15) *which* made no demands on the (16) *intellect.* (17) *As* I watched, I did my best to avoid any (18) *conscious* thinking concerning my (19) *problem,* and (20) *when* I came out of the movie I knew exactly what I would have to do to put the story back on track.

It never failed. — Isaac Asimov, "The Eureka Phenomenon"

Revising parts of speech with a word processor

Use your word processor to improve the wording of your sentences. Make a back-up copy of your draft and then experiment with parts of speech.

Substitute pronouns. Examine your draft for sentences where pronouns, rather than nouns, would create coherence and transition and eliminate repetition. Delete selected nouns and replace them with appropriate pronouns.

Change verb tense. To change the method of development of a paper — for example, from explaining a process to narrating an event, or vice versa — use the "delete" feature to change verb tenses to suit your new purpose.

Add clarifying words and phrases. After finishing a draft, make sentences more specific by inserting concrete, vivid adjectives and adverbs; the word-processing program will automatically reformat your sentences to accommodate these changes.

7 **Understanding Sentences**

Sentences contain at least a subject and a verb, and express a complete thought. Although sentences do not depend on groups of words outside themselves to make their meanings clear, they may contain words, phrases, and clauses, in addition to the essential subject and verb, that enhance their internal clarity. This chapter will help you to recognize the parts that make up sentences and to use these parts to form expressive, coherent sentences.

Quick Reference

Learning about parts and kinds of sentences will give you the technical knowledge you need to analyze and revise your writing.

❯ *Sentences must include a subject and a predicate.*

❯ *Phrases cannot stand alone but must be parts of sentences.*

❯ *Subordinate clauses cannot stand alone but must be joined to independent clauses.*

❯ *Use subjects, predicates, phrases, and clauses to create simple, compound, complex, and compound-complex sentences.*

| 7a | Distinguish among parts of sentences.

A **sentence** consists of at least a subject and verb. As the simplest complete expression of meaning, it is therefore the basic unit of written communication. Understanding the parts of sentences will help you to understand how to express your meaning coherently and effectively.

Subjects

The **subject** of a sentence is the person, place, thing, idea, quality, or condition that acts or is acted upon or that is described or identified in the sentence.

> *subj.*
> *Gauguin* fled to the South Pacific in search of unspoiled beauty and primitive innocence.

The subject can consist of one or more nouns or pronouns, together with any related modifiers. The subject generally appears near the beginning of a sentence, but it can appear in other positions as well. **》》》** *Subjects of sentences can never be part of prepositional phrases. The nouns and pronouns in prepositional phrases serve as objects of the preposition and cannot also be subjects.* **《《《**
Subjects can be **simple, compound,** and **complete.**

Simple Subjects

A **simple subject** consists of a single word.

> *simple subj.*
> *Machiavelli* changed the way rulers thought about governing. (*Machiavelli* performed the action, *change.*)

》》》 *Sometimes the subject* you *is unstated but understood in an imperative sentence (a request or command).*

[*You*] Go!

[*You*] Open the door this minute! **《《《**

Compound Subjects

A **compound subject** consists of two or more simple subjects joined by a conjunction.

compound subject

simple subj.   *simple subj.*

Locke and *Descartes* had different views on knowledge.

Complete Subjects

A **complete subject** contains the simple subject plus any words modifying it: adjectives, adverbs modifying adjectives, and prepositional phrases.

complete subject

simple subj.

The *supplies* for a basic design course need not be expensive.

EXERCISE 7.1 ❭ *Subjects*

Underline the complete subjects in the sentences below. Bracket and label simple subjects; bracket compound subjects and draw an arrow joining the simple subjects within them.

1. The musical, a combination of drama and music, developed as a distinctly American art form.

2. Emerging from vaudeville traditions, productions like George M. Cohan's *Little Johnny Jones* offered engaging tunes like "Yankee Doodle Boy" and "Give My Regards to Broadway" in very predictable plots.

3. However, in 1927, Jerome Kern and Oscar Hammerstein presented *Show Boat,* the first major musical based on a respected novel, and changed musicals forever.

4. *Oklahoma, South Pacific, My Fair Lady,* and *West Side Story* remain the most lasting contributions of the 1940s and 1950s, the golden years of the American musical.

5. In recent decades, British musicals have enjoyed both critical and popular success on Broadway, while American productions have often seemed insipid by comparison.

Predicates

The **predicate** of a sentence expresses the action or state of being of the subject. It states what the subject of the sentence does, what it is, or what has been done to it.

> *predicate*
> As a child prodigy, Mozart *was paraded* through the aristocratic houses of Europe.

A predicate consists of one or more verbs, together with any modifiers or complements. (Complements are discussed on pages 174–84.) Like subjects, predicates can be **simple, compound,** or **complete.** In questions, the parts of the predicate are usually separated by the subject.

Simple Predicates

A **simple predicate** consists of the verb and any auxiliaries.

> *simple pred.*
> Machiavelli *changed* the way rulers thought about governing.

Compound Predicates

A **compound predicate** consists of two or more verbs joined by a conjunction.

compound predicate

simple pred.

Compact discs *have revolutionized* the recording industry and, in all

compound predicate

simple pred.

likelihood, *will replace* albums as the most popular recording form.

Complete Predicates

A **complete predicate** consists of the simple or compound predicate plus all related modifiers — adjectives, adverbs, prepositional phrases, and any complements.

complete predicate

simple pred.

The supplies for a basic design course *need* not *be* very expensive.

EXERCISE 7.2 ❭ *Predicates*

*Underline the complete predicates in the sentences below. Bracket
and label simple predicates; bracket compound predicates and draw
an arrow joining the simple predicates within them.*

1. Professional ice hockey associations were first formed in Canada
   near the beginning of the twentieth century.

2. The first major league, the National Hockey Association, was
   founded in 1910 and included teams only from eastern Canada.

3. The following year, the Pacific Coast League organized teams from
   western Canadian cities, cities from the American northwest, and
   later other American cities.

4. In 1917, the National Hockey Association was reorganized to form
   the National Hockey League.

5. Since then, teams from both Canada and the United States have competed throughout the regular season and have vied for the Stanley Cup, the symbol of the League championship.

EXERCISE 7.3 ❯ *Subjects and Predicates*

Underline and label the simple and compound subjects and predicates in each of the following sentences.

Most tarantulas live in the tropics, but several species occur in the temperate zone and a few are common in the southern U. S. Some varieties are large and have powerful fangs with which they can inflict a deep wound. These formidable looking spiders do not, however, attack man; you can hold one in your hand, if you are gentle, without being bitten. Their bite is dangerous only to insects and small mammals such as mice; for man it is no worse than a hornet's sting.

Tarantulas customarily live in deep cylindrical burrows, from which they emerge at dusk and into which they retire at dawn. Mature males wander about after dark in search of females and occasionally stray into houses. After mating, the male dies in a few weeks, but a female lives much longer and can mate several years in succession. In a Paris museum is a tropical specimen which is said to have been living in captivity for 25 years. — Alexander Petrunkevitch, "The Spider and the Wasp"

Complements

A **complement** completes the meaning of a transitive verb. A **direct object** or an **indirect object** completes the action of the verb; a **predicate noun** or a **predicate adjective** follows a linking verb and restates the subject or describes its state of being.

Complements follow the verb and are part of the complete predicate. They can be simple or compound.

Direct Objects

Direct objects complete the action of a transitive verb by answering the questions *what* or *whom*.

Senator Packhard supported *the doomed Equal Rights Amendment.* (*What* did Senator Packhard support?)

Indirect Objects

Indirect objects indicate to whom or for whom the action of the transitive verb is intended. Indirect objects follow transitive verbs but always precede direct objects.

The librarian handed *Michael* the bibliography.   (*To whom* did the librarian hand the bibliography?)

Predicate Nouns

Predicate nouns follow linking verbs and restate or identify the subject of a sentence.

Agnes De Mille was a skillful and innovative *choreographer.* (*Choreographer* restates the subject, *De Mille.*)

Predicate Adjectives

Predicate adjectives follow linking verbs and modify the subject of a sentence.

De Mille's choreography was sometimes *playful,* frequently *surprising,* and often *austere.*   (*Playful, surprising,* and *austere* describe the subject, *choreography.*)

EXERCISE 7.4 ❯ Complements

Underline the complements in the sentences below and label them as direct objects, indirect objects, predicate nouns, or predicate adjectives. Draw an arrow between the parts of compound complements.

1. The year 1896 was not only a tribute to humanity's best but also a reflection of humanity's worst characteristics.

2. At the Democratic Convention, William Jennings Bryan gave his "Cross of Gold" speech and sparked interest in an uneventful campaign.

3. The British Patent Office granted Guglielmo Marconi a patent for the wireless telegraph.

4. When the United States Supreme Court handed down its *Plessy* v. *Ferguson* decision, it established a "separate but equal" standard that institutionalized racism.

5. Athens, Greece, was the site of the first modern Olympiad.

6. Alfred Nobel was the benefactor of an endowment which began by awarding yearly prizes in peace, science, and literature.

EXERCISE 7.5 ❯ Complements

Underline and label the complements in the following paragraph.

Henry Reed was class valedictorian. He was a small, very black boy with hooded eyes, a long, broad nose and an oddly shaped head. I had admired him for years because each term he and I vied for the best grades in our class. Most often he bested me, but instead of being disappointed I was pleased that we shared top places between us. Like many Southern Black children, he lived with his grandmother, who was as strict as Momma and as kind as she knew how to be. He was courteous, respectful and soft-spoken to elders, but on the playground he chose to play the roughest games. I admired him. Anyone, I reckoned, sufficiently afraid or sufficiently dull could be polite. But to be able to operate at a top level with both adults and children was admirable. — Maya Angelou, "Graduation"

Phrases

Phrases are groups of related words that cannot function as independent sentences because they lack subjects or predicates or both; phrases must be part of a sentence. The three most commonly used kinds of phrases are **prepositional phrases, verbal phrases,** and **appositive phrases;** they function as nouns, adjectives, or adverbs. A fourth kind, **absolute phrases,** modifies whole sentences.

Prepositional Phrases

A **prepositional phrase** consists of a preposition, its object or objects (a noun or pronoun), and any modifiers; it functions most often as an adjective or adverb and less often as a noun.

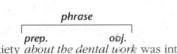

The dog limped *across the yard to the lighted doorway.*   (Both phrases work as adverbs, answering the question *"Where* did the dog limp?")

My anxiety *about the dental work* was intense.   (The phrase works as an adjective, answering the question *"Which* anxiety?")

EXERCISE 7.6 ❯ *Prepositional phrases*

Insert parentheses around the prepositional phrases in the following sentences and then underline the word or words that each phrase modifies.

1. In the last three decades, the once inexact study of weather has become a highly complex science.

2. The National Weather Service currently uses computers to synthesize data it receives from satellites, balloons, ground stations, and airplanes.

3. Once computers at the National Meteorological Center compile this information, it is relayed by a variety of electronic means to regional weather stations where teams evaluate the results.

4. Of particular interest are the findings of the National Severe Storms Forecast Center (NSSFC) in Kansas City, Missouri, for its team channels information about potentially dangerous storms to affected areas.

5. Using data from the NSSFC, local meteorologists issue a wide range of watches and warnings, notably for tornadoes, severe thunderstorms, blizzards, and hurricanes.

6. By providing systematically gathered and carefully organized information, weather forecasters can warn people of danger — saving millions of dollars worth of property and saving thousands of lives.

Verbal Phrases

Verbal phrases combine **verbals** (verb forms used as nouns, adjectives, and adverbs) with complements or modifiers. There are three types of verbals — **gerund phrases, participial phrases,** and **infinitive phrases.** Like verbals, verbal phrases function in sentences as nouns, adjectives, or adverbs.

Verbals.The three types of verbals are **gerunds, participles,** and **infinitives.**

Gerunds are -*ing* forms of verbs that work as nouns.

Reading is my favorite winter sport.

Participles appear in two forms: the present participle (*climbing, going*) and the past participle (*climbed, gone*). See the discussion of participles and the list of irregular verbs on pages 146–151.

Scowling, the tax assessor repeated the question.   (*Scowling* is a present participle modifying *tax assessor.*)

Exhausted, the dancer collapsed into the chair.   (*Exhausted* is a past participle modifying *dancer.*)

Infinitives combine the word *to* with a verb's primary form; they are used as nouns, adjectives, or adverbs.

To win is their only goal.   (*To win* works as a noun — the subject of the sentence.)

The office secretary is an important person *to know*.   (*To know* works as an adjective, modifying *person*.)

Lance was too excited *to sleep*.   (*To sleep* works as an adverb, modifying *excited*.)

Gerund Phrases. **Gerund phrases** combine a gerund and its complements and modifiers; the entire phrase works as a noun.

phrase

gerund   obj.
Climbing Mount Everest was their lifelong ambition.   (The gerund phrase is the subject of the sentence.)

phrase

gerund   obj.
I enjoy *playing* chamber music.   (The gerund phrase is the direct object of *enjoy*.)

phrase

gerund   obj.
Harrison reread the instructions for *assembling* the bicycle.   (The gerund phrase is the object of the preposition *for*.)

EXERCISE 7.7 ❯ *Gerund phrases*

Underline the gerund phrases in the following sentences. Bracket the objects and modifiers.

1. Learning a second language is a complicated task, but it is a rewarding one.

2. The benefits can be as simple as reading a menu in a foreign restaurant, a book in a used-book store, an untranslated quotation in a scholarly work, or a magazine in a library.

3. Working for international corporations is one career option open to people trained in a second language.

4. Traveling outside the United States is especially enjoyable when reading and speaking a country's language is possible.

5. Through studying other languages, people become sensitive to language itself and that sensitivity can increase their effectiveness as thinkers, readers, writers, speakers, and listeners.

Participial Phrases. **Participial phrases** combine a participle and its modifiers; the phrases work as adjectives. Like other adjectives, participial phrases must be placed near the nouns and pronouns they modify.

phrase
part.
Standing on the wooden bridge, Nathan watched small leaves float

phrase
part.
by, *swirling* along in the current.   (The first participial phrase modifies *Nathan;* the second modifies *leaves.*)

phrase
part.
Seated at a table far from the door, Carlos had not noticed his friends' arrival. (The participial phrase modifies *Carlos.*)

EXERCISE 7.8 ❯   *Participial phrases*

Insert parentheses around the participial phrases in the following sentences and label the participles as present or past. Then underline the word that each phrase modifies.

1. Challenged by books like E. D. Hirsch's *Cultural Literacy* and Allan Bloom's *The Closing of the American Mind,* Americans have begun to reassess their educational system.

2. Articles have appeared in the popular media, questioning, on the one hand, the assumptions of these books and, at the same time, criticizing our educational system.

3. Enticed as they are by eye-catching but often misleading headlines and titles, writers have provided misleading clues about the goals of these books.

4. Limited by time and length constraints, television and print journalists have offered elliptical, abbreviated summaries of Hirsch's and Bloom's positions, oversimplifying their statements.

5. Talk-show hosts, by sensationalizing discussions of Hirsch's and Bloom's books, have failed to help viewers address important educational concerns.

6. Such problems in evaluating educational problems, made worse by American tendencies to oversimplify, will persist until Americans consent to read Hirsch's and Bloom's books for themselves.

Infinitive Phrases. **Infinitive phrases** combine an infinitive and its complements and modifiers; these phrases function as nouns, adjectives, or adverbs. When infinitive phrases are used as adjectives, they should be placed near the nouns they modify. When they work as adverbs, however, they can appear in a variety of positions, as can other adverbs.

phrase

inf.   *inf.*

Rachel must learn *to control* her temper if she wants *to get* along

phrase

in this office.   (Both infinitive phrases work as nouns. Both are direct
objects, describing *what* Rachel must learn and *what* she might want.)

phrase

inf.

To be responsible, we must act without prejudice.   (The infinitive
phrase, working as an adjective, modifies *we*.)

phrase

inf.

The experiment was too dangerous *to contemplate* seriously.   (The
infinitive phrase, working as an adverb, modifies the predicate adjective *dangerous*.)

EXERCISE 7.9 ❯ *Infinitive phrases*

*Underline the complete infinitive phrases in the following sentences
and label each phrase as a noun, adjective, or adverb.*

1. It is hard to believe how much wood and how many wood products
   Americans use without being aware of them.

2. To start off our mornings, many of us eat cereals packaged in card-
   board boxes while reading newspapers made from wood pulp.

3. To go about our daily routines, we move between rooms built with
   two-by-fours, walk on hardwood floors, and open wooden doors,
   often oblivious to the structural uses to which wood is put.

4. We talk on the telephone — to convey messages or simply to con-
   verse — without thinking that wood resins are used in the plastic

casing for the phone, let alone that millions of wooden telephone poles help to make such communication possible.

5. Many of us use pencils to write with, paper to write on, and desks or tables to write at — all products of forest-related industries.

6. To conceive of how many trees are necessary to support the activities of even one person is virtually impossible.

Appositives

Appositives explain, describe, define, identify, or restate a noun. They provide either necessary explanation or nonessential information. In the latter case, the appositive must be separated from the rest of the sentence with commas.

The painting *American Gothic* has been amusingly used in many advertisements.   (Because *American Gothic,* the appositive, is necessary to the meaning of the sentence, no commas are needed.)

Mitchell, *a hopelessly disorganized person,* was audited by the IRS and fined one thousand dollars.   (Because the appositive provides nonessential information, it is set off with commas.)

EXERCISE 7.10   ❯   *Appositives*

Combine the following pairs of sentences to form single sentences containing appositives. Be sure to use commas where needed.

Example

The American Kennel Club recognizes over one hundred breeds of purebred dogs. The American Kennel Club is the primary organization of dog breeders.

The American Kennel Club, the primary organization of dog breeders, recognizes over one hundred breeds of purebred dogs.

1. Sporting dogs hunt by smelling the air to locate game. Pointers, setters, retrievers, and spaniels are typical sporting dogs.

2. Working dogs serve or once served as herders, sled dogs, and guards. The group called working dogs comprises twenty-eight separate breeds.

3. Terriers hunt by digging. Their digging is an activity for which their strong front legs seem natural.

4. Nonsporting dogs include nine breeds most usually kept as pets. Many nonsporting dogs are descended from breeds in other classifications.

5. Most toy dogs have been bred down from larger breeds of dogs. Toy dogs are almost always kept only as pets.

Absolute Phrases

Absolute phrases consist of nouns and participles, usually with modifiers, and modify whole sentences rather than individual words. They can be positioned anywhere in a sentence but must be separated from the rest of the sentence by a comma or commas.

Her feet aching from the six-mile hike, Lisa stretched out under the tree to rest.

Lisa stretched out under the tree to rest, *her feet aching from the six-mile hike.*

Lisa, *her feet aching from the six-mile hike,* stretched out under the tree to rest.

EXERCISE 7.11 ❯ *Phrases*

Underline and label the prepositional, gerund, participial, infinitive, appositive, and absolute phrases in the following sentences.

1. Intrigued by the history of Great Britain, many Anglophiles are Americans obsessed by England and English things.

2. To learn about their "adopted" country, Anglophiles often sub-scribe to magazines like *British Heritage.*

3. They read as well materials in books and newspapers that offer in-sight into the English way of life.

4. Many Anglophiles, their daily schedules rearranged, watched the satellite broadcasts of the royal weddings of Charles and Diana and of Andrew and Sarah.

5. Anglophiles, often people who feel displaced in the rush of Ameri-can activities, find pleasure in learning about "that sceptered isle."

6. Visiting England is the lifelong dream of most Anglophiles, but spending time there often spoils illusions that have developed through years of active fantasizing.

EXERCISE 7.12 ❭ *Phrases*

Place in parentheses and label the prepositional, appositive, and ab-solute phrases in the following paragraph. Then underline the gerund, participial, and infinitive phrases and label each one.

When in the winter of 1845–6, a comet called *Biela* became oddly pear-shaped and then divided into two distinct comets, one of the astronomers who observed them, James Challis of Cambridge, averted his gaze. A week later he took another peep and *Biela* was still flaunt-ing its rude duality. He had never heard of such a thing and for several more days the cautious Challis hesitated before he announced it to his astronomical colleagues. Meanwhile American astronomers in Washington D.C. and New Haven, equally surprised but possibly more confident in their own sobriety, had already staked their claim to the discovery. Challis excused his slowness in reporting the event by say-ing that he was busy looking for the new planet beyond Uranus. When later in the same year he was needlessly beaten to the discovery of that planet (Neptune) by German astronomers, Challis explained that he had been preoccupied with his work on comets. — Nigel Calder, "Heads and Tails"

Clauses

A **clause** contains both a subject and a predicate and can be either **independent** or **subordinate.**

Independent Clauses

An **independent clause** (sometimes called a **main clause**) is grammatically complete and can be used alone as a simple sentence or combined with other clauses to form other sentence types (see pages 189–191).

> *subj.   pred.*
> *Eleanor Roosevelt withdrew* her membership from the Daughters of the American Revolution (DAR).

> *subj. pred.*   *subj. pred.*
> The Joad *family lost* their farm, and then *they left* for California. (t wo independent clauses forming a compound sentence)

Subordinate Clauses

A **subordinate clause** (sometimes called a **dependent clause**) contains a subject and predicate but is grammatically incomplete and must be joined to an independent clause to express a complete idea. Subordinating conjunctions and relative pronouns establish this dependent relationship.

> *conj. subj.   pred.*
> *because* she *objected* to the DAR's discriminatory practices

To make a subordinate clause grammatically complete, join it to an independent clause or revise it into a simple sentence by eliminating the subordinating conjunction or relative pronoun.

> *Eleanor Roosevelt withdrew* her membership from the Daughters of the American Revolution (DAR) *because she objected* to the DAR's discriminatory practices.   (complex sentence)

Or:

> *Eleanor Roosevelt withdrew* her membership from the Daughters of
> the American Revolution (DAR). *She objected* to the DAR's discrimina-
> tory practices.   (two simple sentences)

Subordinate clauses function in sentences as nouns, adjectives,
or adverbs, depending on what information they provide.

Noun clause

<pre>
              clause
        ┌──────────────────────┐
        subj.   pred.
</pre>
Whoever wrote this paper should pursue graduate study.   (used as
the subject of the sentence)

<pre>
                                      clause
                        ┌─────────────────────────────────────┐
                            subj.   pred.
</pre>
Even the White House knows *that military spending is out of control*.
(used as the direct object of *knows*)

<pre>
                  clause
        ┌──────────────────────────┐
            subj.   pred.
</pre>
Sell the land to *whoever agrees not to develop it*.   (used as the object
of the preposition *to*)

Adjective clause

<pre>
                clause
        ┌────────────────────┐
            subj.   pred.
</pre>
The armor *that Mordred wore* was rusty and dented. (modifies *armor*)

Adverb clause

<pre>
                        clause
        ┌──────────────────────────┐
            subj.   pred.
</pre>
Jessica paints more carefully *than I usually do*. (modifies *carefully*)

EXERCISE 7.13 ❯ *Clauses*

*Underline the subordinate clauses in the following sentences and in-
dicate whether they are used as nouns, adjectives, or adverbs.*

1. Wherever I hang my hat is home.

2. Don't count your chickens before they hatch.

3. Absence makes the heart grow fonder.

4. All that glitters is not gold.

5. Fools rush in where angels fear to tread.

EXERCISE 7.14 ❯ *Clauses*

*The following paragraph contains a number of subordinate clauses.
Underline them and indicate whether they are used as nouns, adjectives, or adverbs.*

When the credits run at the end of a film, audience members who stay
to read them discover the names of people whose contributions are
sometimes as important to the film as the actors' are. For instance, producers control and organize the entire film production, finding people
who will finance the project and finding creative people who will actually make the film. That directors are in charge of the filming is well known,
but many people do not realize that directors also choose and coach actors and find locations and select technicians. When the filming is finally
completed, editors begin their work. They take thousands of feet of film,
select the best shots, and piece together the version of the film that audiences eventually see. Besides the producers, directors, and editors,
hundreds of other people are involved in the making of a film. Learning
who they are and what they do makes audience members more apprecia-
tive of the combined efforts involved in film making.

| 7b | > | **Distinguish among kinds of sentences.** |

The four basic sentence types are **simple, compound, complex,** and **compound-complex.** Learning to recognize their different structures and purposes and learning to use them will help you improve the effectiveness of your writing.

Classifying Sentences by Structure

Simple Sentences

A **simple sentence** is an independent clause that contains at least one subject and one predicate. Simple sentences may have compound subjects, compound predicates, and compound complements, however, as well as multiple modifiers and phrases.

> *subj.*   *pred.*
> Governor O'Brian attended.   (simple subject; simple predicate)

> *subj.*   *pred.*   *d.o.*   *pred.*   *d.o.*
> Governor O'Brian attended the meeting and made the opening speech.
> (compound predicate, each part having its own direct object)

Compound Sentences

Compound sentences contain at least two independent clauses, each with its own subject and predicate. The clauses are usually joined by a comma and a coordinating conjunction, but they can be joined by a semicolon, with no coordinating conjunction.

> *subj.*   *pred.*   *conj.*   *subj.*   *pred.*
> Bluebirds are getting scarcer, but ornithologists do not know why.

> *subj.*   *pred.*   *subj.*
> Dickens assailed the workhouses in *Oliver Twist;* in *Bleak House* he
>
> *pred.*
> took on the Courts of Chancery.

Complex Sentences

Complex sentences contain one independent clause and one or more subordinate clauses. The clauses are joined by either subordinating conjunctions or relative pronouns.

Subordinate clauses may be positioned at the beginning, middle, or end of the sentence. Each position conveys a different emphasis. Note the placement of commas in the examples.

sub. clause

conj.   *subj.*   *pred.*   *subj.*
Because shortages exist in government-run shops, Soviet citizens

ind. clause

pred.
often purchase goods through the black market.

ind. clause

subj.   *pred.*
Soviet citizens often purchase goods through the black market

sub. clause

conj.   *subj.*   *pred.*
because shortages exist in government-run shops.

sub. clause

conj.   *subj.*   *pred.*
Soviet citizens, because shortages exist in government-run shops, often purchase goods through the black market. (In this case, the subordinate clause interrupts the independent clause.)

Compound-Complex Sentences

Compound-complex sentences contain at least two independent clauses and one subordinate clause.

$$\overbrace{\qquad\qquad\qquad\qquad\qquad\qquad\qquad}^{\textit{sub. clause}}$$

sub. clause   *ind. clause*

conj.   subj.   pred.   *subj.   pred.*
Because the zoo was closed on Monday, we visited the United

ind. clause

conj. subj. pred.
Nations instead, and we visited the zoo on Tuesday.

EXERCISE 7.15 ❯ *Sentences*

Combine the following groups of simple sentences to form compound, complex, or compound-complex sentences. Create at least one sentence of each type. Label your revised sentences.

Example

Hoover Dam supplies water and electricity to Los Angeles and surrounding areas. The dam was originally built to control the flow of the Colorado River.

Although Hoover Dam currently supplies water and electricity to Los Angeles and surrounding areas, it was originally built to control the flow of the Colorado River.   (complex)

1. In the early 1900s, the Palo Verde and Imperial valleys seemed ideal for development. At times floods washed away crops. At other times crops withered.

2. In 1918, the Bureau of Reclamation submitted a report. The report suggested building a dam. The dam would improve water control.

3. Water control was the primary goal for the project. Generating electricity was a secondary goal.

4. The Bureau of Reclamation designed the dam. Six companies worked on the project. It was a joint venture that involved an average of 3,500 workers a day.

5. The finished dam is 726 feet high. It is 1,244 feet long. It contains 4,400,000 cubic yards of concrete. That is enough to pave a one-lane road from New York to San Francisco.

Classifying Sentences by Purpose

In addition to classifying sentences by grammatical structure, writers classify sentences by their purpose.

Declarative Sentences

A **declarative sentence** expresses a statement.

"God does not play dice." — Albert Einstein

Exclamatory Sentences

An **exclamatory sentence** expresses an emphatic statement.

"Give me liberty or give me death!" — Patrick Henry

Imperative Sentences

An **imperative sentence** expresses a command.

"Ask not what your country can do for you — ask what you can do for your country." — John F. Kennedy

Interrogative Sentences

An **interrogative sentence** asks a question.

"What *is* the answer? . . . In that case, what is the question?" — Gertrude Stein

EXERCISE 7.16 ❯ *Sentence structures*

Label each sentence in the following paragraph as simple, compound, complex, or compound-complex.

Rodeo, like baseball, is an American sport and has been around almost as long. While Henry Chadwick was writing his first book of rules for the fledgling ball clubs in 1858, ranch hands were paying $25 a dare to a kid who would ride five outlaw horses from the rough string in a makeshift arena of wagons and cars. The first commercial rodeo in Wyoming was held in Lander in 1895, just nineteen years after the National League was formed. Baseball was just as popular as bucking and roping contests in the West, but no one in Cooperstown, New York, was riding broncs. And that's been part of the problem. After 124 years, rodeo is still misunderstood. Unlike baseball, it's a regional sport (although they do have rodeos in New Jersey, Florida, and other eastern states); it's derived from and stands for the western way of life and the western spirit. It doesn't have the universal appeal of a sport contrived solely for the competition and winning; there is no ball bandied about between opposing players. — Gretel Ehrlich, "Rules of the Game: Rodeo"

EXERCISE 7.17 ❯ *Sentence purposes*

Label each of the following sentences as declarative, exclamatory, imperative, or interrogative. Then experiment, rewriting each sentence in each of the three remaining forms.

1. "Tell me what you eat, and I will tell you what you are." — Anthelme Brillat-Savarin.

2. "Education is what survives when what has been learnt has been forgotten." — B. F. Skinner

3. "One only dies once, and it's for such a long time!" — Molière

4. "How can we know the dancer from the dance?" — W. B. Yeats

Revising sentences with a word processor

Writing with a word processor gives you considerable freedom to make sentence-level revisions. Make a back-up copy of your draft, and then experiment with your writing. Consider, for instance, these specific ways that you can use the computer to try different forms and effects:

Combine sentences. Word processors allow you to combine sets of sentences to create varied sentence types without retyping.

De-combine sentences. If, on rereading your draft you decide that some sentences seem too long or complex, use the computer to de-construct them easily into briefer, more readable sentences.

Revise sentence patterns. Using "block" and "move" commands, transform simple sentences into other, more varied sentence types containing appositives, absolute phrases, subordinate clauses, and other patterns. Try recasting some declarative sentences as exclamatory, imperative, or interrogative sentences.

The freedom to rearrange sentences will be a great help to you during revision. You can always return to your original version by using "block" and "move" functions to retrieve sections of your back-up copy.

8 Sentence Variety

8a ❯ Vary sentence length.

Varying sentence lengths helps writers to achieve effective paragraph rhythm. A paragraph of short sentences can seem undeveloped and choppy; a paragraph of long sentences can seem dense and difficult.

Short Sentences

Although short sentences present one idea clearly, too many of them in succession can make writing seem awkward and simplistic. A few well-placed short sentences, however, can enhance variety and add emphasis.

Our senator maintains two elaborate houses, one in our state and one in Washington. Although I understand the reasons for having two homes, owning two $300,000 residences seems needlessly extravagant. In short, I disapprove.

Medium Sentences

Medium-length sentences allow space to connect ideas and add details, while remaining clear and easy to read. Medium-length sentences are the most versatile and should form the core of your writing.

Although I enjoy televised boxing, I am often dissatisfied with network commentaries. All too often, sportscasters' comments are superficial, pointing out the obvious — like who is winning — rather than helping me to understand the sport.

Long Sentences

Long sentences establish complex interrelationships and include substantial amounts of amplification and clarification. Use long sentences sparingly to emphasize relationships and to incorporate significant details.

For over a century, the *Statue of Liberty,* in all its majesty, has stood at the entrance to New York Harbor, welcoming immigrants, travelers, and returning Americans and symbolizing the freedoms we value.

EXERCISE 8.1 ❯ *Sentence length*

 Expand, combine, or divide the following sentences to achieve variety and effective expression.

Example

Medieval castles, strongly built of native stone, served as homes for the nobility, but in times of brigandage and war they also served as fortresses and as shelters for the peasants who lived nearby.

Medieval castles served as homes for the nobility. Strongly built of native stone, they also served in times of brigandage and war as fortresses and as shelters for the peasants who lived nearby.

1. Sometimes castles served as prisons, treasure houses, or seats of local governments as well because they were secure and centrally located, although access to castles was sometimes limited because some castles, notably those in central Europe, were built on irregular terrain.

2. Some castles are attractive.

3. Some used drawbridges.

4. Battlements, also called parapets, were the tall, structural walls from which soldiers observed the countryside, and during battles these same soldiers positioned themselves in these lofty places to shoot arrows or hurl rocks at the invaders below.

5. Most people know of castles from films.

| 8b | > | **Vary sentence types.** |

Although the four basic sentence structures are **simple, compound, complex,** and **compound-complex,** the effect of these structures varies depending on the types of sentences that writers use: **loose, periodic,** or **balanced.**

Loose Sentences

Loose sentences, the most common type, first present major ideas (the subject and verb) and then provide other information. This pattern is satisfying and easy for readers.

Dr. Zhivago is a typical David Lean film, with panoramic scenes, larger-than-life characters, and universal implications.

Periodic Sentences

Periodic sentences, less common than loose sentences, create suspense and emphasis by placing the main idea or some part of it at the end of the sentence.

> After having spent thousands of dollars and hundreds of hours renovating the townhouse, the Petersons sold it.

Balanced Sentences

Balanced sentences use parallel elements — words, phrases, and sometimes whole clauses — to create interest and emphasis.

> I practiced; I ran; I lost.

> One brother was refined, intelligent, and persuasive, but the other was crude, shrewd, and domineering.

EXERCISE 8.2 ❯   *Types of sentences*

Label each of the following sentences as loose, periodic, or balanced; then revise each sentence into one of the other types.

1. Almanacs, published yearly in book or pamphlet form, include calendars, citations for important dates, information about geography and weather, and a myriad of other facts.

2. Almanacs are informative and practical, yet they are also idiosyncratic and entertaining.

3. Though generally associated with colonial American farmers and navigators, almanacs have as their precedents the works of an unsuspected group: Persian astrologers.

4. Over the years, sailors have relied on the *Nautical Almanac,* farmers have used the *Old Farmer's Almanac,* and amateur weather forecasters have depended on the *Ford Almanac.*

5. With its proverbs, its lists of counties and roads, its advice on planting, its selections of verse, and its astrological information, *Poor Richard's Almanac* is probably the best-known early almanac.

6. Contemporary almanacs are best represented by works such as the *Information Please Almanac,* compendiums of widely divergent statistics on thousands of topics.

| 8c | Vary sentence beginnings. |

Although subjects and verbs in subordinate or independent clauses begin most sentences, writers can create variety by positioning other sentence elements first.

Beginning with Adverbs

Adverbs can appear in many positions in sentences. Using them at the beginning creates variety.

The ornithologist cautiously approached the eagle's nest.

Cautiously, the ornithologist approached the eagle's nest.

Beginning with Adjectives

When an adjective phrase modifies the subject of the sentence, move it to the beginning of the sentence to create variety.

Jason, exhausted and dirty, collapsed in the armchair.

Exhausted and dirty, Jason collapsed in the armchair.

Beginning with Prepositional Phrases

Move adverbial prepositional phrases to the beginning of the sentence.

The pope did not restrict his travel after the attempt on his life.

After the attempt on his life, the pope did not restrict his travel.

Beginning with Verbal Phrases

Verbal phrases (gerund, participial, and infinitive phrases) make effective beginnings. Make certain, however, that the phrases modify the subject of the first clause; otherwise, you will create a dangling modifier.

The monks, worried that the manuscript might be stolen, placed it in a secret vault.

Worried that the manuscript might be stolen, the monks placed it in a secret vault.

Incorrect

Worried that it might be stolen, the manuscript was placed in a secret vault.   (The beginning phrase cannot modify *manuscript;* therefore, it is a dangling modifier.)

Beginning with Conjunctive Adverbs and Transitional Expressions

Create variety by occasionally placing conjunctive adverbs and transitional expressions at the beginning of sentences.

The subscription price for *Architectural Record,* for instance, is almost half of the newsstand price.

For instance, the subscription price for *Architectural Record* is almost half of the newsstand price.

Beginning with Coordinating Conjunctions

Conventionally, coordinating conjunctions join independent clauses in compound sentences, but they can also be used to introduce a sentence closely related to the one preceding it.

International terrorism has made many world travelers more cautious than they used to be, but some travelers seem naively indifferent to potential threats from terrorists.

International terrorism has made many world travelers more cautious than they used to be. But some travelers seem naively indifferent to potential threats from terrorists.

▶▶▶ *Some readers object to the use of coordinating conjunctions to begin sentences. If you use this strategy to achieve variety, do so selectively.* **◀◀◀**

EXERCISE 8.3 **❭** *Varying sentence structure and beginnings*

Most of the sentences in the following paragraph are loose. To make the writing more varied and interesting, combine some sentences, restructure others into periodic or balanced form, and experiment with different sentence beginnings.

  Landscaping serves more than an aesthetic function, even if few people realize it. Small shrubs and bushes protect a building's foundation, sheltering it from summer heat and winter cold. Large shrubs and small trees provide windbreaks for buildings, providing protection, especially in the winter, from strong winds that can affect interior temperatures and subsequently heating costs. Large trees shade a building during the summer, keeping the sun's warming rays off the building's roof and consequently keeping the building cool. Landscaping does improve the looks of a building, often enhancing architectural details and softening harsh lines, but the surprise for many people is that landscaping can pay for itself in energy savings, which means it has practical as well as aesthetic benefits.

Coordination joins two or more independent clauses with a comma and one of the coordinating conjunctions: *and, but, for, nor, or, so,* and *yet.* The resulting compound sentences bring balance and emphasis to writing.

Subordination joins at least one independent clause with at least one subordinate clause, forming a complex sentence that indicates the relative importance of ideas. Different subordinating conjunctions (*after, because, when, until,* and so on) create differences in meaning and emphasis.

Coordination

Linking or Contrasting

To avoid a monotonous series of simple sentences while still giving equal stress to the main ideas, join closely related main clauses with a coordinating conjunction. The resulting compound sentence will give your writing an even, balanced rhythm.

Tamiko does not like watching television, *but* she does like shooting video tapes.

Vail had a foot of fresh snow, *but* Katrina postponed her skiing trip.

Varying Conjunctions

Each of the seven coordinating conjunctions links ideas in a slightly different way. For example, although *but* and *yet* both indicate contrast and are roughly interchangeable, they create slightly different impressions for the reader.

Estella was a heartless girl, *but* Pip loved her anyway.

Estella was a heartless girl, *yet* Pip loved her anyway.   (*Yet* expresses contrast more strongly and is more formal than *but*.)

In another example, *for* and *so* indicate a cause-and-effect relationship but require that clauses appear in a different order. Hence, they achieve different effects.

There is no room for delay, *so* there is no room for doubt.   (With *so*, the cause precedes the effect, and the effect is slightly emphasized.)

There is no room for doubt, *for* there is no room for delay.   (With *for*, the effect precedes the cause, and the emphasis shifts slightly to the cause.)

Avoiding Excessive Coordination in a Series of Sentences

The balance of clauses in compound sentences can create a monotonous rhythm if it is overused. Look, for instance, at this series of coordinated sentences:

Several weeks before the last snowfall, the ground thaws, and the wintered-over spinach turns green. Some of the leaves begin to grow, but most remain dormant for a few weeks more. The plants grow rapidly in the middle of March, and by April we are eating fresh spinach salad.

By the third sentence, an annoying and potentially distracting rhythm has developed. Remember not to rely too much on any one sentence pattern.

Several weeks before the last snowfall, when the ground thaws, the wintered-over spinach turns green. Although some of the leaves begin to grow, most remain dormant for a few weeks more until the middle of March, when the plants grow rapidly. By April we are eating fresh spinach salad.

Avoiding Excessive Coordination Within Sentences

Three or more identically structured clauses in a single sentence can effectively link ideas and create interest and an emphatic rhythm. When clauses are dissimilar in structure or meaning, however, try other methods to join the ideas.

Awkward coordination

Americans have become concerned about stimulants in foods, and they have started using products without caffeine, and to accommodate them restaurants now regularly serve decaffeinated coffees and teas.   (These clauses lack balance. The first two explain trends among Americans, but the third describes an effect of these trends.)

Effective subordination

Because Americans have become concerned about stimulants in foods and have started using products without caffeine, restaurants now regularly serve decaffeinated coffees and teas to accommodate them. (The first two clauses are joined and then related to the effect.)

Effective subordination

Americans, concerned about stimulants in foods, have started using products without caffeine, and to accommodate them restaurants now regularly serve decaffeinated coffees and teas.   (With some necessary rewording, one clause has been reshaped as a verbal phrase.)

Because excessive coordination is distracting and interferes with sentence variety, use your word processor's "search" codes to locate coordinating conjunctions. Determine whether their use is excessive, and experiment with the alternative methods in this chapter for linking ideas and creating variety and emphasis.

EXERCISE 8.4 ❯ *Coordination*

Revise the following sentences to achieve effective coordination and to eliminate excessive coordination.

1. Many American cities are now concerned with maintaining their architectural characters. Building codes control the development of new buildings.

2. Codes often restrict the kinds and sizes of buildings that can be constructed. Architects must design structures that match the scale of existing buildings.

3. Many cities, such as Boston and San Francisco, need the vast commercial space provided by tall office buildings. These skyscrapers often cannot be built in some areas because of protective codes.

4. City dwellers do not want the severe shadows cast by tall buildings. They do not want small, historical, and architecturally interesting buildings dwarfed by monolithic towers.

5. Citizens are now aware that poorly planned cities become unlivable, and, as a result, they have been supportive of new building codes, but city development is now more challenging than it once was, for cities must now grow by controlled, aesthetically consistent patterns.

Subordination

Establishing Levels of Importance

To avoid a monotonous series of simple sentences and to avoid the awkward rhythm of too many compound sentences, join related clauses with a subordinating conjunction. The resulting complex or compound-complex sentence will stress the relative importance of ideas while producing a varied rhythm.

Jessica stripped two coats of shellac and three coats of paint from the table *before* she discovered that the walnut was in excellent condition.

(The sentence emphasizes the multiple stages of stripping over the discovery of the wood beneath.)

Because viewers expect quick overviews with many visual aids, television newswriters must plan brief, attention-getting news stories. (The sentence emphasizes the effect on newswriting of viewers' expectations.)

Using Relative Pronouns

Relative pronouns (*that, which, who,* and so on) embed clauses within sentences, adding clarity and producing variety. The information in the embedded relative clause is clearly less important than the information in the independent clause.

One of T. S. Eliot's best poems is "The Love Song of J. Alfred Prufrock," *which* is also one of his earliest.   (The relative clause embeds secondary but useful information.)

Avoiding Excessive Subordination

When too much secondary information is included in a sentence, ideas can become muddled. Consider the following sentence:

Although many films about adolescence concentrate on the awkward and often unsatisfying relationships that exist between teenagers and their parents, most of these films take a satiric approach, presenting parents as fools or tyrants and, as a result, defusing through laughter much of the tension in the real relationships because the depicted relationships are so extreme, so absurd.

Although grammatically correct, this sentence is poorly planned. Revision into three sentences improves its rhythm and clarity.

Many films about adolescence concentrate on the awkward and often unsatisfying relationships that exist between teenagers and their parents. Most of these films, however, take a satiric approach, presenting parents as fools or tyrants. Because the relationships depicted in these

films are so extreme, so absurd, much of the tension of real relationships is defused through laughter.

EXERCISE 8.5 ❭ *Subordination*

 *Use subordinating conjunctions and relative pronouns to com-
bine the following sets of sentences into a coherent paragraph.*

1. Some people never visit art museums or exhibitions. Their only
   contact with art is through "public art." Public art is sculpture and
   other works displayed in public places.

2. Monuments are one kind of public sculpture. Statues and placards
   are the most common kinds of monuments. These monuments
   commemorate historical events or honor individuals or groups of
   people, such as veterans.

3. People often walk through plazas and courtyards near government
   buildings. Sculpture is often displayed in these areas. This sculpture
   is frequently commissioned by the government.

4. Most people are comfortable with traditional, realistic statuary of
   people. Many people are less at ease with abstract sculpture.

5. Many people say nonrepresentational sculpture doesn't "look like
   anything." In time, some grow more accepting. They learn to enjoy
   modern sculpture's use of form, texture, and material.

6. Sculpture enriches public space. It provides visual and tactile stimu-
   lation. It also sometimes provides pleasure. It even supplies topics
   for conversation.

EXERCISE 8.6 ❭ *Coordination and subordination*

*Revise the following paragraph by using coordination and subordina-
tion to indicate the relative importance of ideas and to improve the variety of the sentences.*

Dermatologists continually warn people about the danger of ultraviolet rays. Many people seem intent on getting dark suntans. During the summer, beaches and pools are crowded with people. These people want to "catch some rays." They smear on creams, lotions, and oils. They can accelerate the sun's natural modification of skin pigments. They want to get deep tans. They lie on towels or stretch out on lounge chairs for hours, oblivious to doctors' stern advice. In most cities, tanning salons are quite popular. "California" tans are not always possible everywhere. For a fee, usually between three and ten dollars, people can lie down and subject themselves to artificial sunlight. This artificial sunlight is produced by ultraviolet bulbs. Many people think a tan looks healthy. Overly dark tans, in fact, cause serious skin damage. This damage can last a lifetime.

Revising for sentence variety with a word processor

Take advantage of the word processor to create needed variety and emphasis in your sentences.

Move sentence elements. Using the "block" and "move" features, shift elements to the beginnings of sentences to create variety. Such moves will require you to change capitalization and punctuation — alterations that are much easier and faster on a word processor than on a typewriter.

Vary sentence structures and lengths. Look for a series of short sentences to combine through coordination or subordination. Look for excessively long sentences to break up. Look for repeated sentence types, and restructure some for greater variety and more effective expression.

9 Emphasis

Emphasis underscores the significance of main ideas and makes supporting ideas and details clear and vivid. To control emphasis, therefore, is to control meaning. The specific choices that writers make to create emphasis depend on their specific purposes. Among other methods — such as choosing words carefully (see Chapters 13 and 14), constructing cohesive paragraphs (Chapter 4), and using subordination and coordination (Chapter 8) — writers emphasize people and actions by writing active sentences, and they emphasize ideas by writing concisely.

Quick Reference

Emphatic sentences stress the most important ideas, allowing readers to concentrate their attention according to the writer's purpose. Control emphasis in the following ways:

> *Write active sentences to stress the doer of an action.*

> *Write passive sentences to stress the receiver of an action or to stress that the doer of the action is unknown.*

> *Strip sentences of all unnecessary words, phrases, and clauses to highlight words crucial to meaning.*

9a ⟩ **Use active and passive sentences to create different kinds and degrees of emphasis.**

Active Sentences

Verbs in the active voice create **active sentences:** the subjects of the sentences act.

phrase

subj.   verb   d.o.
Lin Su invested two thousand dollars in the commodities market.

Passive Sentences

Verbs in the passive voice create **passive sentences:** the subject
of the sentence is acted upon. The subject of a passive sentence
would be the complement if the sentence were active. A passive
verb requires auxiliaries.

              subj.   verb   *phrase*
Two thousand dollars was invested in the commodities market

phrase

by Lin Su.

>>> *A passive sentence does not always specify the person completing the action. When the sentence identifies the person who initiates an
action, the person is named in a prepositional phrase beginning with
by.* **<<<**

Emphasis

Stressing Who or What Acts

An active sentence emphasizes the doer of an action. It establishes
a clear, strong relationship between the subject and verb.

> The *restorer damaged* a portion of the fresco when he cleaned it.
> (The damage is clearly due to the restorer's error.)

When the results of an action are more important than the doer, or
when the doer is unknown, passive sentences effectively express
the meaning.

Irreparable *damage was done* to the fresco during its restoration.

In most cases, however, clarity, precision, and force make the active voice the better choice. Notice the ambiguity in the following passive sentence:

A portion of the fresco was damaged when the restorer cleaned it. (It is not clear that the damage was the restorer's fault.)

The choice of an active or a passive verb allows subtle but significant shifts in meaning and emphasis.

Active

The 1980 eruption of Mount St. Helens destroyed over sixty million dollars' worth of property.   (The use of *eruption* with the active verb *destroyed* emphasizes the violence of nature.)

Passive

Over sixty million dollars' worth of property was destroyed by the 1980 eruption of Mount St. Helens.   (This sentence shifts the emphasis to the loss of property.)

Stressing Action

The passive emphasizes action over the doer of the action; thus, it is especially useful for describing universal or widespread conditions or events.

Passive

Open-heart surgery to repair faulty valves is now commonly performed across the United States.   (The surgical procedure is most important here, not the individual doctors who perform it.)

Active

Doctors across the United States now commonly perform open-heart surgery to repair faulty valves. (This construction emphasizes the doctors who perform the procedures.)

As a general guide to usage, write active sentences when "who is doing what" is most important. When "what is being done" is most important, passive sentences may better serve your purpose.

EXERCISE 9.1 ❯ *Active and passive sentences*

Determine which of the following sentences should be left in the passive voice and briefly state your reasons. Revise the remaining sentences into the active voice.

1. Biographies are often written by people who know their subjects well, either from personal contact or through study.

2. The *Life of Samuel Johnson,* a famous early biography, was written by James Boswell, a personal friend of Johnson.

3. In typical fashion, facts, anecdotes, and quotations were recorded in Boswell's diary and then translated into the biography.

4. When people like Benjamin Franklin choose to write their autobiographies, experiences are often presented to create a positive impression.

5. The lives of famous people like Lincoln were once described reverently by biographers.

6. Balanced treatments of positive and negative qualities are frequently presented by contemporary biographers.

7. A multifaceted view of the Roosevelts' relationship is presented in *Eleanor and Franklin,* a biography of the couple by Joseph P. Lash.

8. An essentially negative portrait of Pablo Picasso emerges in the Stassinopoulos-Huffington biography of the twentieth-century artist.

9. Contemporary autobiographies are usually written by well-known people with the help of professional writers.

10. *Iacocca,* a recent autobiography, was written by Lee Iacocca and a co-writer to chronicle Iacocca's rise in the automobile industry.

9b ▷ Make your writing as concise as possible.

Concise writing expresses meaning in as few words as possible. Such writing is precise, clear, and emphatic. To write concisely, choose concrete, exact words; and avoid needless repetition by eliminating words, phrases, and clauses that do not add meaning. Your sentences need not be short, for some long sentences are concise and some short sentences are not; but, to highlight important ideas, they should contain no extraneous words.

In a first draft, writers may not strive for concision. Rather, they concentrate on developing ideas and connecting them effectively. When revising, however, writers search for the words and expressions that most clearly and concisely express their meaning.

Unnecessary Repetition of Words and Ideas

Deliberate, controlled **repetition,** as in the following example, emphasizes important ideas:

> We forget all too soon the things we thought we could never forget. — Joan Didion

But such effects, if overused, can irritate readers and so should be used rarely.

Avoid unintentional, excessive, or monotonous repetition. In revising your writing, delete unnecessary words and rearrange the sentence to read smoothly.

During the 1930s and 1940s, the studio renowned for film musicals was MGM studio.

In the 1930s and 1940s, MGM studio was renowned for film musicals.

Rely on specific word choices to make your ideas clear. Do not elaborate needlessly. **Redundancy,** repeating ideas, adds useless words and irritates readers.

The smile on Karina's face showed that she was pleasantly elated by the reception of her new poem.   (Where else could a smile be but on her face? Could elation be anything but pleasant?)

Karina's smile showed that she was elated by the reception of her new poem.

Eliminating Wordiness

Eliminating Expletive Constructions

Sentences beginning with expletive constructions (*it is, here is, here are, there is,* and *there are*) weaken the impact of ideas by obscuring the subject and verb. Other, stronger words in the sentence can often better express your meaning. Revise your writing to eliminate expletives. Strike them out and use the remaining, substantive words to present the same idea.

There are three kinds of qualifying exams routinely used by the admissions committee.

The admissions committee uses three kinds of qualifying exams.

Eliminating Wordy Expressions

Wordy expressions bog down writing. Phrases like *at this point in time* and *because of the fact that* add unnecessary words without enhancing either sense or sound. Many such expressions can be shortened or have clear, concise substitutes.

Due to the fact that an accident blocked the road, I was late.

Because an accident blocked the road, I was late.

Concise Alternatives to Wordy Expressions

Wordy	*Concise*
at this point in time	now
by means of	by
in order to	to
in the event that	if
of the opinion that	think
until such time as	until

Eliminating Empty Phrases

Phrases such as *in my opinion, I believe, it seems,* and *I suppose* add little meaning to a sentence but blur its focus and slow its pace. Readers may take these phrases to mean that you are unsure of your ideas or information. Unless your purpose is to compare your opinion with someone else's, such phrases serve no purpose and should be dropped from your writing.

It seems that athletes in triathlons are masochistic.

Athletes in triathlons *seem* masochistic.

Eliminating *to be* Verbs

To be verbs weaken sentences by depriving them of strong verbs and adding words. Many words in English have multiple forms, usually including a verb form that can replace weak *to be* verbs. Examine your sentences containing *to be* verbs for words that might yield verbs.

Research assistants *are responsible for completing* most day-to-day experiments *and recording* the results.

Research assistants *complete* most day-to-day experiments *and record* the results.

Eliminating Nonrestrictive Clauses and Modifying Phrases

Nonrestrictive clauses (clauses not essential to the meaning of the sentence) that contain *to be* verbs can be reduced to appositives (phrases restating a noun or pronoun). Because appositives contain no subject or verb, they are more concise than clauses.

Chemicals found in aerosols have damaged the Earth's ozone layer, *which is our main protection from solar radiation.*

Chemicals found in aerosols have damaged the Earth's ozone layer, *our main protection from solar radiation.*

When it will not affect rhythm or clarity of a sentence, change prepositional and verbal phrases to one-word or multiword modifiers. When multiword modifiers precede a noun, they are often hyphenated.

The colors *of the tapestry* were distorted *by a nearby window made of stained glass.*

A nearby stained-glass window distorted the *tapestry's* colors.

EXERCISE 9.2 ❭ *Concision*

 Through revision, make these wordy sentences concise; note the number of words saved.

1. It is known to scientists who study such matters that an average of four trillion gallons of precipitation falls on the United States each and every day.

2. Falling from the overcast sky, heavy rains and snows fill our lakes, rivers, streams, and waterways, as well as replenish water supplies in our reservoirs.

3. There are some areas of the continental United States that are known to receive annually fewer than five inches of rain each year.

4. Other parts of the United States experience the benefit of more than twenty inches of precipitation or rain in a calendar year.

5. Precipitation — which includes rain, snow, sleet, and drizzle — is crucial to the national well-being of the United States.

6. Most of the people who think about it are aware that water is used to satisfy the needs of people, plant life, and animal life; however, they often fail to consider the fact that water is also in use in important industries.

7. I am of the opinion that water distribution should be under the management of a separate and independent national agency.

8. Until such time as we have a national policy for the management of water supplies, we can expect to have imbalances in the supplies of water in this country.

EXERCISE 9.3 ❯ Concision

! *Make the following paragraph, bloated with useless words, more concise.*

To be capable of understanding the development and use of paper and how that use came about, we must make our way back hundreds of years to China. By most estimates, paper was invented by the Chinese, who created it in 105 B.C. As a matter of fact, it was kept as a secret by the state for hundreds of years. As far as we know, most transcriptions were done on bamboo sheets. The Moors discovered the Chinese invention in A.D. 750. They became aware of it when they were at war with the Chinese. The Moors established and forged the link to Europe. In 1100, there was a paper mill for making paper established in Toledo, Spain. Gradually, the use of paper began to spread across Europe in a slow manner. Paper was able to reach Rome in approximately 1200, and it was a cause for the Catholic Church to feel threatened by the "new" invention. The church opposed the introduction of something that was so unfamiliar. According to the church, documents written on paper were not legally binding due to the fact that the church did not consider paper permanent. Still, paper began to be used by people instead of parchment, which was treated animal skin. People were greatly intrigued and fascinated as well by the new medium, which was cheaper and more convenient than parchment had ever been or could ever be. The use of paper reached English soil by 1400, and then it reached America by 1690. Soon, there was no other universally accepted writing surface that was used everywhere by virtually everyone. At this point in time, we take paper for granted and use it daily. We do not even acknowledge the fact that it was once a revolutionary new invention.

! *Creating emphasis with a word processor*

To create more emphasis in your writing, try these two methods on your word processor.

Find and replace *to be* verbs. Use the "search" commands to check for a variety of *to be* verbs: *am, are, is, was, were,* and others. Not every *to be* verb will need to be replaced, but replacing some with more forceful verbs will make your sentences more emphatic.

Search for and replace expletive constructions. Many word-processing programs allow for multiword searches. If yours does, look for *there is, there are, it is,* and other expletive constructions. Strike them out and revise the sentence by using more forceful subjects and predicates.

10 Parallelism

Parallelism brings symmetry to coordinate sentences and sentence elements; symmetry, in turn, enhances clarity. Parallelism requires that ideas of equal importance be expressed in similar ways or that words or phrases used together in similar ways appear in identical grammatical form: nouns with other nouns, verbs with other verbs of the same tense, predicate adjectives with other predicate adjectives, and so on.

Quick Reference

Parallelism creates clarity by stressing the balance between similar words, parts of sentences, or entire sentences.

> *Independent clauses joined by coordinating conjunctions must be parallel to be grammatical.*

> *Clauses and phrases joined by correlative conjunctions must be parallel to be grammatical.*

> *Prepositions, conjunctions, pronouns, and sentence structures arranged in parallel constructions convey meaning clearly and effectively.*

10a ⟩ **Maintain parallelism in constructions by using coordinating conjunctions:** *and, but, for, nor, or, so,* **and** *yet.*

When a coordinating conjunction is used in a sentence, the joined elements should appear in identical grammatical form.

All her employers found Jan to be intelligent, able, and a hard worker. (*Intelligent* and *able* are predicate adjectives; *hard worker,* a predicate noun, is not parallel.)

All her employers found Jan to be *intelligent, able,* and *hard working.*

To have dreams is important, but living them is even more important. (*To have dreams,* an infinitive phrase, and *living them,* a gerund phrase, are not parallel.)

To have dreams is important, but *to live them* is even more important.

>>> *Double-check sentences using coordinating conjunctions to ensure that elements are parallel. If necessary, list elements in the margin of your draft to check their forms against one another.* **<<<**

| 10b | Maintain parallelism in sentences by using correlative conjunctions: *both . . . and, either . . . or, neither . . . nor,* and *not only . . . but also.* |

Correlative constructions present balanced alternatives that require parallel treatment.

Stacy could either go to the library or could develop photographs. (Because *could* appears before *either, could* is not part of the correlative construction. If an auxiliary like *could* does not appear immediately before the first verb, it should not appear before the second verb.)

Stacy could *either go* to the library *or develop* photographs.

The aim of a teacher should be both to inspire and educate.   (In correlative constructions, infinitive forms must be repeated, not mixed with present-tense verbs.)

The aim of a teacher should be both *to inspire* and *to educate.*

>>> *Double-check sentences using correlative conjunctions to ensure that elements are parallel. If necessary, list parallel elements in the margin of your draft to check their forms against one another.* **<<<**

| 10c | Repeat sentence elements — prepositions, conjunctions, relative pronouns, clauses — for correctness, clarity, emphasis, or effect. |

In brief sentences, prepositions and subordinating conjunctions can sometimes be omitted from the second part of a parallel structure. In longer sentences, repeat prepositions and subordinating conjunctions.

Repetition for Correctness and Clarity

Bela Karolyi coached Phoebe Mills, an exceptional performer on the balance beam and who is also an outstanding performer in the floor exercise.   (Use of the coordinating conjunction *and* requires parallel structures in the phrases it links.)

Bela Karolyi coached Phoebe Mills, *an exceptional performer on the balance beam* and *an outstanding performer in the floor exercise.*

Or:

Bela Karolyi coached Phoebe Mills, *who is an exceptional performer on the balance beam* and *who is also an outstanding performer in the floor exercise.*

When the summer days grow increasingly longer and noticeably hotter and work becomes especially frustrating, I head to the cabin at Bishop's Point for a cool and relaxing break.   (The length of the opening subordinate clause makes the parallel construction difficult to follow without repeating the subordinating conjunction, *when.*)

When the summer days grow increasingly longer and noticeably hotter and *when* work becomes especially frustrating, I head to the cabin at Bishop's Point for a cool and relaxing break.

Repetition for Emphasis and Effect

Throughout a paper or paragraph, varied sentence structures help maintain readers' interest. In some cases, however, closely linked ideas expressed in a series of parallel sentences can create clarity and heighten interest.

His voice quavered audibly; his face blushed hotly; his hand trembled violently.

Consider in detail the parallel structures of these elements:

Possessive Pronouns	Subjects	Verbs	Adverbs
His	voice	quavered	audibly;
his	face	blushed	hotly;
his	hand	trembled	violently.

EXERCISE 10.1 ❯ Parallelism

Revise the following sentences to improve parallelism.

1. "As Ye Plant, So Shall Ye Reap" is a moving essay about the plight of migrant workers and which is somewhat controversial.

2. Over the years, César Chávez has used his political power to draw attention to the harsh treatment of these workers, to garner support from politicians, and orchestrate boycotts of selected produce.

3. Not only are migrant workers exploited in the Southwest but also in other parts of the Sunbelt.

4. The work of these laborers, extremely tedious and which needs to be controlled by labor laws, is traditionally undervalued.

5. To supply better wages and providing better working conditions should be our goal.

EXERCISE 10.2 ❭ *Parallelism*

Locate and correct faulty parallelism in the following paragraph.

Americans like to play it safe, so it is not surprising that they want the places where they play to be safe. Not so very long ago, however, amusement parks were poorly supervised, dirty, and they were rather tasteless. On hot summer Saturdays, American families would head to places with names like Chain-of-Rocks Park to have a good time. Once there, they found that the parking facilities were not only randomly planned but also no guards patrolled the area. The parks themselves were poorly maintained, with litter on the sidewalks, with oil running on the sidewalks, and with food having been left to spoil on the tables. The attendants appeared to be people with nothing better to do and who wash or shave only infrequently. They seemed to be alternately indifferent, callous, or they sometimes appeared to be threatening. Probably because of these unappealing qualities and other safety concerns, the amusement parks of an earlier time have been replaced by well-maintained, clean, and attractiveness of today's Six Flags, King's Island, and Disney parks. Yesterday's grimy and chaotic amusement parks have been replaced by today's safe, sanitized theme parks.

! Achieving parallelism with a word processor

Use your word processor to identify and revise problems with
parallelism.

Locate conjunctions. Because parallelism is most often
required in constructions using coordinating and correlative
conjunctions, use the "search" code to find them. Search for
and or *either . . . or,* for instance, and double-check
parallelism in sentences containing these words.

Make necessary changes. When you discover elements
that are not parallel, use the "delete" code to remove the
nonparallel element and then replace it with a parallel
one.

11 Pronoun Reference

Writers can vary and unify their writing by substituting pronouns for overused nouns. To make their meaning clear, however, writers follow certain patterns of pronoun usage.

Quick Reference

A pronoun must refer clearly to a specific noun, its antecedent; otherwise, the meaning of a sentence can become confused.

> *Make sure that a pronoun has one antecedent, not several.*

> *Be certain that a pronoun's reference is clear, not vague or general.*

> *Make sure that reflexive pronouns have antecedents in the same sentence.*

| 11a | Avoid unclear pronoun references.

Unclear pronoun references result when antecedents are ambiguously placed, broad or vague, or implied rather than stated. Readers associate pronouns with the nearest antecedents. To avoid confusion, be sure that the antecedents of the pronouns you use are specific, clear, and appropriately positioned.

Ambiguous References

Ambiguous references result when more than one noun could be a pronoun's antecedent.

Ambiguous

The scuba instructor gave Patrick a detailed account of the history of the sport. He thought the lecture was a waste of time.   (Did the instructor feel dissatisfied, or did Patrick?)

Clear

Even though he thought the lecture was a waste of time, the scuba instructor gave Patrick a detailed account of the history of the sport. (The rule of nearness suggests that *he* refers to the scuba instructor.)

Vague References

General or broad antecedents result in **vague references** and confused readers.

Vague

The members of Israel's Knesset requested more military aid from the United States. This was approved by Congress.   (Did Congress approve of the request, or did Congress approve the aid?)

Clear

Upon the request of members of Israel's Knesset, Congress approved more military aid.

Implied References

An **implied antecedent** suggests a reference but does so confusingly, leaving to the reader the writer's work of creating clear, precise thought and expression.

Unclear

The Theater-in-the-Round is not very innovative, but they usually do technically polished productions.   (*They* has no direct antecedent.)

Clear

Although the directors at the Theater-in-the-Round are not very innovative, they usually do technically polished productions.

> **11b** Use reflexive pronouns (those ending in *-self* or
> *-selves*) to refer only to the subjects of
> sentences.

Reflexive pronouns serve only as indirect or direct objects.

```
                      reflex.  indir.
        subj.         verb     obj.      d.o.
                        |        |         |
```
Carlotta Monterey gave herself credit for Eugene O'Neill's stability in
his last years.

▶▶▶ *Use a personal pronoun in place of a reflexive pronoun if the subject of the sentence is not the antecedent. A reflexive pronoun should
never be the subject of a sentence.*

Incorrect

Wilbur and myself disagreed about the effectiveness of amplified
sound on stage.

Correct

Wilbur and I disagreed about the effectiveness of amplified sound on
stage. **◀◀◀**

> **11c** Use pronouns to refer to antecedents in the
> same or in the immediately preceding sentence.

When pronouns and antecedents are separated by too many
words, references become vague or unclear. Too-frequent use of a
pronoun becomes monotonous. Alternate between using a noun
and using a pronoun.

Charlie Chaplin began his work in American films with the
Keystone Cops. Although ~~Chaplin's~~ *his* early roles were limited,
they gave him a chance to demonstrate his considerable talents.

Chaplin later showcased his talents in a one-reeler titled *The Tramp*. In that film, ~~Chaplin~~ ^{he} introduced the character that was to win him wide acclaim. ~~He~~ ^{Chaplin} later produced, wrote, directed, and starred in such films as *The Kid, City Lights,* and *Modern Times*.

(Although the entire paragraph is about Chaplin and consequently is not confusing, it is improved by alternating Chaplin's name with pronouns.)

For clarity, observe the convention of restricting pronoun references to sentences within the same paragraph, even when the reference seems clear.

. . . Chaplin later produced, wrote, and starred in such films as *The Kid, City Lights,* and *Modern Times*.
~~His~~ ^{Chaplin's} importance in Hollywood soon became clear. In fact, he, Mary Pickford, and Douglas Fairbanks split from their studios to form the studio United Artists. . . .

EXERCISE 11.1 ❯ *Pronoun reference*

 Clarify the pronoun references in the following sentences.

Example

Although *Macbeth* is based on Scottish history, he modified historical evidence to create a compelling tragedy.

Although *Macbeth* is based on Scottish history, Shakespeare modified historical evidence to create a compelling tragedy.

1. In the opening act, the witches tempt Macbeth and Banquo with promises of greatness. They certainly are strange.

2. Teachers have long felt that *Macbeth* is a Shakespearean tragedy that appeals to students. They find *Macbeth* a valuable introduction to Shakespeare's other, more complicated works.

3. Although *Macbeth* has violence at its core, Nedah, Louis, and myself found the Polanski film version bloodier and more perverse than necessary.

4. The elements of Japanese kabuki theater merge well with the symbolic dimensions of *Macbeth*. They make kabuki productions of *Macbeth* very appealing.

5. In the last act of *Macbeth,* it implies that conditions in Scotland will return to normal.

❗ *Checking pronoun reference with a word processor*

Use "search" codes to locate pronouns; then check for clear antecedents.

Locate personal pronouns. Your subject will determine what pronouns you use most often. Search for these pronouns and examine their use for ambiguous, vague, or implied antecedents.

Locate reflexive pronouns. Search for these pronouns and make certain that their antecedents appear in the same sentences.

---

12 Positioning Modifiers

Modifiers explain, describe, define, or limit a word or group of words. Position modifiers so that the relationship between them and the words they modify is clear.

Quick Reference

Modifiers add vividness and specificity to writing when they are effectively positioned in sentences. Modification is most effective when it adheres to these principles:

> *As often as possible, place modifiers near the words they modify.*

> *Seldom separate subjects and predicates or predicates and complements with long modifiers.*

> *Use modifiers to explain, describe, define, or limit only one word or phrase. If a modifier can conceivably modify several words or phrases, reposition it.*

12a > **Place modifiers to create clarity and smoothness in sentences.**

Modifiers explain, describe, define, or limit a word or group of words. To do so effectively, they must be placed where they create clear meaning.

Positioning Long Modifiers

If a long modifier separates the subject from the verb or the verb from the object, reposition the modifier.

Ineffective

Poe's "The Telltale Heart" is, however disturbing its main premise may be, a spellbinding story.

Effective

However disturbing its main premise may be, Poe's "The Telltale Heart" is a spellbinding story.

Positioning Prepositional Phrases and Subordinate Clauses

Because readers instinctively use nearness as a guide to understanding modification, place prepositional modifiers near the words they modify.

Unclear

Huck and Jim were impressed by the view of the mansion, on the raft. (The mansion was on the raft?)

Clear

On the raft, Huck and Jim were impressed by the view of the mansion.

Unclear

In spite of his successful command of forces in the Pacific, President Truman relieved Douglas MacArthur of his military duties.   (Truman commanded forces in the Pacific?)

Clear

President Truman relieved Douglas MacArthur of his military duties, in spite of his successful command of forces in the Pacific.

Positioning Limiting Modifiers

Limiting modifiers such as *hardly, nearly,* and *only* substantially change the meaning of a sentence. Place them carefully and double-check to see that your intended meaning is clear.

He simply stated the problem.   (Stating the problem is all he did.)

He stated the problem simply.   (He made the problem easy to understand.)

We had time only to meet him.   (We had time for nothing else.)

We had time to meet only him.   (We met no one else.)

Positioning Modifiers near Infinitives

Try not to place a modifier between *to* and an infinitive. Although this usage is common in conversation and is acceptable to some linguists, it is best to avoid split infinitives.

Split infinitive

After rereading "Ode on a Grecian Urn," Ralph began *to quickly prepare* his report.

Always acceptable

After rereading "Ode on a Grecian Urn," Ralph quickly began *to prepare* his report.

12b ⟩ Avoid dangling modifiers.

A phrase that appears at the beginning of a sentence but that does not modify the subject of the sentence is a **dangling modifier.** Sentences with dangling modifiers are unclear and illogical. Eliminate dangling modifiers by repositioning the misplaced phrases.

Dangling

Leaping high above the waves, Michael watched the dolphins. (Michael was not leaping; the dolphins were.)

Clear

Michael watched the dolphins leaping high above the waves.

Dangling

> *When still in high school,* my father expected me to be home by mid-
> night. (You were not out that late when your father was in high
> school. You probably were not even born.)

Clear

> When I was still in high school, my father expected me to be home by
> midnight.

| 12c | > | **Avoid squinting modifiers.** |

Squinting modifiers are words or phrases that could modify either the words before them or the words after them.

Squinting

> Armand said *before ten o'clock* he would reach the summit. (He
> spoke before ten o'clock? Or would he arrive before ten?)

Clear

> Armand said he would reach the summit before ten o'clock.

»»» *When a modifier is in an ambiguous position, you may be able to
clarify the meaning of the sentence by inserting the relative pronoun
that in the appropriate position.*

Ambiguous

> Walter said *during the meeting* Monica misrepresented her case.
> (Did Walter comment during the meeting? Or is that when Monica dis-
> torted her case?)

Clear

> Walter said *that* during the meeting Monica misrepresented her case.
> (Here, *that* clarifies when Monica spoke.)
>
> Walter said during the meeting *that* Monica misrepresented her case.
> (Here, *that* clarifies when Walter spoke.) **«««**

EXERCISE 12.1 ❭ *Positioning modifiers*

The following sentences contain misplaced modifiers. Revise the sentences to make the modification clear and effective.

1. The problems of alcoholism, no matter whether they affect adults, adolescents, or even children, need to be honestly addressed.

2. Drinking is, though acceptable within most groups in American culture, socially, physically, and economically costly.

3. Families and coworkers often fail to honestly assess the drinking habits of alcoholics and, as a result, fail to immediately encourage alcoholics to seek professional help.

4. People who drink often have liver trouble, among other medical and social problems.

5. When inebriated, family members endure the emotional and physical abuse of alcoholics.

6. Alcoholics must admit often that their drinking problems are severe before they can get help.

EXERCISE 12.2 ❭ *Positioning modifiers*

The following paragraph contains a variety of misplaced modifiers. Revise the sentences to make the modification clear and effective.

Helping my uncle with his one-acre garden taught me that victories in the garden are won the hard way. My uncle and I, each morning before it got too hot, would do maintenance work. We would pull small infestations of weeds by hand and then spray, with a postemergent herbicide, larger growths of weeds. Then we would mulch the plants whose foliage did not protect the soil from the sun's drying rays. Using straw and sometimes black plastic sheets, we would, trying not to damage low leaves, encircle the stalks of the plants. Covered with parasitical bugs, we would sometimes have to spray plants with a pyrethrin mixture. Once we got started, we worked often without talking. A few comments seemed to be enough on the growth of the asparagus or the tomatoes. Once, however, Uncle Charles told me during our work sessions I was a conscientious worker when he felt talkative. As the days passed, I began to, because of my own hard work, realize how much effort goes into gardening. I must say that grown with so much care, I now appreciate my fruits and vegetables more than I used to.

Positioning modifiers with a word processor

Use your word processor to improve the effectiveness of modifiers.

Reposition modifiers. When modifiers must be moved, use the "block" and "move" commands to make the changes. You will also need to alter punctuation and mechanics using the "delete" command.

Insert the relative pronoun *that* when *that* is necessary to prevent misreading. Your word-processing program will automatically reformat the sentence.

DICTION

13   Using Meaning and Tone

Through **diction,** the choice and use of words for effective communication, writers make their meanings clear to readers. Specific word choices affect the tone of writing, implying writers' perceptions of themselves, their readers, their subjects, and their purposes in writing.

Quick Reference

Selecting appropriate words requires a strong sense of your purpose and your audience.

❯ *Use formal or informal diction, depending on the tone that you want to achieve in your paper.*

❯ *Choose words that your readers will understand.*

❯ *Select words whose denotations suit your meaning and whose connotations suit your purpose.*

❯ *Use specific words that convey your meaning clearly and efficiently.*

❯ *Use idioms correctly; note especially the correct preposition in phrasal idioms.*

13a 〉 Consider your word choices.

American English consists of many regional and social dialects that can be broadly classified as standard or nonstandard.

Standard English is just that: standard, established usage for speaking and writing. Writers employ its grammatical principles and accepted word choices for most formal writing, including academic and professional; educated readers expect its use in most of what they read. **Nonstandard English** — often used in conversation, fiction, and informal writing — occasionally uses ungrammatical constructions and colloquial, regional, or personal words and expressions.

In the early stages of writing — in planning, organizing, and writing a rough draft — most writers do not pause to consider their diction, standard or otherwise. However, when writers revise a rough draft, word choices become especially important. Use the following guidelines, the Glossary of Usage starting on page 635, and your dictionary to choose the words that best convey the meaning and tone you want.

Formal Diction

Used in most academic and professional writing, **formal diction** differs somewhat from the word choices of everyday conversation. When addressing certain subjects (death, religion, politics, or culture, for example), writers usually select formal diction.

Formal diction generally excludes slang and contractions and uses the third person (*he, she, it, they*). Writers choose the most exact words to express their meaning and organize words carefully to achieve the desired tone. The following paragraph, informal in the first draft, is revised in the second draft to achieve the formal tone suited to the subject.

Informal diction and tone

The effects of divorce on children change with the kids' ages. Little kids, one to four, often don't get it when their parents yell at each other, but they usually know something's wrong. They tend to get down, stopping eating and talking, or to act up, getting loud and wild. Bigger kids, from four to eight, have a better idea of what's going on. Because they don't know any better, they're always asking embarrassing questions like "Why are you and Mommy yelling at each other?" These kids often get edgy, flunk in school, and carry a heavy load of guilt.

Formal diction and tone

The effects of divorce on children vary with the children's ages. Very young children, from one to four, often do not fully comprehend the problems between their parents, but they usually sense the tension. They may become depressed, not eating or talking, or demand attention through loud misbehavior. Older children, from four to eight, more clearly recognize relationships in turmoil. Lacking social adeptness, they often ask embarrassing and candid questions such as "Why are you and Mommy yelling at each other?" These children may become nervous, do poorly in school, and feel responsible for their parents' problems.

Informal Diction

Informal diction is the language of conversation. Most writers use informal diction naturally, especially for subjects like travel, sports, and popular culture.

Informal diction often includes contractions and uses first-person pronouns (*I, me, my,* and so on) and sometimes includes slang and regionalisms. It can serve your purposes well in a non-academic composition, such as a personal-experience paper. The following paragraph, with its personal point of view, effectively employs informal diction.

When I was about eleven, my parents got a divorce. I wasn't surprised. For months before, I had known something was wrong, although I wasn't sure what. Mom and Dad would alternately argue about trivial matters and then turn silent, not speaking to each other for days. Then one day, Dad just quietly moved out. It was a relief for everyone, and now, ten years later, Mom and Dad are good friends.

Diction and Audience

A good idea supported with pertinent examples and facts may confuse readers if the words you choose do not accurately convey your intended meaning. To assess the appropriateness of your diction for your audience, consider these questions:

How well developed are your readers' vocabularies? If your readers are well educated or well read, their vocabularies are probably extensive, and you have a wide choice of words to use to present ideas. On the other hand, if you suspect that your readers' vocabularies are not well developed, you must adjust your diction to present your ideas clearly yet simply.

Do your readers understand the technical vocabulary of the subject? Readers who are familiar with your subject will understand its technical terminology, and you will be able to use it freely. If readers are not familiar with your subject, however, you cannot assume that they will understand its specialized vocabulary, and you will have to define key words or use everyday equivalents for technical terms.

What level of diction will your readers expect? Most readers expect standard diction in most writing; some prefer formal diction for some topics; others prefer informal diction for all topics. If formal diction suits your purpose, you should comply with readers' expectations by omitting slang, contractions, and regionalisms from your writing. If your purpose justifies informal diction, comply with readers' expectations by choosing words freely. Remember, too, that for some subjects, readers expect a well-chosen blend of formal and informal language, a combination often termed moderate diction. To answer questions about the level of particular words or phrases, refer to the Glossary of Usage starting on page 635, to your dictionary, or to a dictionary of usage.

You cannot completely match your word choices with readers' knowledge, needs, and expectations, but you should make an effort to analyze your audience and write in language that they will understand and appreciate.

EXERCISE 13.1   ❯   *Formal and informal diction*

The diction of the following sentences about the novel Native Son *is too informal. Revise the sentences to increase their formality.*

1. Many readers are grossed out when Bigger Thomas bashes the rat in the opening scene of the novel.

2. The Daltons, a filthy rich family, had made a bunch of money by ripping off poor tenants in slum housing.

3. Their daughter Mary and her left-wing friends were into hanging out in restaurants in black neighborhoods.

4. Bigger took off after he accidentally did Mary in.

5. Once the cops nabbed Bigger, he was put on trial and then sent up the river.

| 13b | ❯ | **Select words whose denotations and connotations match your meaning.** |

Words are defined in two ways, by their denotations and by their connotations.

Denotations

Denotations are dictionary meanings — short, specific definitions. They present the explicit meanings of words and exclude the subtle shades of meaning that words acquire from use in specific contexts.

Connotations

Connotations are the secondary and sometimes emotional meanings of words. They suggest meaning beyond the explicit denotation. Connotations can create difficulties for beginning writers who do not consider the implied meanings of the words they choose. Make sure that the connotations of the words you use match your purpose.

Consider Connotations

Two words often share the same denotation (and hence are synonyms) but have distinct connotations. Connotations can be classified as positive, negative, or neutral.

Positive connotation

The *delegation* of students protested outside the administration building.   (*Delegation* implies an orderly, duly constituted, and representative gathering.)

Negative connotation

The *mob* of students protested outside the administration building. (*Mob* suggests lack of control and implies a threat.)

Neutral connotation

The *group* of students protested outside the administration building. (*Group* simply denotes "a number of people.")

EXERCISE 13.2 ❱ *Connotations*

Revise the following sentences to replace words whose connotations seem inappropriate.

1. Airport security has become restrictive in the last few years, as folks who travel a lot have discovered.

2. At every concourse in major airports, people dawdle in lines, waiting to have their carry-on luggage inspected.

3. At these security checkpoints, people sometimes get peeved about passing their stuff through scanning devices, but every once in a while, someone is flabbergasted when his or her luggage sets off the alarm.

4. The security guards interrogate people whose luggage sets off the alarm to see if they have a reasonable excuse, and then the checking continues.

5. Although these security checks are an annoyance, they help to keep air travel inviolate.

| 13c | Select abstract or concrete words to suit your meaning. |

Abstract words name intangibles, such as concepts, qualities, or conditions: *truth, loyalty, laziness, freedom, poverty*. **Concrete words** name tangibles: *fire hydrant, bagel, razor, rabbit, silo*. For some purposes, abstract words effectively present general ideas. The vividness of concrete words, however, adds interest and specificity appropriate to all writing.

Abstract
    Poverty demoralizes people.

Concrete
    Being unable to pay bills, buy suitable clothing, feed one's children well, and buy some small conveniences demoralizes parents who want comfortable homes for their families.

The diagram following illustrates the continuum of specificity.

Most General			*Most Specific*
Games	Card games	Wagering card games	Poker
Trees	Fruit trees	Apple trees	Granny Smith apple trees
Animals	Mammals	Marine mammals	Whales

Whales can be made more exact by specifying *blue whales, sperm whales,* and *killer whales*. Although you may not always have this many alternatives, choose the most specific word possible to clarify your meaning.

1. *Women* in *fiction* are sometimes shrewder than *men*.

2. *Heroines* in *novels* are sometimes shrewder than *heroes*.

3. *Romantic heroines* in *nineteenth-century novels* are sometimes shrewder than *their lovers*.

4. *Catherine* in <u>*Wuthering Heights*</u> is shrewder than *Heathcliff*.

Sometimes a generalization best suits your purpose, in which case the third sentence may be the best. However, do not forget the importance of specificity. Readers of the first sentence could easily and justifiably supply their own details, thinking wrongly, for instance, that the writer means that women in contemporary short stories are sometimes shrewder than their fathers. To avoid such misinterpretation, make your meaning clear through using specific diction.

EXERCISE 13.3 〉 *Specific words*

The following sentences present general ideas. Clarify their meanings by replacing general words with specific ones.

1. Politics is expensive.

2. The crowd at the convention was big.

3. Family members of politicians often have personal problems.

4. The candidate won the election.

5. Television influences politics.

13d 〉 Use the established forms of idioms.

Idioms, groups of words that together establish an idiosyncratic meaning, are often illogical if examined word for word. For example, *break it up,* commonly understood to mean "stop fighting," does not make sense when examined one word at a time. *Break,* to split into two or more pieces, creates a visual image of fighters separating. *It,* though indefinite, clearly refers to the implied subject, *fight. Up* defies explanation unless it is considered part of the idiom *break up.* Other unanalyzable idioms include *pick up (the house), take a shower, fall in love,* and *catch a cold.* Such idioms have developed along with our language, and although they may not make literal sense, they are understood.

All idioms are not equally acceptable in formal writing. If you use an idiom, use it carefully and use its established form. The correct use of many phrasal idioms, such as those in the following list, depends on using the correct preposition. If you are in doubt about which preposition to use, check the list or your dictionary.

Phrasal Idioms

agree with (someone)

agree to (a proposal)

angry with (*not* angry at)

charge for (a purchase)

charge with (a crime)

die of/die from

differ with (meaning "to disagree")

differ from (meaning "to be unlike")

in search of (*not* in search for)

intend to (*not* intend on)

off (*not* off of)

plan to (*not* plan on)

similar to (*not* similar with)

sure to (*not* sure and)

to search for

try to (*not* try and)

wait for (someone or something)

wait on (meaning "to serve")

Whenever you are confused about the meaning of an idiom, consult a dictionary.

EXERCISE 13.4 ❯ *Idioms*

Select the appropriate idioms for the following sentences.

1. The National Geographic Society (NGS), founded in 1888, is a (type of a/type of) organization with diverse interests and goals.

2. On the one hand, the NGS often goes (in search of/in search for) exotic flora and fauna to describe in articles and broadcasts.

3. On the other hand, NGS also (tries and/tries to) make Americans aware of simple but subtle differences between peoples of different cultures.

4. Although the format for NGS television programs does not (differ with/differ from) that of other nature documentaries, they are nonetheless uniformly more fascinating.

5. With over 10.5 million members, NGS will be (sure to/sure and) flourish into the twenty-first century.

| 13e | **Use slang and regionalisms selectively.** |

Both **slang** and **regionalisms** are exclusive, informal vocabularies, intelligible to a restricted group. In the case of slang, the restriction is generally to a social, professional, or cultural group; in the case of regionalisms, the restriction is to a specific geographic area.

Slang tends to change rapidly and to be in use for only brief periods. In speech, slang can be refreshingly direct and shows that speakers are aware of current language trends. If the use of a slang expression becomes broad enough, the expression may be absorbed into acceptable written English. Until that happens, however, slang has little place in formal writing. Slang is so quickly dated and so informal, and its meaning is so often inexact to those outside the originating group, that it does not communicate very clearly.

> That class was *the pits*.   ("A waste," as in peach pits? "A cavity in the ground," as in the La Brea Tar Pits?)

> When I saw how far ahead I was, I felt *wicked*.   ("Evil"? Wicked good? Wicked bad?)

Regionalisms are understood within the bounds of a restricted geographic area, but beyond that area their meaning becomes lost. Like slang, regionalisms should be avoided because they can muddle communication.

Early in November, we ordered the *tags* for our car.   (Although *tags* will be clear to readers from some areas of the East, use the more common expression *license plates* to ensure the understanding of readers from other areas.)

EXERCISE 13.5 ❯ *Slang and regionalisms*

Make a list of five slang terms or phrases and five regionalisms in current use. Then write two sentences for each one. In the first sentence, use the slang or regionalism; in the second, translate the slang or regionalism into standard English.

Example:
rip-off (noun)

The insurance plan to supplement Medicare was a *rip-off.*

The insurance plan to supplement Medicare was a *fraud.*

| 13f | ❯ | **Use euphemisms selectively.** |

Euphemisms are "nice" words substituted for specific words whose connotations are negative, unpleasant, or unappealing. Instead of saying that soldiers were *killed,* a press release might say that they *gave their lives.* Instead of saying that people are being *fired,* a notice might say they are being *let go.* Instead of saying that a customer is *overweight,* a salesclerk might say that she is *full-figured.* Seldom fooled by euphemisms, readers instinctively supply the appropriate translation.

Euphemism	*Translation*
financial enticements	bribes
the oldest profession	prostitution
corporal punishment	spanking
placed in custody	arrested
hair-color enhancer	dye

Some euphemisms establish a buffer around painful feelings — as when *passed away* replaces *died* — but even this use should be infrequent.

EXERCISE 13.6 ❯ *Euphemisms*

Revise the following sentences to eliminate euphemistic words and phrases.

1. Weddings are often not inexpensive displays by people and for people who fail to consider their less-than-genuine behavior.

2. Elaborate and expensive, many weddings must be financed through deferred-payment plans.

3. Even brides who are in the family way often wear traditional white bridal gowns.

4. Many less-than-honest people who do not attend worship services regularly insist on being married in houses of God.

5. Ironically, many of these marriages — begun with such elaborate display — end in marriage dissolutions.

Revising meaning and tone with a word processor

When you are working on a paper, use the word processor's "delete" and "insert" capabilities to adjust the diction.

Make changes as you type the draft. As you reread on the screen, delete words that do not fit naturally in the sentences.

If the right word does not occur to you as you work, use a symbol such as ^ or ~ to mark the place. At a pause in your work, use the "search" function to find the symbols and return to the sentence to consider the appropriate word choice.

Make "hard-copy" changes. Print a copy of the paper, and examine your word choices; then return to your computer to delete ineffective words and substitute better ones.

Ineffective word choices — such as clichés, pretentious and sexist language, and jargon — weaken writing by distracting or irritating readers and by obscuring ideas. Writers need to be aware of and avoid such problems. This chapter addresses the most common difficulties.

Quick Reference

Avoid hackneyed or imprecise word choices that muddy writing and distract readers from central ideas.

❯ *Eliminate clichés and other trite expressions.*

❯ *Use words to clarify your meaning, not to impress readers; avoid pretentious language and jargon.*

❯ *Use figurative language to enliven and illuminate your writing; avoid overused, illogical, or mixed figures of speech.*

❯ *Avoid sexist language; it is often inaccurate and it may be offensive.*

14a ❯ **Avoid clichés and triteness.**

A **cliché** is an overused expression that has lost its original inventiveness, surprise, and, often, meaning. **Triteness** describes words and phrases that have been overused: they are stale, uninteresting, and frequently vague.

Some writers do make effective use of trite or clichéd language. Consider, for example, the following quotation from Joseph Brodsky's essay "Flight from Byzantium": "Dust! This weird substance, driving into your face! It merits attention; it should not be concealed behind the word *dust*." *Weird* can seem trite and vague in some contexts, but here it expresses the surprising strangeness Brodsky felt in encountering the common substance dust in a new way and with a new intensity. Readers, however, will be skeptical of clichéd and trite language. and inexperienced writers should avoid using it.

Clichés

Readers finding clichés in your writing will assume that you did not take the time to think through your ideas or consider original ways to express them.

Complete the following phrases.

last but not ———

beat around the ———

fit as a ———

in the final ———

red as a ———

Most people can supply the missing words easily. If you use such phrases in your writing, your readers will find them equally predictable — and boring. Rather than relying on clichés in your own writing, devise phrases that express your meaning exactly, in your own words.

Triteness

Trite words and phrases have been used so often, and so thoughtlessly, that they have lost all appeal and interest. If you discover trite expressions in your writing, strike them out and replace them with less predictable word choices that create interest in and clarify your ideas.

Trite

The report of the Educational Task Force was *very thorough*. (*Thorough* is so common and used in so many contexts that it hardly clarifies the meaning of the sentence.)

Improved

The report of the Educational Task Force included a general preface, a fifteen-chapter text, and twenty-seven appendixes presenting research data. (The use of details to explain the features of the report improves the clarity of the sentence.)

 Eliminating triteness is especially easy to do on a word processor. Simply delete the trite word or phrase and insert a carefully chosen replacement. If you overuse particular trite expressions, use the "search" function to find and replace them.

EXERCISE 14.1 ❱ *Clichés and trite expressions*

Revise the following sentences to eliminate clichés and trite expressions.

1. Some monuments have struck a chord with the American people and can remind each and every one of us of the value of public memorials.

2. The *Statue of Liberty* is an awe-inspiring national monument, symbolizing how America opened its arms to European emigrants.

3. The simplicity of the Tomb of the Unknown Soldier and the low-key military display puts a lump in the throats of many visitors.

4. One out-of-the-ordinary monument, St. Louis's Gateway Arch, reaches to the sky in a sweeping curve of shiny stainless steel.

5. With its marble as smooth as glass, the Vietnam Memorial is a plain and simple monument honoring the tens of thousands of soldiers who gave their lives for their country.

14b   Avoid pretentious language.

A rich and varied vocabulary is an asset for a writer, but the words used in any given piece of writing must be geared to its specific audience and purpose. Writers who use **pretentious language** use words to impress rather than to communicate with readers. Avoid stilted language, even in formal writing. Not only is pretentious diction dishonest, but it often makes simple ideas difficult to grasp and complicated ideas impossible to understand. If writers do not translate pretentious diction into natural words, readers have to do so.

Pretentious

> *Prior to* the purchase of the *abode,* the Enricos carefully *ruminated* about how *residential payments* would affect their *cash flow.*   (The stilted word choices here, some poorly chosen synonyms and some jargon, require a translation.)

Natural

> *Before* the Enricos purchased the *house,* they carefully *thought* about how *mortgage payments* would affect their *finances.*   (This sentence uses natural diction and is therefore easily understood on the first reading.)

》》》 *Although a thesaurus, or a book of synonyms, may help you to find alternative ways of stating a point, it should be used carefully. Use only words that are a natural part of your vocabulary, avoid clichés, and never choose words whose connotations you do not understand. Using a thesaurus to find impressive or unusual words results in pretentious writing.* **《《**

EXERCISE 14.2   **》**   *Pretentious language*

Revise the following paragraph to eliminate pretentious language and use language that is more natural. (Suggestion: Make this a personal narrative.)

When one participates in commencement ceremonies, one is often fraught with a mixture of emotions. One senses relief because one's time in high school is terminating. Conversely, one feels uncertain about what lies ahead. Some students will seek employment immediately, other students will approach matrimony, and yet other students will pursue additional academic studies. For this diversity of students, commencement exercises symbolize an uncertain transmutation in their lives.

14c ⟩ Avoid jargon.

Jargon is the technical vocabulary of a specialized group. Doctors, mechanics, weather forecasters, teachers, carpenters, and publishers all have special words that they use in special contexts. When they write only for their own group, their use of the group's jargon may be acceptable (perhaps even necessary). When writing for a wide audience, however, writers must translate jargon into common terms.

Jargon	*Translation*
urban open space (city planning)	a city park
precipitation (weather forecasting)	rain, snow, sleet
telephone surveillance (law enforcement)	wiretapping
cost-efficient (business)	economical
merchantable dwelling (real estate)	a house that will sell

Jargon

The city council recommends a systematic program of greening for our arterials as a means to revitalize our declining streetscape.

Translation

The city council recommends that we plant trees along our main streets to make them appear less neglected.

EXERCISE 14.3 ❯ *Pretentious diction and jargon*

 Translate these pretentious, jargon-laden sentences into natural, clear writing.

1. An excessive proportion of American citizenry improvidently pass their days ignoring quotidian dangers to health.

2. The abundance of vehicular collisions attests to the fact that the people of the United States of America are oblivious to safety-inducing guidelines for automobile management.

3. The numbers of persons who imbibe an excess of distilled spirits is also a depression-inducing statistic.

4. The inhalation of toxic fumes from smoking materials, although prohibited in many business establishments, continues to have a negative impact on the health aspect of the male and female population sectors.

5. The personal and private ownership and use of firearms and related paraphernalia account for the accidental demise of scores of people each twelvemonth.

14d ❯ Use figures of speech cautiously.

Figures of speech may be single words, phrases, or longer expressions. They add vitality to writing, most often by making unexpected or suggestive connections between dissimilar things. Metaphors and similes are the most common and useful figures of speech.

Metaphors imply the identity of the things compared.

Dr. Mantera's criticism of the proposal was all thunder and no lightning.   (The implication is that the criticism was mere noise with no illumination or insight.)

Similes are direct comparisons using the connectives *like, as,* or *as if.*

Rob accelerated his car, shifting lanes quickly and rounding corners at high speed — as if he were making the final lap at the Indianapolis 500.

Original and apt figures of speech can enliven your writing, but they should be used to illuminate and clarify your ideas, not to decorate them. Be careful to avoid clichés.

Effective metaphor

Ronald, *a modern Tom Sawyer,* enjoys harmless trickery and mild adventure.

Ineffective metaphor

After the laughter stopped, Bernice gave Rinaldo an *icy* stare.   (The modifier is a cliché.)

Effective simile

Cleo is *like a Duracell battery:* she's always starting something, and it lasts longer than we ever expect.

Ineffective simile

Darryl's grades are solid *as a rock*.   ("Solid as a rock" is a cliché.)

Extended or multiple related figures of speech must present a uniform impression, drawing on logically consistent images, locales, experiences, or circumstances. Without this consistency, the image is confused — often laughably so.

Confusingly mixed

Like an agile deer, the politician leaped into the fray.   (Agile deer do leap, but they are shy animals unlikely to seek conflict. Moreover, "leaped into the fray" is a cliché.)

Logically linked

Like an agile deer, the politician leaped over obstacles to the proposal. (The agile deer leaping over obstacles is a logical, consistent image.)

EXERCISE 14.4 ❭ *Figures of speech*

Revise the ineffective figures of speech in the following sentences.

1. Like good soldiers, athletes get down to the work that training sessions require and rise to the occasion.

2. Swimmers fly through lap after lap during practices, building the tireless endurance necessary in races.

3. Like kangaroos, basketball players jump for balls and then fire them down the court, hoping to hone skills to use in games.

4. With catlike speed, sprinters shoot from starting blocks over and over again, trying to perfect an opening move that will put them miles above the rest.

5. Like trains speeding down the tracks, football linesmen practice rushing and tackling, leaving other players in their wake.

| 14e | Avoid sexist language. |

Sexist language implies, generally through choices of key nouns and pronouns, that the subject applies only to males or only to females. Because it fails to reflect the diversity of contemporary society, sexist language is narrow-minded and inaccurate.

To avoid sexist language, avoid using sex-specific pronouns when the antecedent is not sex-specific and avoid nouns that arbitrarily or from empty tradition restrict meaning to one sex or the other. When choosing nouns, learn to notice the subtle — and sometimes not so subtle — implications of your choices.

Sexist

A psychiatrist is bound by professional oath to keep his patients' records confidential.   (Many psychiatrists are women, so this statement is not accurate.)

Nonsexist

A psychiatrist is bound by professional oath to keep his or her patients' records confidential.   (The use of *his or her* eliminates the sexist bias in the sentence.)

Nonsexist

Psychiatrists are bound by professional oath to keep their patients' records confidential.   (The use of plural forms avoids sexist language.)

Sexist

According to family records, my forefathers came to the United States from France in 1806.   (Fore*mothers* had to come too, or there would not have been any children.)

Nonsexist

According to family records, my ancestors came to the United States from France in 1806.

EXERCISE 14.5 ❯ *Sexist language*

The following passage was written in 1872, when sensitivity to sexist language was not common. Rewrite the passage to eliminate sexist language — but do not change the meaning of the passage.

The blight which threatens theoretical culture has only begun to frighten modern man, and he is groping uneasily for remedies out of the storehouse of his experience, without having any real conviction that these remedies will avail against disaster. In the meantime, there have arisen certain men of genius who, with admirable circumspection and consequence, have used the arsenal of science to demonstrate the limitations of science and of the cognitive faculty itself. They have authoritatively rejected science's claim to universal validity and to the attainment of universal goals and exploded for the first time the belief that men may plumb the universe by means of the law of causation. — Friedrich Nietzsche, *The Birth of Tragedy*

| 14f | ❯ **Avoid neologisms and archaisms.** |

Neologisms, recently coined words or word forms, appear in current speech (and in some journalistic and technical writing) and then very often fade away. In formal writing, avoid using new terms unless nothing else expresses your meaning.

Questionable

Personal computers must be *user-friendly.* (*Computer,* once a neologism, is now standard; *user-friendly* is still jargon, vague to the uninformed, and colloquial.)

Better

Personal computers must be *easy for people to use.*

Archaisms, words once in common use but no longer standard, seem affected and disruptive in contemporary writing.

Words no longer in use — like *yon* ("over there") or *betwixt* ("between"), or words no longer used in a given sense, like *save* in the sense of "except" — make writing artificial and pretentious.

Artificial

We adults sat and reminisced *whilst* the children played along the shore.   (No one says *whilst* any more, and no one should write it.)

Natural

We adults sat and reminisced *while* the children played along the shore.

≫ *Some neologisms are so expressive and apt that they become widely used and universally acceptable.* Stereo, fallout, *and* refrigerator *were once newly coined words that have long since become standard.* **≪**

EXERCISE 14.6 **〉** *Neologisms and archaic words*

Revise the following sentences to eliminate words or phrases that are either too new or too old to be standard usage.

1. Methinks that romance novels deserve more attention from serious readers than they have often received.

2. Betwixt the covers of romance novels as varied as *Wuthering Heights* and *The Lady and the Highwayman,* readers will find quickly paced stories of intrigue and love.

3. The heroines and heroes of these novels are ofttimes innocent, sincere, and trusting people whose lives are threatened by erstwhile friends who are really enemies.

4. With their inherent reliance on historical context, these infotainment novels provide readers with knowledge of past societies, as well as reading pleasure.

5. Although the reading of romance novels does not require much intellectual input from readers, these books provide innocent pleasure and distraction.

!   *Choosing effective words with a word processor*

Beyond general uses of word-processing programs to delete and substitute words, consider these specific approaches:

Replace neologisms. As you check a paper by using a spell-checking program, the program will highlight words not found in its dictionary. Neologisms, because they are new and in limited use, will not appear. The spell checker will draw your attention to these words, and you can then decide whether they or standard substitutes best serve your purposes.

Check for sexist use of pronouns. Use the "search" commands to look for masculine pronouns: *he, him, his,* and *himself.* When the antecedent is not exclusively male, change the pronoun to *he or she, him or her,* and so on, or change the antecedent, pronoun, and verb to plural forms.

GRAMMAR

15 Fragments

Fragments are capitalized and punctuated as if they were sentences, but they are not sentences. They may be phrases lacking subjects or verbs, or they may be subordinate clauses. Four strategies for correcting fragments appear in sections 15a and 15b.

Although fragments are common in speech, notes, rough drafts, and writing that imitates speech, formal writing generally requires complete and grammatical sentences that state ideas fully. The use of fragments for special effect is discussed in section 15c.

Quick Reference

Fragments distract readers and shift their attention away from your ideas to the mechanics of your writing. To avoid this, follow these suggestions:

> ❯ Make sure that your sentences contain subjects and verbs, the basic sentence elements.

> ❯ Be sure to use subordinating conjunctions in complex and compound-complex sentences, not in subordinate-clause fragments.

> ❯ Use intentional fragments selectively for special effect, remembering that excessive use distracts and annoys readers.

15a ❯ Revise fragments that are phrases.

Correct fragments that lack subjects or verbs by supplying the missing element or by combining the fragment with a complete sentence.

Fragments Lacking Subjects

Fragments without subjects may be verb phrases (free-standing predicates and complements); they may also be verbal phrases (phrases using gerunds, participles, and infinitives [see Verbs, pages 178–83]). Eliminate these fragments by adding a subject or by joining the fragment to an appropriate sentence.

Fragment

Brian is addicted to reading mystery novels. Reads one a week.

Complete

Brian is addicted to reading mystery novels. *He* reads one a week.   (A subject pronoun has been added.)

Complete

Brian, who is addicted to mystery novels, reads one a week.   (The fragment has been joined to a related sentence.)

Fragment

Jay has one ambition. To travel around the world.

Complete

Jay's one ambition *is* to travel around the world.   (The infinitive phrase is joined to the sentence.)

Fragments Lacking Verbs

Fragments without verbs are usually subjects and related modifiers, appositives, or absolute phrases. Correct these fragments by adding a verb or joining the appositive or absolute phrase to a nearby sentence.

Fragment

Rachel, an avid collector of china figurines. She pays eighty-five dollars for extra insurance coverage.

Complete

Rachel *is* an avid collector of china figurines. She pays eighty-five dollars for extra insurance coverage.   (A verb has been added.)

Complete

Rachel, an avid collector of china figurines, *pays* eighty-five dollars for extra insurance coverage.   (The fragment has been joined to a related sentence.)

 Use your word processor to correct phrasal fragments quickly and easily by inserting subjects or verbs. Be sure to change capitalization and punctuation as required by the new sentence.

15b   **Revise fragments that are subordinate clauses.**

A subordinate clause must be joined to an independent clause to form a grammatical sentence. Correct subordinate-clause fragments by dropping the subordinating conjunction to form a simple sentence or by joining the subordinate clause to one or more independent clauses to form a complex or compound-complex sentence.

Fragment

Some students have to postpone starting college. Because the cost of attending has risen.

Complete

Some students have to postpone starting college. The cost of attending has risen.   (The subordinate conjunction has been dropped.)

Complete

Some students have to postpone starting college because the cost of attending has risen.   (Here the subordinate clause becomes part of a complex sentence.)

Complete

Because the cost of attending college has risen, some students have to postpone starting.

Your word processor will help you to join phrases and subordinate clauses to related sentences quickly and easily. Use the "block" and "move" features and experiment with ways to reposition these groups of words to form new expressive, grammatical sentences.

| 15c | Use fragments sparingly for special effect. |

Fragments can be effective and acceptable, even in final drafts, when they are used to isolate and thus emphasize a key word or phrase. Use this strategy selectively to achieve emphasis or to supply an answer to a question.

> *G, PG, R, X.* These symbols are used to classify films and to restrict the audiences that see them. Although the coding system represents an admirable effort to protect children, does it work? No. Many parents disregard the implied advice of the rating system, and few theater owners adhere to its guidelines when selling tickets.

EXERCISE 15.1 ❯ *Fragments*

Eliminate the fragments in the following paragraph by adding subjects or verbs or by combining the fragments with complete sentences.

The National Board of Teaching Standards has been formed recently to address matters of teacher training and certification. Because of inconsistencies that exist among states. Some states require prospective teachers to take a pre-professional skills test. To establish the reading, writing, and mathematical skills of future teachers. But not others. All states require expertise in content areas. Approximates that of traditional majors in each subject area. States require additional work in educational theory and practice. Usually fifteen to twenty semester hours of work. These pedagogical courses, ones emphasizing general principles of teaching and general patterns of learning. No matter how theoretically sound these courses may be, inconsistencies exist. Since states establish their requirements individually. As a result, teachers moving from one state to the other may not be fully prepared to meet requirements. Future teachers need the coordinated efforts of state departments of education. To develop uniform educational programs. Especially with prospects of taking the National Teacher's Exam.

EXERCISE 15.2 ❯ *Fragments*

The following paragraph includes a number of fragments. Some are intended for special emphasis, but others are clearly grammatical errors. Correct the ineffective fragments and explain why the others should remain.

New York. St. Louis. Knoxville. New Orleans. Los Angeles. These cities have all hosted those pretentious, glorious, overly expensive, and enjoyable activities known as world's fairs. Filled with exhibits, amusements, and restaurants. World's fairs offer people a chance to learn about the world while enjoying themselves. At these large fairs, nations from around the world build pavilions to showcase their national achievements. Often sending examples of their best technology, art, and historical treasures. Dancers, singers, and musicians. Enjoy seeing native costumes and folk dances that illustrate the diversity of the world's cultures. Sometimes, even specialties of individual fairs have become common later on. St. Louis, the city where the ice-cream cone was invented. It has since become a favorite treat worldwide. World's fairs, originally planned to "bring the world closer together." But do they continue to serve this original purpose? Not really. Because people now travel by airplane and can see the countries of the world. They see much more than can be seen in national exhibits at world's fairs.

16 Comma Splices and Fused Sentences

Comma splices and fused sentences contain two or more independent clauses that are not properly punctuated. In a **comma splice** (also called a **comma fault**), the independent clauses are incorrectly joined with only a comma. In a **fused sentence** (also called a **run-on sentence**), independent clauses are placed one after the other, with no punctuation.

Correct comma splices and fused sentences by changing the punctuation or structure of the sentence.

Quick Reference

Comma splices and fused sentences are never acceptable in writing because they incorrectly merge ideas.

> *Use a period to separate the independent clauses in comma splices or fused sentences.*

> *Use a semicolon, a comma and a coordinating conjunction, or a subordinating conjunction (and a comma if necessary) to join independent clauses.*

> *Remember that conjunctive adverbs may be used only within independent clauses or sentences, not to join them as coordinating or subordinating conjunctions do.*

16a ▷ **Separate the independent clauses in a comma splice or a fused sentence by using a period to form two sentences.**

Comma splice

Many artists and musicians are extremely fashion conscious, they view their clothes as a form of self-expression.

Separate sentences

Many artists and musicians are extremely fashion conscious. They view their clothes as a form of self-expression.

16b   **Join the independent clauses in a comma splice or a fused sentence by using a semicolon to form a compound sentence.**

Fused sentence

In the 1950s, members of English departments felt their programs were too diverse they split into departments of literature, composition, linguistics, and speech communication.

Compound sentence

In the 1950s, members of English departments felt their programs were too diverse; they split into departments of literature, composition, linguistics, and speech communication.

16c   **Correct a comma splice or a fused sentence by using a comma and a coordinating conjunction to form a compound sentence or by using a subordinating conjunction to form a complex sentence.**

Use the coordinating conjunctions (*and, but, for, nor, or, so,* and *yet*) with a comma to link independent clauses grammatically to form a compound sentence. Use subordinating conjunctions (*although, because, since, while,* and others) to join independent clauses to form complex or compound-complex sentences.

Comma splice

The sky diver hurtled toward the ground, she felt no fear.

Compound sentence

The sky diver hurtled toward the ground, but she felt no fear.

Fused sentence

> NASA delayed the shuttle launch the ground crew wanted to check the on-board computers again.

Complex sentence

> NASA delayed the shuttle launch because the ground crew wanted to check the on-board computers again.   (When the subordinate clause ends the sentence, a comma is unnecessary if the meaning is clear.)

Fused sentence

> Many cabinet members work for only four to eight years with the president they continue to work in Washington as consultants to major firms.

Complex sentence

> Although many cabinet members work for only four to eight years with the president, they continue to work in Washington as consultants to major firms.   (When the subordinate clause begins the sentence, a comma is required.)

16d ▷ **Do not mistake conjunctive adverbs for coordinating or subordinating conjunctions.**

Conjunctive adverbs (*besides, furthermore, however, nevertheless, still, then, therefore,* and others) logically connect ideas, but they do not link independent clauses grammatically as coordinating conjunctions do. When a conjunctive adverb appears in a comma splice or fused sentence, correct the sentence by using a period or semicolon to separate the independent clauses.

Comma splice

> Corporate mergers are often like marriages, however, some unfriendly ones are like abductions.

Correct

> Corporate mergers are often like marriages. However, some unfriendly ones are like abductions.

Correct

> Corporate mergers are often like marriages; however, some unfriendly ones are like abductions.   (The use of the semicolon establishes a closer link between the ideas.)

EXERCISE 16.1 ❯ *Comma splices and fused sentences*

Correct these faulty sentences by changing their punctuation or structure.

1. *Rock 'n' roll* is a generic term used to describe a wide variety of musical styles, nonetheless, each musical style remains distinct.

2. The term *pop music* was coined in the 1950s, it describes music that cuts across socio-ethnic lines and appeals to a wide audience.

3. *Acid rock* describes the amplified, electronic music of mid-1960s artists in this subgenre of rock music were often part of the counter-culture of drugs.

4. *Disco*'s emphasis on highly synthesized electronic music with an insistent rhythm made it popular dance music, nevertheless, its popularity faded in only a few years.

5. Black American music, sometimes called *soul music* and sometimes *rhythm and blues,* developed from gospel music its acceptance in conservative white culture attests to the power of music to break down barriers.

6. With its emphasis on shock value, *punk rock* created a brief sensation in the world of music people soon grew tired of being shocked by performers who often lacked musical skill.

EXERCISE 16.2 ❯ *Comma splices and fused sentences*

Correct the comma splices and fused sentences in the following paragraph by adding periods, commas and coordinating conjunctions, semicolons, or subordinating conjunctions.

Book censorship in American high schools has become a standard practice these days, individuals and groups have applied pressure to school boards everywhere. The books that have been censored range widely in subject they range widely in literary quality as well. No book seems to be beyond the reach of book censors. Books treating sexual situations, like *A Farewell to Arms,* have been banned, books that contain questionable language, like *The Catcher in the Rye,* have been banned, too. *The Grapes of Wrath* has been censored in some communities because of its presentation of socialist ideology, *Lord of the Flies* has been removed from libraries because of its violence. Even a book like *Huckleberry Finn* is now being brought into question it has racially demeaning dialect. The American Library Association has come to the defense of these books, however that has not kept them on bookshelves and reading lists in many American high schools.

Revising comma splices and fused sentences with a word processor

Use a word processor to revise comma splices and fused sentences, taking advantage of its ability to make small changes that do not require the retyping of whole sentences.

Separate faulty sentences. Divide comma splices and fused sentences into separate simple sentences. Be sure to change capitalization and punctuation.

Insert coordinating conjunctions to join independent clauses correctly.

Join clauses with subordinating conjunctions. Use the "block" and "move" functions to experiment and find the best placement for clauses and coordinating conjunctions. You may also need to add commas.

17 Agreement

Subjects and verbs agree in number; pronouns and antecedents agree in number and gender.

Quick Reference

Errors in subject-verb or pronoun-antecedent agreement are easy to correct if you remember these basic principles.

❯ *Verbs must agree in number with the subject of the clause or sentence. Do not be misled by intervening words.*

❯ *Let the meaning of the subject (singular or plural) guide your choice of verbs; watch especially compound subjects with and or or, indefinite pronouns, collective nouns, and plural words with a singular meaning.*

❯ *Make sure that pronouns have clear antecedents with which they consistently agree in both number and gender.*

❯ *Let the intended number of the antecedent guide your choice of pronouns; watch especially compound subjects with and or or, indefinite pronouns, collective nouns, and plural words with a singular meaning.*

| 17a ❯ | **Subjects and verbs must agree in number.** |

Verbs agree with the subject of the sentence, not with intervening words. Words that separate subjects and verbs, especially nouns that serve as objects of prepositions, should not influence your choice of verbs.

> The *swallows* of Capistrano *are* becoming noticeably less predictable. (*Capistrano,* a singular noun in a prepositional phrase, does not affect verb choice.)

Compound Subjects Joined by *And*

Compound subjects joined by *and* require plural verbs.

```
          compound subj.     plural verb
    ┌──────────────────────────┐  │
```
The *defendant* and her *counsel were* both angered by the verdict.

⟩⟩⟩ *Compound subjects that are seen as one unit are singular and require a singular verb.*

> "*Tragedy and triumph*" *describes* Britain's lonely resistance to Hitler during the grim days of 1940. **⟨⟨⟨**

Subjects Joined by *Or, Nor, Either . . . Or,* or *Neither . . . Nor*

Or, nor, and so on do not indicate multiple subjects; they indicate alternative subjects. The verb, therefore, should agree with the number of the subjects considered individually.

Singular subjects

> *Either walking or running strengthens* the heart.   (Walking *strengthens;* running *strengthens.*)

Plural subjects

> *Recordings or books* as gifts *please* most people.   (Recordings *please;* books *please.*)

When a compound subject contains both plural and singular elements, the verb agrees with the nearer element.

Singular and plural elements
Neither the designer nor the *engineers accept* the prototype.

Plural and singular elements
Neither the engineers nor the *designer accepts* the prototype.

》》》 *When a singular noun follows a plural noun in a compound subject, the required singular verb, though grammatically correct, may seem awkward. If a sentence seems awkward, revise it.*

The prototype satisfies neither the engineers nor the designer. **《《《**

Indefinite Pronouns

Indefinite pronouns (*anyone, each, either, everybody, none, someone,* and others) have no specific antecedents. Some, such as *both* and *all,* are plural and require plural verbs, but most are singular and require singular verbs. Be especially careful using pronouns like *everyone* or *everybody,* which require singular verbs even though *every-* sounds plural; *-one* or *-body* should guide you.

Somebody *attends* to the correspondence while she is gone.

Both assign papers during the first week of class.

Everyone brings her or his book to class on Friday.

》》》 Every *and* each *used as adjectives require singular verbs, even when the subject is compound.*

Every man, woman, and child *was* evacuated before nightfall.   (*Every* emphasizes the people individually, so a singular verb is appropriate.)

Each actor and musician *was* asked to stand to be acknowledged. (*Each* emphasizes individuals and requires a singular verb.) **◀◀◀**

Collective Nouns

Collective nouns stressing group unity require singular verbs; collective nouns stressing the individuality of group members require plural verbs.

Group unity

The *committee votes* by a show of hands.   (The committee as a whole follows this procedure.)

Individuality of group members

The Supreme Court *act* according to their individual consciences. (Each member acts separately, so the plural form is correct.)

▶▶▶ *If collective nouns stressing individuality sound awkward with plural verbs, revise the sentence by including "members of" or a similar phrase that clearly requires a plural verb.*

The Supreme Court justices *act* according to their individual consciences. **◀◀◀**

Expletive Constructions

Expletive constructions (*here is, here are, there is,* and *there are*) depend for meaning on the noun complement (the noun that follows the construction); the verb in the expletive phrase must agree in number with the noun. A singular noun requires *is;* a plural noun requires *are.*

Here *is* the first *chapter* of my forthcoming novel.

There *are* many unimaginative *programs* on television.

Your word processor will help you locate and check your uses of expletive constructions. Use the "search" codes to find *here is, here are, there is,* and *there are.* Make sure that the verb in each expletive agrees with its noun complement.

Relative Clauses

The relative pronouns (*who, which,* and *that*), when used as the subject of a clause, agree in number with their antecedents.

> Flooding in the spring is a *threat* that *requires* our attention. (*That* refers to *threat,* a singular predicate noun. Consequently, the relative clause requires a singular verb.)

> People once believed in the *pseudo-sciences* of physiognomy and astrology, which *have* now lost their credibility. (*Which* refers to *pseudo-sciences,* a plural object of a preposition. The verb in the relative clause must, therefore, be plural.)

Linking Verbs

Linking verbs agree with the number of the subject, not the number of the predicate noun.

> A major *expense* of operating a school *is* salaries for administrators, teachers, and custodians. (Although *salaries* is plural, the subject of the sentence is *expense,* a singular noun. Therefore, the verb must also be singular.)

Plural Nouns with Singular Meanings

Plural nouns such as *news, politics, electronics,* and *mumps* often have singular meanings. When used in a singular sense, they require singular verbs.

Fractions, measurements, money, time, weight, and volume considered as single units also require singular verbs.

Plural noun

Geriatrics successfully *discredits* the prejudice that senility is inevitable in the elderly.   (*Geriatrics* is a single discipline and requires a singular verb.)

Plural unit

Six hundred dollars seems a reasonable price.   (The dollar amount, considered *one* price, requires a singular verb.)

>>> *Common exceptions to this principle are scissors and trousers. Though units, they are considered plural. When used with the phrase a pair of, however, pair dominates and requires a singular verb.*

The *scissors need* sharpening.   (The logic is that scissors have two functional parts, making the plural verb appropriate.)

This *pair* of scissors *needs* sharpening.   (The word *pair* emphasizes that the parts act as a single unit, making the singular verb necessary.) **<<<**

Titles

Even when the words in a title are plural, the title of a single work requires a singular verb.

Leaves of Grass illustrates the best and worst characteristics of nineteenth-century American verse.   (*Leaves of Grass* is the title of one long poem, so a singular verb is required.)

Words Used as Words

Words used as words require singular verbs. This rule applies even when the word discussed is plural.

Media often inaccurately *substitutes* for *medium*.   (*Media,* a plural noun, requires a singular verb when discussed as a word.)

In news broadcasts, *persons has become* a standard but annoying substitute for the word *people*.   (*Persons,* a plural noun, when discussed as a word requires a singular verb.)

EXERCISE 17.1 ❯ *Subject-verb agreement*

Select the verb that maintains subject-verb agreement.

1. Archaeologists (studies/study) the buildings, tools, and other artifacts of ancient cultures.

2. Every archaeologist, especially field researchers, (know/knows) of a historic site ruthlessly desecrated by treasure-seekers.

3. Despite international agreements, unscrupulous museums or a wealthy private collector (compete/competes) for every major artistic discovery, stolen or not.

4. But laws and international policing (reduce/reduces) yearly the number of destroyed sites and stolen artifacts.

5. Excavations — better controlled than ever by teams of university archaeologists, students, local workers, and national representatives — (proceed/proceeds) slowly these days, avoiding the damage inflicted by yesterday's "grave robbers."

6. *Digs* (is/are) the current jargon used to describe an excavation site.

7. Recent decades (has seen/have seen) few finds of the historical significance of the discovery of Tutankhamen's tomb in 1922, but research in various locales (continue/continues).

8. For archaeologists, five or ten years (seem/seems) a reasonable time to work at a single site, so new finds will be made — but made more slowly than in the past.

EXERCISE 17.2 ❱ *Subject-verb agreement*

> *The following paragraph contains many errors in subject-verb agreement. Correct the misused verbs and then draw arrows to the subjects with which each verb agrees.*

There is more and more adults attending college at a later age. Their motives, either to change careers or to get the education they missed, varies. Anyone walking on a college campus see students in their thirties, forties, fifties, and even sixties carrying books and talking with friends. Almost every class and laboratory now include at least one of these "nontraditional" students. Because their home and job situations and their preparedness differs from those of eighteen- and twenty-one-year-olds, these students face problems that surprises a younger student. Some of these adults organizes their schooling around full-time jobs. Others care for families, as well as attends class. Nobody going to college and getting a degree find it easy, but an adult student with adult responsibilities have extra problems to cope with. As this situation becomes more common, everyone adjust, however, a process that already have begun. Even the media recognize this trend in American education. With humor and sympathy, *Kate and Allie* provide insights into the problems adults face when attending college. Who knows? Given a chance today, maybe even Lucy Ricardo or John Walton might enroll in a class or two.

| 17b | ❭ | **Pronouns and their antecedents must agree in number and gender.** |

Singular antecedents (the words to which pronouns refer) require singular pronouns; plural antecedents require plural pronouns.

sing.   *sing.*
antecedent   *pronoun*
  | |
Genghis Khan ruled *his* vast empire with great cruelty.

plural   *plural*
antecedent   *pronoun*
  | |
Children need encouragement and guidance from *their* parents.

Pronouns must also agree with the gender of their antecedents.

fem. antecedent   fem. pronoun
        | |
Queen Elizabeth II rules *her* empire as a constitutional monarch.

Plural pronouns do not specify gender, but singular pronouns specify masculine, feminine, or neuter gender.

Pronoun Forms

	Subjective	*Objective*	*Possessive*	*Reflexive*
Masculine	he	him	his	himself
Feminine	she	her	hers	herself
Neuter	it	it	its	itself

Pronoun-Antecedent Agreement and Sexist Language

The masculine pronouns (*he* and its variations) were once acceptable substitutes for antecedents whose gender was undetermined and thus might be either male or female. This usage is unacceptable today, even in formal writing, because it excludes women without justification and consequently reinforces stereotypes.

To avoid this problem, use plural antecedents and pronouns when possible or rephrase the sentence. Do not use a plural pronoun like *their* with a singular antecedent; this creates a problem in pronoun-antecedent agreement. Another possible solution, using pronouns in pairs (*he or she, his or hers, he/she,* and so on) should be used sparingly, since it can lead to distracting repetition and awkward rhythm in sentences.

Sexist

A good *surgeon* carefully explains procedures to *his* patients.

Nonsexist but incorrect

A good *surgeon* carefully explains procedures to *their* patients.   (The plural *their* does not agree with the singular *surgeon*.)

Nonsexist and correct

Good *surgeons* carefully explain procedures to *their* patients.   (Here a plural noun is used with a plural pronoun.)

Nonsexist and correct

Good *surgeons* carefully explain procedures to patients.   (Here the possessive pronoun is omitted without substantial loss of meaning.)

Nonsexist and correct

A good *surgeon* carefully explains procedures to *his or her* patients.

To express generalizations based on individual experiences, use a specific antecedent instead of a general noun. That, in turn, will dictate a specific pronoun choice and help you to avoid sexist language.

Dr. Knepper, like all good surgeons, carefully explains procedures to *his* patients.

Compound Antecedents Joined by *And*

Compound antecedents joined by *and* require plural pronouns.

compound antecedent   plural pronoun

Female *whales and dolphins* fiercely protect *their* young.

Antecedents Joined by *Or, Nor, Either . . . Or,* or *Neither . . . Nor*

Compound subjects joined by these words present alternative, not multiple, subjects, so pronouns refer to each subject individually.

Singular antecedents

Neither Gladstone nor Disraeli graciously accepted criticism of *his* plans for the British government.   (Gladstone/*his;* Disraeli/*his*)

Plural antecedents

Did *the Greeks or the Romans* consider Zeus *their* principal god? (Greeks/*their;* Romans/*their*)

When part of a compound antecedent is singular and part is plural, the pronoun agrees with the nearer antecedent.

Singular and plural antecedents

The dean or the *students* must modify *their* terms.   (students/*their*)

If the construction sounds awkward, place the singular noun first or consider rewriting the sentence.

Correct but awkward

The students or the *dean* must modify *her* terms.   (dean/*her*)

Better

If the *dean* will not change *her* terms, the *students* will have to change *theirs.*   (dean/*her;* students/*theirs*)

Indefinite Pronouns as Antecedents

Indefinite pronouns (*anyone, each, either, everybody, none,* and others) are usually singular in meaning and take singular pronouns. However, some indefinite pronouns (*all, most, some,* and others) are plural in meaning and take plural pronouns. Let the number of the indefinite pronoun guide you.

Anyone who works as a war correspondent risks *his or her* life frequently.   (*Anyone* refers to people one at a time, as does the pronoun cluster *his or her.*)

All signed the petition, and then *their* regional representative sent it to national headquarters.   (*All* refers to the signers in the aggregate, so the plural *their* is correct.)

Collective Nouns

When collective nouns stress group unity, they take singular pronouns; when collective nouns stress the group as a collection of individuals, they take plural pronouns.

Group unity

The *audience* showed *its* approval by applauding loudly.   (The audience is perceived as a single unit, creating a unified response.)

Individuality within the group

The *audience* raised *their* voices in song.   (This sentence stresses the many voices of the audience members.)

EXERCISE 17.3 ❯   *Pronoun-antecedent agreement*

! *Insert appropriate pronouns in the following sentences.*

1. Greeks, Romans, Egyptians, Indians, and virtually every other civilized group had one or more methods of keeping _____ dwellings cool in summer months.

2. For example, all of these peoples hung water-soaked mats in _____ doorways to develop cooling moisture.

3. Leonardo da Vinci, with _____ usual inventiveness, created the first mechanical fan in about 1500, _____ power provided by running water.

4. The 1838 British House of Commons was the first to enjoy systematic control of ventilation and humidity during _____ sessions.

5. Neither Alfred Wolff (in 1902) nor Willis Carrier (in 1911) realized the impact _____ work would have on later generations.

6. After 1931, a passenger riding on the Baltimore & Ohio railroad could travel to _____ destination in air-conditioned comfort.

7. When Stuart Cramer first used the phrase *air conditioning* in 1906, _____ almost certainly didn't know that _____ newly coined term would be in universal use today.

8. Few people who live in temperate climates or who work in high-rise buildings would want to give up _____ air conditioning in the summer.

EXERCISE 17.4 ❯   *Pronoun-antecedent agreement*

Most pronouns in the following paragraph have been omitted. Insert appropriate pronouns, maintaining correct pronoun-antecedent agreement.

Everyone who works in the United States must pay _____ income taxes on or before April 15. An employee of a traditional business has _____ taxes withdrawn in each pay period and at the end of the year receives _____ yearly statement, the W2 form. Neither employees nor the employer can decide how _____ tax accounts will be handled, but employees determine what percentage of taxes will be taken from _____ wages. For a self-employed taxpayer, the procedure for determining _____ taxes is not so clear. Artists, writers, free-lance contractors, and other people whose incomes fluctuate must estimate _____ incomes for the year and pay _____ taxes in installments. Anyone who has ever tried to estimate how productive _____ will be in the next year can appreciate the difficulty a self-employed person has in estimating how much _____ will owe at the end of the year. In the past, the self-employed were granted some leniency in paying _____ taxes. However, in 1987, in spite of objections from some of _____ constituents, Congress voted to penalize people whose estimated tax payments were less than 90 percent of _____ taxes due.

▪ Maintaining agreement with a word processor

Use the computer's capabilities to discover and correct errors in subject-verb and pronoun-antecedent agreement.

Use the "search" function to locate *and* and *or* and related conjunctions. Check for agreement problems.

Check pronouns and antecedents. Use the "search" codes to locate specific pronouns. Once you have located them, check the sentence to make sure that the antecedent and pronoun are correctly matched in number and gender. If they are not, change either the pronoun or the antecedent. Check masculine pronouns carefully to avoid sexist use.

Revise agreement errors. Use the "delete" and "insert" capabilities to change verbs and pronouns that do not agree with their subjects or antecedents.

Experiment with solutions to agreement errors. Convert all nouns to plurals, for example, to avoid problems with sexist use of pronouns.

18 Pronoun Case

The case of a pronoun indicates the pronoun's grammatical relationship to the other words in the sentence. Pronoun case is indicated by changes in form (*I, me, or mine*, for example) or by changes in position in the sentence, as in the following example.

```
subj.    obj.  poss.
case     case  case
  |       |     |
I gave them his address.
```

Quick Reference

Follow these rules and suggestions to avoid problems with pronoun case.

▶ *Personal pronouns used as subjects in clauses and sentences require the subjective case (* I, he, we, *and* they, *for example); pronouns used as objects require the objective case (*me, him, us, *and* them, *for example).*

▶ *Use a personal pronoun in the possessive case (*my, his, our, *and* their, *for example) to modify a noun or a gerund.*

▶ *Distinguish among* who *and* whoever *(the subjective-case forms),* whom *and* whomever *(the objective-case forms), and* whose *(the possessive-case form).*

▶ *Do not confuse possessive-case pronouns (for example,* its*) with contractions (for example,* it's*, meaning "it is").*

Nouns and pronouns used as subjects or predicate nouns are in the **subjective case.** Nouns or pronouns used as direct objects, indirect objects, or objects of prepositions are in the **objective case.** Nouns or pronouns used to show ownership are in the possessive case.

Case Forms of Personal Pronouns

	Subjective	*Objective*	*Possessive*
Singular			
1st person	I	me	my, mine
2nd person	you	you	your, yours
3rd person	he, she, it	him, her, it	his, hers, its
Plural			
1st person	we	us	our, ours
2nd person	you	you	your, yours
3rd person	they	them	their, theirs

Case Forms of *Who* and Related Pronouns

Subjective	*Objective*	*Possessive*
who	whom	whose
whoever	whomever	

Most pronouns and all nouns in the subjective case (*someone, Alicia*) form the possessive case by adding *'s* (*someone's, Alicia's*). The objective case is most frequently indicated by change of position.

Personal pronouns and relative pronouns produced with variations of *who* change forms in all three cases.

>>> *Do not confuse possessive-case pronouns that do not use an apostrophe (*his, her, its, ours, your, yours, their, theirs, and *whose) with contractions that sound the same:* it's *("it is"),* there's *("there is"), and* who's *("who is").* **<<<**

<hr>

| 18a | > | **Pronouns used as subjects or as predicate nouns require the subjective-case form.** |

Subjective case

Although *he* got a *D* in freshman composition, Faulkner went on to become one of America's most honored writers.

When a sentence has a compound subject, isolate the parts of the subject to help you choose the appropriate pronoun.

Compound subject

Just after sunrise, Kendal and *she* waded into the stream to fish. (Kendal waded; *she* waded; consequently, *Kendal and she* waded.)

A predicate noun restates the subject and so requires the subjective case. Sometimes, however, this construction sounds excessively formal. Observe this pronoun-case rule in formal writing, but consider revising your sentence for less formal writing contexts. For example, invert the subject and predicate noun.

We discovered that "the mad scribbler" was *he*.   (The predicate noun, signaled by the linking verb *was,* must be in the subjective case.)

We discovered that *he* was "the mad scribbler."   (This sentence sounds less formal but is still correct.)

18b >	**Pronouns used as direct objects, indirect objects, or objects of prepositions require the objective-case form.**

A direct object answers the question *whom* or *what.* An indirect object answers the question *to whom* or *for whom.* Pronouns that answer these questions should be in the objective case.

Direct object

> Susan B. Anthony challenged sexist and racist assumptions; we should respect *her* for that.

Indirect object

> Although Rasputin was feared by the Russian nobility, Czar Nicholas and Czarina Alexandra gave *him* their absolute trust.

Object of preposition

> The Medici family supported the arts in Renaissance Florence; many of the greatest works of Michelangelo, Leonardo, and Botticelli were created for *them.*

≫ *When a preposition has a compound object, isolate the parts of the object to help you choose the appropriate pronoun.*

The contract had to be signed by both *him* and Eileen.   (by *him;* by Eileen) **≪**

18c | **Pronouns showing ownership or modifying a gerund require the possessive-case form.**

Possessive Pronouns Used with Nouns

The possessive pronouns *my, your, his, her, its, our, your,* and *their* modify nouns. They act as adjectives in sentences and are sometimes called pronoun-adjectives.

> Although *my* exam scores and Wilma's were better than *Sasha's* scores, *her* speeches were clearly the best.   (The pronouns in the possessive case serve as pronoun-adjectives.)

Possessive Pronouns Used Alone

The possessive pronouns *mine, yours, his, hers, its, ours, yours,* and *theirs* are sometimes used alone as subjects, predicate nouns, direct objects, indirect objects, or objects of prepositions.

> The blue car outside is *mine; his* is the red one.   (Both pronouns are in the possessive case, but *mine* works as a predicate noun and *his* as a subject.)

Possessive Pronouns Modifying a Gerund

When modifying a gerund (an *-ing* verb that functions as a noun), pronouns must be in the possessive case, serving as pronoun-adjectives.

> I was annoyed by *his* interrupting the speaker.   (The annoyance resulted from the person's *interrupting,* not from the person himself.)

> The director commented that *their* dancing was the best part of the musical number.   (The best part was their *dancing,* not them.)

> **18d** Sentence structure determines the case of pronouns in appositives, with nouns, and in elliptical constructions.

Pronouns in Appositives

When a pronoun in an appositive restates the subject of a clause, use the subjective case. When a pronoun in an appositive restates an object, use the objective case.

> The two assistant managers, Gerald and *he,* were responsible for preparing the quarterly reports.   (Because *Gerald and he* restates the subject of the sentence, the pronoun must be in the subjective case.)

> Certificates of merit were given to the runners-up, Abigail and *her.* (*Abigail and her* restates *runners-up,* the object of the preposition, so the pronoun must be in the objective case.)

We or *Us* with Nouns

When using *we* or *us* with a noun, choose the case that would be correct if the noun were omitted.

> I think that *we* bicyclists should demand special cycling lanes on campus.   (Without *bicyclists,* the clause reads *we should,* a correct use of the subjective case.)

> Organizational policy prohibits *us* committee members from meeting informally.   (*Members* is a direct object, so the adjoining pronoun must be in the objective case.)

Pronouns in Elliptical Constructions

In **elliptical constructions** (constructions in which words are omitted or understood), use the case that would be appropriate if all the words were included. If the pronoun used alone sounds too formal, add the omitted words.

The Piersons arrived twenty minutes later than *we*. (The complete thought is that they arrived twenty minutes later than *we arrived*.)

EXERCISE 18.1 ❯ *Pronoun case*

Supply the correct pronouns in the following sentences.

1. Hans Christian Andersen, the son of a shoemaker, began _____ adult life as an actor.

2. _____ failed on the stage, but because the king granted _____ a scholarship, Andersen was able to begin _____ writing career.

3. _____ writing of novels, plays, and long poems is almost completely forgotten, but almost everyone knows a few of _____ best fairy tales.

4. Ironically, Andersen did not set out to write fairy tales, but _____ wrote _____ first four to make money quickly.

5. Those stories succeeded beyond _____ expectations, and subsequently European nobility and royalty honored _____ for _____ work.

6. Although Andersen's tales may not be as well known as those of the brothers Grimm, _____ use of irony and humor, rather than violence, makes _____ work very appealing.

7. "The Emperor's New Clothes," one of _____ most ironic tales, alienated _____ from some of _____ noble patrons.

8. Today's readers, however, can enjoy the irony without insult and take delight in what was, for _____, a troublesome piece.

9. The best children's writers — and _____ is among them — delight us as children and intrigue us as adults, providing in simple tales some lessons on life.

10. If you think about Andersen as a failed actor who became a world-famous writer of fairy tales, you'll discover why "The Ugly Duckling" was one of ———— favorites; in a professional sense, at least, it was ———— story.

| 18e > | **Distinguish between the subjective-case forms** ***who*** **and** ***whoever*** **and the objective-case forms** ***whom*** **and** ***whomever.*** |

Use the subjective-case forms *who* and *whoever* as subjects of sentences, clauses, and questions. Use the objective-case forms *whom* and *whomever* as direct objects, indirect objects, and objects of prepositions.

Who and *Whoever*

Who among us has not heard of the lost city of Atlantis? (*Who* is the subject of the question.)

Salvador Dali was an artist *who* took delight in shocking his contemporaries. (*Who* is the subject of the clause.)

The foundation will offer a scholarship to *whoever* writes the most creative essay. (*Whoever* is the subject of the clause; although the preposition *to* might suggest that the objective case is required, the whole clause, not the word *whoever,* is the object of the preposition.)

Whom and *Whomever*

Whom should we invite to speak to the alumni? (*Whom* is the direct object of *invite.*)

The board will approve the appointment of *whomever* we select. (*Whomever* is the direct object of the last clause.)

Use the "search" feature to locate *who, whoever, whom,* and *whomever.* Then double-check the sentence to be sure that you have used them correctly. If you have not, use the "delete" and "add" functions of your word processor to make necessary changes.

EXERCISE 18.2 ❯ *Pronoun case*

Use who, whom, whoever, and whomever correctly in the following sentences.

1. The Better Business Bureau, a nonprofit organization, was founded to help people ———————— are victims of questionable business methods and deceptive advertising.

2. Consumers should first address complaints to ———————— has acted in an unbusinesslike manner.

3. The Better Business Bureau is a group to ———————— consumers can turn if they still are not satisfied.

4. The Better Business Bureau will answer questions and suggest strategies to ———————— calls, but it will not take legal action against suspected businesses.

5. Since the Better Business Bureau refers cases to government agencies, however, it helps ensure that businesspeople ———————— are unethical do not continue to exploit consumers.

EXERCISE 18.3 ❯ *Pronoun case*

Indicate whether the italicized pronouns in the following paragraph are in the subjective, objective, or possessive case. Be ready to explain your decisions.

When *I* came out of prison, — for some one interfered, and paid that tax, — *I* did not perceive that great changes had taken place on the

common, such as *he* observed *who* went in a youth and emerged a
tottering and grey-headed man; and yet a change had to *my* eyes come
over the scene, — the town, and State, and country, — greater than
any that mere time could effect. *I* saw yet more distinctly the State in
which *I* lived. *I* saw to what extent the people among *whom I* lived
could be trusted as good neighbors and friends; that *their* friendship
was for summer weather only; that *they* did not greatly propose to do
right; that *they* were a distinct race from *me* by *their* prejudices and
superstitions, as the Chinamen and Malays are; that in *their* sacrifices to
humanity *they* ran no risks, not even to *their* property; that after all *they*
were not so noble but *they* treated the thief as *he* had treated *them,* and
hoped, by a certain outward observance and a few prayers, and by
walking in a particular straight though useless path from time to time,
to save *their* souls. This may be to judge *my* neighbors harshly; for *I*
believe that many of *them* are not aware that *they* have such an institu-
tion as the jail in *their* village. — Henry David Thoreau, "Civil
Disobedience"

19 Verb Tenses

Tenses are the forms of verbs that indicate when things happened or existed in relation to when they are described. Tenses also indicate whether an action or state of being continued over time or whether it has been completed. Tenses are formed through the use of auxiliary verbs and changes in verb endings.

Quick Reference

Verbs, along with subjects, form the core of sentences. The use of effective verbs will strengthen your writing.

> ❯ *Use the correct verb tense and form to express your meaning accurately.*

> ❯ *Use present tense to describe beliefs, scientific principles, works of art, and repeated or habitual actions.*

> ❯ *Use sequences of tenses correctly to clarify the time relations in your writing.*

> ❯ *Use verb mood correctly to indicate your opinion on the factuality or probability of your sentence.*

Regular Verbs

Regular verbs form tenses according to consistent patterns. (For an example of a full conjugation of the verb *to learn,* see page 302.)

To Learn

Present tense	learn(s)
Past tense	learn*ed*
Future tense	*will* (or *shall*) learn
Present perfect tense	*have* (or *has*) learn*ed*
Past perfect tense	*had* learn*ed*
Future perfect tense	*will* (or *shall*) *have* learn*ed*
Progressive tenses	
Present progressive	am (are) learning
Past progressive	was (were) learning
Future progressive	will be learning
Present perfect progressive	has (have) been learning
Past perfect progressive	had been learning
Future perfect progressive	will have been learning

Irregular Verbs

Irregular verbs form tenses through changes in word form.

To Go

Present tense	go(es)
Past tense	went
Future tense	will (or shall) go
Present perfect tense	have (or has) gone
Past perfect tense	had gone
Future perfect tense	will (or shall) have gone

≫≫ *The progressive tenses of irregular verbs (I am going, I was going, and so on) are formed regularly.* **≪≪**

| 19a | Use the simple tenses to describe actions or conditions occurring or completed within the time specified. |

The simple tenses are the **present, past,** and **future.**

Present Tense

Use the present tense to describe events occurring or conditions existing in the present.

He *concedes* your point.

In addition, there are some special uses of the present tense.

Repeated or Habitual Actions

Use the present tense to describe a habitual or frequently repeated action or series of actions or to explain standard procedures.

Air traffic controllers *work* long, tension-filled shifts.

Deposit a coin into the slot; *wait* for the tone; then *dial* the number.

General Beliefs and Scientific Principles

Use the present tense to assert accepted beliefs.

Every child *deserves* adequate nutrition, clothing, housing, and a good education.

Express scientific and other principles in the present tense.

> The force of gravity *determines* the flow of water in rivers and streams.

> *Do* unto others as you would have them *do* unto you.

Descriptions of Works of Art

Use the present tense to describe and discuss works of art — literature, music, dance, painting — prehistoric through contemporary.

> In Coleridge's *Rime of the Ancient Mariner,* the narrator *learns* and compulsively *repeats* to others the lesson of the sacredness of all life.

> Picasso's *Guernica contains* images of chaos and terror.

Past Tense

Use the past tense to describe actions completed or conditions that existed in the past. In writing, you use the past tense more often than any other tense because much of what you write about has already occurred.

> Henry Ford *created* the Model T but, more importantly, *perfected* the industrial assembly line.

Future Tense

Use the future tense to describe actions or conditions that will or are expected to occur or exist in the future.

> The committee *will hold* its next meeting in Geneva, Switzerland.

| 19b | Use the perfect tenses to describe actions or conditions in relation to other actions or conditions. |

The perfect tenses are the **present perfect, past perfect,** and **future perfect.**

Present Perfect Tense

Use the present perfect tense to describe actions that occurred or conditions that existed at an unspecified time in the past or that began in the past and continue to the present.

> Since I *took* a music appreciation class, Beethoven's piano concertos *have been* favorites of mine.   (*Took* is in the past tense because the class is over; *have been* is in the present perfect tense because the preference began in the past and continues to the present.)

Past Perfect Tense

Use the past perfect tense to describe past actions or conditions that were completed before some other past action or condition.

> Until Lincoln *was elected* in 1860, the Republican party *had achieved* very little since its founding in 1854.   (*Had achieved* establishes the limited success of Republicans before the other past event, Lincoln's election.)

Future Perfect Tense

Use the future perfect tense to describe actions that will be completed or conditions that will exist in the future but before a specific time.

> Almost all businesses *will have converted* to computerized bookkeeping by the turn of the century.   (The "turn of the century" is in the future. Converting to computerized booking will also be in the future, but before A.D. 2000.)

| 19c | Use the progressive tenses to describe actions or conditions beginning, continuing, or ending within the present, past, or future. |

Progressive tenses stress the continuing nature of actions or conditions.

> The Japanese *are sharing* a large part of the costs for operating the United Nations.   (The present progressive tense shows a continuous action.)

> The American government *has been supporting* the United Nations since its founding.   (The present perfect progressive tense describes a continuing process that began in the past.)

》》》 *To avoid unnecessary wordiness, use the progressive tenses only when necessary to express continuing actions or states.*

> The president was trying to avert an increase in the minimum wage.

> The president tried to avert an increase in the minimum wage.   **《《《**

| 19d | Use tenses in logical sequences to show precisely and accurately the relationships among actions and conditions. |

Verb tense signals chronology, indicating when actions occurred or conditions existed in relation to when they are described. Logical sequences of tenses clarify the relationship among actions and conditions.

Sequences of present and past tenses cause few problems for writers, but more complicated verb-tense sequences may. Use the following rules for guidance.

Infinitives

Infinitives (*to swim, to subscribe, to record*) assume the tense indicated by the main verb.

> Brainwashing *attempts to convince* people *to give up* their beliefs. (The infinitives coordinate with the present-tense verb.)

> Fidel Castro *led* the revolution *to overthrow* Cuba's dictator and subsequently *guided* the country's efforts *to institute* Communist reforms. (The infinitives automatically coordinate with the past-tense verbs.)

Present Participles

The present participle, like the infinitive, assumes the tense of the main verb.

> *Having* a fixed rate of interest, bonds *appeal* to wary investors more than stocks do.

> *Speaking* to the American people in his first inaugural address, Franklin Roosevelt *reassured* them that "the only thing we have to fear is fear itself."

Past Participles and Perfect Participles

Past participles (*hurried, welcomed, driven*) and perfect participles (*having hurried, having welcomed, having driven*) indicate that the action or condition they describe occurred before that of the main verb.

> *Dressed* as a man, Aurore Dupin (who used the pen name George Sand) *attended* the theater when women were not allowed to go.

> *Having won* a record nine gold medals in Olympic swimming, Mark Spitz retired from competition.

Use of Tenses in a Subordinate Clause

Past Tense or Past Perfect Tense in a Subordinate Clause

When the verb in an independent clause is in the past or the past perfect tense, the verb in the subordinate clause must also be in the past or the past perfect tense.

Once scientists *discovered* that fluorocarbons damage the ozone layer that protects the Earth from ultraviolet radiation, environmentalists *protested* against their use in commercial products.   (The use of the past tense *protested* in the independent clause establishes that this series of actions took place in the past.)

Before bacteria and viruses *were* discovered, diseases *had been explained* in superstitious ways.   (The use of the past perfect *had been explained* establishes that nonscientific explanations existed before the scientific ones.)

Present, Future, Present Perfect, or Future Perfect Tense in a Subordinate Clause

When the verb in the independent clause is in the present, future, present perfect, or future perfect tense, any tense can be used in the subordinate clause. These tenses and combinations of tenses create numerous possibilities for expressing chronological relationships precisely and accurately. Be sure to arrange the tenses logically so that your meaning is clear.

Some scientists currently *think* that exercise *will prolong* life.

Although Molière's *Tartuffe was written* in 1665, its comments on religious hypocrisy and exploitation still *have* meaning today.   (Literature of the past still speaks to contemporary audiences.)

| 19e | Use the mood of a verb to indicate your opinion on the probability or factuality of your sentence. |

Verbs in English may have one of three moods: indicative, imperative, or subjunctive. Grammatical mood does not refer to or equal psychological mood; the word *mood* in the grammatical sense derives from "mode," meaning "manner," the way in which something appears, is done, or happens.

Definition and Use of Moods

Using the **indicative mood,** writers make statements or ask questions about conditions or actions that they consider facts.

> Air travel is one of the safest modes of transportation.

Using the **imperative mood,** writers make statements (commands) about actions or conditions that they consider should or must become facts.

> Buckle your seat belt and observe the no-smoking sign.   (The subject, *you,* is omitted or understood, as is generally the case in the imperative.)

Using the **subjunctive mood,** writers make statements or ask questions about actions or conditions that they doubt, wish for, or consider hypothetical or contrary to fact.

> If the terminal were redesigned, airport security would be easy to maintain.   (Note that *both* clauses express conditional, nonfactual states: The terminal has not been redesigned, and security is not easy to maintain.)

» *Clauses beginning with* if *use the indicative when they describe factual conditions, as in the following example:*

> If the terminal was redesigned, it was difficult to see any improvement. (Both clauses are in the indicative past tense because they describe actual events and perceptions.) **«**

The subjunctive, which can sound extremely formal and even stilted, is now rarely used in English, except for conditional expressions, such as the example above, and other idiomatic expressions, such as the following:

Let it *be*.

God *save* the Queen!

I move that the committee secretary *forward* the report to the mayor.

He asks that his privacy *be* respected.

Forming the Moods

Most expressions in English are in the indicative mood, which is formed using any and all of the verb tenses covered in 19a through 19c above. The imperative mood is formed using the present tense, as in the example above.

Only the subjunctive has distinct forms. The verb *to be* in the subjunctive differs from its indicative forms in both the present and the past tense; the forms, identical in the singular and plural, are, respectively, *be* and *were*.

If the report *be* true, let us act quickly.   (present tense)

If she *were* in charge, she would have acted.   (past tense)

Subjunctive forms for verbs other than *to be* differ from the indicative only in the third person singular of the present tense, in which the -s ending is dropped.

May the weather *continue* clear.

This last example illlustrates the sometimes excessively formal tone of statements in the subjunctive. Often, a correct version in the indicative can be substituted.

If the report is true, we should act quickly.

I hope that the clear weather continues.

>>> *If you choose to use the subjunctive, remember to use the correct forms and to use them consistently in related clauses or sentences.* <<<

EXERCISE 19.1 ❯ *Tenses*

Revise the following sentences, written primarily in the present tense, by changing them into the past tense.

1. The design team for the theater production meet to review the script for the play.

2. They talk about specific concerns and mention any special needs they should consider.

3. The discussion turns to potential problems in lighting the production, as it always does, because the theater — a renovated movie house — is modified less than is needed.

4. The lighting designer says, once again, that the theater will need major electrical work before a computerized lighting system can be installed.

5. Completing the discussion of lighting, the team turns its attention to the set for the play.

6. The play chosen — *Who's Afraid of Virginia Woolf?* — requires a single set, one room in a history professor's house.

7. The designers describe productions they have seen.

8. The costumer describes a production that was done in Baltimore.

9. The lighting designer remembers a collegiate production she saw in Iowa.

10. The director says he wants this set to be more realistic in its details than others he has seen.

11. As is usually the case, the team leaves after the first meeting, having made only a few key decisions.

EXERCISE 19.2 ❯ Tenses

Identify the tenses of the numbered verbs in the following paragraphs. Be prepared to explain why each tense is used.

Are owls truly wise? The Greeks (1) *thought* so, identifying them with Athena, goddess of wisdom. In medieval illustrations, owls (2) *accompany* Merlin and share in his sorcery. In fairytales they rival the fox for cunning. Children's picture books (3) *show* them wearing spectacles, mortarboard, and scholar's gown. Soups and other confections made from owls (4) *have been credited* with curing whooping cough, drunkenness, epilepsy, famine, and insomnia. The Cherokee Indians used to bathe their children's eyes with a broth of owl feathers to keep the kids awake at night. Recipes using owl eggs (5) *are reputed* to bestow keen eyesight and wisdom. Yet these birds are no smarter, ornithologists (6) *assure* us, than most others. A museum guide in Boston once (7) *displayed* a drowsy-looking barn owl on his gloved wrist, (8) *explaining* to those of us assembled there how small the bird's brain actually was. "You (9) [*will*] *notice* the head of this live specimen appears to be about the size of a grapefruit," he said, "but it's mostly feathers." Lifting his other hand, he (10) *added,* "The skull, you (11) *see,* is the size of a lemon. There's only room enough inside for a bird-brain, not enough for Einstein!" We all laughed politely. But I was not convinced. Sure, the skull (12) *was* small. The lower half was devoted to jaw and most of the upper half to beak and eye-holes. Yet enough neurons could be fitted into the remaining space to enable the barn owl to catch mice in total darkness. They can even snatch bats on the wing, these princes of nighttime stealth. We have to invent sonar for locating submarines, radar for locating airplanes; neither (13) *is* much use with mice or bats. Barn owls can also see dead — and therefore silent — prey in light one-hundredth as bright as we would need. Like the ability to saw a board square or judge the consistency of bread dough, that might not

amount to scholarship, but it (14) *is* certainly a wisdom of the body. It
(15) *has worked* for some sixty million years. — Scott Sanders, "Listening to Owls"

EXERCISE 19.3 ❯ *Mood*

*Where appropriate, revise the verbs in the following sentences to cor-
rect their use of mood.*

1. Increasingly, working parents in the United States are asking that
   every employer acknowledges the childcare problem.

2. A single parent especially often wishes a company-operated childcare facility was available at or near his or her place of work.

3. Lateness would probably decline if a parent was able to make one
   trip to a single location, instead of a trip to a childcare facility and
   then a separate trip to work.

4. If Congress was to partially subsidize childcare facilities, many companies might help their employees by providing on-site childcare.

5. But even if a company was to provide on-site childcare, problems in
   assuring sufficient daycare facilities would still exist.

Adjectives and Adverbs

Most writers naturally use adjectives and adverbs correctly. Occasionally, however, they misuse adjectives and adverbs because they do not think carefully about which word they are modifying. The following guidelines should help to solve most problems in adjective and adverb usage.

Quick Reference

Adjectives and adverbs refine the meaning of a sentence, but to do so effectively they must be used correctly.

❯ *Use adjectives to modify nouns and pronouns.*

❯ *Use adverbs to modify verbs, adjectives, and other adverbs.*

❯ *Use positive adjective and adverb forms when no comparison is made; use comparative forms to compare two items; use superlative forms to compare three or more items.*

❯ *Distinguish between troublesome adjective and adverb pairs.*

20a ❯ **Adjectives modify nouns and pronouns.**

Make sure that the word modifying a noun or pronoun is an adjective. Isolate the word and its modifier, placing the modifier first, to see if the pair sounds correct. When you are uncertain, consult a dictionary to find the correct adjective form.

Treasure Island, an *adventure* novel by Robert Louis Stevenson, is a classic of *adolescent* fiction.   (*Adventure* modifies *novel; adolescent* modifies *fiction.*)

Jim Hawkins, the *young* hero, is *resourceful* and *brave.*   (*Young* modifies *hero; resourceful* and *brave* modify *Jim Hawkins.*)

20b	Adverbs modify verbs, adjectives, and other adverbs.

Make sure that the word modifying a verb is an adverb. Isolate the pair of words to see if the pair sounds correct. The adverb should make sense before or after the verb. When you are uncertain of a word's adverb form, consult a dictionary.

H. G. Wells, a political and social reformer in Victorian England, is *best* known *today* for two brief works: *The War of the Worlds* and *The Time Machine.*   (*Best* and *today* both modify *is known.*)

Adverbs that modify adjectives and other adverbs are intensifiers, stressing the specific modifications of the primary modifier. Because some intensifiers — *very, especially, really,* and *truly* — are used so frequently, they may have the paradoxical effect of weakening the impact of your statement. Use them only when they are necessary to your meaning.

Unfortunately, Wells' ingenious science fiction has spawned some *very* bad science fiction films.   (*Very* intensifies the adjective *bad.*)

⟩⟩⟩ *This sentence would be improved if the writer substituted a single, stronger adjective (for example,* appalling *or* dreadful*) or a more specific, descriptive adjective (for example,* boring, unbelievable, *or* exploitative*) for* very bad. **⟨⟨⟨**

| 20c | Use positive, comparative, and superlative adjectives and adverbs correctly. |

Positive Adjectives and Adverbs

Positive adjectives and adverbs imply no comparisons: *recent, soon, clearly, fortunate*.

                                           adj.   *adj.*

The set for *The Passion of Dracula* was *ornate* and *eerie*.

                                           adv.

The scene changes were made *quickly*.

Comparative Adjectives and Adverbs

Comparative adjectives and adverbs establish differences between two similar people, places, things, ideas, qualities, conditions, or actions. Adjectives and adverbs form comparatives in two ways. One-syllable modifiers add the suffix *-er*: *sooner, paler*. (See also the table of irregular adjectives and adverbs on page 318.) Multisyllable modifiers use *more* or *less* to form the comparative: *less easily, more recent*. **》》** *A number of two- and three-syllable adjectives use the -er form (and -est for the superlative). Use the -er and -est forms with multisyllable words that have the following characteristics:*

"Voiced" last syllables: *pretty, narrow*

L sound in the last syllable: *simple*

Accent on the last syllable: *severe*

Consult a dictionary if you are unsure of how to form a specific comparative or superlative. **《《**

                                comp. adj.   *comp. adj.*
                                     | |

The set for *The Passion of Dracula* was *more ornate* and *eerier* than anyone expected.

                                          comp. adv.
                                          |

The scene changes for this production were made *more quickly* than they were for *Hedda Gabler*.

Superlative Adjectives and Adverbs

Superlative adjectives and adverbs compare a person, place, thing, idea, quality, condition, or action with three or more similar items. Superlatives are the most emphatic adjective and adverb forms. One-syllable words form the superlative by adding the suffix -*est* : *soonest, palest*. Multisyllable adjectives and adverbs generally form the superlative by using *most* or *least: least easily, most recent*. (But see also the note on exceptions under the discussion of comparative forms on page 316.)

                              super. adj.   *super. adj.*
                                     | |

The set for *The Passion of Dracula* was the *most dramatic* and *eeriest* one I have seen.

During this production season, the scene changes in *Dracula* were
        super. adv.
          |
made *most quickly*.

Several adjectives form the comparative and superlative irregularly, using neither suffixes nor helping words, but changing their spellings completely.

Positive	Comparative	Superlative
bad	worse	worst
good	better	best
little	less / littler	least / littlest
many much some	more	most
well	better	best
badly	worse	worst

Double Comparatives and Superlatives

Only one change is needed to form the comparative or superlative of an adjective or adverb. To use both a suffix and a helping word is unnecessary and incorrect.

Incorrect

Madonna rose to superstardom *more faster* than even she expected.

Correct

Madonna rose to superstardom *faster* than even she expected.

Incorrect

Kliban's cartoons of cats are the *most funniest* ones I have seen.

Correct

Kliban's cartoons of cats are the *funniest* ones I have seen.

Incomparable Adjectives

Because of their meanings, some adjectives cannot suggest comparisons of any kind. Examples of such words are *central, dead, empty, impossible, infinite, perfect, straight,* and *unique.* Use only the positive form of such modifiers.

Incorrect

James Joyce's *Ulysses* was the *most unique* novel I have read. (*Unique* means "one of a kind.")

Correct

James Joyce's *Ulysses* is a *unique* novel.   (This sentence uses *unique* in its proper, positive form.)

Correct

James Joyce's *Ulysses* was the *most unusual* novel I have read.   (*Unusual* is a quality that can be compared.)

| 20d | Distinguish carefully between troublesome adjective and adverb pairs. |

Use *bad,* the adjective form, to modify nouns and pronouns, even with sensory or linking verbs (*appear, feel, look, smell, taste, sound,* and forms of *to be*). Use *badly* only to modify a verb.

That was a *bad* rendition of *Rhapsody in Blue*.

After sitting in the sun for two hours, Monica felt *bad*.

After dozens of art classes, Anita still painted *badly*.

Use *good,* the adjective form, only to modify a noun or pronoun. Use *well* as an adverb to mean *satisfactory;* use *well* as an adjective to mean *healthy*.

Marco was a very *good* pianist.

The rehearsal went *well* last night.

Although Anton had a slight fever, he said he felt *well* enough to play in Saturday's game.

Other troublesome adjective and adverb pairs appear in the Glossary of Terms.

EXERCISE 20.1   ❯ *Adjective and adverb forms*

Select the appropriate adjective or adverb forms in the following sentences.

1. Current methods of building construction will make homes (affordable/more affordable/most affordable) than they were in the past, without sacrificing quality.

2. Although prefabricated homes have always been (easily/more easily/most easily) constructed than conventionally built homes, they were not always built (good/well).

3. Now, however, factory construction of major structural elements is (increasing/increasingly) impressive.

4. Many home units — like kitchens and bathrooms — are being constructed with their plumbing and wiring embedded in wall units; then these "core construction blocks" are fitted together (quick/quickly/more quickly) in various ways.

5. Because installing plumbing and wiring is (costly/more costly/most costly) than other phases of construction, these "core blocks" keep on-site construction costs (low/lower/lowest).

6. With the money saved from structural costs, a homeowner can concentrate on architectural trim and interior design work that can make his or her home (unique/more unique/most unique).

EXERCISE 20.2   ❯   Adjectives and adverbs

! *Correct the errors in adjective and adverb use in the following paragraph.*

   Tapestries, fabrics with pictures woven into them, were used in medieval churches and palaces more often as decorations but sometimes as insulation in the chilly buildings. The most unique tapestries were produced in Arras, France, where the art of weaving pictures reached its perfectest form in the 1400s. The tapestry makers of Arras worked so good that the word *arras* was soon used as a synonym for *tapestry*. The tapestries that have survived from the 1400s and 1500s are in various states of repair. Some, like the set of tapestries called *The Hunt of the Unicorn*, are in real sound condition. Their colors are still vibrant. The more famous panel of the set shows a unicorn sitting within a circular fence, surrounded by flowers and foliage of the brightest colors. Unfortunately, other tapestries have been treated bad over the centuries, and their colors are faded or their yarns damaged. Weaving tapestries is a most complex craft that has been sporadically and more simplistically revived in the last hundred years, but we will probably never approximate the more intricate and reverential nature of tapestries done in the late Middle Ages.

Using the word processor to evaluate adjective and adverb use

Beyond basic strategies for revision, a word processor can help you to solve special problems with adjectives and adverbs.

Search for intensifiers. Use the "search" codes to find words like *very, really,* and *especially.* Eliminate all of the intensifiers that do not convey crucial meaning.

Search for comparatives and superlatives. Use the "search" codes to find *more, most, less,* and *least.* Then make sure that the comparative or superlative form is aptly chosen. With some word-processing programs, you can search for specific sets of letters, not just separate words. If your program has that capability and if you have special problems with comparatives and superlatives, consider searching for *-er* and *-est* combinations.

PUNCTUATION

21 End Punctuation

Three marks of punctuation end sentences: the period (.), the question mark (?), and the exclamation point (!). These forms of punctuation usually end sentences that have expressed complete thoughts; they also serve a few other purposes.

Quick Reference

End punctuation clearly and simply indicates the end of a sentence and its intended effect.

> *Use periods to end sentences that make statements, issue commands, or ask indirect questions.*

> *Use question marks to end sentences that ask direct questions.*

> *Use exclamation points to end sentences that express strong feeling.*

21a ⟩ **Use periods after sentences making statements, issuing commands, or asking indirect questions.**

Statement
Cigarette smoking is hazardous to your health.

Command
Stop smoking today.

Indirect question

The Surgeon General asked whether the students understood the risks of smoking. (The sentence implies that the Surgeon General asked a question; but the sentence itself is not a question. The word order of the main subject and verb indicates that the sentence is a statement.)

> **21b** ⟩ **Use question marks after direct questions.**

A question mark is one of two indicators of direct questions; the other is inverted word order of the subject and any part of the verb. (Indirect questions end with periods and use normal word order; see section 21a.) The verb in a question may include a helping verb not necessarily present in a statement.

Question

Did the president know of the illegal actions of his advisers?

Statement

The president knew of the illegal actions of his advisers.

》》》 *Some writers use question marks in parentheses to indicate uncertainty. This usage should be avoided in formal writing.*

The Chinese invented paper in A.D. 105(?) but kept it a state secret for hundreds of years.

Better

The Chinese invented paper around A.D. 105 but kept it a state secret for hundreds of years. **《《《**

> **21c** ⟩ **Use exclamation points after sentences and strong interjections to express strong feeling or indicate special emphasis.**

An exclamation point may follow a sentence or an interjection.

Sentence

"I know not what course others may take; but as for me, give me liberty or give me death!" — Patrick Henry

Interjection

"Well! Some people talk of morality, and some of religion, but give me a little snug property." — Maria Edgeworth

Exclamation points should be used sparingly, especially in formal writing. Not many sentences or interjections require the emphasis that exclamation points provide.

EXERCISE 21.1 ⟩ *End punctuation*

! *Add the end punctuation required in the following paragraph, capitalizing where necessary to indicate new sentences.*

Harry Truman, the thirty-third president, was a spirited leader with a penchant for candor he assumed the presidency in 1945, after Franklin Roosevelt's death, and until he left office in 1953 repeatedly challenged assumptions about how presidents ought to behave his presidency was marked by controversy Truman made the decision to drop nuclear bombs on Hiroshima and Nagasaki; he supported the Marshall Plan to help Europe recover from the devastation of World War II; he sent American troops to Korea a sign of his unquestioning acceptance of responsibility for key decisions one of Truman's favorite slogans became nationally known: "the buck stops here" another of his favorites was "if you can't stand the heat, get out of the kitchen" supporters, using

Truman's own flavorful language often shouted this refrain: "give 'em hell, Harry" Truman made many difficult decisions and never attempted to avoid the controversy that resulted or to blame others for his decisions was he a great president that is a judgment best left to history, but he certainly was an honest and an interesting one

Word processing and end punctuation

A word processor will help you to avoid problems with overuse or incorrect use of question marks and exclamation points.

Find and check your use of question marks. Use "search" commands to locate question marks. Check the sentence to make sure that the subject and verb are inverted. If you discover a question mark following an indirect question, revise the sentence or the punctuation.

Find and replace most exclamation points. Use the "search" commands to locate all exclamation points in your papers. For all but the most necessary and emphatic uses, delete the exclamation points and replace them with periods.

22 Commas

Commas separate and clarify the relations among single words, phrases, and clauses. If commas do not appear where they are needed, thoughts can merge or overlap confusingly.

Confusing

As the speaker finished his audience stood to cheer.   (Without a comma after *finished,* the sentence momentarily suggests that the speaker finished the audience.)

Clear

As the speaker finished, his audience stood to cheer.

Quick Reference

Use commas to clarify and separate sentence elements.

❯ *Use commas to separate items in a series.*

❯ *Use commas to separate clauses in compound sentences.*

❯ *Use commas to set off introductory subordinate clauses in complex and compound-complex sentences.*

❯ *Use commas to set off introductory words and phrases that serve as adverbs.*

❯ *Use commas to set off nonrestrictive information.*

❯ *Use commas to set off statements that signal direct quotations.*

> **22a**   Use commas to separate three or more items
> in a series.

Separate a series of three or more parallel words, phrases, or
clauses with commas. Although some writers omit the comma immediately preceding the conjunction, a comma there is always
correct and may prevent confusion.

Nouns or Verbs in a Series

The faces of George Washington, Thomas Jefferson, Abraham Lincoln,
and Theodore Roosevelt are carved into Mount Rushmore.   (Commas
separate each noun in the series.)

A good reporter asks questions directly, listens attentively, and takes
notes accurately and quickly.   (Commas separate all verbs in the
series.)

Adjectives and Adverbs in a Series

When several adjectives independently modify a single noun, use
commas to separate each one. Similarly, when adverbs separately
and equally modify a verb or an adjective, separate them with
commas. No comma separates the last modifier in the series from
the word modified.

The ancient, dilapidated depot is slated for demolition.   (*Ancient*
depot; *dilapidated* depot; each adjective functions independently.)

The ornithologist slowly, calmly, and carefully approached the injured
goose. (*Slowly* approached; *calmly* approached; *carefully* approached; each adverb functions independently.)

»»» *To test the independence of modifiers, reverse the order of the
modifiers or substitute* and *for each comma. If the sentence still makes
sense, the adjectives or adverbs are coordinate and should be sepa-*

*rated by commas. If the sentence does not make sense, the modifiers
are* cumulative *and do not require commas (see section 23d).*

The dilapidated and ancient depot is slated for demolition.   (The
modification is clear, and the sentence makes sense.) **‹‹‹**

Phrases and Clauses in a Series

Phrases

Letters by Churchill, to Churchill, and about Churchill have become
important and valued historical documents.

Clauses

At the turn of the century, the need for social reforms erupted into
pitched battles as muckrakers exposed business corruption, industrial
leaders challenged their accusations, and politicians sided with the
powerful industrialists.

EXERCISE 22.1 ❯ *Commas*

Insert commas where needed in the following sentences.

1. Computers are now commonplace equipment in homes schools
   and businesses.

2. It is amazing how quickly completely and smoothly most people
   have become acclimated to the new technology.

3. Computerized cash registers are now common in grocery stores at
   movie houses in discount stores and even at gas stations.

4. Computers in public and private libraries have made it possible for
   people to search for books print lists of available materials and complete research quickly.

5. Today our mail comes with computer labels our bank statements
   arrive with spread-sheet accounts of transactions and even our grocery store receipts have computer lists of products we've bought.

| 22b | Use commas to separate clauses in compound and compound-complex sentences. |

Compound Sentences

Most independent clauses joined by a coordinating conjunction must be separated by a comma. When the clauses are brief and when no confusion is likely, the comma may be omitted. Using a comma, however, is always correct.

Price supports for dairy products greatly help farmers, and consumers benefit as well.   (Without a comma after *farmers,* the initial reading might inappropriately link *farmers* and *consumers* as direct objects.)

Making mistakes is common but admitting them is not.   (Because these clauses are brief and because confusion is unlikely, the comma may be omitted.)

▶▶▶ *Do not mistakenly place a comma before every coordinating conjunction. Place a comma only before coordinating conjunctions that link independent clauses. Conjunctions that connect only two words, two phrases, or two dependent clauses usually do not require commas.* **◀◀◀**

Compound-Complex Sentences

One comma separates the independent clauses in a compound-complex sentence. When a compound-complex sentence begins with a subordinate clause, however, a comma must also be used to show where the subordinate clause ends and the independent clause begins.

Once people learn to use computers and laser printers, personal publishing becomes possible, and many small organizations print their own materials.

EXERCISE 22.2 ❯ *Commas*

> *Combine these simple sentences to form compound, complex, or compound-complex sentences. Insert any necessary commas.*

1. *Buffalo* is the name usually used to refer to American bison. It is a common name used to describe several hundred kinds of large wild oxen worldwide.

2. Water buffalo in India have been domesticated for centuries. South African buffalo have resisted domestication and run wild. Small buffalo on Pacific islands remain wild as well.

3. In North America, especially on the Great Plains, huge herds of buffalo once roamed. By 1900, the bison population of approximately 20 million was reduced to fewer than six hundred.

4. William Hornaday, an American zoologist, worked to protect the remaining bison. He felt their extinction would be shameful. He encouraged the National Forest Service to build fenced areas for small herds.

5. Today, bison are kept in captivity. They cannot be trained or domesticated. They are of zoological rather than practical interest.

22c	Use commas after most introductory words, phrases, and subordinate clauses.

Introductory Words

Because conjunctive adverbs (*however, subsequently,* and others) and some adverbs are nonrestrictive sentence elements, they must be set off by commas. (See Nonrestrictive Words, pages 334–35.)

Conjunctive adverb

Subsequently, testimony proved that President Nixon was deeply involved in illegal activities.

>>> *A conjunctive adverb used to link compound sentences joined by a semicolon should be followed by a comma.*

Impeachment proceedings seemed imminent; therefore, Nixon resigned from office. **<<<**

Adverb

First, children require good nutrition to grow and learn properly. (The comma prevents confusion; without it, readers might think that *first* is an adjective modifying *children.*)

Introductory Phrases

When a transitional expression (*for example, in other words, in fact,* and others) or an opening prepositional or verbal phrase is used as an adjective or adverb, separate the phrase from the rest of the sentence with a comma.

Transitional expression

For example, most organization newsletters are now generated by laser printers to achieve the look of typeset copy without the cost.

Prepositional phrase

After twenty years of promoting feminist causes, the National Organization for Women has achieved some of its goals but continues to address new ones.   (The comma signals the end of the introductory phrase and the beginning of the main idea of the sentence.)

>>> *If an introductory prepositional phrase is brief and if the meaning is clear without a comma, the comma may be omitted.*

In April Americans pay income taxes. **<<<**

Verbal phrase

Crouching in a makeshift hut of sticks and grasses, Jane Goodall observed the chimpanzees at play.   (The introductory participial phrase is adjectival, modifying *Goodall.*)

Introductory Subordinate Clauses

When a subordinate clause begins a sentence, use a comma to separate it from the independent clause that follows.

> Because mosquitoes are such a problem in southern coastal cities like New Orleans, city workers spray with insecticides each evening. (The comma marks the end of the subordinate clause.)

EXERCISE 22.3   ❯   *Commas*

 Insert commas where needed in the following sentences.

1. Built during the third and fourth centuries the catacombs of Rome are the most famous in the world.

2. Intended for use as burial sites the passages and rooms were used for other purposes too.

3. According to legend early Christians kept the bodies of Saint Peter and Saint Paul hidden for a time in the catacombs.

4. In addition Christians often took refuge in the catacombs because the catacombs were protected by Roman law.

5. Curiously use of the Roman catacombs ceased in A.D. 400.

| 22d | ❯ | **Use commas to separate nonrestrictive information from the rest of a sentence.** |

Restrictive information, essential to the meaning of a sentence, supplies the distinctions that give ideas the specificity intended by the writer. Such information is not set off by commas. Nonrestrictive information does not supply distinctions central to the meaning of a sentence. Because nonrestrictive information can be omitted, it is set off by commas from the rest of the sentence. Nonrestrictive elements may be single words, phrases, or clauses.

Nonrestrictive Words

Conjunctive Adverbs

Use commas to set off conjunctive adverbs. When they appear at the beginning or end of a sentence, use one comma to set them off. When they appear in the middle of a sentence, use two commas.

At end of sentence

Many people admired Nixon's command of international policy. They remained suspicious of his politics, however.

In midsentence

Newspaper reports suggested Nixon's involvement in Watergate. The president, however, claimed he had committed no crimes.

The words *yes* and *no,* mild interjections, and names in direct address

Use commas to separate the words *yes* and *no,* interjections, and names in direct address from the rest of a sentence.

Yes *and direct address*

"Yes, Virginia, there is a Santa Claus." — Francis Church   (The comma after *yes* separates it from the rest of the sentence; the comma after *Virginia* separates this name used in direct address.)

Interjection

Okay, so it was Franklin who said, "In this world nothing is certain but death and taxes."

Nonrestrictive Phrases

Transitional Expressions

Transitional expressions (*for example, as a result,* and so on) are nonrestrictive and should therefore be separated from the rest of the sentence. Use a single comma if the expression appears at the beginning or end of a sentence; use two commas if it appears in the middle of a sentence.

Nixon has, in fact, remained an astute commentator on foreign affairs.

Absolute Phrases

Absolute phrases modify entire sentences. Because these phrases are nonrestrictive, they must be set off by commas. Use a single comma if the phrase appears at the beginning or end of a sentence; use two commas if it appears in the middle of a sentence.

At end of sentence
Franklin Roosevelt was the first president to fly in a commercial airplane, a fact unknown to most people.

In midsentence
Gandhi, the goal of Indian independence achieved, retired from public life.

Prepositional and Verbal Phrases

When prepositional and verbal phrases supply information that is not essential to the meaning of a sentence, use commas to set them off from the rest of the sentence.

Prepositional phrase
J. D. Salinger, above all else, values his privacy.   (The prepositional phrase *above all else* requires commas because it can be omitted without substantially altering the sentence's meaning.)

Verbal phrase

M*A*S*H*, challenging idealized assumptions about war, achieved surprising success.

Appositives

Appositives restate proper nouns. Nonrestrictive appositives add clarifying but not essential information and are set off by commas.

Frank Lloyd Wright, an architect in the early twentieth century, felt that the design of a building should be suited to its surrounding.

Nonrestrictive Clauses

Nonrestrictive clauses that begin with a relative pronoun *(which, who, whose, whom, whoever,* and *whomever)* can be omitted without substantially changing the meaning of a sentence. Because they are not essential, nonrestrictive clauses must be set off by commas.

The Starry Night, which is prominently displayed in the Museum of Modern Art in New York, exemplifies Van Gogh's use of rich colors applied in bold strokes.   (The information in the relative clause is set off by commas because it does not add to the essential meaning of the sentence.)

Picasso, who became one of the most successful and wealthiest artists in the world, started out ignored and impoverished during his early days in Paris.

| 22e | Use commas to set off sentence elements that express contrast. |

Because words and phrases that provide contrasting details do not function grammatically as parts of a sentence, they should be separated from the rest of a sentence by commas.

Shaw's first love was music, not theater.

The BBC, unlike American public television networks, is completely financed by the government.

EXERCISE 22.4 ❯ *Commas*

Insert commas where needed in the following sentences.

1. *Beowulf* which is one of the earliest examples of Anglo-Saxon literature still appeals to those who like adventure stories not only to scholars.

2. The character Beowulf with a combination of heroic and religious qualities goes to the aid of Hrothgar the leader of a noble tribe.

3. The most famous episode of *Beowulf* the battle between Beowulf and the monster Grendel is a marvelous mix of supernatural and traditional Christian elements.

4. *Beowulf* is a historical-literary milestone; it is however a popular classic as well.

5. The plot elements of *Beowulf* — fights with supernatural beasts and tests of moral strength for example — remain standard elements in today's science fiction films perhaps explaining why *Beowulf* remains so popular.

Use commas to set off expressions that signal direct quotations.

[ex]s separate expressions such as *he said* and *she commented*
[ ]e quotations they identify. These expressions can be used
[ ]ginning, in the middle, or at the end of a quotation. Note
[ ]omma precedes the opening quotation mark.

[ ]going battle of wits, Lady Astor once said to Winston Churchill,
[ ]nston, if you were my husband, I should flavor your coffee with
poison."

"Madam," Churchill replied, "if I were your husband, I should drink it."

Or:

"Madam, if I were your husband, I should drink it," Churchill replied.

22g ⮞ **Use commas according to convention in numbers, dates, addresses, place names, and titles.**

For easy reading and comprehension, most numbers of one thousand or more are divided by placing a comma between groups of three digits, moving from the right.

1,271   1,300,000

Dates written in month-day-year order require a comma between the day and the year, and in sentences a comma must also follow the year.

December 7, 1941, marked the beginning of America's involvement in World War II.

If dates are written in day-month-year order, or if only the month and year are given, no comma is needed.

Martin Luther King, Jr., was born on 15 January 1929; his birthday has been designated a national holiday.

The stock market crash of late October 1929 precipitated the Depression.

Addresses written on one line or within a sentence require commas after the street name and between the city and state. Zip codes follow, with two spaces before and no comma after when written on a single line. When written within a sentence, zip codes appear without extra space before and with a comma after. (See Business Writing, Appendix D.)

709 Sherwood Terrace, Champaign, Illinois 61820

Information on the water rights issue is available by writing the newspaper directly at *Courier-Journal,* 822 Courier Road, Wendel, Vermont 05753, to the attention of the editor.

Parts of place names are separated by commas even when they include only city and state or city and country. Within a sentence, a comma also follows the last item in the place name — essentially making the last item an appositive.

Marietta, Georgia   Ontario, Canada

Nestled in the bluffs along the Mississippi River, Elsa, Illinois, is always 10 to 15 degrees cooler than nearby towns and cities.

Titles and academic and professional degrees that follow an individual's name should be set off with commas.

Adele Zimmerman, professor emerita, spoke at the alumni luncheon on Saturday.

Fernando Rivera, M.D., and Sean Mullican, Ph.D., coordinated the county's alcohol-abuse program.

⟫⟫ *When roman numerals follow the name of a private individual, monarch, ship, and so on, no commas are required.*

Louis XIV of France was known as the "Sun King" because of the splendor of his court.

Commas are required with the abbreviations Sr. *and* Jr., *however.*

Louis Gosset, Jr., won critical acclaim for his sensitive portrayal of an extraterrestrial being. ⟪⟪

EXERCISE 22.5 ⟩ *Commas*

Insert commas where needed in the following paragraphs.

A. Although zoos provide opportunities to see many exotic animals up close the facilities for the animals do not always allow them to pursue or visitors to observe natural habits. Rhesus monkeys very small primates do not seem cramped in small places; they do not appear to suffer or experience any ill effects from their confinement. Chimpanzees however seem noticeably depressed in areas that do not allow them to move about freely. Orangutans highly intelligent primates also seem despondent. However the jungle cats tigers and leopards seem to suffer most. They pace in their cages or lie inactive and inattentive. These large primates and big cats which are usually among a zoo's main attractions require more space and some distance from the crowds of eager spectators. In recent years zoo keepers who have the animals' best interests in mind have begun building habitats for these larger animals. Most zoos have paid for these building projects which can be quite elaborate from general funds. Other zoos have launched major advertising campaigns hoping for individual donations. Still others stressing commitment to the community have appealed to major corporations. These large building projects should continue for they provide improved living conditions for large wild animals. As we maintain zoos that entertain and educate people we must also remember that the animals that live there should not suffer for our benefit.

B. Alaska the forty-ninth state joined the Union on January 3 1959. The largest state geographically covering 586412 square miles Alaska is also the least populated with only 479000 people. In fact the entire state has fewer people than many American cities of moderate size let alone Chicago Los Angeles or New York. Yes the contrast in physical size and population presents an anomaly but Alaska's history is full of such anomalies. Juneau its capital city has approximately twenty thousand people making it roughly the same size as Texarkana Arkansas; Augusta Maine; and Winchester Nevada. Alaska has fewer schools than many other states but has the highest teachers' salaries in the nation. Contradictions such as these have always been present. In 1867 when William H. Seward secretary of state arranged the purchase of Alaska for $7200000 most people thought the purchase was foolish. But "Seward's Folly" as the acquisition was called turned out to be not at all foolish. Rich deposits of minerals oil and natural gas have made Alaska one of America's greatest assets. (For more information on Alaska write to the Alaskan Chamber of Commerce 310 Second Street Juneau Alaska 99801.)

Word processing and commas

If you have problems with comma use, a word processor will provide a convenient means for eliminating them.

Check your comma use. Use "search" commands to locate the commas in your writing. Be sure that a comma rule justifies each use; check the position of the comma in relation to the items it separates or sets off from other sentence elements.

Add commas when necessary. Reread your final draft carefully, checking for places where needed commas are missing. Use the computer's ability to insert commas and automatically reformat the altered sentence. Check spacing and capitalization.

---

23 Unnecessary Commas

Commas help to establish meaning by separating elements in sentences. Thus, the use of commas where they are not needed confuses, distracts, and annoys readers and interferes with the communication of ideas.

Quick Reference

Too many unnecessary commas can be as confusing as too few necessary commas.

> *Do not place commas between subjects and verbs or between verbs and complements.*

> *Do not use a comma before a coordinating conjunction joining only two words, phrases, or clauses.*

> *Do not use commas to set off restrictive sentence elements.*

> *Do not use commas before quotations introduced by that or if.*

23a Do not use a comma between a subject and its verb or between a verb and its complement.

In general, no punctuation should break the subject-verb or verb-complement pattern in a sentence. Insert commas only when they are necessary because of intervening elements, such as non-restrictive phrases or clauses, appositives, coordinate modifiers, and transitional words.

Subject and verb

Governments in many countries, control the prices of consumer goods.   (The comma interrupts the subject-verb pattern.)

Governments in many countries control the prices of consumer goods.

Governments in many countries, especially those in the Communist bloc, control the prices of consumer goods.   (The pair of commas is required because a nonrestrictive phrase has been added.)

Verb and complement

Black markets generally develop, in countries where consumer goods are scarce.   (The comma interrupts the verb-complement pattern.)

Black markets generally develop in countries where consumer goods are scarce.

| 23b | Do not use a comma before a coordinating conjunction that joins only two words, phrases, or dependent clauses. |

Words

The Federal Reserve controls the twelve Federal Reserve banks, and regulates the prime interest rate.   (The comma incorrectly separates the elements of a compound verb: controls *and* regulates.*)*

The Federal Reserve controls the twelve Federal Reserve banks and regulates the prime interest rate.

Phrases

The Federal Reserve's goals are to stabilize the national economy, and to help establish international monetary policies.   (The comma incorrectly separates two infinitive phrases joined by *and*.)

The Federal Reserve's goals are to stabilize the national economy and to help establish international monetary policies.

Clauses

Economists note that low interest rates encourage spending, but that they can also fuel inflation.   (The comma incorrectly separates two clauses, each beginning with *that*.)

Economists note that low interest rates encourage spending but that they also fuel inflation.

>>> *Remember that a comma is required between the independent clauses of a compound sentence.*

Low interest rates encourage spending, but they also fuel inflation.

See Chapter 16 for more information and examples. **<<<**

23c >   **Do not use a comma before the first or after the last item in a series.**

Commas separate items in a series, but unless the series is part of a nonrestrictive phrase, no commas should separate the series as a unit from the rest of the sentence.

To earn extra money, to gain experience, and to make important contacts, are reasons recent graduates in education often work as substitute teachers.   (The infinitive phrases form a series that is the subject of the sentence. The commas after *money* and *experience* are appropriate, but the comma after *contacts* separates the compound subject from the verb.)

To earn extra money, to get more experience, and to make important contacts are reasons that recent graduates in education often work as substitute teachers

| 23d | > | **Do not use commas with cumulative modifiers.** |

Cumulative modifiers — adjectives and adverbs that build upon each other to create meaning — should not be separated by commas. They differ from coordinate modifiers, which modify words separately and require separation with commas.

A pulsar is a rotating, neutron star.   (The comma separates cumulative adjectives: *neutron* modifies *star;* but *rotating* modifies the phrase *neutron star.*)

A pulsar is a rotating neutron star.

To test whether modifiers are cumulative, change their order. If the new order makes no sense, the modifiers are cumulative and no commas should be used. The example above would not make sense if it were written "A pulsar is a neutron rotating star."

| 23e | > | **Do not use commas to set off restrictive elements in sentences.** |

Because restrictive elements — whether they are single words, phrases, or clauses — are essential to the meaning of a sentence, they should not be set off by commas.

Words

The musical play, *West Side Story,* is based on Shakespeare's *Romeo and Juliet.*   (The commas are incorrect because *West Side Story* is necessary to the meaning of the sentence.)

The musical play *West Side Story* is based on Shakespeare's *Romeo and Juliet.*

Phrases

Audience members continued to arrive, until well into the first act.   (Because the phrase is essential to the meaning of the sentence, no comma should be used.)

Audience members continued to arrive until well into the first act.

Clauses

Composers and lyricists, who adapt well-known plays, usually strive to maintain the spirit of the original works.   (The commas are not needed because the relative clause is essential; it identifies a particular group of composers and lyricists.)

Composers and lyricists who adapt well-known plays usually strive to maintain the spirit of the original works.

| 23f | **Do not use a comma before an indirect or a direct quotation introduced by *that* or *if*.** |

Because a quotation preceded by the word *that* or *if* functions as a complement, a comma would improperly separate verb and complement.

Mark Twain commented, that Wagner's music is more respected than it should be.   (The subordinate clause following *said* is the direct object of *said*.)

Mark Twain commented that Wagner's music is more respected than it should be.

But:

Mark Twain commented, "Wagner's music is better than it sounds."

23g ⟩ **Do not use a comma after *such as* or *like* or before *than*.**

Such as and *like* are prepositions that introduce examples in prepositional phrases; because these examples serve as objects, no comma is needed. *Than* signals a comparative construction, and it is illogical to separate with a comma the two items compared.

Some humanistic studies such as, philosophy, art history, and dramatic arts require a more scientific approach, than most people think. (The comma after *such as* inappropriately separates the preposition from its objects; the comma preceding *than* interrupts a comparative construction. The commas after *philosophy* and *art history* correctly separate items in a series.)

Some humanistic studies such as philosophy, art history, and dramatic arts require a more scientific approach than most people think.

EXERCISE 23.1 ❯ *Unnecessary commas*

 The following sentences contain far too many commas. Eliminate those that break the flow of the sentences or that obscure the logical connections between ideas.

1. Primary colors like, red, blue, and yellow are the most often used colors in national flags.

2. Interestingly enough, Libya's bright, green, flag is the only solid colored flag, in current use.

3. The small, Arab republic, Qatar, has a simple, black, and white flag.

4. Many countries — such as, Bahrain, Canada, Denmark, Indonesia, Japan, Monaco, Singapore, and Tunisia — use only red, and white, in their flags.

5. Most national flags use three, or four, bold colors, and use simple geometric shapes in their designs.

6. However, the ornate flag, of Sri Lanka, uses four colors, and black, and an elaborate design.

7. Only a few national flags, vary from the traditional, rectangular shape, including those of, Nepal and Switzerland.

8. The most frequently used colors, for flags, are red, white, and blue.

9. The U.S. flag, contains fifty, small, white stars on a blue field, and thirteen, alternating stripes of red and white.

10. As symbols of nations, flags serve, ideological, and political purposes — uniting citizens in times of peace, as well as in times of war.

EXERCISE 23.2 ❯ *Unnecessary commas*

Delete the unnecessary commas from the following paragraph.

We went fishing, the first morning. I felt the same, damp, moss covering the worms, in the bait can, and saw the dragonfly alight on the tip of my rod, as it hovered a few inches from the surface of the water. It was the arrival of this fly, that convinced me, beyond any doubt, that everything was as it always had been, that the years were a mirage, and there had been no years. The small, waves were the same, chucking the rowboat under the chin as we fished at anchor, and the boat was the same boat, the same color green, and the ribs broken in the same places, and under the floor-boards the same fresh-water leavings and débris — the dead helgrammite, the wisps of moss, the rusty discarded fishhook, the dried blood from yesterday's catch. We stared, silently at the tips of our rods, at the dragonflies that came and went. I lowered the tip of mine into the water, tentatively, pensively dislodging the fly, which darted two feet away, poised, darted two, feet back, and came to rest again a little farther

up the rod. There had been no years, between the ducking of this dragonfly and the other one — the one that was part of my memory. I looked
at the boy, who was silently watching the fly, and it was my hands that
held his rod, my eyes watching. I felt dizzy, and didn't know which rod, I
was at the end of. — E. B. White, "Once More to the Lake"

> **!** ***Word processing and unnecessary commas***
>
> If you use unnecessary commas, use the word processor to
> help you avoid this problem.
>
> Check your comma use. Use "search" commands to
> locate the commas in your writing. Check each use,
> making sure that a comma rule justifies it.
>
> Delete unnecessary commas. The word-processing
> program will automatically reformat sentences for you.

24 Semicolons and Colons

Semicolons perform various functions, sometimes acting as commas (separating items in a series) but more often acting as periods (separating closely related independent clauses).

A colon in effect says, "Notice what follows." Colons formally introduce lists, clarifications, and quotations.

Quick Reference

Use semicolons and colons selectively according to convention.

❯ *Use semicolons to join closely related independent clauses.*

❯ *Use colons to introduce lists, clarifications, and quotations.*

❯ *Do not allow colons to separate verbs from complements or prepositions from objects.*

24a ❯ **Use a semicolon between closely related independent clauses not joined by a coordinating conjunction and before a conjunctive adverb that connects independent clauses.**

The use of a semicolon to link closely related independent clauses emphasizes the close relationship between the clauses.

Only a few hundred people in the United States know how to work with neon tubing; most of them are fifty years old or older.

>>> *Remember that the clauses linked by a semicolon must be independent; otherwise, you will create a sentence fragment.* **<<<**

The use of a conjunctive adverb in addition to a semicolon further stresses the interrelationship of the independent clauses.

> Neon signs were once common at stores, restaurants, and gas stations across the country; however, in the sixties and seventies these sometimes garish advertisements fell into disfavor.   (The conjunctive adverb emphasizes the contrast.)

>>> *Remember to include a comma after the conjunctive adverb.* **<<<**

| 24b | > | **Use semicolons to separate equivalent sentence elements that contain commas.** |

Items in a Series

When items in a series contain commas, use semicolons to separate them.

> Sculptors creating works for outdoor display generally use native stone like sandstone, granite, or limestone; metals or alloys like bronze, cast iron, or steel; or imported stone like marble.   (This use of semicolons helps readers identify the elements of the series.)

>>> *Heavily punctuated series can become awkward to read. If your sentence contains too many pauses, break it into briefer, smoother sentences.*

> Sculptors creating works for outdoor display generally use native stone like sandstone, granite, or limestone. Other frequently used materials include metals or alloys like bronze, cast iron, or steel or imported marble. **<<<**

Independent Clauses

A semicolon effectively marks the break between independent clauses containing commas.

> Much of the sculpture commissioned for public plazas is artistically innovative, visually exciting, and technically impressive; but often it does not appeal to the general public because they have grown accustomed to traditional, realistic statuary.   (The semicolon clarifies the balance of the two-part sentence.)

⟩⟩⟩ *Separate clauses into independent sentences if doing so would make reading them easier. Some rewording may be necessary.*

> Much of the sculpture commissioned for public plazas is artistically innovative, visually exciting, and technically impressive. Nevertheless, it often does not appeal to the general public because they have grown accustomed to traditional, realistic statuary. **⟨⟨⟨**

24c ⟩	**Do not use semicolons when other punctuation is required.**

With a Subordinate Clause

Use a comma, not a semicolon, after a subordinate clause at the beginning of a complex or compound-complex sentence.

Incorrect

> Because it had a strong, centralized government; the Roman Empire was able to maintain relative stability, peace, and prosperity for nearly four centuries.   (The semicolon obscures the relationship between the clauses.)

Correct

> Because it had a strong, centralized government, the Roman Empire was able to maintain relative stability, peace, and prosperity for nearly four centuries.

To Introduce a List

Use a colon or a dash, not a semicolon or a comma, to introduce
a list.

Incorrect

> Historians cite several reasons for the decline of Rome; expanded citi-
> zenship, the deterioration of the army, barbarian invasions, economic
> decentralization, and inefficient agriculture.

Correct

> Historians cite several reasons for the decline of Rome: expanded citi-
> zenship, the deterioration of the army, barbarian invasions, economic
> decentralization, and inefficient agriculture.

24d ▷ **Use colons to introduce elements formally
or emphatically.**

Selective use of colons adds clarity and emphasis to writing. Excessive use may be distracting.

To Introduce a Series

The part of the sentence that precedes a colon must be an independent clause, and the items in the series should never be direct
objects, predicate nouns or adjectives, or objects of prepositions.

> The names of six of the Seven Dwarfs reflect their personalities and
> habits: Bashful, Dopey, Grumpy, Happy, Sleepy, and Sneezy.   (The
> colon emphasizes the list; the words that precede the colon form a
> complete sentence.)

To Introduce an Independent Clause That Explains the Preceding Clause

When a complete sentence is needed to explain the meaning of the preceding sentence, use a colon to clarify the relationship. The first word following the colon usually begins with a lower-case letter, which identifies the clause as a clarification. However, the first word following the colon may begin with a capital letter.

> Good song lyrics are like good poetry: both express ideas in rhythmic, elliptical form.   (Without the second sentence, the meaning of the first would not be completely clear; the colon points to the explanatory relationship.)

To Introduce an Appositive at the End of a Sentence

Appositives (restatements of nouns or pronouns) are given special emphasis when they are introduced with colons. This use of the colon stresses the appositive as a necessary explanation of a key word in the main sentence.

> Early astronomers and astrologers assigning names to planets drew primarily on one source: mythology.

To Introduce a Direct Quotation

Direct quotations are formally introduced by colons. Both the introduction and the quotation must be independent clauses. The first word of the quotation is capitalized. (See Quotation Marks, pages 430–31).

> The educational sentiment that Mark Twain articulated would shock many humorless educators: "It doesn't matter what you teach a boy, so long as he doesn't like it."   (The colon, preceded by a complete sentence, emphasizes Twain's comment.)

> **24e** Use colons to separate numerals in time references and Bible citations and to separate titles from subtitles.

Hours and minutes given in numerals are separated by a colon. When the reference is to hours only, spell out the number.

The next flight to Tel Aviv leaves at 2:15 A.M.

We expect to be home by nine o'clock.

Chapter and verse in citations of books of the Bible are separated by a colon.

Genesis 3:23   Luke 12:27

Titles and subtitles are separated by a colon.

Nancy McPhee's *Book of Insults Ancient and Modern: An Amiable History of Insult, Invective, Imprecation, and Incivility (Literary, Political, and Historical) Hurled Through the Ages and Compiled as a Public Service* is a collection of amusing comments, criticisms, and rejoinders.

> **24f** Do not use a colon between a verb and its complement or between a preposition and its object.

Colons should not separate basic sentence elements. To test the accuracy of colon placement, change the colon to a period and drop the words that follow. If the remaining sentence is complete, the colon is correctly placed. If the remaining sentence is incomplete, delete or move the colon or rephrase the sentence.

Incorrect

The names of Enrico's cats are: Winston Churchill, T. S. Eliot, Eudora Welty, and Eleanor Roosevelt.   (*The names of Enrico's cats are* is a fragment; the colon separates the verb from its complement.)

Correct

The names of Enrico's cats are Winston Churchill, T. S. Eliot, Eudora Welty, and Eleanor Roosevelt.

Incorrect

Enrico named his cats after: Winston Churchill, T. S. Eliot, Eudora Welty, and Eleanor Roosevelt.   (*Enrico named his cats after* is a fragment; the colon separates the preposition *after* from its objects.)

Correct

Enrico named his cats after Winston Churchill, T. S. Eliot, Eudora Welty, and Eleanor Roosevelt.

Correct

Enrico named his cats after historical figures and writers: Winston Churchill, T. S. Eliot, Eudora Welty, and Eleanor Roosevelt.   (The prepositional phrase is complete, and the list of names adds clarification.)

EXERCISE 24.1 ❱ *Semicolons and colons*

Correct the errors in semicolon and colon usage in the following sentences.

1. The Mediterranean Sea is bordered to the south by: Egypt, Libya, Tunisia, Algeria, and Morocco.

2. The major ports on the Mediterranean Sea are: Barcelona; Spain, Marseille; France, Naples; Italy, Beirut; Lebanon, Alexandria; Egypt, and Tripoli; Libya.

3. Because the Bering Sea borders both the Soviet Union and the United States; it is often patrolled by military ships from each country.

4. In the Western Hemisphere, gulfs are more common than seas: however, several seas are located off the northernmost coasts of North America.

5. Four seas are named for colors; the Yellow Sea, the Red Sea, the White Sea, and the Black Sea.

EXERCISE 24.2 ❱ *Semicolons and colons*

The following paragraph uses the semicolon as its only form of internal punctuation. Revise the punctuation, reserving the semicolon for places where it works better than any other mark of punctuation.

Ninety-six percent of Americans have eaten at one of the McDonald's restaurants in the last year; slightly more than half of the U.S. population lives within three minutes of a McDonald's; McDonald's has served more than 55 billion hamburgers; McDonald's commands 17% of all restaurant visits in the U.S. and gets 7.3% of all dollars Americans spent eating out; McDonald's sells 32% of all hamburgers and 26% of french fries; McDonald's is the country's largest beef buyer; it purchases 7.5% of the U.S. potato crop; McDonald's has employed about 8 million workers — which amounts to approximately 7% of the entire U.S. work force; and McDonald's has replaced the U.S. Army as America's largest job training organization. — John Love, *McDonald's: Behind the Arches*

Word processing and semicolons and colons

Because semicolons and colons must be used so infrequently and so carefully, you probably will want to check each use. A word processor will help you do that easily.

Locate semicolons. Use "search" commands to locate places where you have used semicolons. Make sure that they separate independent clauses or items in a series that contain commas.

Locate colons. Use "search" commands to locate colons. Double-check their use, especially making sure that they do not separate verbs from their complements or prepositions from their objects.

25 Apostrophes

Apostrophes show possession (usually with an added *s*) and indicate the omission of letters or numbers from words or dates. Errors in the use of apostrophes are easily corrected.

> ### Quick Reference
>
> *Apostrophes have two uses: to show possession and to indicate omission.*
>
> ❯ *Use an apostrophe and an* s *to form the possessive case of words not ending with* s.
>
> ❯ *Use only an apostrophe to form the possessive of words ending with* s.
>
> ❯ *Use an apostrophe to indicate the omission of letters in contractions and numbers in dates.*
>
> ❯ *Do not use apostrophes with possessive pronouns (*yours, theirs*); do not confuse the possessive pronoun* its *with the contraction* it's *("it is").*

25a ❯ **Use apostrophes to form the possessive case.**

Words Not Ending with *S*

Form the possessive of words not ending with *s* by adding an apostrophe and an *s.*

Wyoming*'s* state capitol	Pasteur*'s* discovery
Rockefeller*'s* legacy	a week*'s* wages

360

everybody's last choice   the atom's nucleus

Saturday's game   *A Room of One's Own*

Words Ending with *S*

Many singular nouns end with an *s*: *virus, Chris, albatross*. Most plural nouns also end in *s*: *clocks, scientists, cats*. Both singular and plural nouns ending in *s* form the possessive by adding an apostrophe only; an additional *s* is unnecessary.

Dickens' *Bleak House*   a United Nations' task force

Paris' night life   Brahms' *Requiem*

》》》 *To check whether the possessive form you have used is correct, mentally eliminate the apostrophe and* s *or the apostrophe. The word remaining should be the correct one for your meaning. For example, the phrase* earthquake's *destruction without the apostrophe and* s *refers to only one earthquake; the phrase* earthquakes' *destruction without the apostrophe refers to multiple earthquakes.* **《《《**

Compound Words and Joint Possession

Show possession in compound words or joint possession in a series by adding an apostrophe and *s* to the last noun only.

brother-in-law's objection

General Motors, Ford, and Chrysler's combined profits

the United States and Canada's trade agreement

》》》 *If possession in a series is not joint but individual, each noun in the series must be possessive.*

Angela's, Bert's, and Lionel's fingerprints   (Each person has a separate set of fingerprints.) **《《《**

25b ▷ **Use apostrophes to indicate the omission of letters from contractions and of numbers from dates.**

With apostrophe	*Complete form*
shouldn't	should not
I'll	I will *or* I shall
it's	it is
the '89 champions	the 1989 champions

▶▶▶ *Use contractions and dates with numbers omitted in informal writing only. In formal writing, present words and dates fully.* **◀◀◀**

25c ▷ **Do not use apostrophes with possessive pronouns.**

Possessive pronouns do not require the addition of an apostrophe. Do not be confused by those (*yours, ours, his,* and others) that end in *s.*

Incorrect
   a belief of her's

Correct
   a belief of hers

EXERCISE 25.1 ❯ *Apostrophes*

 Correct the use of apostrophes in the following sentences. Add needed apostrophes and delete unnecessary ones.

   1. Even before people kept record's or conceived of science as a field of study, chemistry exerted its influence on their lives.

2. Early civilizations understanding of elements was primitive — the Greeks' and Romans' four elements were air, earth, fire, and water — but their applications of chemical principles were sophisticated.

3. Today, perhaps, its difficult to understand how much the development of the alloy bronze revolutionized human's lives.

4. During the Middle Ages, alchemists discovered how many chemical compounds work, even though trying to turn metals to gold was a chief preoccupation of their's.

5. By the seventeenth century, scientists studies were more methodical and practical, as was illustrated by Robert Boyles studies' of gases, for example.

6. Even before the development of sophisticated microscopes, John Daltons' theories of atomic elements explained chemical's reactions.

7. Dmitri Mendeleev, Russias foremost early chemist, explained the relationships among elements and devised the periodic tables that still appear on student's tests in classes' in introductory chemistry.

8. Marie Curie's and Pierre Curie's discovery of radium in 1898 further expanded scientist's understanding of chemistry.

9. Alfred B. Nobels' bequest of $9 million made possible awards in science and literature; one of the first five prizes in 1901 was an award for achievement in chemistry.

10. Chemist's work today is aided by sophisticated technology, but their search for knowledge has been shared by scientists' of generation's past.

26 Other Marks of Punctuation

Dashes, hyphens, parentheses, brackets, and ellipsis points serve specialized though important purposes in writing. Used effectively, they help to create emphasis and establish meaning.

Quick Reference

Use specialized marks of punctuation carefully to emphasize elements of your sentences and to clarify your meaning.

> *Use dashes to introduce parenthetical information, to set off material that contains commas, and to mark interruptions in thought, speech, or action.*

> *Use hyphens to divide words, to form some compound words, and to join some prefixes and suffixes to root words.*

> *Use parentheses in pairs to introduce parenthetical information and numbered or lettered sequences.*

> *Use brackets to indicate alterations to direct quotations.*

> *Use ellipsis points to indicate omissions in direct quotations and to indicate hesitation or suspended statements.*

26a ▷ **Use the dash selectively to introduce parenthetical comments, to set off series, and to indicate breaks or shifts in thought, speech, or action.**

A dash, made by typing two hyphens with no space before or after, introduces parenthetical information emphatically and clearly, sets off a series at the beginning or end of a sentence, and marks interruptions in thought, speech, or action.

Parenthetical Comments

Parenthetical comments may be single words, phrases, or clauses inserted into a sentence to explain, amplify, or qualify the main idea. Parenthetical comments are grammatically independent of the rest of the sentence. They are frequently marked by parentheses, but those requiring special emphasis are set off with dashes.

> American military advisers did not acknowledge the strength and tenacity of the Viet Cong — a costly error.

> The reports of atrocities — in particular the My Lai Massacre — changed American attitudes about the war.

Appositives (phrases renaming nouns or pronouns) that contain commas may be set off by dashes (in place of commas) for greater clarity.

> Several presidents — Eisenhower, Kennedy, Johnson, and Nixon — were embroiled in political debates about the necessity of American involvement in Vietnam.   (Because the appositive contains three commas, dashes mark the appositive more clearly than commas would mark it.)

A Series

A list of items placed at the beginning of a sentence for special emphasis is followed by a dash.

> The Tiger, the Mako, the Great White — these "man-eating" sharks deserve our respect more than our fear.

A dash may be used to introduce a list informally.

Jaws portrayed most people's reactions to sharks — ignorance, fear, and irrationality.   (In formal writing, use a colon to introduce a list.)

Shifts or Breaks in Thought, Speech, or Action

Andrew Wyeth's monochromatic paintings — why does he avoid color? — are popular with the American public.   (The dashes mark a shift in thought.)

Because of cover stories and related articles in scholarly and popular magazines, interest in Wyeth's "Helga" paintings and drawings was intense for several months — and then suddenly subsided.   (The dash marks a break in action.)

Selective Use

The use of dashes to show emphasis and discontinuity disrupts the rhythm of writing. Often, other punctuation serves as well.

Too many dashes

The thunderstorm — coming from the southwest — looked threatening — with black and blue clouds and flashes of lightning. Within a matter of minutes — five to be exact — it was upon us. Around our house, the trees — delicate dogwoods, tall maples, and stout pines — bent in the heavy winds — their branches swaying violently. The black sky, the growing roar, the shaking house — all signaled the approach of a tornado — we headed for the basement.   (Only two uses of the dash are required in this paragraph, with the appositive in the third sentence and with the introductory list in the last. The other uses are technically correct, but the use of fewer dashes would call less attention to the mechanics of the paragraph and allow readers to focus on the events described.)

Better

The thunderstorm coming from the southwest looked threatening, with black and blue clouds and flashes of lightning. Within five minutes, it was upon us. Around our house, the trees — delicate dogwoods, tall maples, and stout pines — bent in the heavy winds, their branches swaying violently. The black sky, the growing roar, the shaking house — all signaled the approach of a tornado. We headed for the basement.

EXERCISE 26.1 ❯ *Dashes*

Use dashes to combine each set of sentences into a single sentence.

1. The Distinguished Service Cross, the Navy Cross, the Silver Star, the Distinguished Flying Cross, the Bronze Star, and the Air Medal are awards given to members of the armed forces. These awards all recognize heroism.

2. Soldiers may be recognized for heroic behavior several times. They do not receive additional medals. Instead, they receive small emblems to pin on the first medal's ribbon.

3. Since 1932, the Purple Heart has been awarded to members of the armed forces who were wounded in combat. The medal is gold and purple, heart-shaped, and embossed with George Washington's image.

4. General George Washington established this military decoration in 1782. It was called the Badge of Military Merit. It wasn't given between 1800 and 1932.

5. The Congressional Medal of Honor is our nation's highest military award. The award was authorized in 1861 for the navy and in 1862 for the army.

26b ❯ **Use hyphens to divide words at the ends of lines, to form some compound nouns and adjectives, and to link some prefixes and suffixes to root words.**

Word Division

Hyphens are used to divide words that do not fit in their entirety at the ends of typed or printed lines. Because hyphens must be placed between syllables, one-syllable words cannot be broken. Check your dictionary when you do not know where to divide a word. Other conventions of hyphenation dictate that one or two letters not be isolated on a line and that proper nouns not be divided. When it is not possible or acceptable to hyphenate a word, move the whole word to the next line.

Incorrect

Because of excavation difficulties, the archaeologist thou-ght he'd quit the project.

Correct

Because of excavation difficulties, the archaeologist thought he'd quit the project.

Incorrect

Every year some natural disaster seems to strike Bo-livia.   (Proper names should not be divided; two letters should not be isolated on a single line.)

Correct

Every year some natural disaster seems to strike Bolivia.

Many word processors can hyphenate words, providing an alternative to the sometimes awkward spacing that appears with justified right margins or the ragged edge that appears with unjustified margins. However, consider the workability of the word processor's hyphenation before using it. ■ Check the hyphenation pattern. Does the program introduce hyphens only between syllables? If it does not, do not use the "hyphenation" feature. ■ Check proper names. A

word-processing program will not distinguish proper names
from other words and will inappropriately hyphenate them.
Check for hyphenated proper names and move any you find
to the next line.

Compound Forms

A compound noun is a pair or group of words that together function as a single noun. Noun compounds may be open (*beer mug*),
closed (*headache*), or hyphenated (*hurly-burly*). If you are unsure about how to present a compound noun, consult a dictionary. If the compound does not appear, it should be spelled open.

father figure	grandfather	mother-in-law
raw silk	snowmobile	go-between
medical examiner	notebook	razzle-dazzle

When modifiers preceding a noun work together to create a
single meaning, hyphens emphasize their unity. When the same
modifiers follow the noun, hyphens usually are not needed.

Hyphens necessary	*Hyphens unnecessary*
out-of-the-way resort	a resort that is out of the way
long-term investment	an investment for the long term

▶▶▶ *When an adverb ending in* -ly *is the first word of a compound, omit
the hyphen.*

Margaret Atwood is a highly inventive writer. **◀◀◀**

When spelled out, fractions and cardinal and ordinal numbers
from twenty-one through ninety-nine require hyphens. This rule

applies whether the numbers are used as nouns, modifiers, or complements.

eighty-two recipes

forty-first president

three-fourths of the taxpayers

one hundred thirty-three bandages

Prefixes and Suffixes

Use hyphens to form words with the prefixes *all-*, *ex-*, and *self-* and with the suffix *-elect*. Other prefixes (*anti-*, *extra-*, *inter-*, *mid-*, *non-*, *over-*, *post-*, *pre-*, and *un-*) and suffixes (*-fold*, *-like*, and *-wide*) are generally spelled closed.

Hyphenate	*Spell closed*
all-consuming ambition	*anti* body
ex-department chairperson	*extra* sensory
self-restraint	*mid* point
president-elect	state *wide*

When prefixes are joined to proper nouns or to compounds consisting of more than one word, hyphens are required. The proper nouns are capitalized.

un-American

post-World War II

non-native speakers

pre-Columbian

When a prefix has the same last letter as the first letter of the root word (or when a suffix has the same first letter as the last letter of the root word), hyphens are sometimes used for clarity.

anti-intellectual

bell-like

When the omission of a hyphen would result in ambiguity, a hyphen should be used.

release ("let go")   re-lease ("to lease again")

reform ("to improve")   re-form ("to form again")

unionized ("formed into a union")   un-ionized ("not ionized")

EXERCISE 26.2 **❯** *Hyphens*

Add or delete hyphens to correct the use of hyphens in the following sentences. (Some of the hyphens are used correctly.)

1. In the United States, senators are elected to six year terms, presidents (and their vice presidents) to four year terms, and members of Congress to two year terms.

2. Although these electoral guidelines are un-changed, little else about modern day elections has remained the way our national founders conceived them.

3. In pre-computer elections, hand-tabulated ballots were the norm, and results often were not certain for days.

4. Today, with computer-aided counting, officials post fully three fourths of election returns by mid-night of election day.

5. Television-networks quickly project the results of today's elections, usually on the basis of less than one fiftieth of the ballots cast.

6. Consequently, presidents elect now make victory speeches before mid-night on election day, rather than at mid-morning on the following day. Times have clearly changed.

26c >   **Use parentheses selectively, always in pairs, to introduce parenthetical comments and numbered or lettered sequences.**

Parenthetical Comments

Use parentheses to set off information that is only casually related to the flow of ideas in the rest of the sentence; essential information deserves direct presentation. Do not include long explanations parenthetically.

> Joan of Arc (only seventeen at the time) led military troops to help return the rightful king of France to the throne.   (The information about Joan of Arc's age supplements the main idea; it is appropriately set off by parentheses.)

Parentheses are less emphatic and more disruptive than dashes, which are used for a similar purpose. The overuse of parentheses makes writing seem uneven, incoherent, or immature. To avoid such problems, use parentheses only when no other strategy or punctuation will serve your purpose.

Choppy

> The compass (scratched and cracked) should have been replaced (years ago), but Joaquín (reluctant to spend the money) preferred to keep it as it was.   (The rhythm of the sentence is broken by the disruptive use of parenthetical details, some of which should be incorporated in the main sentence.)

Better

> The scratched and cracked compass should have been replaced years ago, but Joaquín, reluctant to spend the money, preferred to keep it as it was.

》》》 *Although you should use such complex patterns of punctuation sparingly, add clarifications of elements in parentheses using brackets, as in the following example:*

> HMS ("Her [or His] Majesty's Ship") *Reliant* **《《《**

Numbered or Lettered Sequences

The numbering or lettering of steps can help clarify the steps of a complicated sequence of events or a process. Such lists, however, may be more distracting than helpful. Use them with care.

> Freezing green beans involves six steps: (1) snap the ends off the beans; (2) wash the beans thoroughly in water; (3) blanch the beans for two to three minutes in boiling water; (4) cool them in ice water; (5) drain them for several minutes and then pack them into freezer containers; (6) seal the containers, label them, and put them in the freezer.

| 26d | Use brackets selectively, always in pairs, to indicate alterations in a direct quotation. |

Brackets indicate alterations in quoted material. If your typewriter does not have brackets, leave spaces when you type and insert brackets by hand.

Clarification

When quotations out of context are not clear, use brackets to add clarifying information. Add only information that makes the original meaning clear; never add contradictory information or negative comments.

> Davies commented, "The army nurses' judgment in triage [where the medical staff decides which patients to treat first] is paramount, for they must determine a soldier's medical stability in a matter of seconds." (The bracketed material explains a key term, and the brackets indicate that the writer, not Davies, defined *triage*.)

> "If architectural preservationists are unsuccessful in their efforts, most [theaters built in the early 1900s] will probably be demolished by the end of the century," Walter Aspen noted. (In place of the bracketed material, the original read "of these fascinating buildings," an unclear reference outside of the original context.)

Alteration of Syntax

Use brackets to indicate changes in the syntax of a quoted passage. Make only minor changes — changes in verb tense, for instance — that allow you to insert a passage smoothly into the context of your writing. Do not alter the meaning of the original.

> Immigrants were sometimes confused or ambivalent about a new life in the United States. As a journalist noted in 1903, "Each day, thousands of immigrants [moved] through the turnstiles at Ellis Island, uncertain but hopeful." (The brackets show a change from the present tense *move,* which was appropriate in 1903, to the past tense *moved,* which is appropriate in current contexts.)

Notation of Error

When a direct quotation contains an error in grammar or fact, you must still transcribe the wording of the original exactly. However, to indicate for readers that you recognize the error and have not introduced it yourself, insert the word *sic* (Latin for "thus") in brackets following the faulty element.

Adderson noted in her preface, "The taxpayers who [sic] the legislation will protect are the elderly, the handicapped, and those in low-income families." (*Sic* notes that the writer recognized Adderson's misuse of *who* for *whom*.)

>>> *To avoid seeming overly critical or pedantic, use* sic *only when necessary for clarity. The writer of the sentence above, for example, could have avoided using* [sic] *by rephrasing the sentence.*

Adderson noted in her preface that those protected by the legislation are "the elderly, the handicapped, and those in low-income families." **<<<**

26e	Use ellipsis points to indicate omissions from quoted material and to indicate hesitating, trailing, or incomplete statements.

Ellipsis points are three *spaced* periods. Other marks of punctuation (periods, question marks, exclamation points, commas, and so on) are separated from ellipsis points by one space. Place ellipsis points either before or after the original punctuation, depending on the original sentence.

Omissions from Quoted Material

Use ellipsis points in quoted material to indicate where you have omitted extraneous information, parenthetical details, or unnecessary clarifications. Never omit words to change the original meaning of a source.

Original version

"The Ninth Street Station is a superb example of ornate woodworking and stonework. Typical of Steamboat-Gothic architecture, it was designed in 1867 by Fielding Smith. It is a landmark we should endeavor to preserve."

Acceptable cut version

"The Ninth Street Station is a superb example of ornate woodworking and stonework. . . . It is a landmark we should endeavor to preserve." (Note the retention of the period at the end of the first sentence.)

Original version

"Theaters, such as the magnificent edifices built by the Lowe and Fox families, aging public buildings, and deteriorating commercial buildings in prime business locations are often demolished to provide space for new office buildings with little architectural interest."

Acceptable cut version

"Theaters . . . , aging public buildings, and deteriorating commercial buildings in prime business locations are often demolished to provide space for new office buildings with little architectural interest."   (The ellipsis points mark the omission of secondary material; the comma before *aging* is retained to separate the items in the series.)

Original version

"This is a great movie if you enjoy meaningless violence, gratuitous sex, inane dialogue, and poor acting. It is offensive by any standards."

Dishonest cut version

"This is a great movie . . . by any standards."   (This is a misquotation.)

Hesitating, Trailing, or Incomplete Statements

More common in dialogue, especially in fiction, than in expository writing, the use of ellipsis points to indicate hesitating, trailing, or incomplete thoughts and statements can be effective if it is used sparingly.

Woody Allen's *Stardust Memories* was . . . boring.

From the back of the crowded elevator Chie shouted, "I have important news about. . . ." But the doors closed before she could finish.

EXERCISE 26.3 ❯ *Parentheses, brackets, and ellipsis points*

 Correct the faulty use of parentheses, brackets, and ellipsis points in the following sentences.

1. To install a cable converter, simply follow these directions: 1) remove the converter from the box; 2) attach the blue adapter wires to your television set; 3) plug the converter into an electrical outlet; 4) select a channel and test the equipment by turning it on.

2. "The benefits (to those who subscribe to cable services) are amazingly varied, from more programs to better programs," explained Ms. Abigail Fitzgerald, a cable network spokesperson.

3. Most cable subscribers would agree that they are offered more… but is it better?

4. Professor Martínez, media specialist at ASU, commented: "Much of what's offered is junk . . . When *Mr. Ed, Car 54,* and *The Munsters* make it to national rebroadcast, we have to question the uses to which cable is put. Of course, that's the long-standing issue (in television broadcasting)."

5. Then again, people (the American people in particular) have always enjoyed (really enjoyed) some mindless entertainment (*unchallenging* is, perhaps, a better word) to relieve the tension (and frustration) of the day.

EXERCISE 26.4 ❯ *Punctuation review*

 Punctuate the following paragraph.

The Postal Reorganization Act signed into law by President Nixon on August 12 1970 created a government-owned postal service operated under the executive branch of the government the new US Postal Service is run by an eleven-member board with members appointed by the president of the Senate for nine-year terms the Postmaster General who is no longer part of the president's cabinet is selected by the members of the board since 1971 when the system began operating four men have served as Postmaster General Winton M Blount E T Klassen Benjamin F Bailar and William F Bolger but has the postal system changed substantially since the PRA went into effect on July 1 1971 no not to any great extent first class second class third class and fourth class these still represent the most commonly used mailing rates however some services have been added for instance Express Mail which tries to rival Federal Express Purolator and other one-day delivery services guarantees that packages will arrive at their destinations by 300 the day after mailing the prices are steep as one might expect in addition the Postal Service has instituted nine-digit zip codes in some areas for all practical purposes however the business at 29990 post offices throughout the US continues in much the same way it did before the PRA.

Word processing and specialized punctuation

Use a word processor to experiment with varied punctuation and to help you locate and check the correct use of specialized marks of punctuation.

Locate dashes, hyphens, parentheses, brackets, and ellipsis points in your writing. Use "search" codes to find each form of punctuation. Check sentences carefully to make sure that you have used these special punctuation marks correctly.

Experiment with varied punctuation. Because word-processing programs allow you to modify your work without completely retyping, experiment with alternative forms of punctuation to create various kinds of emphasis.

MECHANICS

Capitals

Capitals indicate the beginnings of sentences, signal proper nouns and proper adjectives, and identify important words in titles. Appropriate capitalization contributes to the clarity and correctness of your writing. Since unnecessary capitalization is confusing and annoying to readers, make sure when capitalizing a word that an upper-case letter is required.

Quick Reference

Capitals are used to create special emphasis.

> *Capitalize the first word in every sentence.*

> *Capitalize proper nouns and proper adjectives.*

> *Capitalize first, last, and important words in titles.*

27a > **Capitalize the first word in every sentence.**

Subtitles in foreign films can be as distracting as they are helpful.

>>> *When a complete sentence follows a colon, capitalizing the first word is optional.*

The Declaration of Independence presents an idea we should remember: *All* people are created equal. **<<<**

Apply this rule when quoting a complete sentence.

The senator remarked, *"Initiating* dialogue among national leaders is an important step in solving problems in the Middle East."

>>> *In long, interrupted quotations, only words that begin sentences are capitalized.*

"*Prospects* for peace in the Middle East exist," the senator reiterated, "only if leaders negotiate in good faith." **<<<**

| 27b | Capitalize proper nouns and proper adjectives. |

Proper nouns and proper adjectives refer to specific people, places, and things and are therefore capitalized.

In August, the Benton Teachers' Association voted to strike.   (specific name, capitals required)

But:

In August, the teachers' union voted to strike.   (general noun, no capitals required)

Treat the pronoun *I* as a proper noun.

I want to sail to the Bahamas, but I've got to earn some money first.

Names of specific individuals, races, ethnic groups, nationalities, languages, and places

Proper Nouns	Proper Adjectives
Samuel Johnson	Shakespearean sonnet
Caucasian	Egyptian border
Chicano	Hispanic traditions
New Yorker	of German descent
Portuguese	Portuguese trade

Kenya	Belgian lace
Southern Alps	Alpine village
African-Americans	African-American organization

》》》 *Registered trade names and trademarks, even those for common objects, must be capitalized.*

Coke   Scotch tape   Kleenex   Xerox **《《《**

Names of historical periods, events, and documents

the Age of Reason

the Battle of Bull Run

the Declaration of Independence

Names of days, months, and holidays

Monday   August   Valentine's Day

Do not capitalize the names of seasons (*winter, spring, summer,* and *autumn*).

Names of organizations and government branches and departments

Phi Beta Kappa

Greenpeace

the House of Representatives

the Department of Transportation

Names of educational institutions, departments, specific courses, and degrees

Brown University	Belleville High School
Department of Education	School of Nursing

Aviation Technology 421   Zoology 101

Bachelor of Arts   Doctor of Philosophy

▶▶▶ *General references to academic subjects do not require capitals unless they are languages* (English, Italian) *or use proper nouns or proper adjectives* (American history). *Course titles including numbers, however, require capitals.*

Armand earned *A*'s in every speech course he took, but he was proudest of his *A* in Speech 363. **◀◀◀**

Religious names, terms, and writings

Islam   Christmas   God

Judaism   Torah   Allah

Christians   Koran   Krishna

Buddhists   Ramadan   the Resurrection

Titles used with proper names

Ms. Angélica Sánchez

Dr. Martin Luther King, Jr.

Professor Angela Cambridge

Secretary-Elect Weixlmann

President Roosevelt

but: my history professor

         the former president

Abbreviations, acronyms, and call letters

100 B.C. (or b.c.)   7:30 P.M. (or p.m.)

NAACP   Schedule SE

WZZQ radio   KTVI-TV

Abbreviations and acronyms — including those for organizations, businesses, time designations, and documents — and radio and television station call letters are almost always capitalized.

27c ⟩ **Capitalize the first, last, and other important words in the titles and subtitles of books and other works.**

Words requiring capitals in titles and subtitles of books, plays, films, poems, articles, student papers, and so on are the first and last words and all nouns, verbs, adjectives, and adverbs. Nouns and adjectives in hyphenated compounds are also capitalized. Unless they appear as the first or last word, articles (*a*, *an*, and *the*), coordinating conjunctions, and prepositions of four or fewer letters are not normally capitalized.

Encyclopaedia Britannica   (a multivolume work)

The Sound and the Fury   (a novel)

Cat on a Hot Tin Roof   (a play)

Chariots of Fire   (a film)

"The Emperor of Ice Cream"   (a poem)

"The Book Burning"   (an article)

How to Make Yourself Miserable: Another Vital Training Manual   (a book title and subtitle)

Seventeenth-Century English Poetry   (a hyphenated compound)

EXERCISE 27.1 ⟩ *Capitalization*

Add the capital letters required in the following sentences.

1. art 426 (or english 426) is an interdisciplinary course that offers a survey of important artists and writers.

2. the course is team-taught by dr. nicholas bradford of the english department and ms. marlene jacobs of the art department.

3. during the fall of last year, i took the course to fulfill a humanities requirement.

4. we read a portion of dante's *divine comedy* — but not in italian — and saw slides of michelangelo's frescoes on the ceiling of the sistine chapel, both presenting perspectives on italian religious views.

5. we saw numerous paintings depicting the nativity, the crucifixion, and the ascension and read several religious poems.

6. turning our attention from europe, we saw *habuko landscape* by sesshu, a sixteenth-century japanese painter, and read samples of haiku poetry to learn of the spare but elegant images both create.

7. italian and flemish artists dominated the months of october and november.

8. we learned, however, that by the 1800s, neo-classicism had emerged and artistic dominance had shifted to france, where it remained for over a century; we read corneille's *phaedre* and saw representative paintings by david and ingres.

9. Over thanksgiving break, i took an optional field trip with ms. jacobs and several other students; we went to the art institute of chicago, her alma mater, to view their collection.

10. by the time we studied abstract art, national and artistic boundaries had been broken and painters like picasso and poets like t. s. eliot could be said to draw upon the same aesthetic traditions.

11. when ms. jacobs first said, "the fine arts are symbiotic, each reciprocally influencing the other," i wasn't sure i understood what she meant. now i think i know.

28 **Italics**

Italics distinguish titles of complete published works (except articles, essays, and short stories and poems, which require quotation marks): books; journals, magazines, and newspapers; works of art, the specific names of ships, trains, aircraft, and spacecraft; foreign words used in English sentences; and words or phrases requiring special emphasis.

In a printed text, italics are indicated with slanted type (*like this*), but in a typed or handwritten text, italics are indicated with underlining (like this). The meaning is the same.

Quick Reference

Use italics to create your intended meaning.

❭ *Use italics to distinguish some titles, generally those of complete works.*

❭ *Italicize the specific names of ships, trains, aircraft, and spacecraft.*

❭ *Italicize unfamiliar foreign words and phrases.*

❭ *Italicize words used as words, letters as letters, and numbers as numbers.*

❭ *Italicize words to create special emphasis.*

28a ❭ **Italicize the titles of most complete published works.**

The titles of books, journals, magazines, newspapers, pamphlets, plays, and long poems are italicized. Parts of long works, such as chapter titles, and titles of articles, essays, and short stories and poems are presented in quotation marks. Titles of long musical compositions, albums, films, radio and television programs, paintings, statues, and other artworks are also italicized.

Books

Joseph Heller's *Catch-22*

Zora Neale Hurston's *Their Eyes Were Watching God*

》》》 The Bible, books of the Bible (Song of Solomon, Genesis), and legal documents (the Constitution) are not italicized, although they are capitalized. **《《《**

Magazines and journals

Business Week

American Scholar

Charles Simic's essay "Reading Philosophy at Night" from *Antaeus*

Newspapers

the *Kansas City Star*

the *New York Times*

Long poems

John Milton's *Paradise Lost*

Walt Whitman's *Leaves of Grass*

But: Elizabeth Bishop's brief poem "In the Waiting Room"

Long musical compositions

Igor Stravinski's *Firebird Suite*

Giacomo Puccini's opera *Madame Butterfly*

Albums

Kathleen Battle and Christopher Parkening's *Pleasures of Their Company*

the Beatles' *Abbey Road*

Tracy Chapman's "Fast Car" from her album *Tracy Chapman*

Plays

Neil Simon's *Brighton Beach Memoirs*

Edward Albee's *Zoo Story*

Films

Rainman

The Wizard of Oz

Radio and television programs

All Things Considered

Cheers

》》 Although italic type is required for the name of a television series, the titles of episodes (daily, weekly, or monthly segments) are enclosed in quotation marks.

"Antarctica: Earth's Last Frontier" airs Tuesday at nine on *NOVA*. **《《**

Paintings

Pablo Picasso's *Three Musicians*

Georgia O'Keeffe's *Black Iris III*

Statues

Rodin's *The Thinker*

Michelangelo's *David*

Pamphlets

NCTE's *How to Help Your Child Become a Better Writer*

Roberta Greene's *'Til Divorce Do You Part*

| 28b | Italicize the specific names of ships, trains, aircraft, and spacecraft. |

Only specific names are italicized and capitalized. The names of vehicle types and models are capitalized but not italicized. Abbreviations such as *SS* ("Steamship") and *HMS* ("Her [or His] Majesty's Ship") are not italicized.

Ships

Queen Elizabeth II

HMS *Wellington*

Andrea Doria

But: Starcraft Marlin, cruiser series XL

Trains

Orient Express

Stourbridge Lion

Aircraft

The Spirit of St. Louis

The Spruce Goose

But: Boeing 707

Spacecraft

Apollo I

Sputnik II

28c ⟩ **Italicize unfamiliar foreign words and phrases in English sentences.**

If a foreign word or phrase is likely to be unfamiliar to your readers, italicize it.

> Andrea Palladio made frequent use of *trompe l'oeil* effects and murals in his villa designs.

The English language has borrowed extensively from the vocabularies of other languages. Some terms — such as *coffee, coupon, kasha, cliché,* and *kindergarten* — are fully assimilated into standard American usage and do not require italics. A standard college dictionary will help you to distinguish among unfamiliar, familiar, and assimilated foreign words. If a foreign word or phrase is not found in the dictionary (*cinéma vérité, perestroika*), it is likely to be recently imported or unfamiliar to your readers and should be italicized. If a foreign word or phrase is labeled in the dictionary as foreign (*adiós, coup de théâtre*), it may be unfamiliar to your readers; italics are optional. A word that is not labeled need not be italicized, even though the etymology indicates that it has been borrowed (*coup d'état, kibbutz*). **⟩⟩⟩** *When using any but the most common foreign terms, observe all conventions of spelling, including accents and other marks, found in the original language.* **⟨⟨⟨**

28d ⟩ **Italicize words used as words, letters used as letters, and numbers used as numbers.**

> "The *s* was put in *island,* for instance, in sheer pedantic ignorance." — Bergen Evans

> According to numerology, the numbers *5, 7, 12,* and *13* have occult significance.

28e > **Use italics selectively for emphasis.**

Italics may be used to call attention to words requiring emphasis, to signal a contrast, and to ensure close and careful examination of words by the reader.

> "It makes a world of difference to a condemned man whether his re-prieve is *upheld* or *held up*." — Bergen Evans

Use italics very selectively to create emphasis. Emphasis should be created by effective diction and sentence structure. Overuse of italics dilutes emphasis and may distort the tone of your writing. By mimicking heavily stressed speech, overuse of italics may create an impression of irony or even cynicism that you do not intend. (See also section 29d.)

EXERCISE 28.1 ❯ *Italics*

Supply italics where they are needed in the following sentences.

1. E. D. Hirsch's Cultural Literacy: What Every American Needs to Know — especially its appended list — has created a fascinating controversy since its publication.

2. For instance, Herman Melville's name is on the list, but his famous novel Moby Dick is not.

3. The statues David and the Pietà in St. Peter's Church in Vatican City are listed, but their creator Michelangelo does not appear.

4. Many of the foreign phrases — including ancien régime, bête noire, coup d'état, déjà vu, faux pas, fin de siècle, and tête-à-tête — are French, although a large number are Latin.

5. The Niña, Pinta, and Santa Maria do not appear, but the unfortunate Lusitania and Titanic do.

6. The maudlin poem *Hiawatha* and its author Henry Wadsworth Longfellow both appear, but *Paradise Lost*, the brilliant epic poem, appears without its author John Milton.

7. *Birth of a Nation* is the only film on the list not produced first as a book or play with the same name.

8. The absence of *I Love Lucy*, *The Dick Van Dyke Show*, *The Mary Tyler Moore Show*, *All in the Family*, and *M*A*S*H* makes it clear that popular television culture does not concern Hirsch.

9. Oddly enough, the ampersand (&) appears on the list.

10. Including the novel *Tobacco Road* on the list but not the play *Who's Afraid of Virginia Woolf?* seems arguable, but the enjoyment in lists is in disagreeing with them.

▪ *Word processing and italics*

Word processors allow you to use italics easily, without extra typing.

Choose between slanted italic print and underlining. With some word processors and some printers, italic automatically prints as underlining. Some, however, give you the choice of using slanted italic. Before you choose slanted italic, look at a sample print-out. If the slanted type is difficult to read, choose underlining instead; the meaning will be the same.

Insert codes for slanted italic or underlining carefully. Once you enter a code, be sure to toggle out of the code; otherwise, your printer will continue the italics. If your word processor uses control marks in the text, rather than more visible contrasting bars, give this special attention.

Do not use codes for boldface in place of codes for italics. Many people enjoy experimenting with the typefaces made available by word processors and compatible printers, but boldface print is not an acceptable substitute for italics.

Accents and other diacritical marks are available on most word processors and printers. Learn how they work on yours and practice using them.

Quotation Marks

Quotation marks set off direct quotations and identify the titles of unpublished and short works and chapters and other sections of long works.

> ### Quick Reference
>
> *Use quotation marks in one of three ways:*
>
> ❯ *Use quotation marks to set off direct quotations.*
>
> ❯ *Use quotation marks with the titles of brief works, parts of longer works, and unpublished works.*
>
> ❯ *Use quotation marks to indicate ironic or special use of a word.*

29a **Use quotation marks with direct quotations and with dialogue.**

Direct Quotations

Direct quotations represent spoken or written words exactly; quotation marks indicate where the quoted material begins and ends. In contrast, indirect quotations—often introduced by *that* for statements or *if* for questions—report what people say or ask without using their exact words. Quotation marks are not needed with indirect quotations.

> John Kenneth Galbraith commented, "In the affluent society no useful distinction can be made between luxuries and necessities." (The exact words are enclosed in quotation marks.)

But:

> Galbraith argues that, in an affluent society, the necessary and the de-
> sirable become inextricably mixed.   (The paraphrase of Galbraith's
> comment needs no quotation marks, though it does require attribution
> and documentation.)

Dialogue

In dialogue, a record of a conversation between two or more people, quotation marks indicate the exact words used by each
speaker in turn. By convention, each change of speaker begins a
new paragraph.

> . . . I felt that I was getting a better sense of the language from novels
> than from grammars. I read hard, discarding a writer as soon as I felt I
> had grasped his point of view. At night the printed page stood before
> my eyes in sleep.
> Mrs. Moss, my landlady, asked me one Sunday morning:
> "Son, what is this you keep on reading?"
> "Oh, nothing. Just novels."
> "What you get out of 'em?"
> "I'm just killing time," I said.
> "I hope you know your own mind," she said in a tone that implied
> that she doubted if I had a mind.—Richard Wright, "The Library Card"

| 29b | Place punctuation marks with quotation marks according to convention. |

Periods and Commas

Periods and commas appear before closing quotation marks.

> One of Flannery O'Connor's most haunting stories is "The River."

> "The Circus Animals' Desertion," a late poem by William Butler Yeats,
> describes his growing frustration with poetry.

Semicolons and Colons

Semicolons and colons always follow closing quotation marks.

> As a young poet, T. S. Eliot showed his brilliance in "The Love Song of J. Alfred Prufrock"; readers and critics responded to it enthusiastically.

> One word describes Lewis Carroll's "Jabberwocky": nonsense.

Question Marks and Exclamation Points

Question marks and exclamation points must be placed to maintain the meaning of the sentence. If the material in quotation marks (whether a direct quotation or a title) ends with a question mark, then the closing quotation mark appears last. If your sentence is a question that contains material in quotation marks, then the question mark appears last. The same principles apply to the use of exclamation points with quotation marks.

> Was it Archibald MacLeish who wrote "A world ends when its metaphor has died"?   (The quotation is contained within the question.)

> Have you read Ralph Ellison's "Did You Ever Dream Lucky?"   (The question mark inside the quotation marks serves both the question in the title and the question posed by the sentence.)

》》 *If a quotation ends with a question mark or exclamation point, any other punctuation normally required by the sentence structure may be omitted.*

> I just read Ralph Ellison's "Did You Ever Dream Lucky?"

> "Which is the right road?" he asked, but he received no reply.   (A comma is unnecessary following the question mark.) **《《**

29c ⟩ **Use quotation marks with the titles of brief works, parts of long works, and unpublished works.**

Articles, short stories, short poems, essays, and songs are brief works whose titles should appear in quotation marks. Chapter or unit titles and episodes of television series require quotation marks because they are parts of long works. Titles of unpublished papers or dissertations of any length are placed in quotation marks.

Articles

"Good News Is No News" in *Esquire*

"The New World Through New Eyes" in *Smithsonian*

Short stories

Charles Baxter's "A Fire Story"

Isaac Bashevis Singer's "Gimpel the Fool"

Poems

Emily Dickinson's "Because I Could Not Stop for Death"

Theodore Roethke's "My Papa's Waltz"

Essays

Joan Didion's "Why I Write"

James Thurber's "University Days"

Songs

Sarah Vaughn's "How Long Has This Been Going On?"

George and Ira Gershwin's "Summertime"

Chapter or unit titles

"Theatre of the Orient" in O. G. Brockett's *History of the Theatre*

"Nightmare" in *The Autobiography of Malcolm X*

Episodes of television programs

"The Death of Chuckles the Clown" from *The Mary Tyler Moore Show*

"Captain Tuttle" from *M*A*S*H*

Unpublished papers and dissertations

"Prohibition in the New England States"

"The Poetic Heritage of John Donne"

| 29d | Use quotation marks sparingly to indicate an ironic or other special use of a word. |

Words should be used according to their accepted meanings. The use of quotation marks to indicate irony may confuse and annoy readers. The use of quotation marks with nonstandard words—slang, regionalisms, or jargon—shows that you understand the words' potential inappropriateness in a sentence but does not justify their use. Either use the word with assurance or choose another word. (See also section 28e.)

Ironic use

Who needs enemies with "friends" like these?   (Clearly *friends* is being used ironically. The phrase *so-called friends* would convey the same meaning more clearly.)

Disavowal

The negotiator asked for our "input."   (Placing *input* in quotation marks suggests that the writer knows it is unacceptable jargon, but the disavowal does not make the word acceptable. Unless you are quoting directly, use a better word, such as *reactions, responses,* or *thoughts.*)

EXERCISE 29.1 ❯ *Quotation marks*

 Place the needed quotation marks in the following sentences. Pay attention to their positioning with other punctuation.

1. Running on Empty? an article in *National Wildlife,* stresses that water management should be a universal concern.

2. The opening chapter of *The Grapes of Wrath* contains this central image: The rain-heads [thunderclouds] dropped a little spattering and hurried on to some other country. Behind them the sky was pale again and the sun flared. In the dust there were drop craters where the rain had fallen, and there were clean splashes on the corn, and that was all.

3. Dry as Dust, a local documentary on the plight of the Depression farmers, had special meaning in 1988, when water shortages occurred throughout the midwestern states.

4. The very real fear of drought was softened during the Depression by ironic songs like What We Gonna Do When the Well Runs Dry?

5. Nadene Benchley's dissertation, Deluge or Drought: The Crisis in Water Management, ought to be published, for it contains information many people need to know.

30 Numbers and Abbreviations

Quick Reference

Use numbers and abbreviations according to convention.

❯ *In most instances, write out numbers expressible in one or two words.*

❯ *Use figures for exact numbers starting with 101.*

❯ *Use figures for measurements, technical numbers, and fractions.*

❯ *Use abbreviations sparingly in formal writing; if you use them, use standard abbreviations and forms.*

30a ❯ **In most writing contexts, use the written forms of numbers expressible in one or two words.**

Numbers Expressible in Words

Unless you are writing scientific or technical material, cardinal and ordinal numbers expressible in one or two words should be written out. This rule applies to numbers *one* through *one hundred* (*first* through *one hundredth*) and to large round numbers like *four thousand* (*four thousandth*) and *nine million* (*nine millionth*).

> The Soviet Union has four cities — Moscow, Leningrad, Tashkent, and Kiev — with populations of more than two million.

⟫ *Numbers from twenty-one through ninety-nine must be hyphenated.* ⟪

Numbers at the beginning of a sentence must be spelled out — no matter how many words are needed. If the number is long and awkward, revise the sentence.

Incorrect

115 seniors attended graduation.

Correct

One hundred fifteen seniors attended graduation.

Better

We counted 115 seniors at graduation.

Numbers Expressible in Figures

Exact cardinal and ordinal numbers starting with 101 should be expressed in figures.

The Rogun Dam, the tallest in the world, stands 1,066 feet high.

30b ⟩ **Use abbreviations sparingly in formal writing and only in contexts in which their meaning is clear.**

With few exceptions, abbreviations should not be used in formal writing. Commonly used personal titles such as *Ms., Mr.,* and *Dr.* are acceptable; also acceptable are some commonly used and easily recognizable abbreviations such as *JFK* and *NAACP*. If you are unsure whether your readers will recognize an abbreviation, spell out the words.

If you choose to use a common abbreviation for a person or organization in formal writing, the first mention should include the full name, followed by the abbreviation in parentheses.

Other Numbers Expressible in Figures

Addresses	316 Ridge Place; 1111 West 16th Street
Dates	24 December 1948 (*or* December 24, 1948); 150 B.C.; A.D. 1066
Divisions of books and plays	chapter 3; volume 9; act 2; scene 4
Exact dollar amounts	$3.12; $546 million; $7,279,000
Measurements	8 by 10
Identification numbers	332-44-7709; UTC 88 22495
Percentages	82 percent; 100 percent
Fractions	3/4
Scores	101 to 94
Times	3:15 A.M.; 7:45 P.M. (*but* four-thirty in the morning; nine o'clock)

The Potato Chip/Snack Food Association (PC/SFA) is an international trade association. Like other trade associations, the PC/SFA monitors government actions that affect the business of its members.

〉〉〉 *Many common abbreviations may be written without periods. Check your dictionary for acceptable forms.* **〈〈〈**

Certain specialized writing situations — technical directions, recipes, entries for works cited pages, résumés — use abbreviations to save space; but formal, academic writing should not. Instead, write the words out completely.

Acceptable Abbreviations

Well-known personal names	LBJ (Lyndon Baines Johnson); FDR (Franklin Delano Roosevelt)
Personal titles	John Walton, Jr.; Rebecca Santos, Ph.D.; Ms. Ella Beirbaum; Harold Blankenbaker, M.D.; Dr. Asha Mustapha; Rev. Joshua Felten; Gov. Michael S. Dukakis (*but* Governor Dukakis)
Names of countries	USA, US (*or* U.S.A., U.S.); UK (*or* U.K.); USSR (*or* U.S.S.R.)
Names of organizations and corporations	UNESCO; GE; FAA; AT&T
Words with figures	no. 133 (*or* No.)
Time of day	1:05 P.M. (*or* p.m.)
Dates	1200 B.C.; A.D. 476

Use the spell checker of your word-processing program to help you discover irregular abbreviations.   ■   Run the spelling program. Because spelling programs include only a sampling of abbreviations, only the most common, most generally accepted ones are part of the dictionary. Reconsider your use of any abbreviations that the speller brings to your attention.   ■   Check a dictionary in special instances. If you want to use the abbreviation anyway, check a dictionary to make sure that it is correct.

Unacceptable Abbreviations

	Not	*But*
Business designations	Co. Inc.	Company Incorporated
Units of measurement	lb. cm	pound centimeter
Names of days and months	Fri. Oct.	Friday October
Academic subjects	psych. Eng.	psychology English
Divisions of books and plays	p. chap. sc. vol.	page chapter scene volume
Names of places	L.A. VT	Los Angeles Vermont
Personal names	Wm. Robt.	William Robert
Latin phrases	cf. (*confer*) e.g. (*exempli gratia*) et al. (*et alii*) etc. (*et cetera*) i.e. (*id est*)	compare for example and others and so on, and others that is

EXERCISE 30.1 ❱ *Numbers and abbreviations*

Correct the misuse of number forms and abbreviations in the following sentences.

1. Doctor Ruth Waller, an econ. prof. at UCLA, has written 26 articles and 2 books about Asian-American trade relations.

2. 1 of her books and 14 of her articles are on reserve at the ISU library — to be read by students in Econ. two-hundred and thirty-six.

3. Statistics in one article show that Japan's labor force is well diversified, with eleven percent in agriculture, thirty-four percent in manufacturing, and forty-eight percent in services.

4. Statistics also show that the Am. labor force is not as well diversified: we have seventy percent in services, with close to one-third of those in info. management.

5. By Fri., Dec. twelfth, each of us in the class must prepare a report on a US co. that is affected by Asian-American trade.

EXERCISE 30.2 ❱ *Numbers and abbreviations*

Correct the misuse of number forms and abbreviations in the following paragraph.

Walter E. Disney, better known as Walt, was born Dec. fifth, 1901, in Chicago. After early work at the Chicago Academy of fine arts and at a Commercial Art firm in MO, he moved to Hollywood in nineteen-twenty-three. It was there that he revolutionized US entertainment. 1928 was the year he produced "Steamboat Willie," a short cartoon that introduced Mickey Mouse, as well as the use of soundtracks with cartoons. 10 years later, his studio produced the 1st feature-length animated cartoon, *Snow White and the 7 Dwarfs,* and 2 years later, *Pinocchio.* The success of Disney's films stemmed from their innovations, i.e. their use of animated forms, color, music, voices, and story. After more than 12 successful films, Disney began work in television in 1950. In 55, Disneyland opened outside L.A., and Disney's theme parks created a new standard for amusement parks. Few would have suspected, in nine-

teen-twenty-six, that the man whose first cartoon creation was Oswald
the Rabbit would change entertainment in the US of A.

31 Spelling

Many writers have spelling problems. Although these can sometimes be solved by reliance on familiar spelling rules (for example, *i* before *e*, except after *c*), spelling rules in English have many exceptions because English words derive from so many language groups. When you are uncertain of the spelling of a word, immediately consult a dictionary. Also develop practical strategies for overcoming spelling problems.

Quick Reference

Problems in spelling can be solved in a number of ways.

❯ *Learn to use general spelling rules.*

❯ *Use dictionaries to determine meaning and spelling.*

❯ *Use correct pronunciation to guide spelling.*

❯ *Check the spelling of technical terms carefully.*

> 31a ❯ **Learn to use the general rules that guide spelling.**

Although rules for spelling in English have many exceptions because English incorporates words from many languages, a few basic rules are helpful.

Forming Plurals

The letters that end a singular word dictate how its plural is formed.

Ending letters	Plural ending	Samples	
Consonant plus o	Add -*es*	potato	potatoes
		fresco	frescoes
Vowel plus o	Add -*s*	radio	radios
		stereo	stereos
Consonant plus y	Change *y* to *i* and add -*es*	victory	victories
		melody	melodies
Vowel plus y	Add -*s*	monkey	monkeys
		survey	surveys
s, ss, sh, ch, x, *or* z	Add -*es*	bonus	bonuses
		by-pass	by-passes
		dish	dishes
		catch	catches
		tax	taxes
		buzz	buzzes
Proper name with y	Add -*s*	Gary	Garys
		Germany	Germanys

Adding Prefixes

Some prefixes (*dis-, mis-, non-, pre-, re-, un-* and others) do not change the spelling of the root word.

similar dissimilar restrictive nonrestrictive

See pages 369–370 for exceptions to this rule.

Adding Suffixes

The pattern for adding suffixes depends on the letters that end the root word and those that begin the suffix.

Last letter of root word	First letter of suffix	Pattern	Examples
Silent e	Consonant	Retain the e	achievement resolutely
Silent e	Vowel	Drop the e	grieving sizable
Silent e preceded by a "soft" c or g	Vowel	Retain the e	noticeable changeable
Single consonant in one-syllable word with one vowel	Vowel	Double the consonant	sitting clipping

Distinguishing Between *ie* and *ei*

This familiar, useful poem explains the order of *i* and *e*.

Write *i* before *e*
Except after *c*
Or when sounded like *ay*
As in *neighbor* and *weigh*

31b ▷ **Use dictionaries to determine meanings and spellings.**

Spelling Dictionaries

Spelling dictionaries provide the correct spellings of thousands of words. These specialized dictionaries dispense with pronunciation guides, notes on word origins, definitions, and synonyms.

They generally indicate syllable breaks, however, which are helpful for hyphenating words at the ends of lines. People who have good vocabularies but spell poorly benefit from spelling dictionaries because they offer a quick way to confirm, for example, that *separate* is spelled with two *a*'s and two *e*'s and *develop* does not end with an *e*.

Standard Dictionaries

Words that sound alike, such as *mail* and *male*, may have very different meanings and spellings. Knowing which word has your intended meaning will lead you to the correct spelling. To determine that a word has your intended meaning and that you have spelled it correctly, use a standard dictionary. **》》** *When reading a dictionary definition to select the proper word and spelling, be sure to read all the definitions to find the one you need.* **《《**

The sample from *The American Heritage Dictionary, Second College Edition* (Boston: Houghton, 1985) shown in Figure 1 illustrates common features of a dictionary entry.

| 31c | Use correct pronunciation as a guide to correct spelling. |

The omission of letters in casual speech generally does not interfere with comprehension. Habitual mispronunciation, however, may lead to incorrect spelling. To ensure correct spelling when you write, sound out problem words, stressing all the letters but especially those omitted in speech. For instance, people often pronounce *accidentally* as if it were spelled "accident*ly*." Slowing down to sound out all the letters — *ac·ci·den·tal·ly* — will prevent this spelling problem.

Figure 1   A sample dictionary entry.

af·fect¹ (ə-fĕkt′) tr.v. -fect·ed, -fect·ing, -fects. 1. To have an influence on; bring about a change in. 2. To touch or move the emotions of. 3. To attack or infect, as a disease. —*n.* (ăf′ĕkt′). 1. *Psychol.* a. A feeling or emotion as distinguished from cognition, thought, or action. b. A strong feeling having active consequences. 2. *Obs.* A disposition, feeling, or tendency. [Lat. *afficere, affect-* : *ad-*, to + *facere*, to do.]
—af·fect′less *adj.*

   Synonyms: *affect, influence, impress, touch, move, strike.* These verbs can all mean to produce a mental or emotional effect. To *affect* is to change a person's emotions in some usually specified way. *Influence* implies a degree of control over the thinking and actions, as well as the emotions, of another. To *impress* is to produce a marked, usually favorable, effect on the mind. *Touch* usually means to arouse a brief sense of pathos, whereas *move* suggests profound emotional effect capable of inciting action. *Strike* implies instantaneous mental response to a stimulus such as a sight or an idea.

   Usage: *Affect¹* and *effect* have no senses in common. As a verb, *affect¹* is most commonly used in the sense of "to influence" (*how smoking affects health*). *Effect* means "to bring about or execute": *layoffs designed to effect savings*

E.

F.

G.

H.

A. *Spelling and syllabification*
B. *Pronunciation (guide at bottom of dictionary page)*
C. *Part of speech*
D. *Spelling variations (past tense, present participle, plural)*
E. *Numbered definitions*
F. *Word origins*
G. *Synonyms and antonyms*
H. *Usage note*

31d ▷ **Carefully check the spelling of technical words and British variants.**

Technical Words

If you use specialized words, check them individually. Their spellings are sometimes difficult because we use such words infrequently. Keep a note card handy with a list of the correct spelling of any technical words that you use often.

British Variants

Dictionaries list alternative spellings for some common words, and many times any choice is acceptable if applied consistently. When alternatives are identified as *American* (*Am.*) and *British* (*Brit.*), however, use the American spelling.

American Words with British Variants

American	*British*
center	centre
color	colour
encyclopedia	encyclopaedia
judgment	judgement

》》》 *When using a proper name, maintain the original spelling even if it is British.*

Great Britain's *Labour Party* favors the nationalization of many industries.   (Although the American spelling is *labor,* the proper name of the political party uses the British spelling.) **《《《**

Word processing and spelling

If you use a word processor for writing, take advantage of its spelling program. A spelling program searches a manuscript for words not appearing in its dictionary and highlights them for your attention. Be aware, though, of several minor limitations of some spelling programs.

A spelling program cannot distinguish an error in the choice of homonyms (words that have the same sound but different meaning). As long as a word appears in the program's dictionary, the program will not highlight the word. For instance, the use of *pail* for *pale* and *blew* for *blue* would go unnoticed.

A spelling program cannot identify typing errors if they produce words that are in the dictionary of the program. For instance, the use of *quite* instead of *quiet* would go unnoticed because *quite* is a recognizable English word.

The dictionaries for spelling programs are necessarily general so that many people can use them for many types of writing. Highly specialized words — proper names and technical terms, for instance — may not be included. In such cases, add these specialized words to the word list of the dictionary or check them individually.

Always proofread your writing carefully for spelling errors that are not identifiable by the spelling program.

The following list contains words that many people misspell. Use this list as a brief spelling dictionary as you write.

Commonly Misspelled Words

abbreviate	a lot	arranging
absence	although	article
absolutely	altogether	assassin
absurd	always	assassination
accelerate	amateur	assess
accidentally	ambiguous	association
accommodate	among	athlete
accomplish	amount	athletics
according	analysis	attempt
accumulate	analyze	attractive
accustom	annual	audible
achievement	Antarctic	audience
acknowledgment	anxiety	authorities
acquaintance	apartment	automobile
acquire	apparatus	auxiliary
across	apparent	awkward
address	appearance	bachelor
adoption	appropriate	balance
aggravate	archaic	balloon
aggression	arctic	barring
alleviate	argument	bearing
alley	arising	because
allotted	arithmetic	becoming
allowed	arouse	before

Commonly Misspelled Words

beggar	cemetery	completely
beginning	certain	compulsory
believe	changeable	concede
beneficial	changing	conceivable
benefited	characteristic	conceive
biscuit	chief	condemn
boundaries	choose	condescend
breathe	choosing	condition
brilliant	chose	conjunction
bulletin	chosen	conquer
buoyant	climbed	conscience
bureau	column	conscientious
buried	coming	conscious
burying	commission	considered
business	commitment	consistent
busy	committed	contemptible
cafeteria	committee	continuous
calendar	companies	control
candidate	comparatively	controlled
carrying	compel	convenient
casualties	compelled	cooperate
category	competent	copies
ceiling	competition	corner
celebrity	complaint	corpse

Commonly Misspelled Words

costume	definition	dissatisfy
countries	democracy	dissipate
courteous	dependent	distribute
courtesy	descendant	doctor
cozy	describe	dominant
cries	description	dormitory
criticism	desirable	dropped
criticize	despair	drunkenness
cruelty	desperate	echoes
cruise	destruction	ecstasy
curiosity	develop	efficient
curriculum	developed	eighth
custom	development	eligible
cylinder	diary	eliminate
dealt	dictionary	embarrass
debater	diet	eminent
deceitful	difference	emphasize
deceive	digging	employee
decide	disappearance	encouraging
decision	disappoint	encyclopedia
defendant	disastrous	enthusiastic
deferred	discipline	entrepreneur
deficient	discussion	environment
definite	disease	equipment

Commonly Misspelled Words

equipped	fiery	guarantee
equivalent	finally	guard
especially	financial	guardian
eventually	financier	guest
exaggerate	forehead	guidance
exceed	foreign	handicapped
excel	foremost	handkerchief
excellent	forfeit	harass
exceptional	forty	hearse
excitement	frantically	height
exercise	fraternity	heroes
exhaust	freshman	hesitancy
exhilaration	friend	hindrance
existence	fulfill	hoarse
experience	furniture	hoping
explanation	gaiety	human
extensive	generally	humane
extracurricular	genius	humorous
extremely	genuine	hundredths
exuberance	glorious	hurries
fallacy	government	hygiene
familiar	grammar	hypocrisy
fascinate	grandeur	hysterical
February	grieve	illiterate

Commonly Misspelled Words

illogical	interpret	loneliness
imaginary	interrupt	losing
imagination	irrelevant	magazine
imitative	irresistible	magnificent
immediately	irreverent	maintain
implement	itself	maintenance
impromptu	judgment	maneuver
inadequate	judicial	manual
incidentally	khaki	manufacture
incredible	kindergarten	mathematics
indefinitely	knowledge	mattress
independent	knowledgeable	meant
indicted	laboratory	medicine
indispensable	laid	messenger
inevitable	later	millennium
influential	latter	millionaire
initiate	legitimate	miniature
innocent	leisure	minute
inoculate	library	mischievous
intellectual	license	misspelled
intelligence	lightning	modifies
intentionally	likable	modifying
intercede	likely	momentous
interest	literature	mortgage

Commonly Misspelled Words

mosquitoes	occurred	peaceable
mottoes	occurrence	perceive
mountainous	o'clock	perceptive
murmur	official	perform
muscle	officious	perhaps
mysterious	omission	permissible
naive	omit	perseverance
naturally	omitted	persuade
necessary	opinion	phrase
necessity	opportunity	physical
neither	optimistic	physician
nervous	organization	pierce
nevertheless	original	planed
nickel	orthodox	planned
niece	ought	playwright
ninety	outrageous	pleasant
ninth	overrun	politics
noticeable	paid	possesses
notorious	pamphlet	possessive
obedience	parallel	possible
obliged	parliament	potatoes
obstacle	particularly	practice
occasionally	partner	prairie
occur	pastime	precede

Commonly Misspelled Words

predominant	quarter	repetition
prefer	questionnaire	replies
preference	quiet	representative
preferred	quizzes	reservoir
prejudice	realize	resistance
preparation	really	restaurant
prevalent	recede	reverent
primitive	receipt	rhetoric
privilege	receive	rheumatism
probably	receiving	rhythm
proceed	recognize	ridiculous
professor	recommend	sacrifice
prominent	refer	sacrilegious
pronounce	reference	safety
pronunciation	referred	salary
propaganda	referring	sanctuary
propeller	regard	sandwich
protein	regional	scarcely
psychology	relevant	scene
pursue	religion	scenic
pursuing	religious	schedule
putting	remembrance	scrape
quantity	reminiscence	secretarial
quarantine	rendezvous	secretary

Commonly Misspelled Words

seize	statute	tangible
sense	stomach	tasting
sensible	stopped	technical
sentence	strength	technique
separate	strenuous	temperament
severely	stretch	tenant
shining	struggle	tendency
shriek	studying	than
siege	subordinate	therefore
sieve	subtle	thorough
similar	succeed	though
sincerely	success	thought
sincerity	successful	till
skeptical	suffrage	tired
slight	superintendent	together
sophomore	supersede	tournament
source	suppress	toward
specifically	surely	traffic
specimen	surprise	tragedy
sponsor	suspense	transferred
spontaneous	swimming	tremendous
statement	symmetry	tries
statue	synonymous	truly
stature	taboo	twelfth

Commonly Misspelled Words

typical	vengeance	which
tyranny	victorious	whole
unanimous	view	wholly
undoubtedly	vigilant	whom
unnecessary	vigorous	wiry
until	village	woman
usage	villain	women
useful	volume	won't
using	warrant	worried
usually	warring	worrying
vacancy	weird	writing
vacuum	welfare	written
valuable	where	yacht

32 Tips for ESL Writers

Many ESL writers have the same skills, experiences, and success as native language writers. They also face the same problems as native language writers—plus some additional problems. This chapter identifies some of those additional problems and offers some tips for dealing with them.

32a Use outlining for troubleshooting when writing a rough draft

Outlines (section 2b) can have a double benefit for ESL writers. They can clarify the main features of your paper and the interrelationship among them. They can also highlight key structures and words that distort or obscure meaning and impede development.

Any kind of outline serves this dual purpose, but a **sentence outline** reveals the most language problems during drafting. Each sentence summarizes an important point. The working thesis statement and sentence outline shown below demonstrate one ESL writer's effort to sharpen the fundamental phrasing of a first draft after consulting a peer editor.

Working thesis statement: If you understand the ~~base~~ *origin* and construction of Chinese characters, learning to write in Chinese is not difficult.

I. The Chinese characters ~~make-for-strange~~ *excite curiosity* and ~~frighten~~ *dread* in Westerners learning Chinese.

II. Chinese characters represented things or ideas through *originally* *icons* ~~pictures~~.

III.   Knowing the meaning of some portion of a character is a
       related
       quicker way to master a group of characters.
       common
IV.   It is ~~average~~ in Chinese to create a new character by com-
       ^

       bining several individual characters.

| 32b | **Flag diction problems and move on when writing a rough draft** |

Spending too much time trying to find the right word to express a
particular thought can stall or seriously slow the pace of drafting.
Instead of groping for a word, flag the problem spot and move on.
Use a distinctive method of marking that will be easy to see when
you return to the draft. Circle the item, underline it with a wavy
line, highlight it with a brightly colored marker, or insert a brainstorming list (page 16) of two or three possible choices to be considered later. This simple technique will prevent you from bog-
ging down in the fine points of diction when exploring or
arranging your thoughts is more critical.

| 32c | **Set revision priorities** |

Not all language problems that surface during drafting need immediate attention. Many ESL writers set priorities for tackling their
language problems. They begin with vocabulary and sentence
structure errors that affect the clarity, coherence, and completeness of their draft. They focus on the working thesis statement, on
topic sentences, on sentences containing key generalizations, arguments or assertions, and on transition sentences.

32d ▷ Keep a language log of problems and solutions

Keeping a language log is an efficient way to track problems and ensure that a useful editing procedure or a successful method for dealing with a particular error can be repeated. The log entry contains a description and an example of the problem, plus an explanation of how the error was corrected.

32e ▷ Use lists and word-form tables to improve diction

More than a few ESL writers use lists and tables of idiomatic expressions and irregular forms. Such lists are not all-inclusive. They are limited ro recurring problems that need special attention during revision. Phrasal idioms, irregular plural forms, and mass nouns (nouns that are not readily modified by a numeral) are just three of the many English oddities that can be grouped in lists for easy reviewing.

Phrasal Idioms

agree *with* a person
agree *to* a proposal

charge *for* a purchase
charge *with* a crime

Irregular Plural Forms

Singular	*Plural*
analysis	analyses
half	halves
ox	oxen
woman	women

Mass Nouns

anger
behavior
buttermilk
news
oxygen

Be + Adjective + Preposition	*Verb + Noun + Preposition*
is absent from	has access to
is different from	has patience with
is worried about	take pride in
etc.	etc.

Word-form tables help you distinguish among verbs, nouns, adjectives, and adverbs that come from the same word. You lay out the grid and fill in as many parts of speech as you can. Use a standard dictionary to find any parts of speech you don't know. Write sentences demonstrating the usage of each part of speech. A native speaker can provide valuable information about using a word in context.

Verb	*Noun*	*Adjective*	*Adverb*
separate	separation	separate	separately
		separated	

Verb
|
Don't *separate* yourself from your friends and relatives.

noun
|
I like the idea of the *separation* of church and state in the United States.

adjective
|
We would like *separate* checks, please

Separated spouses met with a marriage counselor each week.

adverb
|
Bob and Mary paid for dinner *separately*.

| 32f | Sentence Structure Tips |

Coordinating Conjunctions and Conjunctive Adverbs

Coordinating conjunctions and conjunctive adverbs often have similar meanings and show similar relationships (section 6f). However, they have different effects on coherence and sentence style. When you use coordinating conjunctions and conjunctive adverbs, always test their appropriateness with a native speaker.

Meaning	Coordinating Conjunctions	Conjunctive Adverbs
Addition	and	also besides furthermore moreover
Contrast	but yet	however instead nevertheless nonetheless
Choice	nor or	instead otherwise
Result/Purpose	so	accordingly consequently therefore thus

Faulty *It* and *There* Expletive Constructions

ESL writers frequently omit or misuse the expletives *it* and *there* (page 639).

Incorrect	*It was* a big political scandal in my country last year.
Correct	*There was* a big political scandal in my country last year.
Incorrect	*Is important* that you understand our customs.
Correct	*It is important* that you understand our customs.
Incorrect	*Are only* two important political parties in the United States.
Correct	*There are only* two important political parties in the United States.
Incorrect	*There was* too dark in the room to read.
Correct	*It was* too dark in the room to read.

It expletives are used in statements or questions about weather, time, distance, or environment.

It was freezing.
Is it time to go?
It was ten miles to the next gas station.
It is a rundown neighborhood.

They also serve as discourse markers, informing the reader that the material in the sentence should be given special attention.

It is important for Americans to realize how difficult English is for a fifty-year-old woman.

It is a sad fact that many international students at our university cannot find decent housing.

There expletives are used in statements or questions about the location or existence of someone or something.

There was a large pothole in the middle of the street.

Is there a God?

There are too few people in the United States who speak a language other than English.

Like *it* expletives, *there* expletives serve as discourse markers. However, they are used in sentences that introduce new material.

There are two reasons why I left my country. (The next sentence would discuss the first reason.)

There are several facts about American universities that Indonesian students need to know. (The next sentence would identify the first fact.)

Misuse of the Passive Voice

When active and passive voice (section 9a and page 652) are fused, ungrammatical and confusing constructions result.

Incorrect   My country *has been studied* its lack of modern technology for too many years.

"My country," the subject and the agent of this sentence, needs to be followed by an active verb. Alternatively, the sentence can be rewritten in the passive voice.

Active   My country *has been studying* its lack of modern technology for too many years.

Passive   My country's lack of modern technology *has been stud-ied* for too many years.

Faulty Relative Clauses

Sometimes ESL writers incorrectly insert a personal pronoun into a relative clause as the subject or object.

Incorrect   AIDS is becoming a worldwide epidemic that *it* needs health-care specialists' immediate attention.

Incorrect   Karl bought American novels that he never read *them*.

The relative pronouns *who, whom, which,* and *that* are used as the subjects or objects of relative clauses. They refer to nouns previously used in the sentence. Thus, no additional personal pronoun is necessary.

subject of clause
|

AIDS is becoming a worldwide epidemic that ~~it~~ needs health-care specialists' immediate attention.

object of clause
|

Karl bought American novels that he never read ~~them~~.

|
subject of clause

Mixed Constructions with Subordinating and Coordinating Conjunctions

Misusing subordinating conjunctions and coordinating conjunctions (section 6f) produces a confusing sentence.

Incorrect   Although he is an honored and well-known intellectual, but Professor Singh is not considered an outstanding teacher.

The sentence gives two different structural signals: "although" is signaling a subordinate clause in a complex sentence; "but" is signaling a contrasting item in a compound sentence. The sentence would be restructured to eliminate one or the other confusing signal.

Complex sentence   Although he is an honored and well-known intellectual, Professor Singh is not considered an outstanding teacher.

Compound sentence   Professor Singh is an honored and well-known intellectual, but he is not considered an outstanding teacher.

Guard against this type of mixed construction in complex sentences containing subordinating conjunctions that express concession and contrast—for example, *although, even though, though, if, even if.*

| 32g | > Grammar and Punctuation Tips |

Definite Versus Indefinite Articles

Determining when the definite article (*the*) or the indefinite article (*a* or *an*) is appropriate can become a frustrating task for someone learning English. Articles indicate whether information is part of a writer's and reader's experiences, and they mark a noun or noun phrase as representing a defined group.

In writing, the **definite article** marks six ways in which a reader could be familiar with the noun. Use the definite article *(the)* when

1. The noun is common knowledge: *the sun, the earth, the clouds, the wind, the rain.*

2. The noun is distinctive to a setting: *the desk* (in the corner), *the file cabinet* (under the window), *the bookcase* (in the office).

3. The noun is distinctive to a particular group: *the priest* (in Saint John's Catholic Church), *the president* (of the United States), *the quarterback* (of the Philadelphia Eagles).

4. The noun is one of the components of a defined unit: *the windows* (of the restaurant), *the doors* (facing Main Street), *the closets* (of a house).

5. The noun has been previously mentioned and has therefore been made familiar to the reader: I saw a man walking his dog. *The man* looked very happy.

6. The relevance of the noun is defined by a modifier, such as a prepositional phrase, a relative clause, or an adjective: *the president* of our amateur radio club, *the woman* who gave me my first book, *the best hunting dog.*

The **indefinite article** usually signals that the reader, the writer, or both have no specific experience with the noun. Use the indefinite article (*a* or *an*) when

1. The noun is part of the writer's experience but not the reader's: I once took classes from *an interesting economics professor.* (The writer, not the reader, took classes.)

2. The noun is assumed to be part of the reader's experience but not the writer's: I remember asking my American roommate if she had *a special knack* for getting good grades without studying. (The writer lacks the "special knack" but assumes that the reader is familiar with it.)

3. The noun is not part of either the writer's or the reader's experience: The university needs *a new tuition policy* for

international students. (The new policy belongs to the university.)

The system that underlies generic uses of articles can also cause problems when writing. A generic article is used to indicate that people or things are members of a group. For example, consider the following two sentences:

We saw *the pandas* at the Columbus Zoo.

The panda is becoming extinct in the wild.

The first sentence refers to specific *pandas* while the second sentence refers to *panda* as a class. There are five structural patterns that are used when writing about generic groups. Three of them make use of articles.

Five Generic Uses

Pattern 1:   The kangaroo is a marsupial. (*The* + Singular Noun) This pattern is the most formal and is often used in technical or informative writing.

Pattern 2:   Kangaroos are marsupials. (Plural Noun) This pattern is used in less formal writing and preferred when discussing simple inanimate objects ("Forks were a novelty in the Middle Ages.").

Pattern 3:   Well, a baby eventually needs sleep. (*A/an* + Singular Noun) This pattern is the most informal and frequently occurs in speech or writing containing personal observations shared by the reader.

Pattern 4:   Protein is found in most beans. (Mass Noun) This pattern is restricted to mass nouns.

Pattern 5:   The ancient Egyptians gave us the first solar calendar. (*The* + Plural Noun) This pattern is not as common, mainly reserved for discussing information about religious, political, national, social, historical, or professional groups.

Using Articles with Place Names

In most instances, no article is used with geographical names: *Asia, Burma, Tokyo, Lake Mead*.

Collective and plural names, however, take *the: the United States, the People's Republic of China, the Rocky Mountains, the Himalayas, the Great Lakes*.

Bodies of water (except individual lakes), land masses, and regions of the world also take *the: the Atlantic Ocean, the Caspian Sea, the Gulf of Oman, the Bay of Bengal, the Mississippi River, the English Channel, the Panama Canal, the Australian continent, the Strait of Hormuz, the Kamchatka Peninsula, the Sahara*.

Commas with Adverb Clauses at the End of a Sentence

In the American system of punctuating, commas setting off adverb clauses at the end of a sentence are usually unnecessary.

Incorrect   I came to study business management, because American business schools are internationally famous.

Correct   I came to study business management because American business schools are internationally famous.

The problem often occurs with the subordinating conjunction *because*. Clauses starting with *as if, unless, though, although, even though, when, whenever, since, while, after,* and *before* should also be checked for unnecessary introductory commas.

Not Versus *No*

Knowing when to use *not* and *no* can be confusing.

> **Incorrect**   The teacher *no keeps* regular office hours.
> Frequently I *not understand* him.

Not is regularly used to make a verb phrase negative and to modify an entire noun phrase.

Verb phrase

Sonja does *not* want to be a student anymore.

Noun phrase

Not a single person came to our meeting.

No is typically used like an adjective.

> He has *no* skills for the job.

> *No* money is available for the movie.

Gerunds Versus Infinitives

Deciding when to use a gerund (page 178) or an infinitive (page 146) in a sentence can be confusing.

> **Incorrect**   Juan enjoys *to talk* with friends late into the night.

> **Correct**   Juan enjoys *talking* with friends late into the night.

> **Incorrect**   Peter hopes *studying* linguistics at MIT.

> **Correct**   Peter hopes *to study* linguistics at MIT.

If you are having problems, this rule may help. Use a *gerund* when the verb indicates that a goal or action has been completed or that a personal observation or statement of fact is being made.

gerund
|
The jury *finished* deliberating on the case.

gerund
|
Many Americans *enjoy seeing* foreign films.

Use an *infinitive* when the verb indicates that completing an action or achieving a goal is essential or desirable.

inf.
|
Many college students *will need* to find jobs this summer to subsidize the costs of their education.

inf.
|
Hammed *wants* to study medicine at an American university after graduation.

Be aware, however, that this rule is not a perfect predictor. The following verbs can be followed by a gerund or an infinitive.

attempt	hesitate	plan
begin	intend	prefer
continue	like	start
dread	love	try
hate	neglect	

Indirect Quotation

Indirect quotation (page 639) is often used in place of a one-sentence direct quotation. To construct an indirect quotation, follow these three steps:

1. Change the point of view of the statement being quoted from first person (*I*) to third person (*he, she, it, they*).

2. Make sure the statement being quoted is introduced by an expression such as *he said, she stated,* or *they argued.*

3. Change the tense of the statement being quoted from present to past. If the quotation contains auxiliary verbs, their tense as well. Change *will* to *would, may* to *might* or *could, can* to *could, will* to *would, must* to *had to,* and *shall* to *would.*

Direct quotation   Professor Zucker, my former history professor, once said, "I shall never fully understood Russian history until I experience a winter in Moscow."

Indirect quotation   Professor Zucker, my former history professor, once said that he would never fully understood Russian history until he experienced a winter in Moscow.

Indirect quotations are often introduced with the word *that.*

Subject-Verb Order in Indirect Questions

Subject-verb order in indirect questions sometimes causes problems.

Incorrect   Sybil can't understand *why is John failing the class.*
Hung can't remember *where does she live.*

In direct questions, the auxiliary verb precedes the subject.

Direct question   Why is John failing the class?
Where does she live?

In indirect questions, the subject and verb are in normal word order; they are not inverted.

Indirect question   Sybil can't understand *why John is failing the class.*
Hung can't remember *where she lives.*

32h ▷ **Verb Tips**

Inappropriate Use of Progressive Tenses

Some verbs describing a state or condition are not ordinarily used in the progressive tenses.

Incorrect   This book *is containing* too many difficult words.
                I *am knowing* this material by heart.

Such verbs are called **stative verbs.** For a list of common stative verbs, see below. Be aware that in some contexts, the progressive-tense form of some of these verbs is correct. If you are uncertain about a specific usage, check with a peer editor.

Common Stative Verbs

appear	have	recognize
appreciate	hear	remember
believe	imagine	see
belong	know	seem
contain	like	smell
cost	look	suppose
desire	love	taste
dislike	mean	think
doubt	measure	understand
entail	need	want
feel	own	weigh
hate	prefer	wonder

Make, Have, and *Get* Used as Causative Verbs

The verbs *make, have,* and *get* are commonly used to express the idea that someone or something causes someone else to act. ESL writers are often frustrated by the complexity of sentence structures with causatives. Here is a list of the most confusing features of their structure. Use it when editing these verbs.

1. Both *have* and *get* can act as passive auxiliaries. In such cases, they are followed by a past participle.

Active causative:	Cynthia had Mike fix her video recorder.
Passive causative:	Cynthia *had* her video recorder *fixed* by Mike.
Active causative:	Mary got her brother to paint her apartment.
Passive causative:	Mary *got* her apartment *painted* by her brother.

2. *Have* takes the infinitive form without *to* in the active voice.

Active causative:	Jill had the mechanic *check* her car thoroughly.
Passive causative:	Jill had her car *checked* thoroughly by the mechanic.

3. *Get* takes a *to + infinitive* form in active voice but changes to a *past participle* in passive voice.

Active causative:	Mary got her brother *to paint* the apartment.
Passive causative:	Mary got the apartment *painted* by her brother.

4. *Make* requires the *be* auxiliary in passive constructions.

Active causative:	Conrad's roommate made him stop smoking in the dorm room.
Passive causative:	Conrad *was* made to stop smoking in the dorm room.

441

5. *Make* requires a *to + infinitive* form in the passive construction.

Active causative: Howard made Jill *buy* him lunch.

Passive causative: Jill was made *to buy* Howard lunch.

Past Participles and Present Participles Used as Predicate Adjectives

The past and present participles of verbs that describe feelings or emotions, such as *amuse, bewilder, disappoint,* and *surprise,* are frequently misused as predicate adjectives (page 175).

Incorrect   The size of American cities is *bewildered* for many international students.

He is *disappointing* in Americans' lack of knowledge of other countries.

Use present participles as adjectives when you want to say that a person, thing, or idea *causes* a feeling or an emotion.

Correct   The size of American cities is *bewildering* for many international students.

Many facts that emerged from the investigation were *surprising.*

Use past participles as adjectives when you want to say that a person *experiences* a feeling or an emotion.

Correct   He is *disappointed* in Americans' lack of knowledge of other countries.

Students who could understand the American comedian were *amused.*

Time Expression with Simple Past and Present Perfect Tenses

Certain time expressions are best used with the simple past tense. Others are best used with the present perfect tense.

Incorrect   Since September, I *studied* in the United States.

Incorrect   Last week I *have watched* the TV program on Arab culture.

Since the present perfect tense signals that an action or state that began in the past continues to the present, expressions such as the following are use to show the time span:

since school started	so far
unit now	these days
up until now	

On the other hand, simple past signals that the action or state ended in the past so time expressions such as the following are used to show how long ago it happened:

yesterday	last week
the other day	a month ago
earlier this week	two years ago
at seven o'clock on Friday	

RESEARCH

33 Choosing and Researching a Topic and Taking Notes

To begin work on a research paper, you need to select a topic to research and write about. The possibilities are many, but some kinds of topics will have more value for you than others because of your interests and experiences. Explore alternative topics, keeping an open mind, and base your selection on a reasoned judgment. Consider topics related to your fields of study; consider topics related to your personal interests; consider topics that raise questions you would like to explore. Whatever your final choice, make sure you are committed to it because you will spend hours reading and thinking and writing about it.

Quick Reference

> Choose a general subject that is interesting, specific, and challenging.

> Narrow the subject to a specific topic by restricting its time period, its locale, or its special circumstances.

> Write a working thesis statement to guide your research.

> Compile a preliminary list of sources and evaluate their potential usefulness.

> Take clear, consistent, and complete notes.

> Avoid plagiarism by accurately identifying material quoted or paraphrased from any source.

Research papers can take two forms: factual, objective surveys of all the literature available on a topic, or interpretive analyses of selected evidence arrayed to support the writer's viewpoint and ideas. An interpretive paper, though primarily concerned with the writer's own ideas and interpretations, cannot ignore contrary evidence. Writers of such papers must be thorough and fair even though they must take a position on their material. Part of the challenge — and pleasure — of research is the constant need to reexamine your evidence in the light of new evidence and your ideas in the light of new ideas. In psychology, sociology, economics, and some other courses, you may be required to write the first type of paper. Ask your instructor for guidelines and, if possible, for an example of a good paper of this type. Since most college research papers, particularly those for composition courses, are of the second type, this text focuses on interpretive research papers.

As you gather and read materials related to your topic, you will be taking notes to record information and ideas to use when you write the final paper. You will find the process of reading source materials and taking notes rewarding and enlightening if the topic intrigues and has value for you.

| 33a | Choose a subject and narrow it to a specific topic. |

Choosing a General Subject

Unless your instructor has assigned a general subject for your research paper, you must begin your work by selecting one. Your major or minor field of study or an academic subject that you enjoy or know well is a good broad subject to begin with. Any subject that you know well or have an interest in can lead you to a good topic. A student who works for Exxon, for example, might write about company policies on or responses to ecologically damaging oil spills.

Guidelines for Assessing General Subjects

The subject should be interesting enough that you are willing to spend hours thinking, reading, and writing about it.

The subject should be of a scope broad or narrow enough to be treated adequately in the space recommended or required.

Enough material should be available to research the subject completely within the time available. Very recent events do not make good subjects because adequate materials are not generally available.

The subject should be challenging but should not require special knowledge that you do not have and do not have time to acquire.

The subject should not be overused; overused subjects are likely to be uninteresting to readers and difficult to research because of the high demand for the source materials.

When you have selected a general subject that meets the above requirements, you should consult with your instructor to be sure that it meets the requirements of the assignment.

Michele, who intends to major in psychology and minor in English, considered these general subjects:

Counseling juvenile delinquents

Using psychological concepts to teach literature

The uses of IQ tests

She eliminated the first because it seemed to require knowledge and experience that she did not have. The first of the remaining subjects seemed too broad. IQ testing was also broad, but it could be narrowed easily, and with a nationally recognized psychology program at her school, Michele knew she could find a wide range of materials.

EXERCISE 33.1 ❭ *General subjects*

List five possible subjects for a research paper. Test them against the guidelines given on page 447. (If you have difficulty with this assignment, skim the index of a textbook in your major or minor field for interesting subjects.)

Example

1. Stained-glass windows

2. Housing and architecture

3. Public sculpture

4. Impressionist art

5. Art in contemporary society

Narrowing a General Subject to a Specific Topic

With a general subject in mind, begin to narrow its focus. A focused topic will help you to determine your thesis. It will also help you to avoid wasting valuable research time reviewing and reading materials that will not fit into the final paper. An hour or two spent skimming reference books to narrow a subject often saves many hours later.

Begin by reading general sources in the library's reference room — various encyclopedias, specialized dictionaries, and fact books — to discover the scope and basic themes and details of your general subject. (See the selected list of general reference works on pages 453–56.) Use this information and the following strategies to narrow your subject to a specific topic:

Limit the scope of your paper to a specific, manageable time span. For example, restrict the topic *assembly-line automobile production* to the *1920s* or *1970s*.

Limit the scope of your topic to a single, specific location. For example, focus the topic *revitalization of cities* on *midwestern cities* or *St. Louis.*

Limit your topic to a specific set of circumstances. For example, the topic *the U.S. presidency* might focus on *the U.S. presidency in wartime.*

These strategies can be combined to achieve even greater focus. For example, a student might research *assembly-line automobile production in Korea in the 1970s* or *the U.S. presidency during the conflict in Vietnam.*

To obtain a general knowledge of IQ testing and to find some themes or details to help her to narrow the general subject, Michele skimmed some of the relevant reference books in the college library. She found that her general subject could be effectively narrowed by examining the uses of IQ tests in particular periods, such as the 1920s or 1950s, or by discussing the uses of IQ tests in the United States or in a specific area of the United States. Michele also found many special circumstances that applied to her subject; for example, she noted evidence of cultural bias in the compilation, administration, and interpretation of the tests. Narrowing the subject by combining the problem of bias with a specific location gave Michele many additional topics. One of them was the effect of cultural bias in the use of IQ tests in the multiethnic communities of southern California.

Michele was most interested, however, in what she read about the evolving concept of intelligence and its effect on the form and use of the tests and in efforts to change limited and stigmatizing ways of assessing intelligence. She was unsure whether a historical or a contemporary perspective would be more effective, but she decided to begin with this topic and to let a structure emerge as she gathered information.

EXERCISE 33.2 ❱ *Specific topics*

Select three subjects from your responses to Exercise 33.1 and write three focused topics by identifying a particular time, place, or special circumstance.

Example

1. Stained-glass revivals in the nineteenth and twentieth centuries

2. The universal appeal of the Impressionists

3. Blockbuster exhibitions and the role of art in contemporary American society

---

33b	❱	**Write a working thesis statement.**

In the same way a working thesis statement guides your planning and drafting for other papers, it guides your planning and drafting for your research paper. For a research paper, which involves intensive reading and thinking, the working thesis statement also helps you to select and evaluate materials.

Your focused topic, stated as a complete statement or question and anchored with details derived from your preliminary research (see pages 464–66 and section 33e), should yield an effective working thesis statement. A student working with the focused topic *the U.S. presidency during the conflict in Vietnam* might develop the following thesis:

> During the conflict in Vietnam, the presidency was forced to a new level of accountability by the peace movement and the media.

After writing your working thesis statement, evaluate its effectiveness. (For more information on thesis statements, see section 1e.) An effective thesis statement has three essential characteristics and may have three optional characteristics:

Essential Characteristics

Identify a specific, narrow topic.

Present a clear opinion on, not merely facts about, the topic.

Establish a tone appropriate to the topic, purpose, and audience.

Optional Characteristics

Qualify the topic as necessary, pointing out significant opposing opinions.

Clarify important points, indicating the organizational pattern.

Take account of readers' probable knowledge of the topic.

》》 *A thesis statement can make research seem a deductive process, one beginning with a general conclusion to support. But research should also be inductive, shaped by and building to a conclusion based on information discovered. Therefore, a question may sometimes be more effective than a statement as a guide to research. When researching, allow new ideas and unexpected information to lead you in promising new directions. Keep an open mind by using your working thesis not as something to be proved but as a controlling idea to be confirmed, refuted, or modified on the basis of your reading in the weeks or months ahead.* **《《**

From her general reading and discussions with her psychology professor, Michele decided to research the misuse of IQ tests over the years in light of the current emphasis on responsible use. Before beginning her focused search for specific, relevant materials, she reviewed her preliminary research notes and formulated her working thesis statement:

> *IQ tests, their use, and the concept of intelligence itself have been constantly challenged, refined, and redefined by scientists and edu-*

cators seeking to use the tests wisely, not to label people but to help
them overcome weaknesses and build on strengths.

Michele planned to use this thesis statement to guide her research;
it would help her to eliminate sources that treated unrelated
aspects of intelligence testing and direct her toward relevant
sources. She kept in mind, however, that her thesis statement
would likely change as she learned more about her topic.

A word processor allows you to revise your working thesis
statement easily as you complete your research. ■ Draft
alternative working thesis statements. Work freely and
quickly, typing as many variations of your thesis statement
as possible. In trying to express the thesis statement in
alternative ways, you may discover different approaches to
your work. ■ Revise your working thesis statement as
you learn more. Because the computer allows you to add
and delete freely, without retyping, review and revise your
thesis statement frequently as you continue your research,
acknowledging changes in your interpretation of the topic.

EXERCISE 33.3 ❯ *Working thesis statements*

*Type three working thesis statements with which you might begin
your research. Discuss them with other students or with your instructor to determine which promises to lead to the most productive research and the best paper.*

Example

1. The revivals of use of stained glass in the nineteenth and twentieth
   centuries owe something to a romantic view of the unromantic
   Middle Ages, when stained glass first came into widespread use.

2. The art of the Impressionists, based on idealized images of leisure
   and pleasure, has natural appeal and wins easy acceptance in a century desperately dedicated to increasing and pursuing both.

3. Entertainment or aesthetic experience? Opinion is divided over the usefulness of blockbuster exhibitions and their ultimate effect on museums and the public. Visitors arrive in record numbers to see Van Gogh, Renoir, Gauguin, but what are they seeing and why?

33c ⟩ **Begin your research in the library.**

If you have not done so already, take a tour of your college library with a staff member. On your own, after a tour or using a map or guide to the library, locate and explore the card catalog area (which includes both traditional and computerized catalogs), the reference room, the periodical and newspaper sections, the stacks and reserve area (where books are shelved), and the circulation desk (where books are checked out). Locate and learn to use microfilm, microfiche, or other viewing devices. Talk to library staff members about other services offered by the library, such as interlibrary loans and computerized databases.

General Reference Works

The reference room in your library contains a number of useful general reference works: major encyclopedias, almanacs, atlases, dictionaries, and compendia of biography, etymology, and quotations. The following lists indicate the variety of material available.

General References

Contemporary Authors. 123 vols. 1967 to date.

Current Biography. 1940 to date.

Facts on File Yearbook. 1940 to date.

National Geographic Atlas of the World. 5th ed. 1981.

New York Times Atlas of the World. 2nd rev. ed. 1983.

Who's Who. 1849 to date.

The World Almanac and Book of Facts. 1868 to date.

Encyclopedias

Collier's Encyclopedia. 24 vols. 1981.

Encyclopedia Americana. 30 vols. 1985.

Encyclopedia International. 20 vols. 1982.

New Encyclopaedia Britannica. 30 vols. 1986.

Art and Music

Apel, Willi. *The Harvard Dictionary of Music.* 2nd rev. ed. 1969.

Encyclopedia of World Art. 15 vols. 1959-68.

Sadie, Stanley, ed. *The New Grove Dictionary of Music and Musicians.* 20 vols. 1980.

Thompson, Oscar. *International Cyclopedia of Music and Musicians.* 11th ed. 1985.

Trachtenberg, Marvin, and Isabelle Hyman. *Architecture: From Prehistory to Post-Modernism.* 1986.

Economics and Business

Greenwald, Douglas. *The McGraw-Hill Dictionary of Modern Economics.* 3rd ed. 1984.

Munn, Glenn G. *Encyclopedia of Banking and Finance.* 8th ed. Ed. Ferdinand L. Garcia. 1983.

Sloan, Harold S., and Arnold Zurcher. *A Dictionary of Economics.* 5th ed. 1970.

History

American History Association. *Guide to Historical Literature*. 1961.

Cambridge Ancient History. 12 vols. 1923–39.

Cambridge Mediaeval History. 9 vols. 1911–36.

Freidal, Frank, and Richard K. Showman, eds. *Harvard Guide to American History*. Rev. ed. 2 vols. 1974.

Langer, William Leonard. *An Encyclopedia of World History: Ancient, Medieval, and Modern*. 5th ed. 1972.

New Cambridge Modern History. 14 vols. 1957–80.

Language and Literature

Baugh, Albert C., ed. *A Literary History of England*. 2nd ed. 1967.

Drabble, Margaret, ed. *The Oxford Companion to English Literature*. 5th ed. 1985.

Encyclopedia of World Literature in the Twentieth Century. Ed. Leonard S. Klein. Rev. ed. 4 vols. 1984.

Hart, James D., ed. *The Oxford Companion to American Literature*. 5th ed. 1983.

Modern Language Association International Bibliography of Books and Articles on the Modern Languages and Literatures. 1922 to date.

The Oxford English Dictionary. Ed. J. A. Simpson and E. S. C. Weiner. 2nd ed. 20 vols. 1989.

Spiller, Robert E. *Literary History of the United States: Bibliography*. 1974.

Philosophy and Religion

Edwards, Paul, ed. *Encyclopedia of Philosophy.* 4 vols. 1973.

Ferm, Vergilius, ed. *An Encyclopedia of Religion.* 1976.

Science and Math

Belzer, Jack, et al., eds. *Encyclopedia of Computer Science and Technology.* 14 vols. 1975–80.

Considine, Douglas, ed. *The Encyclopedia of Chemistry.* 4th ed. 1984.

Gellert, W., et al., eds. *VNR Concise Encyclopedia of Mathematics.* 1977.

Gray, Peter. *The Encyclopedia of Biological Sciences.* 2nd ed. 1981.

The McGraw-Hill Encyclopedia of Science and Technology. 5th ed. 15 vols. 1982.

Thewlis, J., ed. *Encyclopedic Dictionary of Physics.* 9 vols. 1961–75.

Social Sciences

Brock, Clifton. *The Literature of Political Science.* 1969.

Eysenck, Hans Jurgen, ed. *Encyclopedia of Psychology.* 2nd ed. 3 vols. 1979.

Mitzel, Harold, ed. *Encyclopedia of Educational Research.* 5th ed. 4 vols. 1982.

Sills, David L., ed. *International Encyclopedia of the Social Sciences.* 17 vols. 1977.

Winick, Charles. *Dictionary of Anthropology.* 1977.

Card and Computerized Catalogs

Card Catalogs

Card catalog entries list books in each of three formats — author, title, and subject. In a **divided catalog,** cards are filed separately by type. A divided catalog may interfile author and title cards and place only subject cards in a separate catalog. In a **dictionary catalog,** author, title, and subject cards are filed together. Each book in the library's collection is cataloged in at least three ways, making your search for materials easier. For instance, if you need a book by Carl Sagan but cannot remember the title, look under *S* in a dictionary catalog or an author catalog for cards listing the library's holdings of Sagan's books. Similarly, if you want a book titled *The Unheavenly City* but cannot remember the author's name, look under *U* in a dictionary catalog or title catalog to locate the book. (Titles beginning with *a, an,* and *the* are filed under the first letter of the following word.) To locate books on a subject like "solar energy," look under *S* in a dictionary catalog or subject catalog.

Individual catalog cards provide basic information about a book: author, title, publisher, publication date, and call number (the number indicating the book's exact location in the library). They also indicate whether a book contains any special features such as maps, illustrations, or bibliographies. (See Figure 1.) **》》》**
Note accurately the call number of any book you are interested in see-ing. Books are shelved by call number, so this information is essential to locate books in the stacks. **《《《**

Figure 1   Author, title, and subject cards

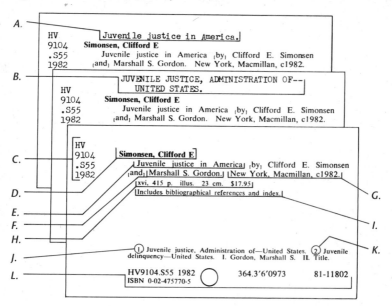

A. Title card heading
B. Subject card heading
C. Library of Congress number
D. Author card heading
E. Title of book
F. Name of second author
G. Publication information: city, company, date
H. Technical information: number of pages in preface, number of textual pages, illustrations, book size, price
I. Additional information: textual apparatus
J. First subject classification
K. Second subject classification
L. Library of Congress number, ISBN number, Dewey Decimal number, On-line Computer Library Center number

Computerized Catalogs

Increasing numbers of libraries list all or part of their holdings in computerized catalogs. In some libraries, books acquired after a certain date appear *only* in the computerized catalog; in other cases, older holdings may not yet have been entered in the computerized catalog. Be sure to check with a librarian to find out how to use the computerized catalog in your library, what it covers, and what will be found only in the card catalog. Computerized catalogs provide the same basic information as card catalogs: author, title, subject, call number, and so on.

A computer system can display simultaneously the information that would occupy several catalog cards. For instance, to research insomnia, you would type the necessary operating commands and then type the subject name, *insomnia.* Within seconds, the computer screen will display the names of the library's books on insomnia. When the list is too long to fit on one screen, you must type a command to see the rest of the list.

Computerized catalogs also make it possible to print out shelf-position lists — print-outs that include a fixed number of sources with call numbers preceding or following a selected call number. Such a printed list is a handy reference when you are beginning research.

Computer searching saves a great deal of time and energy. Take advantage of the new technology if it is available to you.

Periodical Indexes and Bibliographies

Periodicals — magazines, journals, and newspapers — are published at regular intervals, are often intended for expert or informed audiences, and offer up-to-date, specialized discussions of topics. These sources add depth, timeliness, and focus to your research.

Magazines, such as *The New Yorker, U.S. News & World Report,* and *Scientific American,* provide commentary and current information for general audiences. Journals, such as *Critical Inquiry, American Psychologist,* and *October,* are professional or scholarly publications written by and for experts in a given field; they contain specialized, technical information. Magazines usually appear monthly or weekly while journals may appear monthly or quarterly.

A Guide to Magazine Articles

The *Readers' Guide to Periodical Literature* lists articles appearing in hundreds of magazines. Usually located in the reference or the periodicals section, the *Readers' Guide* is printed regularly, is bound yearly, and covers most general-interest magazines. Your library may also have the *Readers' Guide* available on a computerized system.

The *Readers' Guide* alphabetically lists entries by author, title, and subject. Its condensed format uses many abbreviations, which are listed and explained at the front of each volume. Figure 2 (page 461) shows an excerpt from the *Readers' Guide.*

Guides to Journal Articles

To find articles in journals, use the various specialized indexes and bibliographies. Normally located in the reference room, these indexes and bibliographies list entries alphabetically by author, subject, and sometimes title. Indexes and bibliographies differ somewhat in format, but the excerpt from the *Education Index* shown in Figure 3 (page 462) is a fairly representative sample.

Indexes and bibliographies are shelved in the reference room by the call numbers of their subjects. Available guides include the following:

Agricultural Index, 1919–64

The American Humanities Index, 1975 to date

American Indian Index, 1953–68

Figure 2   Sample entries from the *Readers' Guide to Periodical Literature*

A. ──┌ POLITICAL FORECASTING
       └   *See also* ┐
            Public opinion polls┘ ──────────────── *B.*
C. ──   ┌ Beyond the cold war┘ C. Krauthammer. *The New Republic*
            199:14-15+ D 19 '88
            Election prediction: Michael Dukakis will win. M. S.
            Forbes, Jr. il *Forbes* 142:33 N 14 '88
            The next four years [special section] ┌bibl f il *Foreign*┐
            Affairs 67:1-134 Wint '88/'89 ──────────────── *D.*
            Precipitation and presidents [cover story] ┌R. Marshall.┘
F. ──   ┘ il *Weatherwise* 41:263-5 O '88┘ ──────── *E.*
            Vultures [Democrats after losing race by M. Dukakis]
            M. Kondracke. *The New Republic* 199:10+ N 7 '88
            When optimists attract [H. Zullow's political forecasting
            method based on candidates' optimism measurement]
            D. Gelman. il *Newsweek* 112:80 O 17 '88
            POLITICAL INTEREST GROUPS *See* Special interest
            groups

A. Subject heading
B. Cross reference
C. Article title
D. Special information: bibliography, footnotes, illustrations
E. Author
F. Publication information: magazine title, volume number, page numbers, month, year

Applied Science and Technology Index, 1958 to date

The Art Index, 1929 to date

Bibliography and Index of Geology, 1961 to date

Biography Index, 1949 to date

Biological and Agricultural Index, 1964 to date

Book Review Index, 1965 to date

Business Periodicals Index, 1958 to date

Figure 3   Sample entries from *The Education Index*

A. ┌─ Intelligence, Artificial
                    ┌─ *See also*
B. ─────────────┤ Expert systems (Computers)
                    └ Hypertext
C. ─────┌─ Artificial intelligence: a promise of productivity gain
        └─ at the keyboard? G. C. Whyte. *Bus Educ Forum*
            43:11-12 D '88
        Figuring out the rules for how the brain works. J. A.
D. ───────── Turner. por *Chron Higher Educ* 35:A3 O 26 '88
        Investigating AI with BASIC and LOGO. A. Mandell
            and R. Lucking. See issues of The Journal of Computers
            in Mathematics and Science Teaching
        Intelligence, Social *See* Maturity, Social
        Intelligence, Superior *See* Mentally superior
        Intelligence quotient
        Cognitive development and reading achievement in
            pervasive-ADD, situational-ADD and control children.
E. ─────── M. Boudreault and others. bibl *J Child Psychol* ─ F.
        Psychiatry Allied Discip 29:611-19 S '88
        Effect of intrauterine growth retardation (IUGR) on the
            psychological performance of preterm children at
            preschool age. R. Matilainen and others. bibl *J Child
            Psychol Psychiatry Allied Discip* 29:601-9 S '88

A. *Subject heading*

B. *Cross references*

C. *Article title*

D. *Special information: portraits*

E. *Author*

F. *Publication information: journal title, volume number, page numbers, month, year*

Catholic Periodical Index, 1930–33, 1939 to date

Cumulated Drama Index, 1909–49

Dramatic Index, 1909–49

Education Index, 1958 to date

Engineering Index, 1884 to date

Film Literature Index, 1974 to date

General Science Index, 1978 to date

Humanities Index, 1974 to date

Index to Legal Periodicals, 1908 to date

Index to U.S. Government Periodicals, 1974 to date

Industrial Arts Index, 1913–57

MLA International Bibliography of Books and Articles on Modern Languages and Literatures, 1922 to date

Music Index, 1949 to date

Social Sciences Index, 1974 to date

United Nations Documents Index, 1950 to date

Guides to Newspaper Articles

In the reference or the periodicals area, you will find the *New York Times Index, Wall Street Journal Index, London Times Index, Washington Post Index,* and other indexes listing articles published in the newspaper named in the index title. These guides are compiled yearly and arranged alphabetically by subject. If you find a relevant reference in one index, check other newspaper indexes for articles on the subject printed on the same day or a few days before or after. The section from the *New York Times Index* shown in Figure 4 is typical of newspaper indexes.

Figure 4   Sample entries from the *New York Times Index*

AMERICAN SECURITY COUNCIL. See also
United States—Congress (US), F 1

A. ── **AMERICAN SHAKESPEARE THEATER (STRATFORD, CONN). See also**
Theater, F 21, My 11,15   ── *B.*
Theater—Tempest, The (Play), Ap 19

C. ── **Residents of Stratford, Connecticut, oppose state task force's proposal to change name of bankrupt American Shakespeare Theater to American Heritage Theater to expand programs and audiences and achieve solvency;**
D. ── **photos** (S), My 11,II,1:5

May 11 picture caption with article about efforts to
change name of American Shakespeare Theater in   ── *E.*
Stratford, Conn, incorrectly described production of 'The
Tempest' currently playing there, My 15,I,3:2

AMERICAN SILVER MUSEUM (MERIDEN, CONN)
Group of Meriden, Conn, businessmen will open American
Silver Museum in 1988 to display silver crafts that once
made Meriden 'Silver City of the World'; museum is being
touted as anchor in city's $25 million downtown   ── *F.*
G. ── revitalization plan and as tourist draw; photo (M), My 3,
XXIII,16:5

AMERICAN SOCCER AMBASSADORS. See also
Soccer, Ag 2
AMERICAN SOCCER LEAGUE. See also
Soccer, My 8

A. Subject heading

B. Cross references

C. Entry of unusual interest (boldface type)

D. Photograph information

E. Abstract of an important news story

F. Note on length of the article: **(L)** *means over three columns;* **(M)** *means one to two columns;* **(S)** *means less than one column*

G. Publication information: month, day, newspaper section number, page number, column number

---

33d ▷ **Compile and evaluate a preliminary list of sources.**

Compiling a Preliminary List of Sources

A preliminary list of sources generally includes books and a variety of journal, magazine, and newspaper articles. Begin to note possible nonprint sources as well — for example, class notes, interviews, and television documentaries.

On separate 3-by-5-inch note cards, jot down information about each potential source. Note its location. For books, note call number, author, and title. For articles, write down the complete index or bibliography entry. For interviews, documentaries, class notes, and so on, indicate date, title, speaker or producer, and any other relevant identifying information. In addition to the information that is essential for locating or identifying a source, note any special features, such as maps or bibliographies, that might make the source especially useful.

Evaluating a Preliminary List of Sources

Review your preliminary list of sources, using the following guidelines to evaluate their potential usefulness:

Does the author have special credentials? An *M.D., M.A., Ph.D.,* or notice of an affiliation with a university or other organization following the author's name may indicate authority and expertise in the subject at hand.

Does the title of the work suggest a focus appropriate to your topic? The phrasing of a title or subtitle can indicate the author's subject and his or her attitude toward it. A title like *Latin American Civilization: Colonial Period* does not reveal its author's thesis or attitude, whereas *The Colonial Heritage of Latin America: Essays on Economic Dependence in Perspective* does reveal to an extent the book's approach to its subject.

Is the publishing company a reputable one? Most of the books you use have been published by university, academic, or trade presses. You will soon recognize the important publishers in your field.

Are the periodicals well respected by authorities in the field? You may not be able to evaluate a periodical thoroughly, but, depending on your subject and purpose, you will be able to determine the most reliable sources. For example, on issues of national and international importance, the *New York Times* or *Washington Post* are often more authoritative than local newspapers. You will learn which periodicals in your field are most respected by noting which are most frequently cited in the notes and bibliographies of the other works you consult. For academic research papers, the use of popular periodicals, such as *U.S.A. Today* and *Time,* should be kept to a minimum.

Is the publication date recent? For some topics, the currentness of a source is unimportant, but for most topics, sources older than ten or fifteen years are of little value.

Using these guidelines, Michele evaluated Walter Fenno Dearborn's *Intelligence Tests: Their Significance for School and Society* (Boston: Houghton, 1928). Her first instinct was to reject the book because of its publication date; she thought that its information would be outdated. However, Dearborn's credentials as a medical doctor with a Ph.D. and as director of the Psycho-Educational Clinic at Harvard University convinced her that the book deserved a closer look.

EXERCISE 33.4   ❭   *Preliminary list of sources*

Prepare a preliminary list of sources for your paper. Using the card catalog, find at least four books on your topic, including one published within the last two years and one providing an overview of the topic. Using the Readers' Guide, *the appropriate subject index, and one or more newspaper indexes, find at least six articles on your topic. Using the nonprint resources of your library and other local resources — such as businesses, government agencies, and civic and cultural organizations — find two nonprint sources, including one potential interview.*

33e ▷ Evaluate your sources.

Before you begin to read your sources carefully, leaf through them quickly, noting their organization, content, and any tables, maps, photographs, or other illustrations. Do not read each source thoroughly or take notes at this stage; follow the guidelines given below for making a preliminary, general assessment of the usefulness of the materials you have gathered. Once you have a general sense of your sources, you can then read them carefully and take complete and consistent notes, following the guidelines given in section 33f.

Evaluating Books

Books will probably provide the most thorough treatment of your subject, but you should evaluate each one quickly to see if it meets the needs of your research before taking the time to read it closely. After considering the title and subtitle carefully and any information provided about the author's credentials and other writings, review the table of contents. Consider how material is divided and arranged and how much space is allotted to topics that relate to your paper.

Skim the preface, introduction, or the first chapter to get a sense of the author's general approach and the context. Frequently, authors explain their reasons for writing, their strategies for presenting information, or their general interpretations of material in the preface, introduction, or first chapter. These explanations can help you to assess the source's potential value for your paper.

Examine any special sections or appended materials: in-text illustrations, tables, charts, graphs, or diagrams; bibliographies; sections containing special supporting material, such as case studies or lists of additional readings. Reviewing these sections gives you a sense of the book's content and approach. Nontextual materials can be quite useful in providing details, illustrations, and leads to other sources.

Skim a portion of the text that specifically relates to your topic. Do not read it carefully yet, but instead note how the author has developed the content. For example, does the author use examples and facts or narration and description based on personal experience? Does the author explain and support assertions, document facts, and present balanced discussions? Also note the author's style. Is it varied, lively, and interesting? What technical and other vocabulary and tone does it employ? A quick analysis of content and style can reveal whether a source treats the topic seriously and in depth or superficially. (For more information about evaluating sources and forms of argument, see Chapter 5, "Critical Thinking and Writing.")

Evaluating Articles in Periodicals

Articles in magazines, journals, and newspapers can provide you with a great deal of information. To save time, you need to evaluate the potential usefulness of each article you might wish to use before you read it carefully and take notes.

First, read the title and subtitle carefully, assessing what they reveal about the author's content, approach, and tone. Check any note on the author (this may appear at the bottom of the first page or at the end of the article or in a separate section of the journal or magazine). These notes usually state the author's credentials and other publications, which may give you insight into the author's interests and attitudes.

Read any headings that are used to separate sections of the article. Note whether any of the headings indicates content specifically related to your topic.

Skim the article to assess its content and form of presentation. Without pausing over details, skim the article to see if it is specific, current, and complete, and if its style indicates an approach to the topic that will be useful to you.

Check for related materials in the same periodical. Sometimes lists of suggested readings or of people or organizations to contact appear with an article. Issues of periodicals are sometimes organized in whole or in part around a theme, so that a number of articles in the periodical may relate to your topic.

EXERCISE 33.5 ❯ *Evaluating a source*

Look briefly at four sources — two books and two articles from periodicals — and write a brief paragraph describing each. Note especially each source's potential usefulness for your paper.

33f ▷ Take complete, consistent notes.

Establish a uniform system for taking notes. Many researchers use 4-by-6-inch index cards because they are large enough to hold complete notes and easy to distinguish from 3-by-5-inch works cited cards. (For more on works cited cards, see section 33b.) Some writers prefer the generous space of legal pads or loose-leaf paper even though in later stages of planning and writing notes on paper are often more difficult to handle than those on cards.

Use new cards for new ideas; during planning, this will make it easier for you to organize — and reorganize — your notes. At the top of each card, record the following information to help you to identify your sources easily and avoid plagiarism: the author of the source, title (if you are using more than one source by any given author); and the page number of the material you are noting. Make notes on one side of the card only, so that later you do not overlook any information. Fit material on one card, if possible; but if additional cards are necessary, note the author's name, the number of each card, and the total number of cards at the top (for example, "Johnson, Card 2 of 3").

Keep your working thesis in mind as you take notes. Some researchers like to keep a rough outline handy, so that they can take notes with the overall structure of their argument in view and can mark cards with key words to indicate where information fits. **》》** *Be alert as you take notes to unexpected information and ideas that alter or expand your working thesis in new and interesting ways.* **《《** You will want to make note of relevant information (facts, examples, and details) and of ideas (the thoughts and conclusions offered by your sources to interpret or organize their information). You can take notes on both types of material in any of three ways: summaries, quotations, and paraphrases. The sample note cards in figures 5, 6, 7, and 8 present information from this passage from Stephen Jay Gould's *The Mismeasure of Man* (New York: Norton, 1981):

[Terman] reified average test scores as a "thing" called general intelligence by advocating the first of two possible positions (1906, p. 9): "Is intellectual ability a bank account, on which we can draw for any desired purpose, or is it rather a bundle of separate drafts, each drawn for a specific purpose and inconvertible?" And, while admitting that he could provide no real support for it, he defended the innatist view (1906, p. 68): "While offering little positive data on the subject, the study has strengthened my impression of the relatively greater importance of endowment over training as a determinant of an individual's intellectual rank among his fellows."

Goddard introduced Binet's scale to America, but Terman was the primary architect of its popularity. Binet's last version of 1911 included fifty-four tasks, graded from prenursery to mid-teen-age years. Terman's first revision of 1916 extended the scale to "superior adults" and increased the number of tasks to ninety. Terman, by then a professor at Stanford University, gave his revision a name that has become a part of our century's vocabulary — the Stanford-Binet, the standard for virtually all "IQ" tests that followed (175).

Summaries

Summaries present the substance of a passage in condensed form. They are useful means of recording facts, best noted in list or other abbreviated form, as in Figure 5; examples, perhaps noted as a sketch of the original, as in Figure 6; or long arguments, perhaps noted in outline form. Summaries should be entirely in your own words. When taking notes, read the passage carefully, determine what information and ideas you want to record, and express them in lists of words, brief phrases, or short sentences. Do not use any of the original passage without enclosing it in quotation marks. Use quotation marks carefully at the note-taking stage to avoid inadvertently using others' words in your paper without giving proper credit.

Quotations

Quotations reproduce another's work word for word, with the original's exact spelling and punctuation. Quotations should not be overused in your writing and should be sparingly used in your notes. Assess the value of a quotation before you copy it. Ask yourself the following questions:

Is the author's style so distinctive that I could not say the same thing as well or as clearly in my own words?

Is the vocabulary technical and therefore difficult to translate into my own words?

Is the author so well known or so important that the quotation will lend authority to my argument?

Does the author's material raise doubts or questions or make points with which I disagree?

If you answer "yes" to any of these questions, then make note of the quotation. If the material does not fulfill any of these criteria but is significant nonetheless, paraphrase it instead.

Figure 5

Gould   *Tests & Tasks*

<u>*Mismeasure*</u>*, p. 175*

—Binet's 1911 test, 54 tasks, toddlers to teenagers

—Terman's 1916 revision, upward to "superior adults," 90 tasks

—Terman, professor at Stanford U.

Figure 6

Gould   *Stanford-Binet Test*

<u>*Mismeasure*</u>*, p. 175*

Terman made the Binet test more comprehensive, renamed it the Stanford-Binet, and helped to popularize it in the United States.

Always enclose quotations within quotation marks and double-check your note against the original. The copy must be *exact*. Figure 7 shows a sample quotation card.

> **!** Because you can introduce errors each time you write or type a quotation, use a word-processing program to avoid extra recopying or retyping. ■ Prepare a separate file for quotations. Type each quotation into the file and double-check its accuracy against the original. Be sure to label each quotation completely with author, title, and page number. ■ Copy quotations into the draft as needed, leaving a copy in the quotation file in case you change your mind about where or how much of the quotation to use. The use of control codes to copy quotations avoids retyping, which saves time and prevents the introduction of errors.

Figure 7

Gould   *Preconceptions*

<u>*Mismeasure*</u>*, p. 175*

Terman said in 1906:
"While offering little positive data on the subject, the
study has strengthened my impression of the relatively
greater importance of endowment over training as a
determinant of an individual's intellectual rank among
his fellows."

⟫⟫⟫ *When a quotation continues from one page to the next in a source, indicate where the break occurs when you copy the quotation onto your note card (a double slash [//] is a useful indicator for this). This notation is important because when you use the quotation in your paper, you may use only part of it, and you must be able to cite the page reference accurately.* ⟪⟪⟪

Paraphrases

Paraphrases restate a passage in another form and other words; but, unlike summaries, they contain approximately the same amount of detail and the same number of words as the original. If a passage contains an important idea but does not meet the requirements for quotation, restate the idea in your own words, sentence structure, and sequence. When you finish the paraphrase, check it against the original passage to be sure the idea has been completely restated. If you use any phrases or sentences from the original, place them in quotation marks. Intentional or not, unacknowledged borrowing from a source is plagiarism, and most schools impose severe penalties on students who plagiarize.

Figure 8, on page 475, shows a sample paraphrase card.

EXERCISE 33.6 ❯ *Taking notes*

Using the books and articles that your evaluation of your preliminary list of sources determined would be useful, begin taking notes. Summarize, paraphrase, and directly quote from your sources, and make sure that each note card accurately reflects the source and provides full identifying information.

Figure 8

Gould   Stanford-Binet, 1916

<u>Mismeasure</u>, p. 175

Terman was the person responsible for the concept of
"general intelligence" and the widespread use of Binet's IQ
tests. When Terman worked at Stanford, he revised Binet's
test (1911), nearly doubling the number of questions, and
named it the Stanford-Binet (first revision, 1916). It became
the model for later IQ tests.
—the name "became part of our century's vocabulary"

33g ▷ **Do not plagiarize.**

Plagiarism is the use of someone else's words, ideas, or line of
thought without acknowledgment. Even when, as is frequently
the case, plagiarism is inadvertent — the result of careless note
taking, punctuating, or documenting — the writer is still at fault
for dishonest work, and the paper will be unacceptable. You will
remember the seriousness of the offense of plagiarism, and work
to avoid committing it, when you remember that the word *plagiarism* comes from the Latin for "kidnaping." To avoid plagiarizing,
learn to recognize distinctive content and expression in source
materials and learn to take accurate, carefully punctuated and
documented notes.

Common Knowledge

Some kinds of information — facts and interpretations — are known by many people and are consequently described as **common knowledge.** That U.S. presidents are elected for four-year terms is commonly known, as is the more interpretative information that the U.S. government is a democracy with a system of checks and balances among the executive, legislative, and judicial branches of government. But common knowledge extends beyond these very general types of information to more specific information within a field of study. In English studies, for example, it is a commonly known fact that George Eliot is the pseudonym of Mary Ann Evans and a commonly acknowledged interpretation that drama evolved from a Greek religious festival honoring the god Dionysus. Documenting these facts in a paper would be unnecessary because they are commonly known in English studies, even though you might have discovered them for the first time.

When you are researching an unfamiliar subject, distinguishing common knowledge that does not require documentation from special knowledge that does require documentation is sometimes difficult. The following guidelines may help.

What Constitutes Common Knowledge

Historical facts (names, dates, and general interpretations) that appear in many general reference books. For example, George Washington was the first president of the United States, and the Constitution was adopted in 1787.

Literature that cannot be attributed to a specific author. Two examples are *Beowulf* and the Bible; the use of specific editions or translations still may require acknowledgment.

General observations and opinions that are shared by many people. For example, it is a general observation that children learn by actively doing, not passively listening, and a commonly held opinion that reading, writing, and arithmetic are the basic skills to be learned by an elementary school child.

Unacknowledged information that appears in multiple sources. For example, it is common knowledge that the earth is approximately 93 million miles from the sun and that the *gross national product* is the market value of all goods and services produced by a nation in a given year.

If a piece of information does not meet these guidelines or if you are uncertain about whether it is common knowledge, always document the material.

EXERCISE 33.7 ❯ *Common knowledge about your topic*

Make a list of twenty facts, ideas, or interpretations that are commonly known or held about your topic. Beside each item, note into which category of common knowledge it falls.

Special Qualities of Source Materials

A more difficult problem than identifying common knowledge involves using an author's words and ideas improperly. Improper use is often the result of careless summarizing and paraphrasing. To use source materials without plagiarizing, learn to recognize their distinctive qualities:

Special Qualities of Sources

Distinctive prose style: the author's choices of words, phrases, and sentence patterns

Original facts: the result of the author's personal research

Personal interpretations of information, the author's individual evaluation of his or her information

Original ideas: those ideas that are unique to that author

As you work with sources, be aware of these distinguishing qualities and make certain that you do not appropriate the prose (word choices and sentence structures), original research, interpretations, or ideas of others without giving proper credit.

Look, for instance, at this paragraph from Stephen Jay Gould's book:

> If Binet's principles had been followed, and his tests consistently used as he intended, we would have been spared a major misuse of science in our century. Ironically, many American school boards have come full cycle, and now use IQ tests only as Binet originally recommended: as instruments for assessing children with specific learning problems. Speaking personally, I feel that tests of the IQ type were helpful in the proper diagnosis of my own learning-disabled son. His average score, the IQ itself, meant nothing, for it was only an amalgam of some very high and very low scores; but the pattern of low values indicated his areas of deficit.
>
> The misuse of mental tests is not inherent in the idea of testing itself. It arises primarily from two fallacies, eagerly (so it seems) embraced by those who wish to use tests for the maintenance of social ranks and distinctions: reification and hereditarianism (155).

Now look at the following examples of plagiarism and acceptable summaries and paraphrases.

Summaries

Plagiarized

— *tests are often misused.*

— *that's not <u>inherent in the idea of testing</u>.*

478

> — *people use IQ tests for the <u>maintenance of social ranks and distinctions</u>.*

(The underlined phrases are clearly Gould's. To avoid plagiarism, either place key phrases in quotation marks or rewrite them entirely in your own words and form of expression.)

Acceptable

> — *tests are not the problem; the problem is the way people use them.*

> — *the problems develop from unscientific methodology, which is "embraced by those who wish to use tests for the maintenance of social ranks and distinctions."*

(Here, the words and phrases are the writer's, not Gould's. Quotation marks enclose Gould's phrase.)

Paraphrases

Plagiarized

Had Binet's ideas about testing been used, and his IQ tests given as he intended, we would not have seen one of this century's misuses of science. Oddly enough, some school boards in the United States have gone back to Binet's original use of the tests: they are being used to assess children with special needs.

(Changing a few words while retaining the basic phrasing and sentence structure of the original is not acceptable paraphrasing. Gould's thought pattern and prose style still mark the passage.)

Acceptable

We have seen IQ tests misused because scientists have not followed Binet's guidelines for using his tests. Today, some learning disabled students are being assessed effectively, however, because schools are using IQ tests as Binet intended.
— "American school boards have come full cycle."

(Here, the paraphrase presents Gould's idea but does not mimic his sentence structure; the quoted material records a specific phrase for possible use later. Remember that summaries and paraphrases, as well as quotations, require full citations.)

Avoiding plagiarism takes conscious effort, and that effort takes time. Be aware of the special qualities in your source materials, and take notes carefully. By preparing notes properly and then documenting completely, you will avoid plagiarism, which can invalidate your paper and perhaps have other serious consequences, as well.

EXERCISE 33.8 ❯ Practice in note taking

Take notes on the following sets of paragraphs as you would if you were researching their subjects. Include a summary, a quotation, and a paraphrase from each set. Do not plagiarize.

McLoughlin, Merrill, et al. "Men vs. Women." *U.S. News & World Report.* 8 Aug. 1988: 50–56. [The following paragraphs appear on page 52.]

If God created man first, He or She apparently took advantage of hindsight when it came to women. Except for the moment of conception (when 13 to 15 males are conceived for every 10 females), the distaff side simply has a better chance at survival. Spontaneous abortions of boys outnumber those of girls. More males than females die during infancy, youth and adulthood. In every country in the world where childbirth itself no longer poses mortal danger to women, the life expectancy of females exceeds that of males. And in the United States, the gap is growing. A baby girl born today can look forward to nearly 79 years — seven more than a baby boy.

Why? Some of the answers seem to lie deep in the genes. Others doubtless float in the hormones that carry messages from organ to organ, even, some researchers believe, "imprinting" each human brain with patterns that can affect the ways it responds to injury and disease. The research suggests that females start out with some distinct biological advantages.

Fleming, Stuart. "Limning: A Noble Approach to Painting." *Archaeology* May/June 1987: 60, 61, 73. [The following paragraphs appear on page 60.]

During the early years of the seventeenth century, the English philosopher Francis Bacon faced a dilemma. He had gained some public popularity for his outspoken views on social morality, yet thoroughly distrusted the notion that any good could come from having the common people better educated. At the same time, men of science and fellow counselors at court, whom he identified as having the intellectual potential of advanced scholarship, seemed to be entrapped by false traditions of logic and rhetoric. He decried the fact that the dynamic mood of the European industry was being totally ignored by academia. For Bacon, the study of trades and practical experiment held the key to establishment of a universal truth, and he condemned the contrary attitude of his colleagues as one of "vain and supercilious arrogancy."

These seeds of a philosophy that would inevitably elevate the status of craftsmen did not fall on barren ground among the English artistic community. This group well remembered how the Italian Renaissance had enabled painters to shed the social stigma attached to artisans and gain artistic status of a kind previously reserved for poets.

Sagan, Carl. *The Dragons of Eden: Speculations on the Evolution of Human Intelligence.* New York: Random, 1977. [The following paragraphs appear on pages 189 and 191; a double slash (//) indicates the page break.]

In general, human societies are not innovative. They are hierarchical and ritualistic. Suggestions for change are greeted with suspicion: they imply an unpleasant future variation in ritual and hierarchy: an exchange of one set of rituals for another, or perhaps for a less structured society with fewer rituals. And yet there are times when societies must change. "The dogmas of the quiet past are inadequate for the stormy present" was Abraham Lincoln's description of this truth. Much of the difficulty in attempting to restructure American and other societies arises from the resistance by groups with vested interests in the status quo. Significant change might require those who are now high in the hierarchy to move downward many steps. This seems to them undesirable and is resisted.

But some change, in fact some significant change, is apparent in Western society — certainly not enough, but more than in almost any other society. Older and more static cultures are // much more resistant to change. In Colin Turnbull's book *The Forest People,* there is a poignant description of a crippled Pygmy girl who was provided by visiting anthropologists with a stunning technological innovation, the crutch. Despite the fact that it greatly eased the suffering of the little girl, the adults, including her parents, showed no particular interest in this invention. There are many other cases of intolerance to novelty in traditional societies; and diverse pertinent examples could be drawn from the lives of such men as Leonardo, Galileo, Desiderius Erasmus, Charles Darwin, or Sigmund Freud.

Preparing Works Cited Entries

The research process is painstaking, especially when it comes to recording complete and accurate information about sources for use in documenting the final paper. Careful documentation and a complete works cited list provide readers with full information on sources cited in the paper. (See section 35d for information on in-text citations.)

To be useful to readers, citations must be clear and consistent. Therefore, very specific rules of documentation have been devised and must be applied.

Quick Reference

Begin preparing your works cited entries, using the formats shown below, as soon as you begin taking notes. Use 3-by-5-inch cards, a new one for each entry, and keep them current and in a safe place or create a works cited file on your word processor.

❯ *A book by one author*

> *Author's last name, first name. Book title. Additional information. City of publication: Publishing company, publication date.*

❯ *An article by one author*

> *Author's last name, first name. "Article title." Periodical title Date: inclusive pages.*

Guidelines for preparing entries for other types of sources appear on the pages that follow.

> **34a** ▷ **Follow the standard citation format required by your subject.**

Most writing in English and other humanities courses uses the documentation format described in Joseph Gibaldi and Walter S. Achtert's *MLA Handbook for Writers of Research Papers,* third edition (New York: MLA, 1988). This documentation format, known as MLA style, is simple, clear, and widely accepted. Some subjects, however, require other styles of documentation, so always ask instructors, especially in nonhumanities courses, whether MLA style is acceptable. In addition to the *MLA Handbook,* frequently used style guides include the following:

Frequently Used Style Guides

CBE Style Manual. 5th ed. Bethesda: Council of Biology Editors, 1983.

The Chicago Manual of Style. 13th ed. Chicago: U of Chicago P, 1982.

Handbook for Authors. Washington, DC: American Chemical Soc., 1978.

Publication Manual of the American Psychology Association. 3rd ed. Washington, DC: American Psychological Assn., 1983.

Style Manual for Guidance in the Preparation of Papers. 3rd ed. New York: American Inst. of Physics, 1978.

Turabian, Kate. *A Manual for Writers of Term Papers, Theses, and Dissertations.* 5th ed. Chicago: U of Chicago P, 1987.

The most widely used of these alternate styles is that of the American Psychological Association (APA), often the preferred style for writing in the social sciences. Guidelines for using APA style appear in Appendix B.

Prepare accurate and complete works cited entries.

Because works cited entries direct readers to sources used in re-searched writing, these entries must be as complete as possible and presented in a consistent and recognizable format. If the following guidelines do not cover a source you want to use, consult the *MLA Handbook* (see section 34a).

Place works cited entries on 3-by-5-inch note cards, one entry to a card. Carefully copy all information directly from the source, and enter it in the exact format that will eventually be required for your works cited page. Keep cards up-to-date and in a safe place.

Information for Citations

Citations vary in the information they include, but all must follow a consistent arrangement. When you must combine forms (to list a translation of a second edition, for example), use these guidelines to determine the format of the combined entry.

1. *Author (s).* For books, use the name or names with the spelling and in the order shown on the title page. For periodicals, take the author's name from the article itself (it may be at the beginning or the end of the article), not from the contents page. If no author, individual or corporate, is listed, make a note of that fact; the work will be listed by title on the works cited page.

2. *Title.* List titles from part to whole. If you are citing part of a book (for example, a single essay in a collection), list the title of the part before the book title; list the title of an article before the periodical title. Take the title of a book from the title page and the title of a part or an article from the first page of the part or article. Use complete titles, including subtitles.

3. *Additional information.* Include any of the following information (in the order presented here) if it is listed on the

title page of a book or the first page of an article: editor, translator, compiler, edition number, volume number, name of series.

4. *Facts of publication.* For books, take the publisher's name and the place of publication from the title page and the date of publication from the copyright page (immediately following the title page); use the publisher's name in abbreviated form (see examples in section 33c), the first city listed if more than one is given, and the most recent date shown. For periodicals, take the volume number, issue number, and date from the masthead, found at the top of the first page of newspapers or within the first few pages in journals and magazines, often in combination with the table of contents.

5. *Page numbers.* When citing a part of a book or an article, provide inclusive page numbers. Look these up for yourself; do not rely on the table of contents.

Format for Citations

Whether handwritten or typed, works cited entries must consistently follow this format:

1. Begin the first line of the entry at the left margin, and indent all subsequent lines five spaces.

2. Invert the first author's name so that it appears last name first (to make it easy to alphabetize and locate on the works cited list). List additional authors in first-last name order.

3. When no author is named, list the source by title.

4. Cite the complete title; use a colon followed by a single space to separate the title from any subtitle.

5. Separate major sections of entries (author, title, and publication information) with periods. A title ending with a question mark or an exclamation point does not require a period. (See example on page 495.)

6. Double-space entries.

Book by one author

Sagan, Carl. The Dragons of Eden: Speculations on the

    Evolution of Human Intelligence. New York:

    Random, 1977.

Magazine article by one author

Diamond, Jared. "The Price of Human Folly." Discover

    Apr. 1989: 73-77.

Using a word processor to prepare citations is especially helpful because entries can easily be added, changed, or deleted as your research continues, and programs have features that simplify typing. ■ To block-indent second and subsequent lines of each entry, use the program's "block-indent" feature (also called a *hanging paragraph*), instead of using a five-space tab to indent each second and subsequent line individually. ■ Revise entries to adjust the spacing, punctuation, and position of information. Word processors allow you to insert, delete, and rearrange information without retyping. ■ Prepare entries in a separate file. Place works cited entries in a separate file so that you will have easy access to them. Add items to the file in alphabetical order. You can later use "block" and "move" codes to correct alphabetization and then to append the complete file to your research paper.

34c ▷ **Follow the appropriate citation forms for books.**

A Book by One Author

Bloom, Allan.   <u>The Closing of the American Mind</u>.   New

    York: Simon, 1987.

A Book by More Than One Author

Vidich, Arthur J., and Joseph Bensman.   <u>Small Town in</u>

    <u>Mass Society: Class, Power and Religion in a Rural</u>

    <u>Community</u>.   Princeton: Princeton UP, 1968.

(A comma follows the first author's first name. The names of other listed authors are not inverted. The letters *UP*, without periods, abbreviate *University Press*.)

Winks, Robin W., et al.   <u>A History of Civilization:</u>

    <u>Prehistory to the Present</u>.   7th ed.   Englewood

    Cliffs: Prentice, 1988.

(Using *et al.* (meaning "and others") saves space when a work has four or more authors (the Winks book has four). Do not underline *et al.*

A Book with No Author or Editor Named

<u>The Chicago Manual of Style</u>.   13th ed.   Chicago: U of

    Chicago P, 1982.

(When no author or editor is named, list the work by title. Alphabetize under *c*, disregarding the article *the*.)

A Book by a Corporate Author

American Psychological Association. Thesaurus of

Psychological Index Terms. 5th ed. Washington,

DC: APA, 1988.

(The American Psychological Association, or APA, is both author and publisher of this work.)

An Edition Other Than the First

Corbett, Edward. Classical Rhetoric for the Modern

Student. 3rd ed. New York: Oxford UP, 1988.

A Work in Several Volumes

Doyle, Arthur Conan. The Complete Sherlock Holmes. 2

vols. New York: Doubleday, 1930.

(The entry cites the entire series; *volumes* is abbreviated.)

Churchill, Winston S. The Birth of Britain. New York:

Dodd, 1966. Vol. 1 of A History of the

English-Speaking Peoples. 4 vols.

(This entry cites a single, separately titled volume in a series.)

Granville-Barker, Harley. Prefaces to Shakespeare.

Vol. 2. Princeton: Princeton UP. 1975. 2 vols.

(This entry cites a single volume of a series without separate volume titles. The number of the cited volume follows the title; the total number of volumes ends the entry.)

A Work in a Collection by the Same Author

Cohen, Arthur A.   "The Monumental Sculptor."   <u>Artists</u>

    <u>and Enemies: Three Novellas</u>.   Boston: Godine,

    1987.   41-124.

(Note that the page numbers, *41–124,* stand alone without the word or abbreviation for *pages.*)

A Work in a Collection by Different Authors

Tizard, Barbara.   "The Impact of the Nuclear Threat on

    Children's Development."   <u>Children of Social</u>

    <u>Worlds: Development in a Social Context</u>.   Ed.

    Martin Richards and Paul Light.   Cambridge:

    Harvard UP, 1986.   236-56.

Chaucer, Geoffrey.   <u>The Canterbury Tales</u>.   <u>The</u>

    <u>Riverside Chaucer</u>.   Ed. Larry D. Benson.   3rd ed.

    Boston: Houghton, 1987.   23-328.

(Editors' names must be included in entries when they are listed on the title page.)

Articles In Encyclopedias and Other Reference Works

Williams, Edgar Trevor.   "Victoria and the Victorian Age."

    <u>Encyclopaedia Britannica: Macropaedia</u>.   1986 ed.

(List articles from reference works by author's name if it is provided and by title if it is not. If the author's initials appear with the article, check the list of contributors for the full name. Reproduce the spelling of titles of reference works exactly, including, as above, any British spellings. Page numbers are not needed when the reference work is arranged alphabetically.)

```
"Spock, Benjamin."  Who's Who.  1989.
```

(This unsigned article is listed by title, reproduced exactly as given in the heading of the reference.)

```
Moray, Neville.  "Attention."  The Oxford Companion to

     the Mind.  Ed. Richard L. Gregory.  New York:

     Oxford UP, 1987.
```

(Well-known reference works, such as standard dictionaries and encyclopedias, require no information other than the title, edition number [if any], and date. Less well known or recently published reference works, such as this one, should have full publication information.)

A Work in a Series

```
O'Connor, Flannery.  Wise Blood.  Collected Works.  Ed.

     Sally Fitzgerald.  The Library of America Ser.

     New York: Literary Classics of the United States,

     1988.  3-131.
```

```
Strachey, Lytton.  Landmarks in French Literature.

     Oxford Paperback's University Ser. 42.  New York:

     Oxford UP, 1969.
```

(If a work is part of a series, the series title and any number are indicated on the title or copyright page. Abbreviate *series*.)

A Reprint

Palmer, John. The Comedy of Manners. 1913. New York:

Russell and Russell, 1962.

(Reprints are identified as such on the copyright page. List the original publication date after the title, and list the date of the reprinted edition after the publisher's name.)

A Translation

Emphasis on the Work

Mann, Thomas. Death in Venice. Trans. Kenneth Burke.

New York: Modern Library, 1970.

(Abbreviate *Translated by* as *Trans.*)

Aristotle. Rhetoric. Trans. W. Rhys Roberts.

Aristotle: Rhetoric and Poetics. New York: Modern

Library, 1954.

(Placing the translator's name after the title of part of a longer work indicates that the translator translated only that part.)

Emphasis on the Translation

Shepley, John, trans. Interview with History. By

Oriana Fallaci. Boston: Houghton, 1976.

(Use this form only when you are discussing the techniques of translation. Abbreviate *translator* as *trans.*)

A Government Document

United States. Cong. Joint Economic Committee. New

Dimensions in Rural Policy: Building upon Our

```
Heritage.   99th Cong., 2nd sess.   Washington: GPO,

    1986.
```

(Information about sessions and specific committees appears on the title page, which is often the cover of government documents.)

A Preface, Introduction, Foreword, or Afterword

```
Schorer, Mark.   Introduction.   Pride and Prejudice.   By

    Jane Austen.   Ed. Schorer.   Boston: Houghton,

    1956.
```

(Use this form to cite the introduction specifically.)

A Pamphlet

```
How to Feed Your Baby: The First Year.   Evansville:

    Mead Johnson, 1980.
```

(Editorial standards for pamphlets are less consistent than those for books, and some information may be missing. Use *n.p.* for "no place of publication" or "no publisher" and *n.d.* for "no date." The abbreviations are not underlined in the entry.)

A Published Dissertation

```
Rollins, Jeremy.   The Philanthropic Legacies of the

    Robber Barons: Carnegie, Rockefeller, and

    Vanderbilt.   Diss.   Syracuse U, 1986.   Ann Arbor:

    UMI, 1980.   9413756.
```

(The title page indicates whether a dissertation has been published. If it has been, italicize the title. If University Microfilms International [UMI] is the publisher, include the order number, found on the title or copyright page.)

An Unpublished Dissertation

```
Shapiro, Barbara.  "Structure and Form: The

    Architectural Development of Frank Lloyd Wright."

    Diss.  U of Illinois, 1988.
```

(The title page provides all necessary information. Enclose the title in quotation marks because the material is unpublished.)

34d ▷ **Follow the appropriate citation forms for periodicals.**

An Article in a Monthly Magazine

```
Schell, Jonathan.  "Speak Loudly, Carry a Small Stick:

    Foreign Policy in an Age of Ambivalence."

    Harper's Mar. 1989: 39-49.
```

An Article in a Journal with Continuous Paging Through a Single Year

```
Pinsker, Sanford.  "Comedy and Cultural Timing: The

    Lessons of Robert Benchley and Woody Allen."  The

    Georgia Review 42 (1988): 822-37.
```

(The title of the periodical is followed, without intervening punctuation or the abbreviation *vol.,* by the volume number and then by the year in parentheses. Page numbers, without an abbreviation for *pages,* follow a colon.)

An Article in a Journal with Separate Paging in Each Issue

```
Thym, Jurgen.  "The Composer as Evangelist."  American
     Choral Review 30.2 (1988): 7-29.
```

(When issues are paged separately, a period separates the volume number and issue number; both are necessary.)

An Article in a Weekly Magazine or Newspaper

A Weekly Magazine

```
Lewis, Geoff.  "Is the Computer Business Maturing?"
     Business Week 6 Mar. 1989: 68-78.
```

(Abbreviate the month and use the date format as shown above to eliminate a comma. Only May, June, and July are not abbreviated.)

A Weekly Newspaper

```
Barrett, Wayne, and Lynnell Hancock.  "Ten Ways to Save
     the Schools: The Decentralization Debate Begins."
     The Village Voice 28 Mar. 1989: 21-28.
```

An Article in a Daily Newspaper

```
Frankel, Glenn.  "Camp David Accord's Unfulfilled
     Promise."  The Washington Post 25 Mar. 1989: A9.
```

(Editions, such as *morning* or *evening,* when specified in the masthead, must be cited after the date, as in the next entry. Section and page numbers are separated with a colon — *1:9.* If sections are identified by letter, as above, no colon is used.)

An Editorial

"U.S. Judges, Held Hostage." Editorial. <u>The New York</u>

 <u>Times</u> 24 Mar. 1989, national ed.: sec. 1:20.

A Letter to the Editor

Weber, Catherine S. Letter. <u>Newsweek</u> 13 Mar. 1989:

 11-12.

(Do not use titles that publishers may include to get readers' attention. If the letter appears in a journal or newspaper, follow the appropriate format for those types of periodicals after the designation "Letter.")

A Review

Davis, Nancy. Rev. of <u>The American Perception of</u>

 <u>Class</u>, by Reeve Vanneman and Lynn Weber Cannon.

 <u>Contemporary Sociology</u> 18.1 (1989): 26-28.

34e ⟩ **Follow the appropriate citation forms for nonprint sources.**

Finding the documentation information for nonprint sources is usually easy, but sometimes it requires ingenuity. Album jackets provide the manufacturers' catalog number and copyright date. Printed programs for speeches or syllabuses for course lectures provide names, titles, locations, and dates. Information about films or television programs can be obtained from opening or closing credits or from reference books such as *Facts on File* or *American Film Record*. If you have difficulty documenting nonprint sources, ask your instructor or a librarian for help.

A Lecture or Speech

Gould, Stephen Jay. "Pattern and Pathway of Life's
    History." University Speaker Series Lecture.
    Indiana State University. Terre Haute, 14 Mar.
    1989.

Bush, George. Inaugural Address. Washington, 20 Jan.
    1989.

Mitten, David M. Class lecture. "Greek Art and
    Architecture in the West: Southern Italy, Sicily,
    and Campania." Harvard University. Cambridge, 15
    May 1989.

(Use a descriptive word, such as *lecture* or *address*, without underlining, if a lecture or speech has no title.)

A Work of Art

Gauguin, Paul. <u>The Brooding Woman</u>. Worcester Art
    Museum, Worcester, MA.

(The title was provided by the artist.)

Achilles Painter. Muses on Mount Helicon. Private
    collection, Lugano, Switz.

(This entry provides the artist and subject designations that art historians have given this anonymous, untitled vase painting.)

Graphic Work (Maps, Charts, Tables)

Periodic Table of Elements. Table. McGraw-Hill

Encyclopedia of Science and Technology. 6th ed.

1987.

A Film

Casablanca. Dir. Michael Curtiz. With Humphrey Bogart

and Ingrid Bergman. Warner, 1943.

(List films by title, with the director's name immediately following.)

Schulberg, Budd, screenwriter. On the Waterfront.

Dir. Elia Kazan. With Marlon Brando and Eva Marie

Saint. Horizon-American, 1954.

(If your paper emphasizes the work of a particular contributor, list the film under his or her name.)

A Television Broadcast

Special Programs

The Great American Fourth of July and Other Disasters.

Writ. Jean Sheperd. American Playhouse. PBS.

WGBH, Boston. 16 Mar. 1982.

(List special programs by title, followed by the name of the writer, director, or producer — whichever contributor suits your purpose. Capitalize but do not underline the series title. Include the name of the network and the date on which the program was broadcast.)

Regular Programs

"Politics, Privacy, and the Press." <u>Ethics in America</u>.

    PBS. WNET, New York. 4 Apr. 1989.

(Episodes of regular programs are listed by title, placed in quotation marks. After the appropriate contributor's name [if any], include the title of the series, underlined.)

A Radio Broadcast

<u>All Things Considered</u>. Natl. Public Radio. WBUR,

    Boston. 30 Mar. 1989.

A Recording

The Beatles. <u>Sgt. Pepper's Lonely Hearts Club Band</u>.

    Capitol, SMAS 2653, 1967.

(Alphabetize this entry by *Beatles,* not *The.* Use *n.d.* if no date is shown on the recording's label or packaging.)

Parker, Charlie. "Don't Blame Me." <u>The Very Best of</u>

    <u>Bird</u>. Audiotape. Warner, J5A 3198, 1977.

(Song titles are enclosed in quotation marks. Media other than long-playing records are noted after the title of the complete recording.)

Mozart, Wolfgang Amadeus. Serenade in B Flat, K. 361,

    "Gran Partita." Compact disk. Netherlands Wind

    Ensemble. Philips, 420 711-4, 1986.

(Designations of musical works by type, key, or number are neither underlined nor quoted.)

Netherlands Wind Ensemble. Serenade in B Flat, K. 361,

"Gran Partita." By Wolfgang Amadeus Mozart.

Compact disk. Philips, 420 711-4, 1986.

(This entry emphasizes the performers rather than the composer.)

A Performance

The New Moon. By Sigmund Romberg. With Richard White,

James Billings, and Leigh Munro. Cond. Jim

Coleman. New York City Opera. Wolf Trap, VA.

23 June 1989.

(In addition to title, author, location, and date, provide whatever other information suits the purpose of your paper.)

An Interview

Haroldson, Thomas B. Telephone interview. 14 Dec.

1988.

(List entries for interviews by the last name of the person interviewed; include the type — *personal* or *telephone,* for example — and the date of the interview.)

Doctorow, E. L. Interview. Fresh Air. Natl. Public

Radio. WBUR, Boston. 14 Mar. 1989.

(For a broadcast interview, indicate the program, network, local station, and date on which you heard the interview.)

Computer Searches

"Salk, Jonas." <u>American Men and Women of Science</u>.

   15th ed. Bowker, 1983. Dialog file 314, item

   0112528.

(Information about the original source, presented according to convention, is followed by the access numbers that are used to retrieve information stored by computer services.)

EXERCISE 34.1 ❯ Compiling a works cited page

From these ten sets of scrambled information, produce ten sample works cited cards. Keep them to use in a later exercise.

1. pages 47–48; Margaret Mead; *Redbook*; "Double Talk About Divorce"; May 1968.

2. 2nd edition; edited by J. Gipson Wells; "Some Thoughts on Divorce Reform"; Paul Bohannan; in *Current Issues in Marriage and the Family;* 1979; New York; Macmillan Publishing Company; pp. 249–63.

3. *Marriage in the United States;* originally published in 1867; Auguste Calier; Arno Press; New York; 1972; 3rd edition.

4. KNOW, Inc.; Pittsburgh; *'Til Divorce Do You Part;* 1972; pamphlet; Roberta Greene.

5. Page 3; "Data Shows Marriages Up, Divorces Down"; section A; March 16, 1983; *Washington Post.*

6. 1984 edition; "Divorce and Separation"; *Facts on File.*

7. Radnor, Pennsylvania; *Inside Divorce: Is It What You Really Want?;* Chilton Book Company; 1975; Edmond Adceo and Robert Burger.

8. Columbia Pictures; starring Dustin Hoffman and Meryl Streep; 1979; *Kramer vs. Kramer;* directed by Robert Benton.

9. Personal interview with Rebecca Stahl; February 19, 1988.

10. Number 1; pages 1–10; "Divorce Is a Family Affair"; March 1971; volume 5; Jack C. Westman and David W. Cline; *Family Law Quarterly.*

35 Organizing, Writing, and Documenting the Research Paper

After weeks of gathering information, organizing and writing the research paper may seem an enormous undertaking. It is. It is also an exciting stage in your work because you now are ready to bring your information and your ideas together in a clear and convincing paper.

Quick Reference

❯ Reread your notes and organize them into groups that correspond to logical divisions of your topic.

❯ Write a rough draft based on this organization, working with one group of notes at a time.

❯ Integrate source material smoothly with your ideas.

❯ Use parenthetical notes to provide readers with information about your sources.

❯ Revise the rough draft to clarify organization and content, to improve style, and to correct technical errors. (See Chapter 3, "Revising," for revision checklists.)

❯ Prepare and submit the final copy according to your instructor's or other standard guidelines.

35a ❭ Organize your notes.

The basic patterns of organizing a research paper resemble patterns used for other papers. (See Chapter 4, "Paragraphs," to review patterns of organization.) Your note taking has given you a wealth of material; now you need to arrange that material in the way that will best present your thesis to your readers.

Reread Your Notes

To begin, review your notes. Though time consuming, rereading all notes will help you to see the scope of your materials and the connections among ideas distilled from your sources. A complete grasp of your materials is crucial as you revise your thesis statement, prepare an outline, and sort your materials.

Revise Your Thesis Statement

Examine your working thesis statement. Based on the information gathered during research, test the validity of your thesis statement:

Does it identify your topic clearly?

Does it present a valid judgment?

Does it incorporate necessary qualifications and limitations?

Does it state or imply that you have acknowledged opposing views?

Is it worded effectively?

If you cannot respond "yes" to these questions, revise the thesis statement.

Use the Revised Thesis to Develop a Rough Outline

Once your thesis statement is clearly and effectively worded, type a clean copy and use it to help you construct a rough outline for your paper. What major categories does the thesis statement imply? Use them as the basis of a rough outline with which to sort your note cards into meaningful groups dictated by your thesis and ideas. Michele's thesis statement, in revised form, looked like this:

In a process that began with the first intelligence test and continues today, the tests, their use, and the concept of intelligence itself have been constantly challenged, refined, and redefined by scientists and educators seeking to use the tests wisely, not to label people but to help them overcome weaknesses and build on strengths.

This thesis statement clearly implies at least three major areas of emphasis: the history of intelligence tests, uses of the tests, and new directions in their use. Allowing for an introduction and conclusion and placing in rough order the most important of her discoveries about her topic, Michele created this rough outline:

Introductory paragraphs/thesis statement

History of tests

— *Binet and Simon*

— *Terman*

— *Otis*

— *Wechsler*

Uses of tests

— *Learning context*

— *Social misuses*

— *Judicial misuses*

New directions

— *Current trends/new directions*

Concluding paragraphs/where should we be heading?

》》》 *Remember that you can revise your outline if you discover a better way to arrange materials as you write the rough draft.* **《《《**

Although you are only sketching your research paper when you are composing a rough outline, preparing it on a word processor has advantages. ■ Type your rough outline on your word processor and then take a break. Return to the outline and print it out, examining it, and then make any necessary changes. Revise it and print a new copy. It will be much easier to evaluate your outline if it is typed rather than handwritten. ■ Write alternative versions. Prepare different versions of the rough outline, experimenting with the arrangement of information and ideas. Print two versions side by side and compare their clarity, balance, and emphasis. ■ Save the rough outline. The structure of the rough outline — and even some of its phrasing — can be used later in devising your formal outline.

Sort Your Notes

Using the major headings of your rough outline, sort your notes. First, find a roomy place — a large table in the library, the floor in your family room, the bed in your room. Make label cards using the major topics from your rough outline. Spread them out and then sort your note cards into the appropriate major topic groups.

If a note fits in more than one group, place the card in the most appropriate group and place a cross-reference card (for example, "See Parker quotation, p. 219 — in *childhood*") in each of the other appropriate groups. Expect to have a stack of notes that do not logically fit into any group. Label them *miscellaneous* and set them aside. You may see where they fit as you continue working.

Use paper clips, binders' clips, rubber bands, or envelopes to keep groups of notes together.

Allow a few days to organize and perhaps reorganize your notes. Sorting cards involves analyzing, reconsidering, and re-arranging. Expect temporary chaos.

Prepare a Formal Outline

After sorting cards into major topics, use the topics to decide on the arrangement of information within sections of your paper. Take each group of cards and organize them into a clear, logical sequence. Creating a formal outline is generally the most useful way to accomplish this. (To review outlining, see section 2b.)

Through a formal, detailed outline derived from her notes, Michele evolved the structure of her paper, including chronological organization of material on test history and topical organization of material on test uses. Her formal outline appears on pages 531–37.

> Using the word processor, expand your rough outline to produce the formal outline of your paper. ■ Introduce the elements of a formal outline: roman numerals, upper-case letters, arabic numerals, and lower-case letters to indicate levels of detail. ■ Add clarifying information. Insert details that will guide you in writing the rough draft.
> ■ Insert your revised thesis statement. Using the "block" and "move" codes, copy your thesis statement into the file that contains your formal outline and place it at the top, below the title. ■ Use the "outline" feature of your word processor to arrange material easily into the correct format.

35b > Write the rough draft.

With notes, revised thesis, and formal outline in hand, you are ready to begin writing the rough draft. The rough draft of a research paper, like the rough draft of any paper, will be messy and inconsistent, sketchy in some places and repetitive in others. That is to be expected. In fact, writing the draft of a research paper may present even more problems than writing other papers because of its greater length and complexity. To help with the process of drafting the research paper, remember the drafting strategies that you developed in writing other kinds of papers. (For a complete discussion, see section 2c.)

General Drafting Strategies

Gather all your materials together.

Work from your outline.

Remember the purpose of your paper.

Use only ideas and details that support your thesis statement.

Remember your readers' needs.

Do not worry about technical matters.

Rethink and modify troublesome sections.

Reread sections as you write.

Write alternative versions of troublesome sections.

Periodically give yourself a break from writing.

Beyond these general principles, which apply to all writing, there are specific principles that apply to writing a research paper and take into account its special requirements and demands:

Drafting Strategies for Research Papers

Allow ample time to write. Begin writing as soon as you can and write something every day.

Work one section at a time. Work steadily, section by section. When you come to a section that is difficult to write or for which you need more information, leave it for later and move on to the next section. Remember to look for necessary new material as soon as possible.

Give special attention to introductory and concluding paragraphs. Ideas for introductory and concluding paragraphs may occur at any time during the writing process. Consider several strategies and select the one most clearly matched to the tone and purpose of your paper.

Give special attention to technical language. Define carefully any technical language required in your paper. Thoughtful definition and use of important technical terms will help you to clarify your ideas as you draft your paper.

Think of your paper by section, not by paragraph. Because of the complexity of material in a research paper, discussions of most topics will require more than one paragraph. Keep that in mind and use new paragraphs to present subtopics.

Use transitions to signal major shifts within your work. The multiparagraph explanations required for key points can make it difficult for readers to know when you have moved from one key point to another. Consequently, emphasize transitions in your draft; you can refine them during revision if they are too obvious.

Incorporate your research notes smoothly so that they are an integral part of your paper. Material from sources should support, not dominate, your ideas. Incorporate source material as needed to support your thesis; do not simply string notes together with sentences. (For a complete discussion of incorporating research notes, see section 35c.)

As you write, remember that a research paper should present your views on a subject, based on outside reading and interpretation; it should not just show that you can collect and compile what others have said about the subject. Develop your own ideas fully. Be a part of the paper: add comments on sources and disagree with them when necessary. Do not be a stenographer. Be a thinker and a writer.

If possible, compose at the computer. "Add," "delete," "move," and "reformat" features will give you flexibility as you prepare your rough draft. You will also be able to print "clean" pages to review and revise later. ■ Drafting a research paper is a complex process, but a few suggestions may simplify your work. ■ Create a file for your draft and copy your thesis statement into it. ■ Copy quotations from your quotation file into the paper as you need them. By copying quotations into the file, rather than retyping them, you will save time and avoid introducing new errors.
■ Keep in mind the kinds of changes that you can easily make during revision. You will be able to move or change words, phrases, sentences, paragraphs, or whole sections; check spelling; change format and spacing; use "search and replace" procedures; and add full documentation.

35c ▷ Incorporate notes smoothly into the research paper.

The information from your note taking — summaries, quotations, and paraphrases — must be incorporated smoothly into your research paper, providing clarifications, explanations, and illustrations of important ideas. Use your notes selectively to substantiate your points, not simply to show that you have gathered materials, and provide your own commentary on the central ideas. Your readers should know why you have included the source material you did.

Summaries

Summaries are probably the easiest kind of researched material to incorporate in your paper because such information fits into your own sentences. Remember that sentences containing summarized facts and ideas require parenthetical notes (see section 35d) that identify the sources of the information. Information that is common knowledge, however, does not require an identifying note (see section 33g for a discussion of common knowledge).

Quotations

Use quotations selectively to add clarity and emphasis to a research paper, not to pad its length. Overquoting reduces the effectiveness of a paper because it suggests that the writer has depended too heavily on other people's ideas.

Never "float" a quotation and expect readers to know why it was worth quoting. Instead, frame the quotation with your own ideas and provide a brief evaluative comment. The examples given below demonstrate an effective pattern for introducing quotations: identify the author and source (book, article, interview, and so on) and explain the quotation's relevance to the discussion. Numerous verbs may be used to introduce quotations.

Verbs Used to Introduce Quotations

add	explain	reply
answer	mention	respond
claim	note	restate
comment	observe	say
declare	reiterate	stress
emphasize	remark	summarize

Quotations of prose and poetry can be either brief and included within the text of a paragraph or long and set off from the paragraph text.

Brief Prose or Verse Quotations

Include prose quotations of four or fewer typed lines (approximately forty-five words) within the paragraph text. Enclose them in quotation marks. For example:

```
Binet's IQ test has been under attack for decades.  Yet

many of the most vocal critics have not objectively

considered Binet's intended use for the test.  Accord-

ing to Stephen Jay Gould, in The Mismeasure of Man,

Binet designed his test "as a practical guide for

identifying children whose poor performance indicated a

need for special education" (152).
```

To vary the pattern, references can be placed at the end of the quoted material or, if not disruptive, in the middle of it. For example:

```
Binet's IQ test has been under attack for decades.  Yet

many of the most vocal critics have not objectively

considered Binet's intended use for the test.  "He

devised his scale," Stephen Jay Gould states in The

Mismeasure of Man, "as a practical guide for identify-

ing children whose poor performance indicated a need

for special education" (152).
```

To use very brief segments of a quotation, a phrase or a part of a sentence, incorporate the material into your own sentence structure. Although derived from the same passage as the quotation used above, this example demonstrates use of only part of the original:

> Binet's IQ test has been under attack for decades. Yet
> many of the most vocal critics have not objectively
> considered Binet's original use for the test. Stephen
> Jay Gould, in his book The Mismeasure of Man, stresses
> that Binet's primary purpose was to separate "children
> whose poor performance indicated a need for special
> education" (152).

Punctuate such quotations according to the requirements of the entire sentence. Do not set such quotations apart with commas unless your sentence structure requires commas.

Incorporate verse quotations of three or fewer lines in the same way. Use quotation marks and indicate the poem's line divisions with a slash (/) preceded and followed by one space. Retain the poem's pattern of capitalization.

> Tennyson stresses Ulysses' longing to pursue unreach-
> able goals, even in the face of old age and death: "And
> this gray spirit yearning in desire / To follow knowl-
> edge like a sinking star, / Beyond the utmost bound of
> human thought" ("Ulysses" 30-32).

Long Prose or Verse Quotations

To incorporate prose quotations of five or more typed lines, or approximately forty-five words, set the quotation off from the body of the paragraph. Indent the quotation ten spaces from the left margin and double-space it; do not enclose it within quotation marks. If a clause introduces the quotation, follow it with a colon, as in this example:

Binet's IQ test has been under attack for decades. Yet many of the most vocal critics have not objectively considered Binet's intended use for the test. Stephen Jay Gould offers this clarification in <u>The Mismeasure of Man</u>:

> Not only did Binet decline to label IQ as inborn intelligence; he also refused to regard it as a general device for ranking all pupils according to mental worth. He devised his scale only for the limited purpose of his commission by the ministry of education: as a practical guide for identifying children whose poor performance indicated a need for special education. (152)

To quote four or more lines of poetry, follow the pattern for long prose quotations: indent ten spaces, double-space the lines, and omit quotation marks. Follow the poet's line spacing as closely as possible, as in this example:

Dante Gabriel Rossetti presents a lush, sensuous view of the afterlife in his poem "The Blessed Damozel":

> The blessed damozel leaned out
> From the gold bar of heaven;
> Her eyes were deeper than the depth
> Of waters stilled at even;

```
        She had three lilies in her hand,

            And the stars in her hair were seven.

        (1-6)
```

Such images of heaven must have shocked tradition-bound

Victorians.

Punctuation with Quotations

Single Quotation Marks. Quotations within brief quotations are to
be enclosed within single quotation marks. Place the material you
are quoting in double quotation marks (" ") and change the
source's punctuation to single quotation marks (' '), as in this example:

```
Gould explains Binet's IQ scoring this way: "The age

associated with the last tasks he could perform became

his 'mental age,' and his general intellectual level

was calculated by subtracting this mental age from his

true chronological age" (149-50).
```

>>> *In long quotations that are indented ten spaces and not enclosed
within quotation marks, any quotation marks within the source material
remain double.* **<<<**

Brackets. Use brackets to clarify words or phrases in a quotation.
For example, the bracketed phrase in the passage below substitutes for the word *he,* which was used in the original but has no
antecedent in the quotation or its introduction.

```
Gould explains Binet's IQ scoring this way: "The age

associated with the last tasks [a school boy] could

perform became his 'mental age,' and his general intel-
```

```
lectual level was calculated by subtracting this mental

age from his true chronological age" (149-150).
```

Bracketed information can substitute for the original word or words or appear in addition to the original material: "the tasks he [a school boy] could perform." If your typewriter does not have brackets, leave space for them and add them neatly by hand.
》》》 *If a quotation requires extensive use of brackets, use another or express the information in your own words.* **《《《**

Ellipses. Use ellipsis points (three spaced periods) to show where words are omitted from a quotation. Omissions from the middle of a sentence do not require any punctuation other than ellipses. Omissions from the end of a sentence, however, require a fourth period (the sentence's end punctuation). The first period immediately follows the last letter of the last word.

```
Gould notes: "[Binet] devised his scale . . . as a

practical guide for identifying children whose poor

performances indicated a need for special education"

(152).
```

》》》 *It is not necessary to use ellipses at the beginning or end of a quote because readers know that quotations come from more complete sources. However, readers cannot be expected to know when something has been omitted from the middle of a passage.*

Unnecessary ellipses
Gould notes that Binet developed ". . . a practical guide for identifying children whose poor performances indicated a need for special education" (152). **《《《**

Paraphrases

Notes that paraphrase a source's ideas in your own words can simply be incorporated into your paper where they fit. A one-sentence paraphrase should be followed immediately by a parenthetical note. Longer paraphrases, especially background information taken from a single source, should be placed in a separate paragraph with parenthetical documentation at the end. So that readers do not assume that the documentation applies only to the ideas expressed in the last sentence, identify the author and source at the beginning of the paragraph. For example:

> Stephen Jay Gould, in The Mismeasure of Man,
> provides a useful summary of Binet's position on IQ
> testing. According to Gould, Binet opposed theories
> that heredity set limits on a student's achievement.
> For him, a student's score on the test did not estab-
> lish his or her worth as a student or as a person.
> Rather, Binet wanted to use IQ tests to pick out slow
> learners and help them through better planned and
> better focused education (152).

35d ⟩ Use parenthetical notes to document your research.

A research paper must include internal documentation to identify clearly which materials come from which sources and where facts, quotations, or ideas appeared in original sources. In the past, note numbers (one half-space above the line) at the end of sentences indicated when information, ideas, and quotations came from source materials. Those note numbers corresponded to full citations placed either at the bottom of the page (footnotes) or gathered at the end of the paper (endnotes). Numbered notes are still seen in older books and articles. Simplified, less repetitive methods of citation are more commonly used today.

Acknowledging the repetitive nature of full note citations, the Modern Language Association (MLA), following the lead of the American Psychological Association, now briefly identifies sources in the paper in parentheses. See section 34a for a discussion of MLA and other style guides.

Consistency of References

Parenthetical references must correspond to an entry in the list of works cited. If a works cited entry is listed under the author's name, the text reference must cite the author, not the title, editor, translator, director, or any other agent. Readers can thus match information in parenthetical references with the information in works cited entries.

Basic Forms of Parenthetical Notes

To avoid disrupting the text, parenthetical notes use the briefest possible form to identify the relevant source: the name of the author or the title under which the source appears in the list of works cited and, for print sources, a page number. In the interests of clarity and economy, writers may incorporate some of the necessary information into their sentences. For example:

```
Between 1851 and 1861, more than 150,000 white settlers
moved westward into land previously claimed by the
Santee Sioux (Brown 38).
```

Or:

```
Brown notes that between 1851 and 1861, more than
150,000 white settlers moved westward into land previ-
ously claimed by the Santee Sioux (38).
```

In-text references can also be used to identify specific authors, when citing more than one author with the same last name ("Dee Brown notes"), or to identify specific works, when citing more than one source by the same author ("In *Bury My Heart at Wounded Knee,* Brown notes'). In these cases the parenthetical note contains only the page number, as in the second example given above.

Print Sources

For any print materials listed by author's name (books, articles, pamphlets, and so on), generally use the author's last name and the page number.

```
Coexisting with illiteracy we often find innumeracy,

"an inability to deal comfortably with the fundamental

notions of number and chance" (Paulos 3).
```

Or:

```
John Allen Paulos states that coexisting with illitera-

cy we will find innumeracy, "an inability to deal

comfortably with the fundamental notions of number and

chance" (3).
```

In some special circumstances, the rule of including the author's last name and the page reference is superseded:

Special circumstance	*Rule and sample*
Two authors with the same last name	Include first and last name: (John Paulos 3), distinct from (Miguel Paulos 217)
Two works by the same author	Include a shortened version of the title: (Paulos, *Innumeracy* 3), distinct from (Paulos, *Mathematics* 76)
Two authors	Include both last names: (Vidich and Bensman 321)
Three authors	Include all last names, separated by commas: (Adams, Atwan, and Ford 17)
Four or more authors	Include the last name of the first author and *et al.,* without underlining: (Lewis et al. 27)
Corporate author	Include the organization as "author": (APA 256)
Multivolume works	Include the volume number after the author's name: (Churchill 1: 8)
Reference books	Include the author's name or a shortened form of the title, depending on how the work appears in the works cited list; no page numbers are required: (Williams) or ("Primates")
Poetry or drama in verse	Include the author's name, a short title (if necessary), and line (not page) numbers: (Arnold, "Stanzas" 67–72)

>>> *Remember that any information given in the text should be omitted from the parenthetical reference.* **<<<**

Nonprint Sources

Cite nonprint sources, for which no page numbers can be given, by title or "author" (lecturer, director, writer, producer, performer, or interview respondent), as they appear in the list of works cited. Such citations, however, are often clearer if worked into the text of your paper.

A depressing and patronizing view of homemakers has
even permeated musical theater, where this image
emerges:

        Here's to the girls who play wife

        Aren't they too much!

        Keeping house but clutching

        A copy of "Life"

        Just to keep in touch. (Sondheim, "Ladies")

Or:

A depressing and patronizing view of homemakers has
even permeated musical theater, where this image
emerges in Stephen Sondheim's "The Ladies Who Lunch":

        Here's to the girls who play wife

        Aren't they too much!

        Keeping house but clutching

        A copy of "Life"

        Just to keep in touch.

》》》 *Because nonprint sources require such limited information in parenthetical notes, it is often possible to incorporate all needed information in the written text.* **《《《**

Punctuating Parenthetical Notes

Without disrupting the text, place parenthetical notes as close as possible to the material they explain — usually at the end of the sentence but before the end punctuation. Allow one space before the opening parenthesis.

Paraphrases and Summaries

```
Jefferson and Latrobe modified the original design of

the White House by adding terraces in 1807 (Pearce 17).
```

Brief Quotations

For brief quotations, place the note *outside* the quotation marks but *before* the end punctuation, a change from the usual pattern of placing end punctuation before the closing quotation marks.

```
Individual occupants, from Jefferson to Roosevelt, have

modified the building to suit their tastes.  Thus,

present features of the White House "form a living link

with the building's past" (Pearce 17).
```

Long Quotations

For long, set-off quotations (indented ten spaces and not enclosed in quotation marks), place a period at the end of the quotation, followed by two spaces and then the parenthetical note not followed by additional punctuation.

The limited press coverage of the Kitty Hawk flight was probably the result of earlier notable failures:

> Just nine days before Kitty Hawk, the secretary of the Smithsonian Institution, Samuel Langley, had tried to launch a winged contraption from the roof of a houseboat on the Potomac River in Washington, D.C. . . . But while boatloads of reporters and government officials watched expectantly, the craft had left its catapult and plunged nose first into the Potomac. (Century 88)

35e ▷ Revise the rough draft into a final draft.

After writing the draft of the paper, set it aside for at least two or three days and longer if possible. Then reread it carefully. Consider the paper's organization, content, and style. Your ideas should be clearly expressed, logically organized, and effectively supported with appropriate and illuminating facts, quotations, and paraphrases smoothly and accurately incorporated. Leave time in your schedule to rework your paper, strengthening undeveloped sections by expanding them, clarifying confusing sections by rewriting them, and focusing overly long sections by cutting unnecessary material. For more information on this stage of the writing process, see Chapter 3, "Revising."

Evaluate the Rough Draft

Using the guidelines given below, assess your rough draft or consider having a peer editing session with someone in your class. Make revisions according to your assessment of the paper's strengths and weaknesses.

Introduction

Is the title interesting, accurate, and appropriate?

Is the introductory strategy interesting and appropriate to the tone and subject of the paper?

Is the thesis statement clear?

Is the length of the introduction proportionate to its importance and to the length of the entire paper?

Organization

Is the organizational pattern appropriate to the subject?

Are topics and subtopics clearly related to the thesis?

Is background information complete and well integrated?

Are interpretations of and conclusions from research clearly stated?

Content

Is the thesis statement clearly developed throughout?

Are topics adequately supported by facts, ideas, and research?

Are quotations and paraphrases well chosen to support the thesis?

Is material from sources smoothly and accurately incorporated?

Style

Is the tone of the paper consistently serious and appropriate for a college paper?

Are sentences clear and logical?

Are sentences in the active voice when possible?

Are sentences varied in length and type?

Is the diction appropriate and consistent?

Are any unfamiliar terms clearly explained?

Mechanics

Is correct grammar used throughout?

Is spelling correct throughout?

Are capitals, italics, and punctuation used correctly throughout?

Are parenthetical notes correctly placed and punctuated?

Conclusion

Does the conclusion restate the main ideas of the paper or offer a final interpretation or illustration of them, without repetition?

Does the concluding strategy leave the reader with the impression of a thorough, thoughtful paper on a meaningful subject?

Prepare the List of Works Cited

Separate the source cards containing the works cited entries for *sources used in the paper* and alphabetize them. Double-check the form of the entries (see section 33b), and then type the list of works cited, starting on a new page. (See page 571 for an illustration of the correct format.)

If you have more than one source by the same author, do not repeat the name for each source. Arrange the sources in alphabetical order by title and type the full name in the first entry and three hyphens followed by a period in place of the name in subsequent entries:

```
Gould, Stephen Jay.  Ever Since Darwin: Reflections in

     Natural History.  New York: Norton, 1977.

---.  The Mismeasure of Man.  New York: Norton, 1981.

---.  The Panda's Thumb: More Reflections in Natural

     History.  New York: Norton, 1980.
```

> If you have prepared your citations on the computer, your job will be simple: all you will need to do is add the heading "Works Cited," alphabetize the entries, and double-check the form of each entry. (See the example on pages 571–73.)

35f ▷ Prepare and submit the final manuscript.

The manuscript format for the research paper varies only slightly from that for other papers. (See Appendix A, Manuscript Form.) The margins, the heading, and the paging are the same, and double-spacing is still required throughout. Because the research paper has additional parts and because parenthetical notes complicate typing, however, allow extra time to prepare the final copy. Do not assume that typing and proofreading a research paper is a one-night process.

Type carefully. Type at an unhurried pace, proofreading and correcting pages before you remove them from the typewriter. Keep the finished pages nearby to double-check when necessary. Type the list of works cited, if you have not already done so, using the guidelines given on pages 525–26. When the final copy is complete, proofread it carefully for typing errors and make any small corrections neatly in black ink.

If you have prepared your paper using a word processor, you will be able to make final changes quickly and easily. ■ Insert paging codes. If you have not already done so, create a "header" that includes your last name and a page code. ■ Print a draft copy. Examine this copy to check the general presentation and format. If you need to alter anything — move a list so that it all appears on the same page, for example — do so now. ■ Print a high-quality copy to submit. Use a letter-quality printer, if possible, to produce the final manuscript.

After preparing the final manuscript of your paper, make a high-quality photocopy as insurance against damage or loss. **》》》** *If you have worked on the computer, you can print yourself an extra copy; you should make a disk copy, and perhaps a back-up disk copy as well, as insurance against loss.* **《《《**

If your instructor suggests a specific way to present the manuscript, follow those guidelines carefully and completely. If your instructor does not suggest a specific procedure, secure the pages with a paper clip in the upper left corner (outline first, then text, and then works cited pages) and place them in a 9-by-12-inch manila envelope with the identifying information from the first page of the paper typed on the outside. It is important to protect the manuscript in this way against damage or loss of pages.

35g ⟩   **A sample research paper.**

The following paper, written by a freshman in a composition class, demonstrates many important aspects of writing and documenting a research paper.

An Optional Outline

Not all instructors will expect an outline with the final copy of the research paper, but some will. On those occasions when you must submit an outline, place it at the beginning of the paper.

Examine Michele Newton's outline for her paper on intelligence testing, considering especially these important features:

1. On each page, the student's last name and the page number are given in the upper right corner.

2. A standard heading is provided, with the student's name, instructor's name, course number, and date.

3. The complete title of the paper is given.

4. The introduction (and conclusion), separated from the outline, appear without roman numerals.

5. The full thesis statement is presented.

6. A traditional outline format is used. Roman numerals indicate major divisions; upper-case letters, arabic numerals, and lower-case letters indicate subdivisions.

1.

2. Michele Newton

Dr. Robert Perrin

English 105

6 April 1990

3.   Intelligence Testing:

Avoiding the Sargasso Sea

4. INTRODUCTION

5. <u>Thesis statement</u>: In a process that began with the
first intelligence test and continues today, the
tests, their use, and the concept of intelligence
itself have been constantly challenged, refined, and
redefined by scientists and educators seeking to use
the tests wisely, not to label people but to help
them overcome weaknesses and build on strengths.

6. I.   Alfred Binet and Theodore Simon produced the
first well-known intelligence test (1905).

A. Test design

1. Individually administered

2. Thirty subtests

B. Innovations

1. Subtests to produce average score

2. Concept of intelligence quotient

a. Mental age

b. Chronological age

7. Roman numeral divisions are complete sentences; subdivisions are in topic-outline form.

An outline of a research paper serves as a "table of contents" and clearly and completely describes the information presented in the paper.

7. II. Lewis M. Terman revised the Binet-Simon test to
   create the Stanford-Binet (1916).

   A. Test emphasis

      1. Arithmetical skills

      2. Verbal skills

      3. Social variables

   B. Uses of the test

      1. Identify the retarded

      2. Label the feeble-minded

      3. Characterize criminals and delinquents

      4. Acknowledge superior children

      5. Determine vocational fitness

III. David Wechsler developed the Wechsler-Bellevue
     Intelligence Scale (1939) and the Wechsler
     Intelligence Scale for Children (1949).

   A. Test design

      1. Academic tests

         a. Verbal

         b. Arithmetical

      2. Performance tests

   B. Innovations

      1. Composite scores

      2. Increased reliability

IV. Historically, intelligence tests have been given
     and interpreted outside a learning context.

  A. Anthony--Mexican American five-year-old

     1. Average score (national group)

     2. Exceptional score (Spanish-speaking
         group)

  B. Cultural and social biases

     1. Deprives children

     2. Limits possibilities

     3. Deprives society

V. The social consequences of misused IQ scores
    should not be ignored.

  A. Undue emphasis on scores

     1. Low scorers--not challenged

     2. High scorers--often pressured

  B. Uncertain predictors

VI. The judicial system has misused the results of
     IQ tests.

  A. Carrie Buck (1927)

     1. Scored in feeble-minded range (standards
         then)

     2. Sterilized by court order

  B. Supreme Court ruling until 1972

VII. Current trends in intelligence testing suggest flexibility in test design and caution in the use of tests.

    A. Alternative methods

        1. Sensory tests

        2. Observations

        3. Ongoing assessment of patterns

    B. Attempts to redefine general intelligence

        1. Academic

            a. Verbal

            b. Arithmetical

        2. Spatial

        3. Physical

        4. Musical

        5. Social

        6. Interpersonal

    C. Applied intelligence

        1. Contextual

        2. Adaptable

        3. Insightful

CONCLUSION

1. Begin page numbering on the first page. In the upper right corner, one-half inch from the top of the paper, type your last name, followed by a space, and then the page number. Position the page number flush against the one-inch margin on the right.

2. Use the same heading for the research paper that you use for other papers: the writer's name, instructor's name, course number, and date. Double-space the heading and place it within the normal one-inch margins in the upper left corner.

3. Two line spaces down from the heading, center the title. If the title runs to a second line, center both lines. Allow two line spaces between the title and the first paragraph of the paper.

4. Michele introduces her paper with a long quotation. It is indented ten spaces from the left. The ellipsis points indicate the omission of the phrase "for example." The parenthetical note follows the closing period.

5. Michele provides a transition from the introductory quotation and establishes a historical context for her discussion.

1. Michele Newton

2. Dr. Robert Perrin

   English 105

   6 April 1990

3.   Intelligence Testing:

              Avoiding the Sargasso Sea

4.   If . . . the impression takes root that

           these tests really measure intelligence,

           that they constitute a sort of last judg-

           ment on the child's capacity, that they

           reveal "scientifically" his predestined

           ability, then it would be a thousand times

           better if all the intelligence testers and

           all their questionnaires were sunk without

           warning in the Sargasso Sea. (Eysenck and

           Kamin, Controversy 90)

       Walter Lippmann, a prominent columnist and

   social philosopher of the first half of the twentieth

   century, wrote this provocative statement in 1922.

   But during their eighty years of use, intelligence

   tests have always generated controversy. Today,

   psychologists and educators continue to debate what

   the tests can measure, how they should be designed,

6. Michele merges a brief quotation with her sentence. The parenthetical note includes only the author's name because the material appeared in an encyclopedia, for which page references are not required. The full quotation reads, "Binet conceived intelligence as the sum of all thought processes involved in mental adaptation."

7. After describing historical definitions of intelligence, Michele provides a current definition, establishing a transition to her thesis statement.

8. Michele's thesis statement comes at the end of her introductory paragraphs. It is presented in one sentence but establishes the qualified opinion that will focus her paper.

9. Michele begins the body of her paper by describing the early work of Alfred Binet and Theodore Simon, the first people to devise intelligence tests. This opening establishes the chronological-historical context for her later discussions.

and how their results should be used--and not
misused.

   At the turn of the century, when the first
intelligence tests were administered in large num-

6. bers, intelligence was thought to be the "sum of all
thought processes involved in mental adaptation"

7. (Durost). Today, although there are many definitions
of intelligence, most theorists agree that intelligence is expressed through the potential of the
person being tested, rather than through the sum of

8. fully developed skills. In a process that began with
the first intelligence test and continues today, the
tests, their use, and the concept of intelligence
itself have been constantly challenged, refined, and
redefined by scientists and educators seeking to use
the tests wisely, not to label people but to help
them overcome weaknesses and build on strengths.

9.   Alfred Binet, director of the psychology laboratory at the Sorbonne, and Theodore Simon, a noted
French physiologist, were looking in new directions
when they designed and administered the first
well-known intelligence tests to French school children in 1905 (Guilford 4). The thirty subtests of

10. Michele summarizes the general skills tested by the 1905 Binet-Simon scale; this general information is considered common knowledge.

11. Rather than quoting long sections of Guilford's book, Michele composed a brief list of representative subtests. Because her list was not a quotation, she did not indent it ten spaces but aligned it with the left margin as is done with tables and charts. Michele identifies the source of the paraphrased information in her list with a parenthetical note. Notice that no punctuation separates the author's name from the page number.

12. Dearborn's interpretation of the innovations in the Binet-Simon test covers three pages in the original source. Michele chose to summarize it briefly and give Dearborn credit for the interpretation.

the 1905 Binet-Simon Intelligence Scale were designed
10. and individually administered to measure memory,
reasoning, numerical facility, comprehension, time
orientation, and the ability to combine ideas into
meaningful patterns of thought. The following subtests, abstracted from the complete Binet and Simon
test, indicate the skills expected of the average
five-year-old:

11. Recognize food (choice between wood and chocolate)
Seek food (in response to chocolate wrapped in paper)
Follow simple orders to repeat gestures
Point to objects (head, nose, etc.)
Recognize objects in pictures
Name objects in pictures
Repeat three digits
Resist suggestions
Define simple words (Guilford 4-5)

Binet and Simon improved on earlier tests in two
ways: (1) the use of multiple subtests to produce an
"averaged" score and (2) the introduction of the
12. concept of "mental age" (Dearborn 65-67). The
child's average score, termed mental age (MA), and
age in years, termed chronological age (CA), were

13. An equation (or table, diagram, or other kind of visual support material) is presented within the paper, where it has the most impact, not at the end of the paper. A parenthetical note is placed at the lower right side, but within the regular one-inch margin. The note includes the author, a comma, and a brief title followed by the page reference to distinguish this source from another by Eysenck and Kamin also cited in the paper.

14. The numbers, computation, and IQ scores incorporated here are not documented. Using the equation cited above, Michele compiled these figures herself.

15. Rather than redraw the curve of test scores, Michele photocopied the original and used rubber cement to insert it into her text. Below the insert, she typed the parenthetical citation. (Large-scale drawings, graphs, and so on, can be reduced to a convenient size using a photocopy machine.)

Newton 4

employed in the equation shown below to produce the
child's <u>intelligence quotient</u> (IQ).

13.
$$IQ = \frac{\text{Mental Age (MA)}}{\text{Chronological Age (CA)}} \times 100$$

(Eysenck and Kamin, <u>Controversy</u> 16)

(To avoid decimals, the result of division is multi-
plied by 100.) For example, a child with an MA of 7

14. and a CA of 7 would have an IQ of 100, the average
score; a child with an MA of 9 and a CA of 7 would
have an IQ of 128, an above-average score; a child
with an MA of 7 and a CA of 9 would have an IQ of 77,
a below-average score. The general interpretation of
the scores follows this pattern:

15.

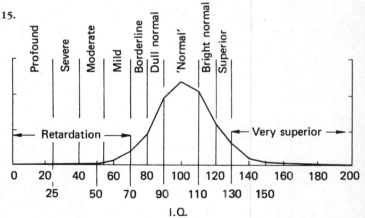

(Eysenck and Kamin, <u>Structure</u> 58)

16. In this section, Michele comments on the material she cites. She does not merely present the source material and expect readers to interpret it. This active, thoughtful summation helps Michele to help her readers understand her topic.

17. This transition paragraph establishes the link between the Binet-Simon test and its revised version, the Stanford-Binet. The transition makes the paper's structure clear for readers and adds interesting information.

18. Because Terman's name is indicated in the introductory phrase, it is not required in the parenthetical note. Notice as well the use of *sic,* without italics, within the quotation; *sic,* which means "thus," indicates that a grammatical, mechanical, or logical error exists in the original. In this instance, *sic* reassures readers that Michele knows that *less* should be in the comparative form: *lesser.*

19. Incorporating Terman's explanation of what supplemental information is useful in determining intelligence allows Michele to establish balance in her discussion, acknowledging that test designers knew that variables other than test scores were important. This list, a direct quotation, is indented ten spaces.

16. This clear mathematical expression of discrepancies
between ability and age as a seemingly scientific,
objective numbered score made the Binet-Simon Intelligence Scale widely popular.

17.   Binet and Simon's work prompted others to explore IQ tests, most notably Lewis M. Terman, an
American psychologist working at Stanford University.
In 1916, Terman adapted the Binet-Simon test, creating the Stanford-Binet Intelligence Scale.

      Terman's test, designed for American school
children, evaluated primarily arithmetical and verbal
skills, though Terman claimed to treat test results
within a broad context. In The Measurement of

18. Intelligence he wrote, "There are no tests which are
absolutely pure tests of intelligence. All are
influenced to a greater or less [sic] degree also by
training and by social environment" (135). Terman
suggested gathering this supplemental information:

19.   1. Social status

            2. The teacher's estimate of the child's
                intelligence

            3. School opportunities, including years
                in attendance, regularity, retardation

20. Michele points to a gap between Terman's theory and his practice, allowing her ideas to emerge in her use of sources.

21. Michele uses the subject headings in one of Terman's chapters to help her to summarize the points he made in a lengthy discussion without taking up too much space.

[working below grade level], or

acceleration, etc.

4.   Quality of school work

5.   Physical handicaps, if any   (135)

20.   But Terman's acknowledgment of these variables did

not guarantee that of test administrators or inter-

preters. Further, Terman's questions, following the

Binet-Simon pattern closely, did not incorporate the

variables in the scale itself. Consider the skills

required of a three-year-old on the Stanford-Binet:

1.   Name parts of body.

2.   Name familiar objects.

3.   Name objects in pictures.

4.   Classify self as boy or girl.

5.   State family name.

6.   Repeat 6-7 syllables (sentences).

7.   Repeat 3-digit sequences. (Terman

142-50)

Although it followed the Binet-Simon model, the

21.   Stanford-Binet claimed a larger purpose. Terman

suggested, in a chapter called "The Uses of

Intelligence Tests," that the Stanford-Binet be used

to identify retarded children and children of superi-

or ability, to assess the feeble-mindedness of

22. Another careful transition moves forward Michele's discussion of the historical development of testing. Such transitions help to hold together lengthy discussions.

23. The dates for Wechsler's tests may be considered common knowledge. Because Michele reasoned that the specific names for his tests are not common knowledge, she documented them.

24. In presenting charts or lists, reproduce the format of the original as exactly as possible, as Michele has done here.

those with mental defects (morons, imbeciles, etc.) and of delinquents and criminals, to place students into classes by ability, and to determine the vocational fitness of people of all ages (3-21). With such broad claims for a single test, it is no wonder that the Stanford-Binet was seen as a panacea for what ailed American education, the legal system, and business.

22. From the 1940s, the most widely used tests have been David Wechsler's Wechsler-Bellevue Intelligence Scale (WBIS), designed in 1939 for adults, and the Wechsler Intelligence Scale for Children (WISC) developed in 1949 (Guilford 8-9). Wechsler's tests,
23. administered in groups, emphasized verbal skills but also assessed performance skills, as shown in this list of subtests:

24.
    Verbal Tests:

    Information

    Comprehension (to measure judgment or
        common sense)

    Arithmetic

    Digits Forward and Backward

    Similarities (state how two given things
        are alike)

25. Michele summarizes the ideas presented in this passage:

> *Durost*   *Wechsler Tests*
>
> *"Intelligence Testing"*
> *"[The Wechsler tests] were easier to administer and
> provided three distinct IQ's (intelligence
> quotients)—one for the entire test and one each for
> two groups of subtests, one group consisting of
> verbal tests, the other of performance tests. The
> Wechsler tests were also supposed to yield insights
> concerning emotional problems."*

26. Having conducted an interview, Michele quotes Jill Lowery
     after first providing her name and credentials. Because an
     interview is a nonprint source (which will not have page
     numbers) and because the source is identified in the text, no
     note is required.

Vocabulary

Performance Tests:

Picture Completion (state what is missing
    in each picture)

Picture Arrangement (put four pictures from
    a conic strip in correct temporal order)

Object Assembly (jigsaw puzzles)

Block Design (construct color-pattern
    designs in duplication of given pat-
    terns)

Digit Symbol (code substitutions, each of
    nine simple symbols to be substituted
    for its digit mate)

(Guilford 9)

25.
    Three scores were tabulated--an average of both tests
    and individual scores for each part--and, at least in
    theory, the test was thought to give insight into the
    emotional stability of the person taking the test
26.
    (Durost). According to Jill Lowery, a fourth-year
    doctoral student in clinical psychology and instruc-
    tor at Indiana State University, the Wechsler Scales

27.
Michele uses an effective transition to move from the first section of her paper — the historical overview — to the second section — the uses and misuses of intelligence tests.

28.
Michele prepares to cite an example of the potential misuse of intelligence tests by providing readers with pertinent information about the case study.

29.
Michele chooses to begin a quotation in midsentence, merging the quotation with her own introductory comment. Notice that within the material she quotes (identified by double quotation marks) Michele places single quotation marks around the words that were quoted in the original. Michele also inserts *and* to make the sentence read smoothly. Brackets show that the addition is hers.

are the most generally accepted tests because they
"have a very rich research history which supports
their validity and reliability."

27.
      Psychologists and educators continue to revise
standard intelligence tests and to research their
effectiveness, but this is only one area of inquiry.
Of equal importance is how the tests are to be
used--and how to avoid the misuses of the past.

      One fundamental error in the use of IQ scores
has been using them outside a context. As part of an
extensive study, Jane R. Mercer, a sociology professor at the University of California, examined the

28.
case of a five-year-old Mexican-American boy,
Anthony, who scored 105 on the Wechsler Scale for
Children. His score, only slightly above average in
a general test group, is twenty-one points above
average if compared to the scores of other children
from Spanish-speaking homes. Considered out of his
socio-linguistic context, Anthony would move along

29.
the same "relatively slow path of the tens of millions of 'ordinary' children, perhaps never realize
his abilities, [and] probably never go to college"
(Krasner 1). Considered within his context, however,

30. Although Alan Coulter is credited with the comment quoted here, his remarks appeared in an article by another author. Consequently, the parenthetical note must include the last name of the author of the article, plus the page number.

Anthony ranks among the top five percent in intelligence.

For so many children like Anthony, raw scores do not give a complete picture of the child's potential. By relying on scores alone, schools and society cheat themselves and their children out of hope for the
30. future. Alan Coulter, acting director for special education in the New Orleans School District, commenting on one-dimensional uses of IQ scores, says, "IQ tests are just labeling people without leading to achievement" (Levine 55).

An IQ label has little to do with a person's general behavior or productivity. Nevertheless, low scorers are often labeled slow and placed in special classes, even if outside school they function as well as other, so-called average children their age. Children labeled slow may find it difficult to move into regular classes because the expectations of parents, peers, and teachers are fixed by the label (Krasner 1). High scorers are also labeled on the basis of a single test score, even though high scores do not always predict success in school, college, or

31. Here, Michele introduces another section of her paper — the judicial misuses of intelligence tests — and illustrates her point by using an interesting case in which the Supreme Court upheld sterilization laws.

Newton 11

the workplace. R. J. Herrnstein, psychology professor at Harvard University, notes in IQ in the
Meritocracy, "A low IQ predicts poor performance more
reliably than a high one predicts good performance"
(113). In an ironic reversal of the harmfully low
expectations of children with low scores, parents'
and teachers' expectations for academic and other
achievement from children with high scores may be too
great (Roberts 94).

31.

Society seems to follow the lead of the schools.
At one time, even the judicial system misused IQ
scores. In 1927, the Supreme Court upheld sterilization laws in Virginia, using intelligence test scores
for justification. The case, Buck v. Bell, centered
on Carrie Buck, a young mother who had scored a
mental age of nine on the Stanford-Binet Intelligence
Scale; her mother, then fifty-two, had scored a
mental age of seven; Carrie's child, though apparently untested, was also considered "feeble-minded"
(Gould 335). Oliver Wendell Holmes, Jr., wrote the
majority opinion:

> We have seen more than once that the public
> welfare may call upon the best citizens for
> their lives. It would be strange if it

32. Rather than quote a passage that would have contained a quotation, Michele selected isolated information from this passage:

Gould   *Supreme Court Ruling*

<u>*Mismeasure*</u>, *p. 335*
" 'Over 7,500 sterilized in Virginia,' the headline read. The law that Holmes upheld had been implemented for forty-eight years, from 1924 to 1972."

---

33. Michele introduces the last section of her paper — new directions in the use of intelligence tests — smoothly and clearly.

> would not call upon those who already sap
> the strength of the state for these lesser
> sacrifices. . . .   Three generations of
> imbeciles are enough.   (Gould 335)

32. Carrie Buck was sterilized under Virginia law, although she would not be considered mentally retarded
by standards set today.   This shocking story becomes
even more so when one considers that the law that
justified Carrie Buck's sterilization, and the ster-
ilizations of some 7,500 others, was not overturned
until 1972 (Gould 335-36).

33.   Today, theoretical, clinical, and educational
psychologists are searching for alternatives to
existing intelligence tests and for more holistic
ways to interpret their findings.   Art Levine, in
"Getting Smart About IQ," noted that school psychologists are looking for "alternatives to IQ tests for
children in need of special help.   They're using a
bewildering variety of academic and sensory tests,
interviewing parents and even analyzing how students
conduct themselves on the playground with friends"
(55).   Katherine Lindenauer, a psychologist with the
Los Angeles School District, offered this comment on
the new method of assessment: "It's more challenging.

It's more complex. But you learn a good deal about the youngsters" (Levine 55). Psychologists are learning to look at the child as an individual and not as an intelligence test score. Dr. Francis Roberts, columnist for Parents magazine, gave the mother of a two-year-old exhibiting above-average intelligence this advice:

> Rather than focusing on test scores, center attention on your child. If you plan on nursery school for your very bright child, look for a staff that values differences among children, as well as a program that does not uniformly press for early academics, that encourages children to explore varying activities and interests, and that allows able children to pursue a specific interest or project in some depth. (94)

Reuven Feuerstein, an Israeli psychologist whose methods are being used in Detroit's special education classes, gives similar advice. Refusing to evaluate children on timed, pressured IQ tests, Feuerstein observes them completing tasks at their own pace. The child's educational future is thus determined not

34. A reference to a source by two authors must include the names of both authors, without additional punctuation. If a third author were included, commas would separate the first two names but would not appear between the last author's name and the page number.

by a test score but by close observation of individual learning patterns. The psychologist-observer diagnoses problems and recommends educational "treatments." During a one-year period, eight children out of eleven labeled mildly retarded had been promoted to a more advanced class (Levine 55). Linda Roland, the special education teacher in charge of the Detroit classroom, said, "I felt I was failing my students and they were failing me. [Now,] they have a future" (Levine 55).

Many intelligence researchers concur that intelligence can no longer be considered a single, universal concept accurately defined by a single test. Psychologists talk not about intelligence but about intelligences (Goleman 24). In 1983, Howard Gardner published Frames of Mind, describing the major intelligences. He includes standard academic skills such as linguistic and logical-mathematical skills, but he extends the traditional definition by including spatial skills, bodily grace, musical gifts, social

34. skills, and interpersonal skills (Walters and Gardner 5-12). More recently, Gardner expanded the seven categories into twenty (Goleman 24).

35. Although Michele had written down Sternberg's exact words, she decided that the quotation did not merit inclusion and chose to paraphrase it. The original quotation is shown below:

Levine   *Applied Intelligence*

"Getting Smart," p. 53
Robert Sternberg, Yale University psychologist, says:
"There are a lot of successful people who didn't do well on IQ tests. The tests put too little emphasis on practical and creative skills."

---

36. Michele begins her concluding paragraphs with a transition sentence that returns to Binet and Simon, allowing her to stress the connections among ideas in her paper.

Another innovator in the search for alternatives
to traditional IQ testing is psychologist Robert
Sternberg of Yale University. Sternberg has found
35. that many successful people did not score well on
intelligence tests; in fact, one-third of the professionals Sternberg interviewed scored below average on
intelligence tests administered in childhood (Levine
53-54). In place of traditional tests, Sternberg
suggests three types of thinking ability as criteria
to assess intelligence: the ability to learn from
context, rather than from specific instruction;
mental flexibility, the ability to adapt to new or
unusual ideas; and insight (Goleman 25). Gardner,
Sternberg, and others in the field argue that traditional IQ tests define intelligence too narrowly and
that narrow concepts encourage misapplication of test
results. Psychologists, educators, and parents, they
maintain, should focus on determining an individual
child's strengths (through a wide range of tests,
observations, and interviews) and not on one-
dimensional labels (Goleman 27).

36. Definitions of intelligence have changed enor-
mously since the time of Alfred Binet and Theodore
Simon. Efforts continue to refine and redefine the

37. Continue page numbering, using last name and page number, through the works cited list.

38. Michele returns to Walter Lippmann for another quotation to "frame" her paper.

37.   Newton 16

concept of intelligence and to find ways to use
individual assessments wisely--tc help people reach
their potentials, not burden them with labels.

     In a response to a 1922 article written by Lewis
38. B. Terman, Walter Lippmann said:

                    I hate the impudence of a claim that in
                    fifty minutes you can judge and classify a
                    human being's predestined fitness for life.
                    I hate the pretentiousness of that claim.
                    I hate the abuse of scientific method which
                    it involves.   I hate the sense of superior-
                    ity which it creates, and the sense of in-
                    feriority which it imposes.   (Lippmann 42)
Although Lippmann's comment was very bold in 1922, in
the more than sixty years that have passed, psychologists have come to agree that intelligence is not
one-dimensional and cannot be judged adequately by
traditional intelligence tests alone.

39. Center the title "Works Cited." Include in the list only sources providing material actually incorporated in the paper. (A works consulted page would include not only sources cited in the paper itself but also any sources read during the process of research.)

40. Alphabetize the list of sources by the first word of each entry, not including *a, an,* and *the.* Provide complete information for each entry, following exact patterns of organization and punctuation (see pages 488–501). Begin the first line of each entry at the normal left margin and indent second and subsequent lines five spaces. Double-space the entire list.

41. List multiple sources by the same author separately. Alphabetize them by title. In second and subsequent entries, omit the author's name, replacing it with three hyphens followed by a period.

39.   Works Cited

40. Dearborn, Walter Fenno. Intelligence Tests: Their

Significance for School and Society. Boston:

Houghton, 1928.

Durost, Walter N. "Intelligence Testing."

Encyclopedia Americana. 1985 ed.

Eysenck, H. J., and Leon Kamin. The Intelligence

Controversy. New York: Wiley, 1981.

41. ---. The Structure and Measure of Intelligence. New

York: Springer-Verlag, 1979.

Goleman, Daniel. "Rethinking the Value of

Intelligence Tests." New York Times 9 Nov.

1986, sec. 12: 23-27.

Gould, Stephen Jay. The Mismeasure of Man. New

York: Norton, 1981.

Guilford, J. P. The Nature of Human Intelligence.

New York: McGraw, 1967.

Herrnstein, R. J. I.Q. in the Meritocracy. Boston:

Little, 1971.

Krasner, William. Labeling the Children.

Washington: U. S. Dept. of Health, Education,

and Welfare, 1977.

Newton 18

Levine, Art. "Getting Smart About IQ." <u>U.S. News &
World Report</u> 23 Nov. 1987: 53-55.

Lippmann, Walter. "The Great Confusion [A Reply to
Terman]." <u>The IQ Controversy: Critical
Readings</u>. Ed. N. J. Block and Gerald Dworkin.
New York: Pantheon, 1976. 39-42.

Lowery, Jill. Personal interview. 8 Nov. 1988.

Roberts, Francis. "Testing the Gifted Preschooler."
<u>Parents</u> Nov. 1986: 94.

Terman, Lewis M. <u>The Measurement of Intelligence:
An Explanation of and a Complete Guide for the
Use of the Stanford Revision and Extension of
the "Binet-Simon Intelligence Scale."</u> Boston:
Houghton, 1916.

Walters, Joseph M., and Howard Gardner. "The
Development and Education of Intelligences."
<u>Essays on the Intellect</u>. Ed. Frances R. Link.
Alexandria, VA: Assn. for Supervision and
Curriculum Development, 1985. 1-21.

APPENDIXES

Appendix A
Manuscript Form

Over the years, writers have developed fairly consistent methods for presenting manuscripts of any type of material and any length. These methods, although not inflexible, have become the expected standard. It is wise to adhere to them.

Accepted guidelines for typed manuscripts (on typewriters and word processors) and handwritten manuscripts are included below. **》》》** *Before submitting handwritten work, always check with your instructor to be sure that it is acceptable.* **《《**

Paper

Typed Manuscript. Use white, medium-weight, $8^{1}/_{2}$-by-11-inch paper. Avoid onion-skin paper and erasable paper. (If you must type on erasable paper, submit a high-quality photocopy on medium-weight paper.) When using a word processor, use letter-quality (not draft-quality) paper, or submit a photocopy on medium-weight paper.

Handwritten Manuscript. Use good, white, standard $8^{1}/_{2}$-by-11-inch paper, preferably with lines. Never submit work on torn-out spiral-notebook paper without first trimming the edges.

Ribbons and Pens

Typed Manuscript. Use a black ribbon and remember to clean your typewriter keys periodically. With word processors, use a letter-quality printer or use the correspondence-quality mode on a dot-matrix printer.

Handwritten Manuscript. Use a blue or black pen for handwritten work unless advised otherwise. Make sure that your pen does not blob or skip.

Typing and Handwriting Formats

Typed Manuscript. Double-space throughout to make papers easy to read and to allow space for corrections and additions. Use only one side of each page.

Handwritten Manuscript. Write on every other line unless given other advice. Write on only one side of each page, clearly and carefully forming letters.

Margins

Typed Manuscript. Leave one-inch margins *on all sides* of the page. Word-processing programs automatically establish "default" margins; if they are not wide enough, reset them.

Handwritten Manuscript. Leave one-inch margins *on all sides* of the page.

Indentions

Typed Manuscript. Indent the first word of a paragraph five spaces from the left margin. Do not skip extra lines before beginning a new paragraph.

Handwritten Manuscript. Indent the first word of a paragraph one inch from the left margin.

Headings and Title

Typed Manuscript. In the upper left corner of your paper, within the one-inch margins, type your name, the instructor's name, the course number, and the date. (Your instructor may also require section or assignment numbers.) Then double-space and type the paper's title, centered. Capitalize all important words in the title, but do not italicize it or place it in quotation marks. Double-space again and begin the first paragraph.

Handwritten Manuscript. Include the same information on hand-written as on typed work. Begin writing your name on the top line of your paper in the upper left corner.

Paging

Typed Manuscript. In the upper right corner of each page, one-half inch from the top, type your last name and the page number, separated by a space. Then double-space and continue the text of the paper. If you are using a word-processing program that automatically places page numbers at the bottoms of pages, insert additional commands to position your last name and the page number at the top. (Check your program's instructions for adding "headers.")

Handwritten Manuscript. On the top line, in the upper right corner of each page, write your last name and the page number.

Proofreading

Typed Manuscript. Proofread typed manuscripts for grammar, usage, and mechanics. Use this handbook. Check carefully for typing errors.

Handwritten Manuscript. Proofread handwritten manuscripts for grammar, usage, and mechanics and to check legibility. Re-form any unclear letters.

Corrections

Typed Manuscript. Make corrections neatly. Use correction fluid or tape. Draw a single line through words you delete at the last minute. Words accidentally omitted may be inserted *above the line*. Use a caret (∧) to indicate where they belong. Whenever possible, type corrections; otherwise insert them neatly by hand using black ink. If you are using a word processor, reopen the file, make all revisions, and then print a clean copy to submit.

½" Davis 1

Ronald Davis

1" → Dr. L. C. Nichols

English 231

6 September 1990

Title of the Paper

_____

_____

_____

_____

_____

_____

_____

_____

_____

_____

_____

_____

_____

1"

1"   ½" Davis 2

1"

_____

Handwritten Manuscript. Follow the guidelines given above, inserting corrections by hand.   **》》**   *More than two or three corrections on a page makes the writer look careless and the page messy. Retype such pages. Also, check with your instructor to see if he or she places a limit on the number of corrections permissible.* **《《**

Submitting the Manuscript

Typed Manuscript. Submit manuscripts according to your instructor's guidelines. If you receive no specific guidelines, secure the pages with a paper clip in the upper left corner. Place lengthy papers in a 9-by-12-inch manila envelope with your name and course information typed or written on the outside. Always make and keep a photocopy of your paper before submitting it.

Handwritten Manuscript. Follow the guidelines given above for typed manuscripts.

A Final Word on Manuscript Form

If you have difficulty following these guidelines or those presented by your instructor, see him or her before you prepare the final copy of a paper.

Appendix B
APA Documentation Style

In fields such as psychology, education, public health, and criminology, researchers follow the guidelines given in the *Publication Manual of the American Psychological Association,* third edition (Washington, DC: APA, 1984), to document their work. Like MLA style (see pages 483–573), APA style encourages brevity in documentation, uses in-text parenthetical citations of sources, and limits the use of numbered notes and appended materials. The two styles, however, vary in their requirements for the organization of manuscripts and the forms for some notes.

The information that follows is an overview of APA style. If your major or minor requires APA style, you should acquire the APA manual, study it thoroughly, and follow its guidelines carefully.

Paper Format

MLA	*APA*
No separate title page: Identification and title placed on the first page of the paper.	*Separate title page:* Includes a descriptive title, author's name and affiliation, and running head. The running head is a shortened version of the paper's title. Center it at the bottom of the title page. In the upper right corner, put the first two or three words of the paper's title. Below that short title, flush against the right margin, put the page number. The title page is always page one.

Paper Format

MLA	*APA*
No abstract.	*Abstract:* On a separate page following the title page, a 75-to-150-word paragraph describing the major ideas in the paper.
Introduction: A paragraph or series of paragraphs used to present and interest readers in the topic of the paper.	*Introduction:* A paragraph or series of paragraphs used to define the topic, present the hypothesis (or thesis), explain the method of investigation, and state the theoretical implications (or context.)
Body: A series of logically connected paragraphs that explore the main idea through various patterns of description, illustration, and argument.	*Body:* A series of paragraphs that describe study procedures, the results obtained, and interpretations of the findings.
In-text parenthetical documentation: Author and page number, unless title is necessary to distinguish among multiple works by one author.	*In-text parenthetical documentation:* Author and date for summaries and paraphrases; author, date, and page number for quotations.

Paper Format

MLA

List of sources: Cited sources fully identified in a listing entitled "Works Cited."

Appendix: Seldom included.

APA

List of sources: Cited sources fully identified in a listing entitled "References."

Appendix: Included when related materials (charts, graphs, illustrations, and so on) cannot be incorporated in the body of the paper.

Manuscript Format

MLA

Type: Any standard typeface — typewriter or printer.

Margins: One-inch margins at top and bottom and on left and right. Right-justified margins are acceptable.

Paging: Author's last name and page number placed in the upper right corner.

APA

Type: Any standard typeface — typewriter or printer. Dot-matrix type without descending letters is unacceptable.

Margins: One-and-one-half-inch margins at top and bottom and on left and right. Right-justified margins are unacceptable.

Paging: The first two or three words of the title placed in the upper right corner. Two lines below the short title, put the page number. Omit the author's name.

Manuscript Format

MLA	*APA*
In-text headings: Not recommended except in very long papers.	*Headings:* Recommended for divisions and subdivisions of the paper.
Corrections: Neat handwritten corrections acceptable; typed corrections preferred.	*Corrections:* Must be typed; handwritten corrections unacceptable.

Citation Format

APA formats for citations in lists of references and in the text differ from MLA formats. Below are listed several basic APA forms. Differences from MLA format are noted and cross references to the MLA model in Chapter 34 are provided.

Reference List Format

A Book by One Author

```
Sullivan, M.  (1976).  International relations: Theo-
     ries and evidence.  Englewood Cliffs, NJ:
     Prentice-Hall.
```

(Use initials for the author's first name. After the author's name, place the publication date in parentheses, followed by a period. Capitalize only the first word of the title and of the subtitle and any proper nouns and proper adjectives. For MLA form, see page 488.)

A Book by More Than One Author

Vidich, A. J., & Bensman, J. (1968). <u>Small town in</u>

    <u>mass society: Class, power and religion in a rural</u>

    <u>community</u>. Princeton: Princeton University Press.

(Invert the names of all authors. Insert an ampersand [&] before the last author. Spell out the names of university presses. For MLA form, see page 488.)

A Book by a Corporate Author

Council on Environmental Quality. (1981). <u>The global</u>

    <u>2000 report to the president</u>. Washington, DC: Gov-

    ernment Printing Office.

A Work in a Collection by Different Authors

Dingwall, R., & Eekelaar, J. (1986). Judgrents of

    Solomon: Psychology and family law. In Martin

    Richards and Paul Light (Eds.), <u>Children of social</u>

    <u>worlds: Development in a social context</u> (pp. 55-73).

    Cambridge: Harvard University Press.

(Do not enclose the title of a short work in quotation marks. *In* introduces its source. The editor's name, the abbreviation *Eds.* [capitalized and placed in parentheses] followed by a comma, the collection title, and inclusive page numbers for the short work [given in parentheses] are provided. Abbreviate *pages.* For MLA form, see page 490.)

An Article in a Monthly Magazine

Angier, N. (1981, Nov.). How fast? How high? How far?

    <u>Discover</u>, pp. 24-30.

(Give the year of publication followed by a comma and the month and day [if any]. Abbreviate *pages*. For MLA form, see page 494.)

An Article in a Journal with Separate Paging in Each Issue

```
Sills, T.  (1981).  Socrates was executed for being

    innovative.  English Journal, 70(7), 41-42.
```

(Italicize the name of the journal [but not the comma following it] and the volume number. The issue number in parentheses immediately follows the volume number; no space separates them. No abbreviation for *pages* accompanies the inclusive page numbers. For MLA form, see page 495.)

An Article in a Daily Newspaper

```
Oppenheim, C.  (1982, Mar. 19).  San Francisco transit

    running in the red.  Chicago Tribune, p. 4.
```

(Invert the date. Do not include information on the edition or section. For MLA form, see page 495.)

A Lecture or Speech

```
Brent, H.  (1981, Nov. 21).  Teaching composition

    theory in the People's Republic of China.  Paper

    presented at the meeting of the National Council of

    Teachers of English, Boston, MA.
```

(Italicize the title of the speech. Follow the title with the name of the sponsoring organization and the location, separated by commas. For MLA form, see page 497.)

Nonprint Materials

```
Fosse, B. (Director).  (1972).  Cabaret [Film].  Los
    Angeles: Allied Artists.
```

(List entries by the name of the most important contributor [director, producer, speaker, and so on]; note the specific role in full in parentheses following the name. Identify the medium [film, filmstrip, slide show, tape recording] in brackets after the title. The place of production precedes the name of the production company. For MLA form, see page 498.)

Text Citation Format

One Author

```
   Greybowski (1985) noted that . . .
```

Or:

```
In a recent study at USC (Greybowski, 1985), partici-
pants were asked to . . .
```

Multiple Authors: First Citation

```
Calendrillo, Thurgood, Johnson, and Lawrence (1967)
found in their evaluation . . .
```

Multiple Authors: Subsequent Citations

```
Calendrillo et al. (1967) also discovered . . .
```

Corporate Authors: First Citation

```
. . . a close connection between political interests
and environmental issues (Council on Environmental
Quality [CEQ], 1981).
```

Corporate Authors: Subsequent Citations

. . . in their additional work (CEQ, 1981).

Quotations Within the Text

First Option

She stated, "The cultural awareness of a student depends, by implication, on the cultural awareness of the
parents" (Hermann, 1984, p. 219).

Second Option

Hermann (1984) added that "enrichment in our schools is
costly and has little bearing on the later lives of the
students" (pp. 230-231).

Third Option

"A school's responsibility rests with providing solid
educational skills, not with supplementing the cultural
education of the uninterested," stated Hermann (1984)
in her summary (p. 236).

1. APA form requires a separate title page. (For MLA form, see page 531.)

2. In the upper right corner of every page, APA style requires a short title consisting of the first two or three words of the paper's title. The short title (which does not necessarily have the same wording as the running head; see item 4 below) identifies each page in the event that any pages go astray. The page number appears on the line below the short title, aligned on the right. (For MLA form, see page 531.)

3. The title, subtitle (if any), and the author's name and affiliation are centered on the page. If a title runs over to a second line, the runover line is also centered. (For MLA form, see page 531.)

4. Near the bottom of the title page, center and type the label "Running head," followed by a colon and a shortened form of the title.

1.   Intelligence Testing

2.   1

3.   Intelligence Testing:
                         Avoiding the Sargasso Sea
                              Michele Newton
                          Indiana State University

4.   Running head: INTELLIGENCE TESTING

5. The second page of a manuscript prepared in APA style is an abstract, a 75-to-150-word paragraph describing the major ideas presented in the paper. The page is titled "Abstract." (In MLA form, there is no equivalent to the abstract.)

5.

Abstract

Since 1905, when Binet and Simon produced their
well-known intelligence test, the underlying concepts
of testing have changed. Terman's revised test
(1916) assessed children of all levels of ability,
and Wechshler's tests (1939 and 1949) assessed multiple abilities in a physical, social, and environmental context. Intelligence tests are no longer used
merely to identify the mentally deficient (whether
for remediation or, as sometimes happened, sterilization); students of all ability levels are now tested
on many life and academic skills within a social
context. The concept of intelligence, too, has been
constantly challenged, refined, and redefined: it
now incorporates multiple intelligences, from problem
solving to creativity. Intelligence tests are no
longer used to limit and label people but to help
them overcome weaknesses and build on strengths.

6. The text of the paper begins on page three. (For MLA form, see page 531.)

7. Repeat the title and subtitle at the top of the third page, centered and worded as on the title page. Double-space and begin the body of the paper. (For MLA form, see page 531.)

8. Indent long quotations five spaces from the left margin. Double-space them. (For MLA form, see page 531.)

9. Parenthetical notes for long quotations follow the closing punctuation. This reference to a source by two authors shows their last names joined by an ampersand (&). The publication date, preceded and followed by commas, follows the authors' names. The page number, with the abbreviation *p.,* appears last. (For MLA form, see page 531.)

6.

7.   Intelligence Testing:

Avoiding the Sargasso Sea

8.   If . . . the impression takes root that

these tests really measure intelligence,

that they constitute a sort of last

judgment on the child's capacity, that they

reveal "scientifically" his predestined

ability, then it would be a thousand times

better if all the intelligence testers and

all their questionnaires were sunk without

9.   warning in the Sargasso Sea. (Eysenck &

Kamin, 1981, p. 90)

Walter Lippmann, a prominent columnist and

social philosopher of the first half of the

twentieth century, wrote this provocative state-

ment in 1922. But during their eighty years of

use, intelligence tests have always generated

controversy. Today, psychologists and educators

continue to debate what the tests can measure,

how they should be designed, and how their

results should be used--and not misused.

At the turn of the century, when the first

intelligence tests were administered in large

10. If an author's name is mentioned in the text, only the publication date of the source, in parentheses, is required. In parentheses at the end of the quotation, but before the closing punctuation, indicate the page on which the information appears. (For MLA form, see page 559.)

11. Parenthetical notes for brief quotations follow the closing quotation mark but precede the end punctuation. (For MLA form, see page 559.)

12. When an author's name is not given in the text, include the author's name, the publication date of the source, and a page citation (if needed) in parentheses. (For MLA form, see page 559.)

10. the workplace. R. J. Herrnstein (1971), psychology professor at Harvard University, notes in IQ in the Meritocracy, "A low IQ predicts poor performance more reliably than a high one predicts good performance"

11. (113). In an ironic reversal of the harmfully low expectations of children with low scores, parents' and teachers' expectations for academic and other achievement from children with high scores may be too

12. great (Roberts, 1986, p. 94).

Society seems to follow the lead of the schools. At one time, even the judicial system misused IQ scores. In 1927, the Supreme Court upheld steriliza- tion laws in Virginia, using intelligence test scores for justification. The case, Buck v. Bell, centered on Carrie Buck, a young mother who had scored a mental age of nine on the Stanford-Binet Intelligence Scale; her mother, then fifty-two, had scored a mental age of seven; Carrie's child, though appar- ently untested, was also considered "feeble-minded" (Gould, 1981, p. 335). Oliver Wendell Holmes, Jr., wrote the majority opinion:

> We have seen more than once that the public
> welfare may call upon the best citizens for

13. The short title and page number appear on all pages of the reference list and on any appendix pages. (For MLA form, see page 571.)

14. Center and type the title "References" at the beginning of the list of sources. APA requires that all sources included on the reference list be cited in the text. (For MLA form, see page 571.)

15. For a book by a single author, list the author's name first, inverted and followed by a period. Include the publication date in parentheses, followed by a period. Italicize (underline) book titles but capitalize only the first word of the title and of the subtitle and any proper nouns or proper adjectives. (For MLA form, see page 571.)

16. A citation for an article in a book (in this case a reference book) begins with the author's name, followed by the publication date in parentheses. (If an article has no author, begin the entry with the article title, not enclosed in quotation marks, followed by the publication date in parentheses.) Use the word *In* before the title of the complete source. (For MLA form, see page 571.)

17. When a source has more than one author, invert the names of all the authors, not just the first. Use commas to separate the names, and place an ampersand (&) before the name of the last author. (For MLA form, see page 571.)

18. For an article in a periodical, the author's name is followed by the year, month and day (if any) of publication. The article title is not placed in quotation marks, and only the first word of the title, proper nouns, and proper adjectives are capitalized. The name of the periodical is both italicized and capitalized. Inclusive page numbers are listed with the abbreviation *pp*. (For MLA form, see page 571.)

13.   Intelligence Testing

                                                     17

14.   References

15. Dearborn, W. F. (1928). Intelligence tests: Their significance for schools and society. Boston: Houghton Mifflin.

16. Durost, W. N. (1985). Intelligence testing. In Encyclopedia Americana.

17. Eysenck, H. J., & Kamin. L. (1981). The intelligence controversy. New York: Wiley.

    Eysenck, H. J., & Kamin. L. (1979). The structure and measure of intelligence. New York: Springer-Verlag.

18. Goleman, D. (1986, Nov. 9). Rethinking the value of intelligence tests. New York Times, pp. 23-27.

    Gould, S. J. (1981). The mismeasure of man. New York: Norton.

    Guilford, J. P. (1967). The nature of human intelligence. New York: McGraw-Hill.

    Herrnstein, R. J. (1971). I.Q. in the meritocracy. Boston: Little, Brown.

    Krasner, W. (1977). Labeling the children. Washington, DC: U.S. Dept. of Health, Education, and Welfare.

Appendix C
Writing Essay Exams

To study for an essay exam, reread course materials (books, articles, classroom notes), review important concepts. and memorize specific information related to major topics. This work is best done over a period of days or weeks.

When confronted by the exam, consider the following strategies for writing effective responses.

Point Values

Apportion your writing on each question according to its point value. For instance, if a question is worth ten points out of a possible one hundred, devote no more than ten percent of the total exam time to your response; if a question is worth fifty points out of one hundred, spend approximately half of the exam time writing your response. Spending disproportionate time on one question may leave you little time for other parts of the exam.

Multiple Questions

To respond to two or more essay questions, pace your writing. Decide, on the basis of point values, how much time each question deserves and write accordingly. An extended response to one question worth ten points and a brief, superficial response to another worth ten points may yield only fifteen points, whereas balanced discussions of both questions would probably yield more points.

Optional Topics

When given alternative questions, construct a brief topic outline for each choice, to see which essay would be most substantial. A few moments spent outlining will help you to select the questions to which you can respond most completely and effectively.

Careful Reading

Many essay questions provide an implied topic sentence for a paragraph essay or thesis statement for a longer essay. Focus your work by developing the idea presented in the question. Follow instructions carefully. Describe, illustrate, compare, contrast, evaluate, analyze, and so on according to instructions.

Style and Technical Matters

To guarantee that responses are grammatically correct, well worded, complete, and free from errors in punctuation and mechanics, adjust your writing strategies. Either write slowly, to make your sentences clear, complete, and free from errors in a first draft, or allow time to make corrections and revisions after you have written your response. For either approach, pacing is crucial.

Organization and Development

A response to an essay question is like a brief paper: It requires an introduction, a body, and a conclusion, although the development and length of each part will depend on the type of question and its point value. A ten-point and a fifty-point essay on the same question will require very different degrees of development, but the structure of each response will be similar. Before an essay exam, quickly review the patterns of development in Chapter 4 (description, examples, facts, comparison and contrast, analogy, cause and effect, process analysis, classification, and definition); you will then be able to organize your responses appropriately according to the pattern explicitly or implicitly required by the question.

Varied Organization

For an illustration of how the organizational pattern of an essay question response varies with the form of the question, examine the topic outlines below, which clearly show the differences in structure required by the two questions. The first question implicitly requires a comparison and contrast structure. The second explicitly requires an analysis structure. The full essay responses would also require appropriate support.

QUESTION

Which is more effective: the impromptu or the extemporaneous speech?

Introduction (thesis): Though both impromptu and extemporaneous speeches are flexible, the planning required for extemporaneous speeches makes them more coherent, more fully developed, and more effective.

I. Impromptu

    A. No written manuscript

    B. Words chosen while speaking

    C. Minimal preparation

    D. Unrehearsed

II. Extemporaneous

    A. No written manuscript

    B. Words chosen while speaking

    C. Substantial preparation

    D. Rehearsed

Conclusion: Extemporaneous speeches are generally more effective because they are more organized and substantive.

QUESTION

Of the four speech-making techniques, choose the one you believe is the most useful and analyze the factors contributing to its effectiveness.

Introduction (thesis): Because they are at once organized but flexible, extemporaneous speeches are the most effective.

   I. Preparation

     A. Reading

     B. Thinking

     C. Selecting

     D. Organizing

  II. Presentation

     A. Flexible

        1. Change examples

        2. Adjust to audience

        3. Add or drop material

     B. Personal

        1. Suited to audience's needs

        2. Suited to speaker's needs

        3. Not manuscript bound

        4. Better contact with audience

Conclusion: Because of advantages in planning and presentation, extemporaneous speaking is generally the most effective.

Degree of Development

For an illustration of the similar structures but different degree of development of essay responses with different point values, examine the samples below, prepared as part of an hour-long exam.

QUESTION

What are the four speech-making strategies and how do they differ?

Ten-point response

There are four basic speech-making strategies. Impromptu speeches are presented on the "spur of the moment"; the speaker has no time to organize or rehearse. Extemporaneous speeches are organized in outline form but are not written word for word. Manuscript speeches are written in advance and then read from a written or typed copy. Memorized speeches are written in advance and then learned word for word, to be presented without a written copy. These four strategies allow speakers to suit their presentations to their speaking situations.

Fifty-point response

Situations for speech making vary and speakers, as a result, choose among four different speech-making strategies to present their ideas most effectively.

Impromptu speeches are given on the "spur of the moment"; the speaker has no chance to organize or rehearse. These highly informal speeches are often unfocused (because they are unplanned) and ineffective (because they were not rehearsed), but they are the usual kinds of speeches given at organization meetings and in class discussions.

Extemporaneous speeches are given from prepared outlines, but they are not completely written. Rather, speakers decide what to discuss and what details or examples to use, and then they choose words as they speak. Extemporaneous speeches have the advantage of being organized, but at the same time they are flexible, allowing speakers to modify what they say to suit the needs of their audiences. For this reason, they are often the most effective speeches at informal meetings.

Manuscript speeches are written in complete form and then read, much like a newscast. Because they are prepared in advance, manuscript speeches are well organized and carefully worded. If they are also well rehearsed, manuscript speeches are effective in formal speaking situations because they present an exact, well-worded version of the speaker's ideas.

Memorized speeches are written in complete form and then committed to memory. Because they are carefully prepared, they often present solid content, but few speakers can memorize a lengthy speech and deliver it well. In addition, memorized speeches are not flexible and only work in highly formal circumstances, like awards ceremonies and formal banquets.

Because of the differences among these four speech-making strategies — in organization, presentation, and flexibility — they provide speakers with a number of ways to share ideas with audiences.

Timed Practice

Before writing an essay exam, practice composing under time pressure. Using notes from class, write and respond to sample essay questions. Use a timer and write several practice responses over several days' time. If necessary, allow yourself extra time to respond to a question, gradually reducing the time until it approximates the time available for the exam. Practice will quicken your writing pace while helping you to study for the exam.

Appendix D

Business Writing

Business Letters

Like a good paper, a business letter should be clearly organized and carefully written in support of a stated or implied thesis. Business letters differ from papers, however, in format and purpose.

When writing business letters, be sensitive to tone. In most instances, you will be writing to solve a problem or to ask for help. A moderate tone, formal but friendly, will work best. Do not be harsh or demanding in an initial letter, but if a problem continues, use a firmer tone in later correspondence.

The following guidelines and example (see page 608) describe a modified block-form letter, which is appropriate for most purposes.

General Guidelines

Use high-quality, white $8^{1}/_{2}$-by-11-inch paper.

Type the letter, using a fresh black ribbon. If your are using a word processor, use a letter-quality printer.

Maintain wide margins on all sides.

Single-space within paragraphs. Double-space between paragraphs. Do not indent the first words of paragraphs; position them flush with the left margin.

Proofread the final copy carefully for spelling, punctuation, mechanics, grammar, and typing errors.

Fold the letter in thirds and place it in a legal-size envelope.

Letter Format

Your Address. Use the address at which you wish to receive follow-up correspondence. Do not include your name with the address; type it beneath your signature at the end of the letter.

The Date. Use the date on which you plan to mail the letter.

Inside Address. Name the person to whom you are writing and include his or her title if you know it. If the letter is addressed to a company, begin this section with the name of the company and then use the complete business address.

Salutation. This greeting should be specific rather than general. Begin with *Dear,* followed by the name of the person and a colon (not a comma). Use general titles (*Mr., Ms.,* or *Dr.*) with the person's name. Use *Mrs.* or *Miss* only when you know that a woman prefers to be addressed in one of those ways. When you do not know the name of the person to whom you are writing, use "Dear Madam or Sir"; avoid "To Whom It May Concern."

Introductory Paragraph. Like a paper, a business letter needs an introductory paragraph. The first paragraph should establish the context for the letter. Be concise but specific. Include answers to the important questions that your correspondent might ask: What do you want to discuss? When did it take place?

Body Paragraph or Paragraphs. Middle paragraphs should provide a description of the problem. They should be clearly written, with careful word choices and specific details. Essentially, these paragraphs give you a chance to present your case, and they must therefore be precise and convincing. If you have tried to solve the problem, describe the strategies you have used, again supplying detailed information and descriptions.

Request for Action. The closing paragraph should ask for help in solving the problem. Be reasonable. If alternative solutions are acceptable, explain them.

Closing. Use a reasonably formal, standard closing, such as *Sincerely, Sincerely yours,* or *Yours truly.* (Align the closing with your address.)

Signature. Sign your name in ink in a space that is at least four lines deep, so that it does not look cramped.

Typed Name. Aligned under the closing, type your name as you wish it to appear in return correspondence.

Envelope Format

Return Address. Include your full return address in the upper left corner of the envelope.

Mailing Address. Address the envelope fully. Include the person's name and title (if applicable) and the full business address, including zip code.

Postage. Be sure to use sufficient postage.

The Résumé

A résumé is a brief listing of important information about your academic credentials, work experience, and personal achievements. The title "Résumé," "Curriculum Vitae," or simply "Vita" in

```
Alicia Hudson
1627 Lafayette Avenue                                  stamp
Topeka, KS   66603



              Aaron Steinmann, Service Director
              Museum Reproductions, Incorporated
              392 Hazelwood Drive
              Chicago, IL   60607
```

1627 Lafayette Avenue
Topeka, Kansas 66603
February 27,1990

Aaron Steinmann, Service Director
Museum Reproductions, Incorporated
392 Hazelwood Drive
Chicago, Illinois 60607

Dear Mr. Steinmann:

On November 16, 1989, I ordered several small pieces of
statuary from your Fall 1989 sale catalog: <u>Child with
Rabbit</u> (#097444), <u>Sleeping Cat</u> (#097118), and <u>Swan</u>
(#097203).

On December 3, 1989, my insured package was delivered by
UPS, and I excitedly opened the cartons to examine my
newest collector's items. Two of the statues were in
excellent condition, but the third, <u>Child with Rabbit</u>,
was not. The glaze on the rabbit and the base was
streaked and irregularly colored. These flaws in the
finish disappointed me greatly, especially since that
piece alone had cost $54.

I immediately called the service number listed on the
invoice. Your representative instructed me to repack the
statue and return it for a replacement. I did so the next
day--December 4, 1989--enclosing a photocopy of the
invoice (#1784229). More than two months have passed, and
I have yet to receive my new <u>Child with Rabbit</u> statue.

I would appreciate receiving my statue soon (since I have
already paid for it), or I would like to know the reason
for the delay. If you are unable to send me the statue, I
would appreciate your crediting my account for $54. Thank
you for your help in solving my problem.

Sincerely,

Alicia Hudson

Alicia Hudson

academic work, or the general designation "Data Sheet" in almost any context, sometimes appears as a heading at the top of the page. Such a title is probably unnecessary, however, because employers are familiar with this form. A résumé is commonly submitted with a job application letter to obtain an interview and sometimes submitted with admissions or scholarship applications, funding requests, project proposals, and annual personnel reports, and in other situations when you need to document your accomplishments.

Because a résumé must make a strong, favorable impression — suggesting the caliber of employee or student you are — you should prepare it carefully. Start by analyzing your goals and background; then gather together pertinent information. Consider the following discussion and modify the format and content of the samples on pages 615 and 616 to emphasize your individual strengths and fit your own needs. Do not be too "creative" or "artistic" with your résumé unless your job objective is in a field like advertising, graphic design, or art education.

Sections

Heading. Center your name at the top of the page. Use capitals, underlining, italics, boldface, or special lettering to make your name stand out.

Address. List your current mailing address in standard postal form, including zip code, and your full phone number, including area code. If you expect to change addresses soon, or if you spend time in two places (such as at college and at home), include both addresses, and indicate when you use each.

Personal Information. Include information on age, marital status, health, height, weight, and so on, *only* if it in some way is pertinent to your objective (for example, if the job has requirements about physical size, such as for a police officer or flight attendant). Employers and agencies can no longer demand such information and may not legally use it when assessing applications. Provide a photograph only if you are asked to do so.

Statement of Objectives. If you are applying for a specific position or purpose, state your immediate objectives and long-range goals. This statement is important because it serves as the controlling thesis for the description of your qualifications. Everything in the résumé should be relevant to your objective. Your statement of objectives should include the job title(s) of the position(s) you are seeking, the types of skills you possess or the types of duties you can perform, and your career goals. If the résumé is a general data sheet and its purpose is simply to list information, the career objective statement may be omitted.

Education. Students or recent students who have little work experience generally describe education before experience. Specify degrees, majors, minors, names and locations of schools, month and year of graduation (your anticipated date of graduation is acceptable), and grade point average (overall, major, or junior/senior). If specific schoolwork — important courses, term projects, or research papers — is relevant to your objective, briefly note it. If you have a college degree, you need not mention high school unless you did exceptionally well (such as being class valedictorian) or the school is prestigious or might interest the employer for some other reason (because it is in the same city, for instance). List honors and awards with education, or list them in a separate section for emphasis if they are numerous and impressive. Extracurricular activities are sometimes included here, but they too can be developed into another section if they warrant such treatment. Internships, co-op training, observation programs, conference workshops, and so on might be described as part of your education or considered as professional experience and listed in that section. The latter is a good idea if you have little relevant work experience.

Experience. Experience may appear after education, if it is not impressive or extensive, or before education, if it is impressive or recent. Arrange experience either chronologically (to show progress or promotion) or in descending order of importance, and list job titles, names of businesses or organizations (including the military), locations (not necessarily full addresses), dates of employment, and duties. Using active verb phrases, provide specific details about relevant skills employed, including technical skills, such as methods (double-entry accounting) and equipment (computers) used, and note improvements or suggestions that you contributed. If your work experience is not directly relevant to the objective of your application, mention responsibilities and accomplishments involving such general skills as communication, leadership, organization, problem solving, and money handling. Do not fail to mention volunteer work, internships, and other nonpaying experience.

Activities, Interests, and Hobbies. List activities specifically related to your objective, such as memberships in professional, fraternal, and community organizations. Mention special participation, contributions, and official positions. Other interesting activities (such as participation in organized sports, challenging hobbies, reading preferences, and cultural interests) may be included to show your habits and character.

References. List two to four recent employers and teachers who are willing to describe your qualifications and recommend your work. Supply their full names, titles, and work addresses and phone numbers. Be sure to contact them for permission before using them as references.

If you do not want to list your references on the résumé (perhaps because of limited space), note that references are available upon request. Use your college's career development and placement service, which will maintain a placement file that includes your letters of reference, transcripts, and data sheets. If you use your school's placement service, list the full address and phone number of the office at the bottom of your résumé.

Format

Length. Unless you have an exceptional amount of experience and education, limit your résumé to one page. If you must go to a second page, arrange the information so that you have two full and evenly balanced pages, not a page and a third. Do not split a major section between pages.

General Appearance. Make the résumé attractive, balanced, and scannable. Do not cramp information in dense blocks. Rather, divide information into discrete, parallel sections. Be consistent in your use of indentation, alignment, capitalization, boldface, underlining, parentheses, and other devices that identify similar kinds and levels of information. Use lists and columns, but make minimal use of patterns that create obvious vertical lines. Leave at least one-inch margins and double-space between sections, but avoid blocks of "white space" (large, unused areas).

Headings. Use headings that clearly describe the information in each section. Position the main headings at the left margin or center them. Headings positioned at the left margin are very noticeable, but they can create a wide strip of white space down the side and make the résumé look imbalanced. Centered headings create a better balanced design and allow more efficient use of space, and they show up clearly if they are set off in some way (underlined, boldfaced) and if adequate space is left between sections. Subheadings can further indicate and emphasize areas of special interest, but too many levels of headings will make the résumé look choppy.

Arrangement. Arrange the sections and the items within each section so that the information flows in a logical and emphatic order. One way is to start with the most relevant and impressive accomplishments and follow a descending order of importance throughout. Chronological order is appropriate when you have only a few items to mention (two part-time jobs, for instance). Reverse chronological order is effective when you have many degrees, experiences, and activities to present — especially if the most recent ones are the most important. Alphabetical order might be useful for listing references, organizations, and courses, but usually even these are best presented in order of importance.

Style. Abbreviate sparingly, using only standard abbreviations (such as for state names in addresses) and acronyms (such as professional organizations). Avoid first-person pronouns and complete sentences. Use active verb phrases. Instead of saying, "I was responsible for training new crew members," you need only write, "Trained new crew members."

Typing

Print Quality. Use standard elite or pica type, not an unusual typeface, such as italic. If you use a word processor, print the final résumé on a letter-quality (not a dot-matrix) printer.

Type with a fresh, black ribbon on heavy bond paper to produce a clear and attractive copy. Single-space within and double-space between sections.

Corrections. Use correction fluid or tape when you make changes. When you make photocopies to submit, these corrections will not show on the copy, whereas smudges on erasable paper will.

Proofreading. Proofread carefully to make sure that your résumé is free of spelling and typing errors. It represents you, so it must be "letter perfect."

Photocopying

Have high-quality photocopies made at a reliable copy shop. Consider having your résumé copied on fluorescent white bond paper, "parchment" paper, or some other special-purpose paper so that it will be distinctive. Spending a little extra money might be worth the investment.

Figure 1.   Standard Résumé Format

SANDRA K. BOYER

Present Address   After May 15, 1990
363 Maehling Terrace   431 N. Seventh St.
Alton, IL   62002   Waterloo, IL   62298
(618)465-7061   (618)686-2324

CAREER OBJECTIVE

Music teacher and orchestra director, eventually
leading to work as a Music Program Coordinator for a
school district.

EDUCATION

Bachelor of Science in Education: May 1990. Freemont
College, Alton, IL. Major: Music education. Minors:
Music theory and business. G.P.A.: 3.87 on a 4.0 scale.
Alpha Alpha Alpha, music honorary society (secretary,
1984-1985). Division 1 Ratings: violin, viola,
clarinet; Division 2 Ratings: cello, oboe

MUSICAL EXPERIENCE

Waterloo Community Orchestra (1983-1986): first violin,
1986; 10-17 performances each year, Waterloo Arts
Festival; classical and popular music
Waterloo Community String Ensemble (1986): coordinator;
8 performances each year, Waterloo Arts Festival;
classical music
Freemont College Orchestra (1987-present): second
violin, 1987-1988; first violin, 1988-present; student
conductor, 1989; 10-20 performances each year;
conducted 3 concerts; classical and popular music

WORK EXPERIENCE

Appointment secretary and sales clerk. Carter's Music
Shop, Waterloo, IL (1984-1986): coordinated 65 lessons
each week; demonstrated and sold instruments and music
Sales clerk. Hampton Music, Alton, IL (1987-present):
demonstrated and sold instruments and music

REFERENCES

Available upon request from the Placement Center,
Freemont College, Alton, IL   62002   (618)461-6299,
extension 1164; file #39261

Figure 2. Alternate Résumé Format

RÉSUMÉ
Sandra K. Boyer

ADDRESS

  School: 363 Maehling Terrace   Home: 431 N. Seventh St.
              Alton, IL 62002   Waterloo, IL 62298
  School phone: (618)465-7061   Home phone: (618)686-2324

EDUCATION

  1982-1986:   Benjamin Thomas High School, Waterloo, IL
  1987-   :   Freemont College, Alton, IL; will graduate May 1990.
                  Major: Music education. Minors: Music theory and
                  business

EXTRACURRICULAR ACTIVITIES

  1982-1986:   Benjamin Thomas High School Orchestra (1st violin,
                  1981-1983)
                  Benjamin Thomas High School String Ensemble (student
                  coordinator, 1982-1983)
  1987-   :   Freemont College Orchestra (2nd violin, 1987-1988; 1st
                  violin, 1988-present; student conductor, 1989)
                  Alpha Alpha Alpha, music honorary society (secretary,
                  1984-1985)

WORK EXPERIENCE

  1982-1983:   Carter's Music Shop, Waterloo, IL 62298; part-time
                  appointment secretary and sales clerk
  1983-   :   Hampton Music, Alton, IL 62002 (837 Telegraph and
                  Alton Square shops); sales clerk

REFERENCES

  Dr. Glendora Kramer, Professor of Music and Orchestra Director,
     Freemont College, Alton, IL 62002, (618)461-6299, extension
     2110
  Mr. Philip Sheldon, Manager, Hampton Music, 837 Telegraph, Alton, IL
     62002, (618)466-6311
  Mrs. Rhonda Travis, Music Instructor, Benjamin Thomas High School,
     Waterloo, IL 62298, (618)686-5534

Appendix E

by Deborah Barberousse
Horry-Georgetown Technical College

Writing About Literature

Preparing to Write

Preparing to write can be just as important as actually writing the paper. Good preparation will simplify the entire writing process and help you write a better paper.

Choosing What to Write About

Not everyone responds to every literary work in the same way. Some pieces you will like, others you will not and some works will leave you ambivalent, just as certain authors will strike a chord with you and others will not. Most teachers, recognizing that writing about literature reflects individual reactions and interpretations, will allow you some freedom in selecting authors, literary works, and topics. Whenever possible, you should write about a work that appeals to you on some level.

However, even when you have been assigned a specific author or literary work, certain aspects of that author's writing or certain elements within the work are likely to appeal to you. For example, Ernest Hemingway's short story "Hills like White Elephants" may not be one of your favorites in terms of theme, but you may be fascinated with the way in which Hemingway uses simple prose, allowing emotion to be communicated almost entirely by the direct actions of the characters. If so, you have the basis for a well-focused paper about literature.

Reading Critically

Once you have chosen an author or a literary work about which to write, you need to read critically, looking for anything that seems especially meaningful or significant.

Marking Passages. One of the best ways to read critically is to mark passages with a pencil, underlining and making margin notes as you proceed. This method is effective because it keeps the work and your notations about it directly linked. But use it only if the book you are marking is your own.

Using Index Cards. Another good method of critical reading involves using index cards—also known as note cards—to note meaningful and significant details. When using index cards, be sure to put page number or line number notations on each card so that you can easily find passages if you need to review them in the context of the entire work.

Index cards work well because as you begin to write your paper you can arrange the cards to reflect the organization of your paper, thus ensuring that your notes are used effectively and at the appropriate place in your paper.

Photocopying. You may photocopy specific passages of a work (not an entire work) for reference, according to copyright laws. Then, as you begin writing your paper, you may choose to make notes on the photocopied sheets rather than in the book itself.

What should you note as you read? The list depends on where you plan to go with your paper. You may have an idea about your thesis before you begin reading critically and marking, or one may begin to form as you look at the work critically.

Your notations might identify particular uses of these elements:

- language
- symbolism
- irony
- structure
- tone
- dialogue
- character

- description
- plot movement
- imagery
- foreshadowing
- epiphany
- theme development

You should note anything that strikes you as significant. It is better to mark a passage when you first read it than to hunt later for something that you vaguely remember. Also, through your notations, you may find the way to proceed with your paper. After you have developed a clear and focused thesis, you can review the work and disregard notations that are not relevant.

Approaches

Once you have chosen a literary work and have read it critically, it is important to determine the approach you will take in writing about it. Most literary essays fall into one of three categories: **explication, analysis,** and **comparison/contrast.**

Although the approaches differ to a great extent, all have one element in common: the intent of each is to show how the author has carried out or furthered the theme, or message, of the work.

Asking yourself a series of questions about specific literary elements in the work(s) under consideration will help you discover which elements to discuss in your paper and what approach to take:

1. Are there any **allusions** that seem significant?

2. Are there any **symbols** in the work? How has the author used **symbolism**? Can any of the symbols be interpreted in different ways?

3. What **images** are particularly strong?

4. Is there any **irony** in the work? How has the author used irony to express his or her meaning?

5. How has the author used language (**connotation, figures of speech**) to express his or her meaning?

6. What is the **tone** of the work? How is the tone significant to the reader's understanding of the message?

7. Is the **plot** of the work significant?

8. If the work is poetry, is the overall **structure** of the poem significant?

9. Has the author used **foreshadowing**? How is the foreshadowing significant?

10. How has the author used **sound** to express his or her thoughts?

11. What is especially significant about the **characters and characterization**? Are any minor characters significant to the development of the theme? Have any of the characters experienced an **epiphany**?

12. How is **setting** used in the work?

13. Does the **point of view** of the **narrator** play an important role in the reader's understanding of the work?

14. How is **dialogue** used to express the action or meaning?

15. What is the **theme** of the work? Is there more than one major theme?

16. How do any or all of these elements work together to create the meaning?

Explication

To **explicate** means to explain. An **explication essay** requires the writer to explain a meaning or meanings in a work of literature. An essay based on this approach moves carefully through a work of literature, or sometimes through a passage, calling attention to details and noting every element that furthers the author's theme.

Explication works best with poetry. An explication of a poem moves through the work, sometimes line by line, sometimes passage by passage, noting its complexities.

Because explication involves such attention to detail, it generally is not the best approach to writing about entire short stories, novels, or plays. Yet such works of literature can benefit from explication when the writer's focus is limited to selected passages or scenes. In dealing with these works, the writer should identify and explain a particular descriptive passage, a key scene, a conversation, or a **monologue**. Explication used in this way is an excellent strategy to show how minute details contribute dramatically to the whole.

The organization of an explication essay is the most obvious and simple of the three approaches. Because explication involves explaining, it is best simply to begin at the beginning of the work or passage and proceed to the end. The organization of the essay essentially reflects the organization of the work.

One final but important note about explication must be made. Explication does not mean paraphrasing, or rewording. A paper that simply restates the author's words, line by line or passage by passage, will be not only boring to the reader but also insulting to the author. Although sometimes it may be necessary to paraphrase in order to clarify, a **paraphrase** should not be the basis of the paper.

Analysis

To **analyze** means to separate a subject into its elements as a means to understanding the whole. An **analysis essay**, therefore, looks not at the entire work but rather at how the author has used one or several elements to carry out or further a theme.

A well-written analysis paper has a specific focus on the element or elements under discussion and clear organization. Two basic methods of organization work well and can be easily modified to suit the purpose of the paper.

One-Element Organization. The writer first identifies one element or technique that the author uses to advance the theme of the work. The writer then discusses the various ways in which that element is used.

Several-Elements Organization. The writer first identifies several elements or techniques that the author uses to advance the theme of the work. The writer then discusses each element individually.

Comparison/Contrast

To **compare** means to show how two subjects are alike, to **contrast** means to show how two subjects are different, and to **compare and contrast** means to show how two subjects are both alike and different. A **comparison/contrast essay** may involve any one of three approaches: it may compare, it may contrast, or it may do both.

An essay based on this approach may deal with two subjects within one literary work, two or more works that have the same subject or the same basic theme, two or more works by the same author, two authors and their works, or one work compared to or contrasted with a particular style of writing. The approach works well whether you are writing about short stories, novels, poetry, or drama.

As with analysis, the key to a well-written comparison/contrast essay lies in organization. It is important not only to identify the two subjects to be discussed but also to determine the basis of the comparison/contrast.

Generally, it is best to identify several ways in which the subjects can be compared/contrasted. Finding a basis for comparison/contrast isn't as hard as you might think. You do this sort of thing all the time. For example, if you were considering which of two colleges to attend, you would establish a basis of comparison/contrast to help yourself make the decision. You might compare/contrast the two schools on the basis of cost, programs offered, and location. You will use the same way of thinking when you write a comparison/contrast essay.

It is important to identify clearly the manner in which the subjects will be compared/contrasted. Otherwise, your discussion may go in too many directions and be confusing to the reader.

A comparison/contrast essay may be organized in one of two basic patterns. The patterns limit and direct the focus of your essay, resulting in a clearly stated, logically organized paper.

Parallel Method. Using this organization, the writer first discusses one of the subjects under consideration according to the identified bases of comparison/contrast and then discusses the second subject according to the same bases.

Point-by-Point Method. Using this organization, the writer discusses each basis of comparison/contrast, giving examples from the two subjects.

Just as you have preferences in reading literature, you will find that you also have preferences in approaches to writing about literature. Although your paper should follow one basic approach, it is certainly possible for you to use one or both of the other approaches within your paper. A comparison/contrast paper may include some explication as well as some analysis, and an analysis paper may include some explication and some comparison/contrast.

Although approach is important, it should not dictate your choice of literature. Instead, the literature under discussion should dictate your choice of approach. Critical reading of the work you intend to write about can lead you to ask pertinent general questions, besides the questions you ask about individual literary elements. For example:

1. How have the author's life experiences affected the work?

2. Is there some particular historical significance to the work? Does it reveal something about a specific time or place?

3. Can we compare the work of one author with that of another author writing on the same subject? Can we find a basis of comparison or contrast for two or more works by the same author?

4. Does the work set forth some universal theme of love, death, or human nature?

Your answers may point to the approach you should take. But neither the questions nor the approaches they lead to are intended to constrict your creativity and imagination. Rather, they serve as guides and patterns that you can and should modify to suit your purpose and the literary work under discussion.

The Structure

A paper about literature is no different in form from any other type of essay. Most essays have a three-part structure:

- an introduction with a thesis statement
- a body made up of several supporting paragraphs
- a conclusion

By asking yourself a series of questions about each part of your essay, you can ensure that your paper will have a clear and effective organization.

The Introduction and Thesis Statement

1. Have I started my discussion of the topic in fairly broad terms rather than jumping right into my thesis statement?

2. Does my introduction identify the work of literature to be discussed and the author?

3. Does my introduction narrow the focus more and more, directing the reader's attention to a clear and narrow thesis statement?

4. Does my thesis statement express the controlling idea of the essay?

5. Is my thesis stated in one tightly focused sentence, and is that sentence located near the end of the introductory paragraph?

The Body

1. Have I selected an appropriate number of main points to support my thesis effectively, and have I developed one point per paragraph?

2. Have I developed clear support for my thesis in each body paragraph?

3. Have I adhered to the standards of good paragraph writing in each paragraph, and does each have a clearly focused topic sentence?

4. Has each body paragraph explained (explication), analyzed (analysis), or compared/contrasted (comparison/contrast) the work(s) or author(s) under discussion, according to the approach I have selected?

5. If I am using explication, does the body of my paper reflect the organization of the work or passage itself?

6. If I am using analysis or comparison/contrast, have I saved my strongest point for the last body paragraph?

7. Have I supported the topic of each paragraph with material from the work(s) under discussion?

8. Does the body of my paper have continuity, and does it flow logically from one point to the next, employing clear transition?

The Conclusion

1. Have I started the concluding paragraph with the general idea of my thesis?

2. Have I avoided simply restating the thesis?

3. Have I used the concluding paragraph to summarize or to draw a conclusion based on my thesis and on the body paragraphs?

4. Have I worked toward a more generalized discussion of the topic near the end of my conclusion?

In addition to ensuring a clear organization, these checklists can help you maintain the focus of your essay and enable you to create an effective, logical discussion.

Quotation and Documentation

A subject that greatly concerns student writers is how to use and document quotations from the work(s) they are writing about. Although documentation is not a difficult process, it is a critical part of writing and must be handled according to accepted standards.

Most teachers prefer that literary papers use **MLA documentation style,** which is universally accepted within the humanities. Many composition and literature textbooks contain a section on MLA documentation, and most college bookstores sell manuscript documentation booklets. If you do not have a copy of the MLA documentation guidelines, you need to obtain one before writing a literary paper. See Chapters 34 and 35 for a fuller discussion of MLA requirements.

Use of Quotations and Paraphrasing

Although MLA guidelines are quite specific and complete, a few points are especially important to remember.

- You must give credit to all sources you use (cite), including the work(s) under discussion, by using parenthetical documentation within the paper and including a Works Cited page at the end.

- You should integrate paraphrases and quotations with your own discussion and interpretation.

- You should use direct quotations when it is important to reproduce the words exactly as they are written so as not to lose something vital. Otherwise, you should paraphrase.

- Quotations of fewer than four typed lines should be enclosed in quotation marks and worked into your paragraph like any other sentence. Parenthetical documentation of the source goes at the end of the sentence. Be *sure* to use quotation marks to indicate directly quoted material.

- Quotations longer than four typed lines should be set off by indenting them ten spaces from the left margin. Such quotations should be double-spaced like the rest of the paper. They should not be enclosed in quotation marks. Parenthetical documentation follows the quotation.

Parenthetical Documentation

The MLA guidelines include instruction in how to use **parenthetical documentation** to cite references within the paper. Parenthetical documentation is simply a set of parentheses containing identification of the source; it follows the cited material.

Each literary form—fiction, poetry, and drama—uses a different form of parenthetical reference. It is important that you recognize and use the appropriate form.

- When citing a passage from a short story or novel, indicate the page number.

Example   "It is impossible to say how first the idea entered my
              brain; but once conceived, it haunted me day and night"
              (37).

- When citing a part of a poem, indicate the line number(s).

  Example   "The only other sound's the sweep / Of easy wind and
              downy flake" (11–13).

Note: When quoting lines from poetry, use a slash (/) to indicate the end of a line as it is printed in your source.

- When citing a part of a classic play, indicate the act, scene, and
  line numbers.

  Example   "There are more things in heaven and earth, Horatio, /
              Than are dreamt of in your philosophy" (1.5.166–67).

Note: If the play you are citing is a verse play, use a slash (/) to
indicate the end of a line. Otherwise, use no slashes.

- When citing a part of a modern play, indicate the act and page
  number.

  Example   "I am not a dime a dozen! I am Willy Loman, and you are
              Biff Loman" (2.1421).

- If you are using more than one source for your paper, such as
  two poems, you will need to provide more detailed parenthetical information, according to MLA guidelines, or you will need
  to indicate in the text of your paper which source you are
  referring to in order to avoid confusion.

  Example   In "Stopping by Woods on a Snowy Evening," Frost
              describes the quiet of an evening in the country by
              explaining "The only other sound's the sweep / Of easy
              wind and downy flake" (11–13). In contrast, the city
              nights speak more loudly. Frost explains in "Acquainted

with the Night" that he has ". . . stood still and stopped
the sound of feet / When far away an interrupted cry /
Came over houses from another street" (7–9).

Works Cited Page

Also included in the MLA guidelines is instruction in how to document your sources on a Works Cited page. The Works Cited page
comes at the end of your paper and lists all the sources you have
used.

Strictly speaking, your essay should conclude with a Works
Cited page listing in MLA style all the sources you have used.
However, if you have used only one source, such as your textbook, your teacher may prefer that you use simple parenthetical
references as described above and omit the Works Cited page. If in
doubt, you should ask your teacher which method he or she prefers.

Smooth Use of Quotations

Quotations from the literature under discussion should be
worked into your paper smoothly. You can best accomplish this
by weaving a quotation into your own sentence. When you do so,
you may need to omit words from the work you are quoting in
order to write a sentence with correct verb or pronoun agreement.
Use ellipsis points—three spaced periods—to indicate the omission of words from a quotation (as in the correct example below).

It is not a good idea simply to quote a passage and then add a
sentence telling what the passage means. Instead, try to present
the quotation and explanation in the same sentence.

Incorrect   "I put my forehead down to the damp, seaweed-smelling
                sand" (2). This is an example of Robert Bly's metaphorical
                language in his poem "In Rainy September."

Correct   Robert Bly uses metaphorical language in his poem "In
                Rainy September" when he describes how he put his

forehead ". . . down to the damp, seaweed-smelling sand"
(2).

Correct documentation is an integral part of writing about literature. Careful attention must be paid to documentation in order to avoid plagiarism and to avoid confusing the reader.

Writing About Stories or Novels

If you plan to write about a short story or novel, read the work thoroughly and carefully, all the while noting your overall reaction and trying to determine the author's message. Critical reading will help you determine the point you want to make in your paper and, in turn, the approach you will take.

Because of the length of most short stories and novels, explication may not be the best approach, unless you plan to explicate selected passages in order to make your point. Analysis and comparison/contrast, however, usually work quite well. No matter which approach you choose, here are some key elements for you to consider:

- plot
- characters
- setting
- point of view

- symbolism
- irony
- theme
- tone

Sample Student Essay

The following student essay is based on Jose Donoso's short story "Paseo" and uses analysis. The writer takes into account how one element of the story, symbolism, is used in several ways in order to create the whole.

The writer organized the essay so that each body paragraph analyzes a different interpretation of a single symbol:

1. Introduction and thesis: Jose Donoso's short story "Paseo" uses multiple interpretations of a single symbol, the dog.

2. The dog representing emotion

3. The dog representing disorder

4. The dog representing madness

5. Conclusion

Jane Perry

Ms. Barberousse

English 102, Section 1

11 December 1994

The Object of Her Affections

The use of symbolism has long been a technique by which an author can present far more than the literal meaning of a story. However, symbols are not always easily defined; indeed, it is sometimes possible that one symbol in a story may be endowed with multiple meanings, all of which lead the reader to a greater understanding of the author's message. Such is the case in Jose Donoso's short story "Paseo." The story is told from the point of view of a grown man looking back on the isolated, frightened child he was. As the boy's jealousy focuses on the attention gained by a nondescript but persistent dog, Donoso leads us into the realm of multiple symbolism.

Perhaps most obviously, the dog represents emotion. The boy in the story grows up with cold people in a house that is "not happy" (316) and that expresses "an absence, a lack, which because it was unacknowledged was irremediable" (316). The boy wishes for more from his family. "I wished," he tells us, "that their confined feeling

might overflow and express itself in a fit of rage, for
example, or with some bit of foolery" (317). Of course,
he knows it is not to be. The dog that his Aunt Mathilda
adopts, however, represents the opposite of repressed, or
perhaps nonexistent, emotion. "Her whole body, from her
quivering snout to her tail ready to waggle, was full of
an abundant capacity for fun" (323). It is the dog's
expression of emotion that permeates Aunt Mathilda's cold
exterior and provokes her to express emotion of her own.
Yet, still, the boy is isolated, perhaps more so, as his
jealousy takes hold. As he watches his aunt stroke the
dog sleeping on her lap, he realizes the extent of his
own isolation and feels the loss of any hope that he,
too, might be the recipient of her affection:

>On seeing that expressionless hand reposing
>there, I noticed that the tension which had
>kept my aunt's features clenched before, re-
>lented, and that a certain peace was now soft-
>ening her face. I could not resist. I drew
>closer to her on the sofa, as if to a newly
>kindled fire. I hoped that she would reach out
>to me with a look or include me with a smile.
>But she did not. (324)

In addition to emotion, the dog also represents
disorder and its effect on constrained order. Dedicated
to her brothers, one of whom is the father of the boy in
the story, Aunt Mathilda is the creator of order in the
house, one whose focus is frightening in its rigidity and
in her insistence on perfection. Defects cannot be
tolerated and, as the boy relates, ". . . when she saw
affliction about her she took immediate steps to remedy
what, without doubt, were errors in a world that should
be, that had to be, perfect" (317). Yet, with the dog's
appearance there are "things that can neither be explained nor resolved" (319). The dog itself is a walking
representation of disorder:

>It was small and white, with legs which were
>too short for its size and an ugly pointed
>snout that proclaimed an entire genealogy of
>misalliances: the sum of unevenly matched
>breeds which for generations had been scouring
>the city, searching for food in the garbage
>cans and among the refuse of the port. (320)

Mathilda, surprisingly, grows more and more attached
to the dog, and with her attachment comes the beginning
of chaos. The chaos starts with simple things, such as
Mathilda losing at billiards and no longer remembering

the order of the shooters, but it progresses to the point
that she loses "the thread of order" (323) that has been
the thread of her life. Eventually, the disorder so
dissolves the very core of Mathilda that her midnight
strolls extend to her disappearance.

In retrospect, the dog also represents madness, a
madness that results when the spontaneity of the dog
disrupts the rigid world of the adults. The boy specu-
lates on the first look that passes between the dog and
his aunt and feels that look "contained some secret
commitment" (320), and her half-hearted attempt to make
the dog go away seems "a last effort to repel an en-
croaching destiny" (320). When the dog first makes
Mathilda laugh, the boy is surprised, but not amused,
because he ". . . may have felt the dark thing that had
stirred it up" (324). It is that unnamed dark thing that
permeates the boy's jealousy and causes him to imagine a
sinister influence in the dog. When he perceives in his
aunt "an animation in her eyes, an excited restlessness
like that in the eyes of the animal" (326) after one of
her evening walks with the dog, the boy begins to feel
concern rather than jealousy. His aunt, formerly a
fortress of routine and order, has become a mystery of
the night:

> Those two were accomplices. The night pro-
> tected them. They belonged to the murmuring
> sound of the city, to the sirens of the ships
> which, crossing the dark or illuminated
> streets, the houses and factories and parks,
> reached my ears. (326)

One night upon hearing his aunt come in, the boy
recognizes the final influence the dog and the madness it
represents are to have on his aunt. "I went to bed
terrified, knowing this was the end. I was not mistaken.
Because one night . . . Aunt Mathilda took the dog out
for a walk after dinner, and did not return" (327).

Who is to say whether the aunt's disappearance is a
manifestation of her madness or simply a rebellion on her
part, an affirmation of the life she has never before
experienced? Yet, in the boy's mind, she is dead, and
her death has been brought about by the dog and all it
symbolizes. The repression of emotion in his aunt has
been freed by something not human, and in doing so it has
brought disorder to order and madness to composure.

Works Cited

Donoso, Jose. "Pasec." <u>The Riverside Anthology of
Literature.</u> Ed. Douglas Hunt. 2nd ed. Boston:
Houghton, 1991. 315-27.

Writing About Poetry

Poetry is perhaps the oldest form of literature. It has been used throughout the ages as a form of history, an expression of religion, and a presentation of images and emotions. Whatever its form, poetry is intended to create in us the experience that is being expressed.

Because poetry is so rich in language and its subtleties, it lends itself to all three literary approaches. Explication provides an excellent opportunity to explore the artistry and talent involved in employing a wide range of elements and techniques to create the whole. Analysis, too, is an excellent approach for a paper based on poetry, where the discussion is narrowed to just one or several basic elements or techniques. Also, poetry is often the basis of comparison/contrast papers in terms of subject, theme, and authors. Whether you are explicating, analyzing, or comparing/contrasting, key elements to consider when writing about poetry include

- speaker
- sound
- imagery
- figures of speech
- connotations

- symbolism
- irony
- structure
- tone
- theme

Sample Student Essay

The following student essay is based on Louise Bogan's poem "The Dream" and uses explication. The organization of the essay is simple, following the organization of the poem itself. The writer takes into account how all the elements of the poem work toward carrying out the poet's theme.

The essay examines the four stanzas of the poem and its overall structure:

1. Introduction and thesis: Louise Bogan's poem "The Dream" is about fear, and Bogan's message—the message of the dream, in fact—is that fear can be tamed through trust.

2. First stanza

3. Second stanza

4. Third stanza

5. Fourth stanza

6. Overall technical structure

7. Conclusion

Marvin Poplin

ᴍs. Barberousse

English 102, Section 1

4 December 1994

Taming the Beast

Dreams have long been the basis for extensive analysis, their meanings interpreted and reinterpreted. Some
people believe that dreams reflect our repressed emotions, providing a necessary outlet for the negative
aspects of our reality. Others· find answers through
dreams, believing that dreams provide simple solutions to
seemingly complex issues in our lives. Louise Bogan, in
her poem "The Dream," describes a dream that expresses
both repression and solution. It is a poem about fear,
and Bogan's message--the message of the dream, in fact--
is that fear can be tamed through trust.

In the first stanza of the poem the speaker describes the fearful dream she had. Bogan introduces the
symbol of a mighty horse that embodies the fear and
retribution carried from the speaker's childhood, fear
and retribution that have been ". . . kept for
thirty-five years . . ." (3). Bogan effectively uses
metaphorical language as she describes the fear personi-
fied in the horse as it ". . . poured through his mane"

(3) and the retribution as it ". . . breathed through his
nose" (4). The source of her fear is unclear, but it may
be that the horse is a symbol of life that can be both
beautiful and terrifying. The imagery created when the
speaker tells us, ". . . the terrible horse began / To
paw at the air, and make for me with his blows" (1-2)
describes a sense of entrapment as life corners her and
spews forth the repressed fear and retribution, emotions
that must be faced.

The speaker's shame at her cowardice is clear in the
second stanza as she describes how she ". . . lay on the
ground and wept" (5). It is at this point that Bogan
introduces another symbol in the poem, a woman who ". . .
leapt for the rein" (6). The stranger's strength and
courage seem so alien to the speaker that she refers to
her as a "creature" (6), something not shackled by human
fears. Perhaps this other woman represents the speaker's
alter ego, a side of her yet to be set free. Nonetheless, Bogan creates a dramatic contrast between the
speaker's inability to respond to her fear as she "lay
half in a swound" (7) and the other woman's determination
as she "Leapt in the air, and clutched at the leather and
chain" (8).

In the third stanza, the other woman advises the speaker to give the horse a token as a gesture of peace. "Throw him, she said, some poor thing you alone claim" (9). In effect, she tells the speaker to surrender to her fate and to approach life with love. The speaker's long-held sense of hopelessness and fear is further contrasted to the possibility of a fresh approach to life as she tells the stranger, ". . . No, no . . . he hates me; he's out for harm, / And whether I yield or not, it is all the same" (11-12).

Yet, face to face with her fears, perhaps shamed by the courage of the other woman, the speaker yields at last in the final stanza of the poem. The imagery created is one of coldness, the coldness that resides in the heart of fear. She describes her act of courage and the fear still inherent in that act when she explains, ". . . I flung the glove / Pulled from my sweating, my cold right hand" (14-15). With that act, the imagery changes from cold to warmth as suddenly as does the beast who, like life that ". . . no one may understand" (15), came to her side and ". . . put down his head in love" (16). After thirty-five years, the beast is tamed.

Like dreams so often are, Bogan's poem is a simple one, not only in the narration of the dream, but also in

the metrical pattern and the rhyme scheme of the poem.
Rarely is a regular iambic beat achieved in the poem,
thus reinforcing the theme of confusion. Yet, at the end
of the poem, when the meaning is clear, the last line
contains three successive iambs in "put down his head in
love." Also, after a routine rhyme scheme of abab in the
first three stanzas, Bogan introduces new tension in the
last stanza with an abba rhyme scheme. The word "love"
comes fresh and unexpectedly to rhyme with "glove," just
as Bogan's poem points out that with trust comes peace,
often just as fresh and unexpectedly.

   Louise Bogan points out in her poem that life is
rarely as predictable as we might like, but it must be
faced, regardless of our fears. Like the speaker, we may
be surprised by the gentleness and peace we find when we
face life head on, offer it our love, and surrender to
its power--just as it surrenders to ours.

Works Cited

Bogan, Louise. "The Dream." <u>The Riverside Anthology of</u>

   <u>Literature.</u> Ed. Douglas Hunt. 2nd ed. Boston:

   Houghton, 1991. 730.

Writing About Drama

Since its ancient beginnings, drama has been used as a literary vehicle to express the condition of humankind. Through the unfolding of events in a play, human existence is played out through a cause and effect relationship. The biggest difference between drama and other forms of literature is that drama is intended to be seen as it is acted on a stage, a fact that is critical to interpretation as a play is read.

Explication may not be the best approach for a paper about drama unless you plan to explicate a key scene, a conversation, or a monologue. Used in this way, explication can be an excellent way to show how minute details in a play contribute dramatically to the whole. Analysis works quite well as an approach to writing about drama because it is possible to analyze how a playwright uses a single element or several elements to set forth a specific theme. Theme also serves as an excellent starting point for the comparison/contrast approach to drama, whether expressed historically or through character. An essay based on drama typically includes a discussion of one or more of these basic elements:

- dialogue
- plot
- characters
- conflict

- setting
- symbolism
- dramatic conventions
- theme

Sample Student Essay

The following student essay is based on Aristotle's definition of tragedy and Arthur Miller's play *Death of a Salesman*. The writer uses comparison. Although Miller's play is a modern one, the writer shows that it can be viewed as an Aristotelian tragedy.

The essay uses the point-by-point method of organization. Each of Aristotle's defining points of tragedy is a basis of comparison:

1. Introduction and thesis: Arthur Miller's great twentieth-century tragedy, *Death of a Salesman*, in spite of its modernity, can be successfully compared to the Aristotelian description of traditional tragedy.

2. The tragic hero

3. The hero's tragic flaw

4. The hero's recognition of the truth about himself

5. Redemption

6. Conclusion

Della Smith

Ms. Barberousse

English 102, Section 1

1 December 1994

<u>Death of a Salesman</u>: A Modern Tragedy

In the fourth century B.C., Aristotle set forth his description of dramatic tragedy, and for centuries after, tragedy continued to be defined by his basic observations. It was not until the modern age that playwrights began to deviate somewhat from the basic tenets of Aristotelian tragedy and, in doing so, began to create plays more recognizable to the common people and, thereby, less traditional. Even so, upon examination, the basic plot structure of some modern tragedies actually differs very little from that of the ancient classics. Arthur Miller's great twentieth-century tragedy, <u>Death of a Salesman</u>, in spite of its modernity, can be successfully compared to the Aristotelian description of traditional tragedy.

According to Aristotle, the protagonist, or tragic hero, of a tragedy is a person of great virtue and of high estate, usually a member of a royal family. The tragedy then carries the protagonist from his position of esteem and happiness to one of misery. Although Miller's

protagonist, Willy Loman, is not of high estate, he is
the head of his household. His wife, Linda, aware though
she is of his failings, sees him as ". . . the dearest
man in the world . . ." (1.1373). Furthermore, he is a
man whose intentions to be the best salesman possible are
honorable, although misguided. It must not be overlooked
that prior to the twentieth century, almost all literature had as its protagonist someone of high estate. The
typical protagonist of the modern age, however, is one
whose main conflict is survival, and that conflict is
certainly true of Willy Loman. Linda summarizes the
plight of the modern tragic hero when she says, "A small
man can be just as exhausted as a great man" (1.1374).

Aristotelian tragedy further defines the tragic hero
as one who has a tragic flaw or frailty that is very
often the error of pride. It is this tragic flaw that
causes the hero's downfall. Willy Loman's tragic flaw is
certainly bound by his pride, a pride that will not allow
him to recognize that he is not the salesman he has
always dreamed of being. As a result, he becomes further
and further detached from reality, believing more in his
dreams than in reality. When Linda tries to get Willy to
slow down his travels and work in New York, he tells her,
"I'm the New England man. I'm vital in New England"

(1.1347). Yet, Willy has just returned from another unsuccessful New England sales trip. His pride will also not allow him to recognize that he is no longer respected by his sons, nor have they become the great successes he has dreamed of for them. When Biff, Willy's older son, momentarily falls for his brother's sporting goods business scheme, Willy tells them, "I see great things for you kids, I think your troubles are over. But remember, start big and you'll end big" (1.1379).

The Aristotelian hero eventually recognizes the dark truth to his life. With this recognition comes, both for the hero and the audience, further recognition that the downfall has resulted from acts for which he is responsible. After all, the hero is capable of making choices. Willy, too, is capable of making choices, but as Biff states in the Requiem, "He had the wrong dreams. All, all wrong" (2.1425). As Willy seems to slip further and further from reality toward the end of the play, he actually comes closer to the truth about himself than ever before. In his delusionary discussion with his brother Ben, Willy plans his suicide, and Ben mentions that it might be seen as cowardly. Willy replies, "Why? Does it take more guts to stand here the rest of my life ringing up a zero" (2.1417)? Even though he quickly

slips back to his destructive pride, the mirror has been
faced and Willy has seen a zero. His very act of suicide
indicates that he knows he cannot regain the respect of
Biff nor can he provide for his family, as he has pre-
tended for so long. It is only through his death that he
can make something of himself for them.

Traditional tragic heroes find a form of redemption
in their suffering, and through that suffering the audience learns moral lessons and experiences a catharsis.
Perhaps Willy is most notably a true tragic hero in that
his tragic flaw, his battle to be what he is not, is one
that is carried out wrongly but for all the right reasons, as is typical of the traditional tragic hero.
Traditional heroes are also victims to some degree,
victims of their own flaw and victims of a force greater
than themselves. In Willy's case, his destructive pride
in being what he is not comes about, at least in part,
because of misguided definitions of success. Biff tries
to stop Willy's spiraling fall as he pleads with his
father to ". . . take that phony dream and burn it before
something happens" (2.1422). However, Willy's definition
of success has been too wrapped up in money for too long.
As audience members of traditional tragedies experience a
catharsis, so does Biff, as he learns from his father's

mistakes and realizes that the key to success lies in
knowing who he is. Perhaps it is only through Biff's
recognition of the truth that Willy is redeemed, though
not as he planned. Biff asks Willy, "Why am I trying to
become what I don't want to be . . . when all I want is
out there, waiting for me the minute I say I know who I
am" (2.1421)?

Tragedy did not end with the modern age. Instead,
it has found new form and is perhaps more recognizable
with the common man as its protagonist. Traditional
tragedy is intended to create in the audience pity and
terror for the tragic hero's condition. Most of us see
enough of ourselves in Willy that we sympathize with him,
even when we disagree with him. Furthermore, it is
difficult for late-twentieth-century Americans not to
feel terror when considering how the forces that destroyed Willy might destroy us as well. Perhaps that
fear is, indeed, the very heart of the tragedy Arthur
Miller created.

Works Cited

Miller, Arthur. <u>Death of a Salesman.</u> <u>The Riverside</u>

    <u>Anthology of Literature.</u> Ed. Douglas Hunt. 2nd ed.

    Boston: Houghton, 1991. 1345–1426.

Getting It Right

Although writing about literature is just like any other form of expository writing, certain conventions, or standards, must be considered. These conventions ensure that you make your point clearly with appropriate references to sources and with adherence to specific style guidelines (MLA).

Literary Essay Conventions

- Use the present tense when discussing works of literature and events within those works.

- Use the past tense only when discussing events that happened in the past, whether in the author's life or in the story itself.

- Work quotations into your paper smoothly, conforming to correct sentence structure and grammatical form. Quotations should not be overlong, nor should they intrude on the text of your paper; instead, they should become part of the text, acting as support for your points.

- Use parenthetical documentation for all quotations, and include a Works Cited page following MLA documentation style.

- Identify works of literature correctly: titles of novels and plays should be underlined; titles of short stories and poems should be enclosed within quotation marks.

- Avoid contractions and colloquialisms.

- Write objectively, avoiding reference to yourself. Expressions such as "I think," "In my opinion," and "I believe" tend to weaken your point. Your essay is, by its very nature, an expression of your opinion, supported with specific and concrete references to the work.

Once you are sure that you have adhered to the conventions of literary essays in your paper, it is important that you proofread and edit for clarity and correctness.

Editing Guidelines

- Review your essay to determine if your thesis is narrow enough and states something other than the obvious.

- Make sure that your basic organization allows you to develop your thesis fully and logically.

- Make sure that you have supported each of your main points with specific and concrete references from the work(s) under discussion.

- Check your documentation style against MLA standards.

- Edit for grammar, spelling, and typing errors.

Manuscript Form

Correct manuscript form is another important consideration. The MLA format is usually acceptable. However, it is always a good idea to ask your instructor how he or she prefers you to handle issues such as typing, whether to have a title page, and whether to include a Works Cited page (see pages 577–581).

Literary Terms

Allusion   An indirect reference to another work of art, a person, or an event.

Analysis   A method by which a subject is separated into its elements as a means to understanding the whole. An analysis essay approaches a work of literature by examining one or several key elements.

Character   An imagined person appearing in a work of fiction, poetry, or drama.

Characterization   The method by which characters in a work of literature are made known to the reader.

Comparison A discussion concerning how two or more persons or things are alike.

Conflict A struggle among opposing forces in a literary work.

Connotation The set of implications and associations that a word carries regardless of its literal meaning.

Contrast A discussion concerning how two or more persons or things are different.

Dialogue Conversation between characters.

Drama A play.

Dramatic Conventions Customary methods of presenting an action by means of devices that an audience is willing to accept.

Epiphany A moment of insight when a character suddenly realizes something previously unrecognized about life or about himself or herself.

Explication A method of explaining. An explication essay explains the meaning or meanings in a work of literature.

Fiction Stories that are at least partially imagined and not factual.

Figures of Speech Words that mean, in a particular context, something more than the dictionary definitions.

Foreshadowing An indication or hint of something yet to come.

Imagery The use of words or groups of words that refer to the senses and sensory experiences.

Irony An effect created when statements or situations seem at odds with how things truly are.

Metaphor An implicit comparison of a feeling or object with another unlike it. Example: He is a snake in the grass.

Metaphorical Language Language that draws comparisons between things that are essentially unalike. Metaphorical language is most often created through the use of metaphor, simile, and personification.

MLA Documentation Style The standardization of references to sources established by the Modern Language Association of America. Although other documentation styles exist, MLA is universally accepted within the humanities.

Monologue An extended speech by one character in a literary work.

Narrator The person telling the story in a work of literature.

Novel A long fictional narrative.

Paraphrase A restatement in your own words of what you understand a poem or some other passage to say.

Parenthetical Documentation A set of parentheses containing identification of the source of cited material.

Personification A figure of speech in which nonhuman things are said to have human characteristics. Example: The car died on the hill.

Plot The planned sequence of events in a literary work.

Poetry A form of writing in which the author writes in lines using either a metrical pattern or free verse.

Point of View The position of the narrator in relation to the events that occur.

Prose Any form of writing that is not poetry.

Setting The background in which a literary work takes place. Time, place, historical era, geography, and culture are all part of the setting.

Short Story A brief fictional narrative.

Simile   A comparison of a feeling or object with another unlike it, using the term "like" or "as." Example: He eats like a horse.

Summary   A brief restatement in your own words of the main idea of a literary work.

Symbol   Something concrete representing something abstract.

Symbolism   The use of symbols to give a literary work a message greater than its literal meaning.

Theme   The message, or main idea, of a literary work.

Tone   The expression of a writer's attitude toward a subject in a literary work and the creation of a mood for that work.

Glossary of Usage

This brief glossary explains the usage of potentially confusing words and phrases. Samples illustrate how the words and phrases are used. To check words or phrases not included here, consult a dictionary.

A, An Use *a* before a consonant sound; use *an* before a vowel sound. For words beginning with *h*, use *a* when the *h* is voiced and *an* when it is unvoiced. (Sound out the following examples carefully.)

a locket   **a** historical novel

an oration   **an** honest mistake

Accept, Except *Accept* means "willing to receive"; *except* means "all but."

Hoover rightfully would not **accept** the blame for the Stock Market Crash of 1929.

No elected official in the United States earns more than $200,000, **except** the president.

Accidentally, Accidently Use *accidentally,* the correct word form. The root word is *accidental,* not *accident.*

The curator **accidentally** mislabeled the painting.

Advice, Advise *Advice,* a noun, means "a suggestion or suggestions"; *advise,* a verb, means "to offer ideas" or "to recommend."

Lord Chesterfield's **advice** to his son, though written in 1747, retains its value today.

Physicians frequently **advise** their cardiac patients to get moderate exercise and eat wisely.

Affect, Effect   *Affect,* a verb, means "to influence"; *effect,* a noun, means "the product or result of an action;" *effect,* a verb, means "to bring about, to cause to occur."

The smallness of the audience did not **affect** the speaker's presentation.

One **effect** of decontrol will be stronger competition.

To **effect** behavioral changes in some house pets is no small task.

Agree to, Agree with   *Agree to* means "to accept" a plan or proposal; *agree with* means "to share beliefs" with a person or group.

Members of the Writers' Guild would not **agree to** the contract's terms.

Although I **agree with** the protesters' position, I cannot approve of their methods.

All ready, Already   *All ready* means "all are prepared"; *already* means "pre-existing" or "previous."

Ten minutes before curtain time, the performers were **all ready.**

Volumes A through M of the *Middle English Dictionary* are **already** in print.

All right, Alright   Use *all right,* the correct form.

The Roosevelts clearly felt that it was **all right** for their children to be heard as well as seen.

All together, Altogether   *All together* means "all acting in unison"; *altogether* means "totally" or "entirely."

Synchronized swimming requires participants to swim **all together.**

Life in a small town is **altogether** too peaceful for some city dwellers.

Alot, A lot   Use *a lot,* the correct form. Generally, however, use more specific words: *a great deal, many,* or *much.*

The senator's inflammatory comments shocked **a lot** of his constituents.

The senator's inflammatory comments shocked **many** of his constituents.

Among, Between   Use *among* to describe the relationship of three or more people or things; use *between* for two.

Disagreements **among** the lawyers disrupted the proceedings.

Zoning laws usually require at least forty feet **between** houses.

Amount, Number   Use *amount* for quantities that cannot be counted separately; use *number* for items that can be counted. Some concepts, like time, use both forms, depending on how elements are described.

The **amount** of money needed to restore Ellis Island was surprising.

The contractor could not estimate the **amount** of time needed to complete the renovations.

We will need a **number** of hours to coordinate our presentations.

In the 1960s, a large **number** of American elm trees were killed by Dutch elm disease.

An   See **A.**

And/or   Generally, avoid this construction. Instead, use either *and* or *or.*

Anxious, Eager   *Anxious* means "apprehensive" or "worried" and consequently describes negative feelings; *eager* means "to anticipate enthusiastically" and consequently describes positive feelings.

For four weeks, Angie was **anxious** about her qualifying exams.

Lew was **eager** to see the restaging of *La Bohème.*

As, As if, Like   Use *as* or *as if,* subordinating conjunctions, to introduce a clause; use *like,* a preposition, to introduce a noun or phrase.

Walt talked to his cocker spaniel **as if** the dog understood every word.

Virginia Woolf's prose style is a great deal **like** that of her father, Leslie Stephens.

As, Because, Since   *As,* a subordinating conjunction, establishes a time relationship; it is interchangeable with *when* or *while. Because* and *since* describe causes and effects.

As the train pulled out of the station, it began to rain.

Because (**Since**) the population density is high, housing is difficult to find in Tokyo.

Awful   Generally avoid using this word, which really means "full of awe," as a negative description. Instead, use *bad, terrible, unfortunate,* or other similar, more precise words.

Bad, Badly   Use *bad,* an adjective, to modify a noun; use *badly,* an adverb, to modify a verb.

Napoleon's winter assault on Russia was, quite simply, a **bad** plan.

Although Grandma Moses painted **badly** by conventional standards, her work had charm and innocence.

Because, Due to the fact that, Since   Use *because* or *since; due to the fact that* is merely a wordier way of saying the same thing.

Beef prices will rise **because** ranchers have reduced the size of their herds.

Before, Prior to   Use *before* in almost all cases. Use *prior to* only when the sequence of events is drawn out, important, and legalistic.

Always check your appointment book **before** scheduling a meeting.

Prior to receiving the cash settlement, the Jacobsons had filed four complaints with the Better Business Bureau.

Being as, Being that, Seeing as Use *because* or *since* instead of these nonstandard forms.

Beside, Besides *Beside* means "next to"; *besides* means "except."

In Congress, the vice president sits **beside** the Speaker of the House.

Few of Georgia O'Keeffe's paintings are well known **besides** those of flowers.

Between See **Among.**

Borrow, Lend, Loan *Borrow* means "to take something for temporary use"; *lend* means "to give something for temporary use"; *loan* is primarily a noun and refers to the thing lent or borrowed.

People seldom **borrow** expensive items like cars, furs, or electronic equipment.

Many public libraries now **lend** compact discs and video tapes.

The **loan** of $5,000 was never repaid.

Bring, Take *Bring* means "to transport from a distant to a nearby location"; *take* reverses the pattern and means "to transport from a nearby location to a distant one."

Soviet dissidents **bring** to the United States tales of harsh treatment and inequity.

American scholars working in Europe must **take** computers with them because the machines are not readily available at many European universities.

Can, May *Can* means "is able to"; *may* means "has permission to." *May* is also used with a verb to suggest a possible or conditional action.

Almost anyone **can** learn to cook well.

Foreign diplomats **may** travel freely in the United States.

I **may** learn to like escargot, but I doubt it.

Can't help but   Avoid this phrase, which contains two negatives, *can't* and *but;* instead rewrite the sentence, omitting *but.*

We **can't help** wondering whether the new curriculum will help or hinder students.

Center around, Center on   Use *center on. Center around* is contradictory because *center* identifies one position and *around* suggests many possible positions.

If we can **center** our discussions **on** one topic at a time, we will use our time productively.

Compare to, Compare with   *Compare to* stresses similarities; *compare with* stresses both similarities and differences.

Jean Toomer's novel *Cane* has been **compared to** free verse.

In reviews, most critics **compared** the film version of *Amadeus* **with** the original play by Peter Shaffer.

Complement, Compliment   *Complement,* normally a noun, means "that which completes"; *compliment,* either a noun or a verb, means "a statement of praise" or "to praise."

A direct object is one kind of **complement.**

One of the highest forms of **compliment** is imitation.

The renovators of the Washington, D.C., train station should be **complimented** for their restraint, good taste, and attention to detail.

Continual, Continuous   *Continual* means "repeated often"; *continuous* means "without stopping."

In most industries, orienting new workers is a **continual** activity.

A **continuous** stream of water rushed down the slope.

Could of, Should of, Would of   Use the correct forms: *could have, should have,* and *would have.*

The athletic director **should have** taken a firm stand against drug use by athletes.

Council, Counsel   *Council,* a noun, means "a group of people who consult and offer advice"; *counsel,* a noun or a verb, means "advice" or "to advise."

The members of the **council** met in the conference room of the city hall.

Following the meeting, they offered their **counsel** to the mayor.

Ms. Reichmann **counsels** the unemployed at the Eighth Avenue Shelter.

Different from, Different than   Use *different from* with single complements and clauses; use *different than* only with clauses.

Most people's life styles are **different from** those of their parents.

Our stay in New Orleans was **different than** we had expected.

Disinterested, Uninterested   *Disinterested* means "impartial" or "unbiased"; *uninterested* means "indifferent" or "unconcerned about."

Olympic judges are supposed to be **disinterested** evaluators, but most are not.

Unfortunately, many people are **uninterested** in classical music.

Due to the fact that   See **Because.**

Each and every   Generally, avoid this repetitious usage. Use *each* or *every,* not both.

Eager   See **Anxious.**

Effect   See **Affect.**

Enthusiastic, Enthused   Use *enthusiastic,* the preferred form.

William was **enthusiastic** about his volunteer work for the Special Olympics.

Etc.   Except in rare instances, avoid the use of *etc.,* which means "and so forth." Normally, either continue a discussion or stop.

Every day, Everyday   *Every day,* an adjective-and-noun combination, means "each day"; *everyday,* an adjective, means "typical" or "ordinary."

Nutritionists suggest that people eat three balanced meals **every day.**

Congested traffic is an **everyday** problem in major cities.

Exam, Examination   *Exam,* a conversational form, and *examination,* a formal variation, are interchangeable.

The CPA **exam** (**examination**) is given three times a year.

Except   See **Accept.**

Farther, Further   *Farther* describes physical distances; *further* describes degree, quality, or time.

Most people know that it is **farther** to Mars than to Venus.

The subject of teen-age pregnancy needs **further** study if we intend to solve the financial and social problems that it creates.

Fewer, Less   Use *fewer* to describe physically separate units; use *less* for things that cannot be counted.

Fewer than ten American companies have more than one million shareholders.

Because the cost-of-living raise was **less** than we had anticipated, we had to revise our budget.

Finalize, Finish   Generally, use *finish* or *complete,* less pretentious ways of expressing the same idea.

Fun   As an adjective, *fun* should be used in the predicate-adjective position, not before a noun.

White-water rafting is dangerous but **fun.**

Further   See **Farther.**

Good, Well   Use the adjective *good* to describe someone or something; use the adverb *well* to describe an action or condition.

A **good** debater must be knowledgeable, logical, and forceful.

We work **well** together because we think alike.

Has got, Have got   Simply use *has* or *have.*

Major networks **have** to rethink their programming, especially with the challenge of cable networks.

He or she, Him or her, His or hers, Himself or herself
Use these paired pronouns with indefinite but singular antecedents; avoid awkward constructions like *he/she* or *s/he.* Generally, however, use plurals or specific nouns and pronouns when possible.

Each person is responsible for **his or her** own actions.

People are responsible for **their** own actions.

President Bush is responsible for **his** and **his staff's** actions.

Hopefully, I Hope   Use *hopefully,* an adverb, to describe the *hopeful* way in which something is done; use *I hope* to describe wishes.

Marsha **hopefully** opened the envelope, expecting to find a letter of acceptance.

I hope the EPA takes stronger steps to preserve our wildlife.

Imply, Infer   *Imply* means "to suggest without stating"; *infer* means "to reach a conclusion based on unstated evidence." They describe two sides of a process.

Chancellor Michaelson's awkward movements and tentative comments **implied** that he was uncomfortable during the interview.

We **infer,** from your tone of voice, that you are displeased.

In, Into   *In* means "positioned within"; *into* means "moving from the outside to the inside." Avoid using *into* to mean "enjoys," an especially nonsensical colloquialism.

Investments **in** the bond market are often safer than those **in** the stock market.

As the tenor walked **into** the reception room, he was greeted by a chorus of "bravos."

Infer   See **Imply.**

Irregardless, Regardless   Use *regardless,* the accepted form.

Child custody is usually awarded to the mother, **regardless** of the father's competence.

Its, It's, Its'   *Its,* a possessive pronoun, means "belonging to it"; *it's,* a contraction, means "it is"; *its'* is nonstandard.

After the accident, the quarter horse favored **its** right front leg.

It's unlikely that the government will increase educational spending.

Kind of, Sort of   Use *rather, somewhat,* or *to some extent* instead.

Lay, Lie   *Lay* means "to place something"; *lie* means "to recline." Some confusion is typical because *lay* is also the past tense of *lie.*

In hand-treating leather, a tanner will **lay** the skins on a large, flat surface.

People with migraine headaches generally **lie** down and stoically wait for the pain to subside.

Lead, Led   *Lead* is the present-tense verb; *led* is the past-tense form.

The clergy used to **lead** quiet lives.

Montresor **led** the unsuspecting Fortunato into the catacombs.

Learn, Teach   *Learn* means "to acquire knowledge"; *teach* means "to give instruction." These are two sides of the same process.

Children **learn** best in enriched environments.

Experience **teaches** us that hard work is often the key to success.

Less   See **Fewer.**

Lie   See **Lay.**

Like   See **As.**

Loan   See **Borrow.**

Loose, Lose   *Loose,* an adjective, means "not tight or binding"; *lose,* a verb, means "to misplace."

In tropical climates, people typically wear **loose,** lightweight garments.

Overcooked vegetables **lose** vitamins, minerals, texture, and color.

May   See **Can.**

May be, Maybe   *May be,* a verb, means "could be"; *maybe* means "perhaps."

The use of animals in research **may be** legal, but it raises ethical questions.

Maybe Van Gogh was mad; if so, his work is the result of an inspired madness.

Number   See **Amount.**

Off of   Use *off* by itself; it is perfectly clear.

> During re-entry, a number of tiles came **off** the first space shuttle.

On account of   Use *because* or *since,* briefer ways of saying the same thing.

Passed, Past   Use *passed* as a verb; use *past* as a noun, adjective, or preposition.

> Malcolm X **passed** through a period of pessimism to reach a time of optimism in his last months.

> The **past,** as the saying goes, helps to determine the present.

> Thoughtful people often reflect on their **past** actions and inactions.

> The ambulance raced **past** the cars, hurrying from the fire site to the hospital.

People, Persons   Use *people* when referring to a group, emphasizing anonymity; use *persons* to emphasize unnamed individuals within the group.

> **People** who lobby for special-interest groups must register their affiliations with Congress.

> Several **persons** at the hearing criticized the company's environmental record.

Percent, Percentage   Use *percent* with a number; use percentage with a modifier.

> Over fifty **percent** of the government's money is spent on Social Security and defense.

> A large **percentage** of divorced people remarry.

Persons   See **People.**

Pretty   *Pretty* means "attractive" or "pleasant looking"; do not use it to mean "rather" or "somewhat."

Principal, Principle   *Principal,* an adjective, means "main" or "highest in importance"; *principal,* a noun, means "the head of a school"; *principle,* a noun, means "a fundamental truth or law."

The **principal** difficulty of reading the novels of Henry James is sorting out his syntax.

The **principal** in the satiric novel *Up the Down Staircase* seems oblivious to the needs of his students.

The **principle** of free speech is vital to American interests.

Prior to   See **Before.**

Quotation, Quote   *Quotation,* the noun, means "someone else's material used word for word"; *quote,* the verb, means "to use a quotation." In conversation, *quote* is often used as a noun; in formal writing, however, distinguish between these two forms.

In his speeches and essays, Martin Luther King, Jr., frequently incorporated **quotations** from the Bible.

In his poem "The Hollow Men," T. S. Eliot **quotes** from *The Heart of Darkness,* a brief novel by Joseph Conrad.

Reason, Reason why, Reason is because   *Reason,* used by itself, is sometimes unclear; *reason why,* a more complete expression, is generally preferred. *Reason is because* is repetitive, because *reason* itself implies a connection.

Literature about AIDS often explores the **reasons why** the general public reacts so irrationally to the disease.

Respectfully, Respectively   *Respectfully* means "showing respect" or "full of respect"; *respectively* means "in the given order."

George Washington **respectfully** declined to be named king of the newly independent colonies.

671

These cited passages were submitted by Joshua Blaney, Andreas Church, and Joanna Meredith, **respectively.**

Seeing as   See **Being as.**

Set, Sit   *Set* means "to place or position something"; *sit* means "to be seated."

The photographer **set** the shutter speed at 1/100th of a second.

Many civil rights demonstrators refused to **sit** in segregated sections of buses, theaters, and government buildings.

Shall, Will   *Shall,* which indicates determination in the future tense, was once clearly distinguished from *will,* which merely describes future actions or conditions. Past distinctions between these forms are disappearing, and *will* is used in almost all cases. *Shall* remains standard, however, for questions using the first person.

Many animals raised in captivity **will** die if released into the wild.

"**Shall** I compare thee to a summer's day?" — Sonnet 18, William Shakespeare

Should, Would   Use *should* to explain a condition or obligation; use *would* to explain a customary action or wish.

Universities **should** not invest funds in companies whose policies conflict with their own.

When asked a pointed question, John Kennedy **would** often begin his response with a humorous remark to ease the tension.

Should of   See **Could of.**

Since   See **As, Because.**

Sit   See **Set.**

Sort of   See **Kind of.**

Suppose to, Supposed to   Use *supposed to,* the standard form.

Affirmative Action policies are **supposed to** ensure fair hiring practices nationwide.

Take   See **Bring.**

Teach   See **Learn.**

That, Which, Who   Use *that* to refer to people or things, but usually to things; use *which* to refer to things; use *who* to refer to people.

The musical work **that** set the standard for CD size was Beethoven's *Ninth Symphony.*

O'Neill's *Long Day's Journey into Night,* **which** won the 1957 Pulitzer Prize, was published posthumously.

People **who** cannot control their tempers are irritating and sometimes dangerous.

Their, There, They're   *Their,* a possessive pronoun, means "belonging to them"; *there,* usually an adverb, indicates placement; *they're,* a contraction, means "they are."

Legislation is pending to give artists royalties whenever **their** work is sold for profit.

Put the boxes over **there,** and I will open them later.

Investment banks should monitor **their** loan-granting policies more carefully.

Theirself, Theirselves   Use *themselves,* the standard form.

The members of Congress hesitated to vote **themselves** a raise.

There   See **Their.**

They're   See **Their.**

Threw, Through, Thru   *Threw,* the past tense of the verb
throw, means "hurled an object"; *through* means "by way
of" or "to reach an end"; *thru* is a nonstandard spelling of
through.

In a pivotal scene in *Hedda Gabler,* Hedda **threw** Lovborg's manuscript into the fire.

Blue Highways is a picaresque account of William Least Heat Moon's
travels **through** the United States.

Till, Until, 'Til   Both *till* and *until* are acceptable; *'til,* though
slightly archaic, is also admissible; watch spellings and punctuation.

There will be no peace in the Middle East **till (until)** religious groups
there become more tolerant of each other.

To, Too, Two   *To* is a preposition or part of an infinitive; *too*
is a modifier meaning "in extreme" or "also"; *two* is the number.

In Cold Blood was Truman Capote's attempt **to** create what he called a
nonfiction novel.

James Joyce's *Finnegan's Wake* is **too** idiosyncratic for many readers.

China gave the Washington Zoo **two** pandas who were promptly
named Yin and Yang.

Try and   Use *try to,* the accepted form.

Producers of music videos **try to** recreate the essence of a song in visual form, with mixed success.

Uninterested   See **Disinterested.**

Until   See **Till.**

Use to, Used to   Use *used to,* the standard form.

Painters **used to** mix their own paints from pigments, oils, and bond-
ing agents.

Utilize, Utilization   Generally use *use,* a shorter, simpler way of expressing the same idea.

Wait for, Wait on   *Wait for* means "to stay and expect"; *wait on* means "to serve."

In Beckett's famous play, Vladimir and Estragon **wait for** Godot.

Because of severe bouts of asthma and allergies, Marcel Proust was frequently bedridden and had to be **waited on** most of his life.

Weather, Whether   *Weather* means "conditions of the climate"; *whether* means "if."

In the South, rapid changes in the **weather** can often be attributed to shifts in the Gulf Stream.

Citizens must pay taxes **whether** they like it or not.

Well   See **Good.**

Whether   See **Weather.**

Which   See **That.**

Who   See **That.**

Who/Whom, Whoever/Whomever   Use *who* and *whoever* as subjects; use *whom* and *whomever* as objects.

Doctors **who** cannot relate well to patients should go into research work.

Whoever designed the conference program did a splendid job.

To **whom** should we submit our report?

Contact **whomever** you wish. I doubt that you will get a clear response.

Who's, Whose   *Who's,* a contraction, means "who is" or "who has"; *whose,* a possessive pronoun, means "belonging to someone unknown."

We need to find out **who's** scribbling graffiti on the walls.

A spelunker is someone **whose** hobby is exploring caves.

Will   See **Shall.**

Would   See **Should.**

Would   **of** See **Could of.**

Glossary of Grammatical Terms

Absolute Phrase See **Phrase.**

Abstract Noun See **Noun.**

Active Voice See **Voice.**

Adjective A word that modifies or limits a noun or pronoun by answering one of these questions: *what kind, which one, how many, whose.*

> **Distilled** water makes the best ice cubes.

A **regular adjective** precedes the word it modifies:

> The **velvet** dress cost two hundred dollars.

A **predicate adjective** follows a linking verb but modifies the subject of the sentence or clause:

> Ladders should be **sturdy** and **light-weight.**

An **article** (*a, an, the*) is considered an adjective:

> **A** good friend is **a** good listener.

A **demonstrative adjective** can show closeness (*this, these*) or distance (*that, those*) and singularity (*this, that*) or plurality (*these, those*):

> All of **these** books will not fit in **that** bookcase.

A **pronoun-adjective** is a pronoun that modifies a noun:

> **Somebody's** car is parked in **my** space.

Adjective Clause See **Clause.**

Adjective Phrase See **Phrase.**

Adverb A word that modifies a verb, adjective, adverb, clause, phrase, or whole sentence by answering one of these questions: *how, when, where, how often, to what extent.*

Roberto enunciates **carefully.**   (*Carefully* modifies *enunciates,* telling how.)

He is **usually** soft-spoken.   (*Usually* modifies *soft-spoken,* telling when.)

He sometimes speaks **too** softly.   (*Too* modifies *softly,* telling to what extent.)

Frequently, he has to repeat comments.   (*Frequently* modifies the whole sentence, telling how often.)

Adverb Clause   See **Clause.**

Adverbial Conjunction   See **Conjunctive Adverb.**

Agreement   The matching of words according to number (singular and plural) and gender (masculine, feminine, and neuter). A verb takes a singular or plural form depending on whether its subject is singular or plural. A pronoun must match its antecedent (the word it refers to) in gender as well as number. A demonstrative adjective must match the number of the word it modifies (*this* and *that* for singular, *these* and *those* for plural).

Antecedent   The word to which a pronoun refers.

Rachel changed the tire herself.   (*Rachel* is the antecedent of the reflexive pronoun *herself.*)

Appositive   A word or group of words that restates or defines a noun or pronoun. An appositive is positioned immediately after the word it explains.

Nonrestrictive appositives clarify proper nouns and are set off by commas:

Crest, **the best-selling toothpaste,** is recommended by many dentists.

Restrictive appositives are themselves proper nouns and require no commas:

The toothpaste **Crest** is advertised heavily on television.

Article See **Adjective.**

Auxiliary Verb Same as Helping Verb. See **Verb.**

Balanced Sentence See **Sentence.**

Case The form that a noun or pronoun takes according to its grammatical role in a sentence.

Subjective case describes a word used as a subject or predicate noun:

She drives a Mazda 626.

Objective case describes a word used as a direct object, indirect object, or object of a preposition:

The small size is just right for **her.**

Possessive case describes a word used to show ownership:

Her Mazda is cherry red.

Most nouns and pronouns change only to form the possessive case (by adding an apostrophe and *s: cat's, someone's*). Personal, relative, and interrogative pronouns, however, change form for all three cases.

Clause A group of words that has a subject and predicate.

An **independent clause** is grammatically complete; when used separately, it is indistinguishable from a simple sentence:

Dinosaurs had small brains.

An independent clause can be joined to another clause with a coordinating conjunction, a subordinating conjunction, or a semicolon.

A **subordinate clause** also has a subject and predicate, but it is not grammatically complete; it must be joined to an independent clause:

> **Although dinosaurs had enormous bodies,** they had small brains.

A subordinate clause can function as an adjective, an adverb, or a noun.

An **adjective clause** modifies a noun or pronoun:

> We want a television **that has remote control.**

An **adverb clause** modifies a verb, an adjective, another adverb, a clause, a phrase, or a whole sentence:

> Jason gets up earlier **than I usually do.**

A **noun clause** functions as a noun:

> **Whoever finds the wallet** will probably return it.

Collective Noun   See **Noun.**

Comma Fault   See **Comma Splice.**

Comma Splice   Independent clauses incorrectly joined by a comma:

Einstein's brain has been preserved since his death, the formaldehyde has damaged the tissue.

Common Noun   See **Noun.**

Comparative Degree   See **Degree.**

Complement   Words or groups of words that complete the meaning of a sentence.

A **direct object** follows a transitive verb and answers these questions: *what, whom:*

> Jason rented some **skis.**

An **indirect object** follows a transitive verb, is used with a direct object, and answers these questions: *to what, to whom:*

Jason gave **me** skiing lessons.

A **predicate noun** follows a linking verb and restates the subject of the sentence or clause:

Jason is a patient **instructor.**

A **predicate adjective** follows a linking verb and modifies the subject of the sentence or clause:

Nevertheless, the lessons were **frustrating.**

Complete Predicate See **Predicate.**

Complete Subject See **Subject.**

Complex Sentence See **Sentence.**

Compound Two or more words, phrases, or clauses that work together as one unit. **Compound words:** *dining room, razzle dazzle.* **Compound subject: Shimita** and **Amir** were married on Tuesday. **Compound predicate:** We **attended** the wedding but **skipped** the reception.

Compound-Complex Sentence See **Sentence.**

Compound Predicate See **Compound.**

Compound Sentence See **Sentence.**

Compound Subject See **Compound.**

Concrete Noun See **Noun.**

Conjunction Words that join words, phrases, and clauses. Conjunctions link compound words, explain alternatives, show contrast, clarify chronology, and explain causal relationships.

A **coordinating conjunction** (*and, but, for, nor, or, so,* or *yet*) links equivalent sentence parts:

Stenographic **and** typing skills are required for the job.

A **subordinate conjunction** (*although, because, until,* and others) introduces a subordinate clause in a sentence:

Although Todd could type, he could not take shorthand.

A **correlative conjunction** (*either . . . or, neither . . . nor,* and others) links equivalent sentence parts and provides additional emphasis:

He will **either** learn shorthand **or** look for other work.

Conjunctive Adverb   An adverb used to link ideas logically; it does not make a grammatical connection as a traditional conjunction does and must therefore be used in an independent clause:

The experiment lasted two years; **however,** the results were inconclusive.

Coordinating Conjunction   See **Conjunction.**

Correlative Conjunction   See **Conjunction.**

Dangling Modifier   An introductory modifier that does not logically modify the subject of the sentence:

Charred from overcooking, we could not eat the steaks.

Degree   The form that adjectives and adverbs take to show degrees of comparison. **Positive degree** is a direct form, with no comparison: *simple.* **Comparative degree** compares two items: *simpler.* **Superlative degree** compares three or more items: *simplest.*

Demonstrative Adjective   See **Adjective.**

Demonstrative Pronoun   See **Pronoun.**

Dependent Clause   Same as Subordinate Clause. See **Clause.**

Direct Address   The use of a noun to identify the person or people spoken to; the noun is set off by commas and restricted to speech or writing that approximates speech:

Friends, it is time for us to voice our opinions.

Direct Object   See **Complement.**

Direct Quotation   Using someone's exact words, taken from speech or writing, in speech or writing. Quotation marks indicate where the quoted material begins and ends:

Jim often says, **"Writing is never finished; it is only abandoned."**

An **indirect quotation** reports what people say without using direct wording; an indirect quotation is often introduced with *that* for statements and *if* for questions:

Jim asked **if I understood what he meant**.

Double Negative   Nonstandard use of two negative words within one construction. See also **Can't help but** in the Glossary of Usage.

He **didn't** do **no** work on the project.

Elliptical Construction   A construction that omits words (usually verbs and modifiers) that are considered understood:

Gorillas are more intelligent than chimpanzees [are].

Expletive Construction   A construction (*there is, it is, there are,* and *there is*) that functions as the subject and verb of a sentence or clause but depends on a complement to create meaning:

There are too many desks in this office.

Fragment   A group of words improperly presented as a sentence, with a capital letter at the beginning and with end punctuation. A fragment can lack a subject or a verb:

Left her baggage in the terminal.

It can be an unattached subordinate clause:

> Although the clerk had said the bags were ready.

It can be an unattached phrase:

> Stood at the baggage claim area for ten minutes.

Fused Sentence   Two or more independent clauses placed one after the other with no separating punctuation:

The vegetables at Trotski's Market are always fresh those at Wilkerson's are not.

Future Perfect Tense   See **Tense.**

Future Tense   See **Tense.**

Gender   Three classes of nouns and pronouns based on sex: masculine (*Roger, he*), feminine (*Blair, she*), and neuter (*tractor, it*).

Gerund   See **Verbal.**

Gerund Phrase   See **Phrase.**

Helping Verb   Same as Auxiliary Verb. See **Verb.**

Imperative Mood   See **Mood.**

Indefinite Pronoun   See **Pronoun.**

Independent Clause   Same as Main Clause. See **Clause.**

Indicative Mood   See **Mood.**

Indirect Object   See **Complement.**

Indirect Quotation   See **Direct Quotation.**

Infinitive   See **Verbal.**

Infinitive Phrase   See **Phrase.**

Intensive Pronoun   Same as Reflexive Pronoun. See **Pronoun.**

Interjection   A word that expresses surprise or emotion or that provides a conversational transition:

> **Well,** I don't want to go either.

Interrogative Pronoun   See **Pronoun.**

Intransitive Verb   See **Verb.**

Irregular Verb   See **Verb.**

Linking Verb   See **Verb.**

Loose Sentence   See **Sentence.**

Main Clause   Same as Independent Clause   See **Clause.**

Misplaced Modifier   A modifier incorrectly placed in a sentence; the word, phrase, or clause it modifies is not clear:

> Jason said before midnight he would have his paper done.

Modifier   A word, phrase, or clause used as an adjective or adverb to limit, clarify, qualify, or in some way restrict the meaning of another part of the sentence.

Mood   A verb form that allows writers to present ideas with proper meaning.

Indicative mood presents a fact, offers an opinion, or asks a question:

> The baby **has** a fever.

Imperative mood presents commands or directions:

> **Call** the doctor.

Subjunctive mood presents a conditional situation or one contrary to fact:

I wish she **were feeling** better.

Nominative Case   Same as Subjective Case. See **Case.**

Nonrestrictive Element   An appositive, phrase, or clause that supplies information that is not essential to the meaning of a sentence. A nonrestrictive element is separated from the rest of the sentence by commas:

Cabaret, **my favorite film,** is on Cinemax next week.   (appositive)

Michael York, **with charm and humor,** played the leading male role. (phrase)

Marisa Berenson, **who is better known for her modeling than for her acting,** played the wealthy Jewish woman who came for English lessons.   (clause)

Noun   A word that names a person, place, thing, idea, quality, or condition. A **proper noun** names a specific person, place, or thing: *Elijah P. Lovejoy, Versailles, the Hope Diamond.* A **common noun** names a person, place, or thing by general type: *abolitionist, palace, jewel.* A **collective noun** names a group of people or things: *team, herd.* A **concrete noun,** either common or proper, names something tangible: *Mrs. Mastrioni, clinic, credit card.* An **abstract noun** names an intangible quality or condition: *honesty, nervousness.*

Noun Clause   See **Clause.**

Noun Marker   Same as Article. See **Adjective.**

Number   Two classes of nouns, pronouns, and verbs: singular (one) and plural (two or more). A noun in the plural form usually ends with *s: problem* (singular), *problems* (plural); a verb in the third-person singular form ends with *s*: *she cares* (singular), *they care* (plural); a demonstrative pronoun in the plural form ends with *se*: *this rabbit* (singular), *these rabbits* (plural).

Objective Case   See **Case.**

Object of a Preposition   A noun or pronoun that a preposition links to the rest of the sentence:

> The electrical outlet is behind the **couch.**   (*Couch* is linked to *is*, telling *where*.)

Parallelism   The use of the same form for equivalent verbs in the same tense, a series of similar verbals or predicate nouns, and so on:

> Congressman Abernathe **denied** the charges, **questioned** the evidence, **produced** full records, and **received** a formal apology.   (all past-tense verbs)

Parenthetical Expression   A word or group of words that interrupts the pattern of a sentence, separating elements and adding secondary information. Such expressions are separated by parentheses or dashes:

> Seeing *Cats* on Broadway was expensive — **the tickets were thirty-five dollars each** — but worthwhile.

Participial Phrase   See **Phrase.**

Participle   See **Verbal.**

Parts of Speech   The classification of words into eight categories according to their use in sentences: noun, pronoun, verb, adjective, adverb, conjunction, preposition, and interjection. Each part of speech is separately defined in this glossary.

Passive Voice   See **Voice.**

Past Participle   See **Verbal.**

Past Perfect Tense   See **Tense.**

Perfect Tenses   See **Tense.**

Periodic Sentence   See **Sentence.**

Person   Three classes of nouns, pronouns, and verbs that indicate the relationship between the writer and the subject. **First person** (*I am, we are*) indicates that the writer writes about himself or herself; **second person** indicates that the writer writes about and to the same people (*you are*); **third person** indicates that the writer is writing to an audience *about* someone else (*she is, they are, Mitch is, the researchers are*).

Personal Pronoun   See **Pronoun.**

Phrase   A group of words that cannot function independently as a sentence but must be part of a sentence. A whole phrase often functions as a noun, adjective, or adverb.

A **prepositional phrase** consists of a preposition (*above, during, under,* and others), its object, and any modifiers: *above the front doorway, during the thunder storm, under the subject heading.* A prepositional phrase can function as an adjective or adverb:

> The woman **next to me** read **during the entire flight.**   (*Next to me* is adjectival, modifying *woman; during the entire flight* is adverbial, modifying *read.*)

A **gerund phrase** combines a gerund and its complements and modifiers; it functions as a noun:

Conducting an orchestra requires skill, patience, and inspiration. (*Conducting an orchestra* is the subject of the sentence.)

A **participial phrase** combines a participle and its modifiers; it functions as an adjective:

From her window, Mrs. Bradshaw watched the children **playing under her maple tree.** (*Playing under her maple tree* modifies *children.*)

An **infinitive phrase** combines an infinitive and its complements and modifiers; it functions as a noun, an adjective, or an adverb:

To succeed as a free-lance artist is difficult. (noun)

Supplies **to use in art classes** are costly unless I get them wholesale. (adverb).

To make ends meet, I work part time at a bank. (adjective)

An **absolute phrase** modifies a whole sentence or clause. It contains a noun and a participle and is separated from the rest of the sentence by a comma:

All things considered, the recital was a success.

Positive Degree See **Degree.**

Possessive Case See **Case.**

Predicate A word or group of words that expresses action or state of being in sentences; it consists of one or more verbs, plus any complements or modifiers.

A **simple predicate** is the single verb and its auxiliaries, if any:

Iago mercilessly **destroyed** the lives of Othello and Desdemona.

A **complete predicate** is the simple predicate, plus any complements or modifiers:

Iago **mercilessly destroyed the lives of Othello and Desdemona.**

Predicate Adjective   See **Complement.**

Predicate Noun   See **Complement.**

Preposition   A word that establishes a relationship between a noun or pronoun (the object of the preposition) and some other word in the sentence:

After his term **in** office, Jimmy Carter returned **to** Plains, Georgia. (*Term* is linked to *Carter; office* is linked to *term; Plains, Georgia* is linked to *returned.*)

Prepositional Phrase   See **Phrase.**

Present Participle   See **Verbal.**

Present Perfect Tense   See **Tense.**

Present Tense   See **Tense.**

Progressive Tense   See **Tense.**

Pronoun   A word that substitutes for a noun (its antecedent). A **personal pronoun** refers to people or things: *I, me, you, he, him, she, her, it, we, us, you, they, them.* A **possessive pronoun** shows ownership. Some possessive pronouns function independently: *mine, yours, his, hers, its, ours, yours, theirs*; some must be used with nouns: *my, your, his, her, our, your, their.* A **reflexive pronoun** shows that someone or something is acting for itself or on itself: *myself, yourself, himself, herself, itself, ourselves, yourselves, themselves.* An **interrogative pronoun** is used to ask a question:

who, whom, whoever, whomever, what, which, whose. A **demonstrative pronoun** is used alone: *this, that, these, those.* An **indefinite pronoun** has no particular antecedent but serves as a general subject or object in a sentence: *another, everything, most, somebody,* and others. A **relative pronoun** introduces an adjective or noun clause: *that, what, which, who, whom, whoever, whomever, whose.*

Proper Adjective   An adjective derived from a proper noun:

Belgian lace, Elizabethan sonnet.

Proper Noun   See **Noun.**

Quotation   See **Direct Quotation.**

Reflexive Pronoun   Same as Intensive Pronoun. See **Pronoun.**

Regular Verb   See **Verb.**

Relative Pronoun   See **Pronoun.**

Restrictive Element   An appositive, phrase, or clause that supplies information necessary to the meaning of a sentence. A restrictive element is not set off by commas:

The police show ***Cagney and Lacey*** was critically successful but only moderately popular. The problems **that two female detectives might face** were dealt with honestly.

Run-on Sentence   See **Fused Sentence.**

Sentence   An independent group of words with a subject and predicate, with a capital at the beginning, and with end punctuation. It expresses a grammatically complete thought. For most purposes, sentences are classified by their structure.

A **simple sentence** contains one independent clause and expresses one relationship between a subject and predicate:

The test flight was a success.

A **compound sentence** contains two or more independent clauses joined by a comma and a coordinating conjunction or by a semicolon:

The test flight was a success, and we began production on the jet.

A **complex sentence** contains one independent clause and one or more subordinate clauses:

Although there were some problems, the test flight was a success.

A **compound-complex sentence** contains at least two independent clauses and one subordinate clause:

Although there were some problems, the test flight was a success, and we began production on the jet.

In addition, a sentence can be classified by the arrangement of its ideas. A **loose sentence** presents major ideas first and then adds clarifications:

The bus was crowded with students, shoppers, and commuters.

A **periodic sentence** places the major idea or some part of it at the end:

Although we wanted a car with power steering, power brakes, power windows, automatic transmission, air conditioning, and quadraphonic sound, we couldn't afford one.

A **balanced sentence** contains parallel words, phrases, or clauses:

> Jeremy was irresponsible, undisciplined, and rowdy, but his brother Jerod was responsible, disciplined, and reserved.

Sentence Fragment   See **Fragment.**

Simple Predicate   See **Predicate.**

Simple Sentence   See **Sentence.**

Simple Subject   See **Subject.**

Simple Tenses   See **Tense.**

Subject   The people, places, things, ideas, qualities, or conditions that act or are described in an active sentence or that are acted upon in a passive sentence.

A **simple subject** is the single word or essential group of words that controls the focus of the sentence:

> **Oppenheimer and Teller,** participants in the Manhattan Project, disagreed about the development of the hydrogen bomb.

A **complete subject** is the simple subject, plus all related modifiers, phrases, and clauses:

> **Oppenheimer and Teller, participants in the Manhattan Project,** disagreed about the development of the hydrogen bomb.

Subjective Case   Same as Nominative Case. See **Case.**

Subjunctive Mood   See **Mood.**

Subordinate Clause   See **Clause.**

Subordinating Conjunction   See **Conjunction.**

Superlative Degree   See **Degree.**

Tense   The modification of main verbs to indicate when an action occurred or when a state of being existed. **Simple**

tenses include the **present** (*he plans, they plan*), **past** (*he planned, they planned*), and **future** (*he will plan, they will plan*). **Perfect tenses** include the **present perfect** (*he has planned, they have planned*), **past perfect** (*he had planned, they had planned*), and **future perfect** (*he will have planned, they will have planned*). The **progressive tenses** indicate habitual or future action (*he is planning, he was planning, he will be planning, he had been planning, they are planning, they were planning, they had been planning, they will have been planning*).

Transitive Verb   See **Verb.**

Verb   A word or group of words that expresses action or a state of being. For most purposes, verbs are classified by their function. An **action verb** expresses physical or mental action:

The cat **pounced** on the mouse. I **thought** it was cruel.

A **linking verb** expresses a state of being or condition and joins the subject with a complement:

The cat **seemed** indifferent to my reaction. Cats **are** skillful predators.

An **auxiliary verb** is used with a main verb to form a verb phrase, commonly used to clarify time references, explain states of being, or ask questions:

We **will** stay on schedule.

Things **could** be worse.

Can you play the harpsichord?

All verbs are classified by the way they form basic verb parts. A **regular verb** forms the past tense by adding *-ed* or *-d* and maintains that form for the past participle: *talk, talked, had talked; close, closed, has closed*. An **irregular verb** follows varied patterns and may change for each form: *go, went, has gone; sing, sang, had sung*.

Verbal   A verb form used as a noun, adjective, or adverb. A **gerund** is an *-ing* verb form that functions as a noun; the form of a gerund is the same as the present participle:

Hiking is my favorite sport.

An **infinitive** is a verb form that uses *to;* it functions as a noun, adjective, or adverb:

To open his own shop is Gerhardt's dream.   (noun)

Raising enough money is his biggest obstacle to overcome.   (adjective)

Gerhardt is too committed **to give up.**   (adverb)

A **participle** is a verb form that uses *-ing, -ed, -d, -n,* or *-t;* it functions as an adjective or adverb. A **present participle** ends in *-ing:*

Beaming, Clancey accepted the first-place trophy.

A **past participle** ends in *-ed, -d, -n,* or *-t;* a past participle can also help form a verb phrase:

The window pane, **broken** by a baseball, must be replaced.   (adjective)

We have **broken** that window many times.   (part of main verb)

See also **Phrase.**

Verb Phrase   See **Phrase.**

Voice   The form of a transitive verb that illustrates whether the subject *does* something or has something *done to it.*

Active voice indicates that the subject acts:

Roy Hobbs **hit** the winning home run.

Passive voice indicates that the subject completes no action but is instead acted upon:

The winning home run **was hit** by Roy Hobbs.

Word-Processing Index

General Index

Boldface numbers refer to section numbers; other numbers refer to pages.

General Index

General Index

CORRECTION SYMBOLS

ab	**30b**	Abbreviation	lc	**27**	Lower case
act	**9a**	Active voice	ms	**Appendix A**	Manuscript form
adj	**6d, 20**	Adjective	mod	**12**	Modifier
adv	**6e, 20**	Adverb	md	**19e**	Mood
agr	**17**	Agreement	n	**30a**	Numbers
⌄	**25**	Apostrophe	¶	**4**	Paragraph
awk		Awkward	//	**10**	Parallelism
[ ]	**26d**	Brackets	( )	**26c**	Parentheses
cap	**27**	Capitals	pas	**9a**	Passive voice
ca	**18**	Case	.	**21a**	Period
coh	**4b**	Coherence	pred	**6c, 19**	Predication
:	**24d–f**	Colon	p	**21–26**	Punctuation
,	**22, 23**	Comma	?	**21b**	Question mark
cs	**16**	Comma splice	" "	**29**	Quotation marks
cp	**6d, 6e, 20c**	Comparison	red	**9b**	Redundant
comp	**1, 2, 3, 4**	Composition	ref	**11**	Reference
con	**9b**	Concision	res	**32–34**	Research
dm	**12b**	Dangling modifier	;	**24a–c**	Semicolon
–	**26a**	Dash	ss	**7**	Sentence sense
ℓ		Delete	su	**7**	Sentence unity
d	**13, 14**	Diction	sp	**31**	Spelling
doc	**33, 34**	Documentation	sub	**7a–b, 8d**	Subordination
	Appendix B		t	**6c, 19**	Tense
. . .	**26e**	Ellipsis points	trans	**4b**	Transition
emph	**9**	Emphasis	⌒		Transpose
!	**21c**	Exclamation point	u	**4a**	Unity
frag	**15**	Fragment	⊙	**22**	Unnecessary comma
fs	**16**	Fused sentence	us	**Glossary of Usage**	Usage
gr	**6, 7**	Grammar			
hy	**26b**	Hyphens	var	**8**	Variety
id	**13d**	Idiom	vb	**6c, 19**	Verb form
∧		Insert	wc	**13, 14**	Word choice
ital	**28**	Italics	w	**9b**	Wordiness
log	**5**	Logic	ww	**13b, 13d**	Wrong word